THE CONDITIONS OF FREEDOM

THE
CONDITIONS
OF
FREEDOM

Essays in
Political
Philosophy

HARRY V. JAFFA

THE JOHNS HOPKINS UNIVERSITY PRESS
Baltimore and London

Copyright © 1975 by The Johns Hopkins University Press
All rights reserved. No part of this book may be
reproduced or transmitted in any form or by any means,
electronic or mechanical, including photocopying,
recording, xerography, or any information storage and
retrieval system, without permission in writing
from the publisher.
Manufactured in the United States of America

The Johns Hopkins University Press, Baltimore, Maryland 21218
The Johns Hopkins University Press Ltd., London

Library of Congress Catalog Card Number 74-24389
ISBN 0-8018-1631-9

Library of Congress Cataloging in Publication data
will be found on the last printed page of this book.

To the Memory of
Lieutenant (j.g.) William A. Pedersen,
United States Naval Reserve
Born July 15, 1945   Died September 15, 1970
Claremont Men's College, Class of 1968

CONTENTS

PREFACE

Billy Pedersen was one of my students at Claremont Men's College. We had formed a friendship of the kind that young men and older ones sometimes do form when they are fellow hobbyists or fellow enthusiasts of a sport (bicycling in our case). Many mornings saw the two of us, before dawn, wheeling eastward through the foothills of the San Gabriel Mountains.

When the pace slackened, and when the ride was over, we talked constantly of a wide variety of subjects, most of them political. Yet I cannot recall that military service was a question or a problem in his mind, although no generation in American history was ever so racked or tormented by it as was his. He was neither an objector himself nor belligerent toward those who did object. Yet he was a highly intelligent young man, as capable as any of examining the opinions of those about him. His patriotism was so natural to him that I think he was hardly aware of it.

Billy volunteered for the Naval Air Service. He volunteered for the helicopter corps. He volunteered for service in Vietnam. When his tour of duty there was completed, he learned that his replacement would not arrive at the unit for ten days. Rather than subject the men with whom he had served to extra duty, he volunteered once more, to serve until his replacement arrived. On the second day after answering this final call, he was killed in action.

Besides numerous lesser decorations, Billy was awarded the Navy's Air Medal, with strike/flight numeral "25," indicating twenty-five strike-flight awards. He also received the Navy Commendation Medal, with Combat "V."

Billy Pedersen was a scholar, an athlete, an officer, and a gentleman. He was one of those "golden lads" of whom A. E. Housman wrote, who went to war, not gaily, but without a doubt that freedom and duty spoke with a single voice. Had he lived, he might have served his country with distinction in any other post of honor or responsibility. It is with deep affection and deep gratitude that I dedicate to his memory THE CONDITIONS OF FREEDOM.

Harry V. Jaffa
The Salvatori Center for the Study of Freedom
Claremont Men's College
Claremont, California
October 14, 1974

THE CONDITIONS OF FREEDOM

ESSAYS

1 | LEO STRAUSS: 1899-1973

We are met here today to honor the memory of Leo Strauss. It is fitting that we should do so. But honor depends upon the competence—if not the virtue—of those who give it, as well as upon the excellence of him who is to receive it. A great man once said of his teacher that he was such a one as bad men had no right even to praise. We cannot admit that we doubt our own wisdom without casting one as well upon him whom we would honor. Still, no one would have insisted more rigorously upon the necessity of both doubts than Leo Strauss.

Willmoore Kendall called Strauss the greatest teacher of politics since Machiavelli. I do not think that we—or at least I—know enough about politics to know who was its greatest teacher, either before or after Machiavelli. But I think I know what Kendall meant by that assertion, and why it is eminently plausible. For it was Strauss who, in a long series of works culminating in *Thoughts on Machiavelli,* laid bare the Machiavellian roots of modernity, and of the specific teachings of the great moderns. Strauss proved beyond a reasonable doubt that, with very few apparent exceptions, the great political philosophers after Machiavelli—for example, Spinoza, Hobbes, Locke, Montesquieu, Rousseau, Hegel, and Marx—were all, in the decisive respects, disciples of Machiavelli. All of them attempted in their doctrines to guarantee the actualization of a certain kind of just or legitimate regime by taking their bearings, not by that regime which is everywhere best, but by what all men actually everywhere are. They tried to assure the fulfillment of the goal of political life by lowering that goal.

Kendall rightly observed that Strauss would not have been able to penetrate the Machiavellian origins of modernity had he not himself transcended those origins. Machiavelli had denied that political life can be understood best or guided best by what is highest. Yet Strauss, notwithstanding his respect, or even awe, of Machiavelli's greatness, quietly denied that denial. No brief quotation can epitomize the vast sweep of Strauss's work, but I commend to you the following for its concise simplicity—indeed, for the classic grandeur—with which it denies Machiavelli's most fundamental denial. It is taken from the preface to the 1968 translation of *Spinoza's Critique of Religion.* "It is safer," wrote Strauss, "to try to understand the low in the light of the high than the high in the light of the

Remarks delivered at Bridges Chapel, Claremont, Calif., Nov. 3, 1973. Reprinted by permission from *National Review* 25, no. 49 (December 1973): 1353–55.

low. In doing the latter one necessarily distorts the high, whereas in doing the former one does not deprive the low of the freedom to reveal itself fully as what it is." Clearly, all of the state-of-nature theorists and all the historical schools tried to understand decent civil society—the high—in the light of the most indecent and powerful passions. Kant's doctrine of the Categorical Imperative would seem to be that point in modern philosophical thought furthest removed from Machiavellianism. In it, every consideration of personal advantage, every element of expedience, would seem to be removed. But what is the "good will" celebrated by Kant? Is it not an abstraction from that view of morality that is drawn from the distinction between mere interestedness and disinterestedness? And is not this view blind to the difference between noble and base interests? Is not Kant's attempt to "democratize" morality, by getting rid of the wise man as the judge of the moral man, an attempt to present the high in the light of the low? There are other and even stronger proofs that, in the decisive respects, Kant too was a Machiavellian.

Strauss never thought that Machiavelli, or his greatest disciples themselves, understood the high merely or simply in the light of the low. Had they done so, they could not have created works of such complex beauty, and Strauss thought that Machiavelli's works were very beautiful. The distinction between the wise few and the unwise many was as fundamental to Machiavellianism as to the classics. Political philosophy, Strauss often said—and wrote—was constituted essentially by permanent questions to which there were no final answers. The great moderns agreed with the great ancients, both as to the permanence of these questions and of the loftiness of the life devoted to their consideration. But they did not think that the kind of man devoted to this life—the man of utmost refinement—could be the prototype of the political man. They placed more confidence upon institutions, institutions whose dark foundations would be laid by unrefined men, institutions which would incorporate their refined understanding of political reality, but whose success would not require such understanding for its operation. Still, only theoretical men could have denied so comprehensively to theory its sovereign role, or have constructed such theoretical books to enshrine that denial. The contemplation of the modern—or Machiavellian—alternative itself, in the light of the permanent questions, belongs to the horizon of classic thought. The tragedy of that alternative is that it points toward the annihilation of that very horizon within which its greatness is visible.

On what we may call the practical level, Strauss's career was constituted by the articulation of the difference between ancients and moderns. For it was by this difference that he provided us with the bearings for understanding "where we are, and whither we are tending." On the purely theoretical level, it turned rather upon the difference between reason and revelation. These two principles represented the most fundamental alternatives to the most permanent of questions, concerning how man ought to live. Modernity itself was seen by Strauss as the most determined—and comprehensive—of human efforts to escape from the dilemma arising from the conflicts engendered in political life by these rival and ambiguous principles. Within the Jewish community, Spinoza was the greatest authority for that new conception both of reason and revelation, in which all hitherto insoluble differences were to be reconciled. Spinoza, as the philosophic founder of the critical-historical study of the Bible, was a founder—if not *the* founder—both of liberal Judaism and liberal Christianity. He was moreover the first great political philosopher who may be said to have been a proponent of liberal democracy, of that regime which, among its other advantages, transcends the age-old differences of race and religion and allows men to become fellow citizens under a rule of law on a ground supplied by natural right.

When Strauss wrote that first book on Spinoza he was, as he tells us in that same preface, "a young Jew born and raised in Germany who found himself in the grips of the theological-political predicament." What was that predicament? The Weimar Republic was a liberal democracy, says Strauss, which "proclaimed its moderate, non-radical character: its resolve to keep a balance between dedication to the principles of 1789 and dedication to the highest German tradition." In short, the Weimar regime represented, in a high degree, that resolution of the human problem that modernity at its best had promised. Strauss never failed to see the weakness of the Weimar regime as a paradigm of the weakness not merely of German liberal democracy, but of modernity. While he never failed to appreciate all the particular reasons for the tragedy of German liberalism, he never thought that the deepest and, in the long run, the strongest reason for that tragedy was merely German. No one appreciated better than he—nor was anyone more grateful than he—for the strength no less than the decency of Anglo-American democracy. But he began his Walgreen lectures in 1949 with a prophecy, that what was happening here would not be the first time, that a nation, defeated on the field of battle, had imposed the yoke of its thought upon its conqueror. Still, that thought was radically modern, rather than radically German.

The young Strauss knew the weakness of the Weimar Republic. He knew the vulnerability of the German Jewish community—also the most liberal in Europe—should Weimar fail. But neither he nor anyone else could guess that the regime that would replace it would have no other clear principle, as he says, than murderous hatred of the Jews. Strauss was certainly attracted then by political Zionism. But political Zionism was an attempt to provide a political solution to a problem originated by religious differences, the very differences that liberalism was designed to transcend.

It was essentially a liberal solution, however, since it was based on an idea of nationality—of humanity and culture—divorced from Jewish orthodoxy. But there was no idea of Jewish nationality or culture possible that did not point to Jewish orthodoxy as its core. Political Zionism proved to be a self-contradiction. In this context, Strauss's Jewish studies led him, not merely to a more profound understanding of Spinoza, but beyond Spinoza to that greater Jewish thinker, Maimonides. And it was Maimonides who pointed the way for him to Farabi and, ultimately, to Socrates. Henceforth his Jewishness would not take the form of any political commitment as such, but of a quiet pride in a tradition that he now knew incorporated the highest as well as the most sacred wisdom.

The establishment of the state of Israel, Strauss thought, "procured a blessing for all Jews everywhere regardless of whether they admit it or not." But it did not solve the Jewish problem. That problem was at bottom the problem arising from the challenge of revelation itself, which science had not refuted, and for which the ethics of humanity was no substitute. The Jews, whose heritage made them the highest symbols of the demand of God himself that men live on the highest level, had become symbols of that cosmopolitanism which ultimately represented the lowering of the goals of political life in the interest of the universal and homogeneous state. The Nazis had singled out the Jews as representatives of international banking and international communism, the ostensibly degenerate symbols of the lowered goals of modern cosmopolitanism. But the Nazis were not Christians. Their hatred of the Jews was a hatred of the entire tradition of the west. Hitler's romantic longing for the Middle Ages was an irrational longing for a noble past purged of the reality of its struggle with reason and revelation. The Jewish problem was, in the end, the human problem.

Strauss did not believe that the principles of reason and revelation could ever be reduced, one to the other. Nor did he believe in the possibility of a synthesis, since any synthesis would require a higher principle than either, a principle which regulated the combination. Catholic Christianity, which found its highest expression in Thomas Aquinas, attempted such a synthesis. Strauss admired the magnificence of Thomas' efforts, and he saw in them a great humanizing and moderating of Catholic theology. Perhaps the greatest gain from the Thomistic synthesis was that Aristotle, after being a forbidden author, eventually became a recommended one. But only in traditional Judaism did the idea of revelation, and of a tradition undivided and uncompromised by syncretism, find its full expression. And Western civilization at its highest expressed the tension between Greek rationalism and Jewish revelation.

Strauss may in the end be best remembered for his works on Socrates, the preoccupation of his last years. For Socrates was the man who seemed to have discovered, or have invented, political philosophy. For he was the man who either first asked the questions which form its core, or at least first asked them in such a way as to make their asking itself a way of life. The Socratic way of life was a continual demonstration that the rulers of Athens—and, of course, of every political regime anywhere—did not really know the things that they thought they knew, knowledge of which was implied in every action they took. By implying that statesmen should know what they needed to know, Socrates intimated that every existing regime was defective, and that it had a duty to transform itself into something better—ultimately into the best regime. That, of course, implied a disloyalty to Athens sufficient to justify Socrates' execution. Yet Strauss did not think Socrates' teaching was utopian, in the sense that he taught that everyone should strive to introduce the best regime. Socrates confessed that he knew nothing, and that knowledge of ignorance is, or should be, moderating, if not humbling. Statesmanship informed by the awareness of ignorance is not likely to aim at final, much less at universal, solutions which imply that we actually do know what we do not know. The best regime is not a political regime; it lives in speech and not in deed. But it *is* the best, and we need not transform the world in order to live there: we need only transform ourselves. No one who has experienced the magic of Leo Strauss's teaching can doubt that the best regime not only is possible, but that it has been actual. Nor can he doubt that whatever amelioration of our condition is possible will come about by the influence of its spirit on those who exercise political power.

I have been asked to say a word about my own studies of Lincoln and the American regime, in their relationship to Strauss. The most obvious connection is between Strauss's many expositions of Locke, and Locke's massive influence on America. Locke certainly represented modernity in its soberest form, although Strauss was careful to emphasize Locke's ultimate, if concealed, insobriety. But Strauss also thought that American politics, at its best, showed a practical wisdom that owed much to a tradition older than Locke. Indeed, Locke's exoteric teaching, which emphasized that older tradition, was taken with the greatest seriousness in America. But the American regime was not formed only by Locke. Many a frontier log cabin, which had in it no philosophical works whatever, had the King James Bible—and Shakespeare. And Shakespeare was the great vehicle within the Anglo-American world for the transmission of an essentially Socratic understanding of the civilization of the West.

Most American studies begin, and properly so, with the Constitution. The Constitution does not define the regime, but it is the most public and visible expression of it. It is part of the defect of modern politics that it looks to the character of the law, more than to the character of the men who make and enforce the law, however intimate the connection between them necessarily is. However admirable the character of the American Constitution, it was not, I thought, the most admirable expression of the regime. The Constitution is the highest American thing, only if one tries to understand the high in the light of the low. It is high because men are not angels, and because we do not have angels to govern us. Its strength lies in its ability to connect the interest of the man with the duty of the place. But the Constitution, in deference to man's nonangelic nature, made certain compromises with slavery. And partly because of those compromises, it dissolved in the presence of a great crisis. The man—or the character of the man—who bore the nation through that crisis, seemed to me—and Strauss gave me every encouragement to believe it—the highest thing in the American regime. The character of Lincoln became intelligible, not on the basis of *The Federalist*—profound as that work is—but on that of the *Nicomachean Ethics*. In the final analysis, not only American politics, but all modern politics, must be clarified on the basis of classical political philosophy. That is because "It is safer to try to understand the low in the light of the high than the high in the light of the low. In doing the latter one necessarily distorts the high, whereas in doing the former one does not deprive the low of the freedom to reveal itself fully as what it is."

We leave to others—more detached and more objective—the judgment of Strauss's place among the political philosophers. For us who have had the privilege of knowing him as a teacher and as a friend, we can only say: of the men we have known, he was the best, and the wisest, and the most just.

2 | WHAT IS POLITICS?
An Interpretation
of Aristotle's *Politics*

Aristotle was born in 384 B.C. in the seaport town of Stagira in Thrace. His father was Nicomachus, a court physician to the royal family of Macedon. Aristotle came to Athens in 367 and entered the school of Plato where he remained until the latter's death in 347. He lived in Assos in the Troad (347-344), in Lesbos (344-342), and for about six years at the Macedonian capital of Pella (342-336), during which time his famed association with the young Alexander occurred. In 335 he returned to Athens where he founded his own school, the Lyceum. In the anti-Macedonian reaction that swept Athens and other Greek cities after the death of Alexander in 323, Aristole was indicted for impiety and fled to Chalcis in Euboea (his mother's birthplace), reportedly saying that "Athens must not sin a second time against philosophy." He died there not long afterward, in 322.

Aristotle's political philosophy is to be found primarily in two books: the *Nicomachean Ethics* and the *Politics*. An evidently earlier and less definitive work is the *Eudemian Ethics,* the fourth, fifth, and sixth books of which are identical with the fifth, sixth, and seventh books of the *Nicomachean Ethics.* An exhaustive study of Aristotle's political philosophy would include a careful examination of similarities and differences in the two ethical treatises, as well as consideration of a smaller and less scientific work called by the tradition *Magna Moralia.* Finally, we must note the famous 158 constitutions (or regimes) said to have been collected by Aristotle, according to ancient catalogues, and which are referred to in the last paragraph of the *Nicomachean Ethics.* Of these, only one has survived. Fortunately, it is the Athenian constitution or, more accurately, a constitutional history of Athens accompanied by an account of the constitution in Aristotle's time. In this essay we will limit ourselves, in the main to Aristotle's *Politics,* with such supplementary consideration of the *Nicomachean Ethics* as is necessary to establish the context within which the political treatise (in the narrower sense of the word "political") occurs

The subject of Aristotle's *Politics* is the *polis* or political community. There is no single English word that will translate *polis,* and to

Reprinted by the kind permission of the publisher from Harry Jaffa, "Aristotle: 384-322 B.C.," in Leo Strauss and Joseph Cropsey (eds.), *History of Political Philosophy,* 2nd ed. (Chicago: Rand McNally & Co., 1972).

understand why is indispensable to any introduction to Aristotle's political philosophy. The *Politics* begins with a definition of the *polis,* and the student who reads this as a definition of the "state," with all the connotations alien to Aristotle in that expression, is apt to be estranged forever from his thought. Our word "politics," although a noun, is the plural form of the adjective "politic.". A parallel instance is the word "athletics," formed from the adjective "athletic." Now athletics is what athletes do. The Greek noun *athlētēs*—from which athletic and athletics derived—survives virtually unaltered in our language. We know what athletics is because we know what an athlete is. The latter is a concrete subject of observation while the former is an abstract general characterization of his activities. But the Greek noun *polis,* which does not survive in our language, is to politics what athlete is to athletics. Politics, the abstract general characterization derived from the Greek survives, but *polis,* the concrete subject, does not.

As we have observed, the usual translation of *polis* is "state."[1] But *polis* and "state" are not even logical equivalents. According to Aristotle, "community" is the genus and "political community" a species. The specifying characteristic of the political community or *polis* is that it is the community that includes all other human communities, while itself being included by none. Because of its all-inclusiveness, the *polis* includes or assimilates within its own end or purpose the end or purpose of every other form of community. The scope of the state is quite different, as we see when we consider the term "state" as it occurs familiarly today in such antinomies as "the individual and the state," "church and state," or "state and society." It is clear that the state, whether separated from or combined with a church, is never understood to include by itself, as an element of its own definition, the function of a church. The purpose of a state, as state, is never understood to be that of providing for the eternal welfare of its citizens or subjects, however much it may assist a church or churches in providing for it. If the functions of church and state happen to be united in the same body, as for example in the Vatican or the British queen in Parliament, they are still distinct from each other. They are as distinct as, to use an Aristotelian example, the functions of a tragic chorus are distinct from those of a comic chorus, although the human beings who comprise the two choruses may be the same. The decisive consideration is this: the end or function of the state—e.g., to secure the rights to life, liberty, and the pursuit of happiness—when added to the end or function of the church—e.g., to direct men to their eternal welfare—constitute an aggregate of ends or functions different from that of either taken

---

[1] Frequently this is rendered "city-state," meaning a very small state with an urban center. This, however, only compounds confusion, because it implies that a *polis* is a particular kind of state.

separately. But the concept of the *polis* is such that there is no process of addition by which one could alter, in either a quantitative or a qualitative sense, its end or function.

It is a common error to suppose that, because the *polis* includes all other communities, the end or function of the *polis* is simply the aggregate of the ends of the communities it embraces, with the addition of the end we attribute to the state. This error is expressed in the attempt to explain the comprehensiveness of the *polis* by saying that it "is" simultaneously church and state. In this view, the reason why the end of the *polis* cannot be altered by any process of addition is that it is by definition the sum of the ends it embraces. But the *polis*, while it embraces the ends of all lesser forms of community, is not the sum of them, because it is in no sense an aggregate. Aristotle sometimes conceives of the *polis* upon the analogy of a living organism.[2] Just as the function of the human organism cannot be conceived as the sum of the functions of heart, liver, hand, and brain, so one cannot conceive of the function of the *polis* as the sum of any parts or components. The function of the human organism is not a sum for the same reason that it cannot be divided and allocated among its parts. It is a whole of which heart, liver, hand, and brain are parts. But it is not a mathematical whole. Without all the parts the whole cannot perform its function, or cannot perform it so well; but the function performed by the whole is a function of the whole alone. What we mean by a whole man can never be resolved into his physiological components.

Polis, we have said, is logically not the equivalent of "state" because *polis* is the species of community which includes by definition all other (and hence lesser) forms of community. "State" is not the comprehensive form of community, if indeed it can be understood as a species of the genus community at all.[3] The state, and the law of the state, can certainly be better understood as a species of contract. By the *polis* is meant a radically different relationship of the political community to human gregariousness than is meant by these contemporary terms. The *polis* cannot *be* simultaneously church and state because the definition of the *polis* implies a quasi-organic relationship between the subordinate functions of subordinate associations within the *polis* to the superordinate function of the *polis*, a relationship which excludes the very idea of what we understand by either church or state.

As both "church" and "state" are excluded from what Aristotle

[2] One must, however, be careful not to identify Aristotle's use of such analogy with the organismic theories of the nineteenth century, which attribute to the state actual qualities of a real organism.

[3] See below, p. 47, for the Sophist Lycophron's definition of law; from W. D. Ross (ed.), Aristotelis *Politica*, Oxford Classical Texts (Oxford: Oxford University Press, 1957), 1280^b 10.

understands by *polis,* so also are "society" and "individual." The term "society" as used in present-day social science, may be like *polis*—as "state" is not—in that it is frequently taken to refer to the totality of the forms of human association. But it is never conceived to be a unified authoritative whole, as is the *polis.* Sometimes society is conceived simply as an aggregate of all forms of community within a specified locality, sometimes as an organic or quasi-organic unity. But whatever the unity attributed to society, it is not the kind of unity which gives its identity to the *polis.* For the unity of the *polis* is like that of the human organism, in that it is the result of a capacity for deliberate rational purpose. Whatever rationality the eye of the beholder may discover in society, it is never deliberate rational purpose; for the presence of such purpose necessitates government, and the very idea of society was conceived to express the idea of human gregariousness without particular reference to government.

What we mean today by "individual" is logically implied by, and is correlative with, "state," "church," and "society," but is utterly incongruent with *polis.* Modern individualism conceives each human being to have a sphere of privacy wherein are generated activities and ends which the state, as state, can never order or direct to their completion and perfection. Because of this essential incompetence of the state in certain areas, other forms of community, of which the church is the most familiar and convenient, although by no means the sole example, are both possible and necessary. There is a familiar aphorism today, that the state exists for the individual and not the individual for the state. The most common characterization of totalitarianism in the Western world is that it reverses this order and treats the individual as if he exists for the state. One must not, in approaching Aristotle, attempt to characterize his thought in terms of such an aphorism, because it is not possible to substitute *polis* for state. It makes no more sense to say that the *polis* exists for the citizen, or the citizen for the *polis,* than to say that the mind exists for the man or the man for the mind. According to Aristotle man exists ultimately for the sake of the good life, and the good life is the same for one man and for a *polis.* The means-end relationship we predicate of state and individual does not subsist between man and *polis,* and all inferences which assume such a relationship are false.

The *Politics* begins by defining the *polis* as follows:

Since we see that every *polis* is a community, and that every community is established for the sake of some good—since all do everything for the sake of what seems to them good—it is clear that as all communities aim at some good, the one that does so in the highest degree and aims at the most authoritative of all goods is the community which is the most authoritative of all and embraces all others: this is the one called the *polis* or the political community.[4]

What are the elements of this definition? First there is this syllogism: Every *polis* is a community; every community aims at some good; therefore every *polis* aims at some good. The minor premise is itself the conclusion of an implied syllogism: Every community is constituted by common action; every action aims at some good; therefore every community aims at some good. To understand the definition of the *polis* we must then grasp with utmost firmness the meaning and the implications of the proposition that every action aims at or intends some good.

This proposition applies, in Aristotle's whole doctrine (or perhaps we should say, doctrine of the whole), to all motion in the universe, but we will consider it only as it refers to voluntary human action. Every human agent acts voluntarily only as he intends something that, insofar as it is a motive for him to act, appears to him to be something good. A hungry man eats because relieving his hunger seems to him to be good. The man who would eat when he is hungry must work that he may have food. Work that may itself not otherwise be desired is nonetheless motivated by a seeming good, namely, food. The student studies that he may learn and learns that he may know. His end is knowledge, which may be desired for its own sake or for the sake of some work which it will enable him to do. This work may be desired for its own sake, or for its consequences (e.g., money or food), or for both. The thief may steal even as the honest man works, that he may eat. Stealing may be evil as honest work is good, but the good for the sake of which the one steals and the other works may nonetheless be the same, namely, eating. In short, all human action originates in desire for something which moves to action by its appearance of desirability or goodness. Desire implies a sense of deficiency in the agent; that which is desired appears to the agent as capable of overcoming the sense of deficiency. As such, it appears to him as good, and becomes thereby the motive for voluntary action.

The question arises, however, as to what is the relationship among the many things that are desired as good. The answer given in the first book of the *Nicomachean Ethics,* with an elaborateness and subtlety which we cannot begin to reproduce, runs somewhat as follows. There are three kinds of ends. First, those which are purely instrumental, which are desired only for their consequences and never for themselves. Money is the most conspicuous example; medicinal drugs is another. Second, there are those good things which would be desired even if they had no further consequences, but in fact are desired as well because they contribute to

---

[4] Ibid., 1252^a 1-6 (trans. Harry V. Jaffa).

the acquisition of other goods. Seeing and hearing are examples of faculties whose activities we delight in for themselves, but which are also means to nearly all the other good things in life, as indeed is health altogether. Honor, pleasure, reason, and every virtue are also things which we would choose, and do choose, for their own sakes, but which are also chosen for their further consequences or advantages. The final class of good is that which is chosen only for its own sake and never for the sake of anything else. Of these three classes it is clear that the merely instrumental, as such, are less valuable than those which are final, meaning thereby the goods which are or can be chosen for their own sakes; and the more final an object of choice is, in comparison with one which is either entirely or partly instrumental, the more inherently valuable it is.

Intrinsic to the distinction between instrumental and final ends and vital to its comprehension is the distinction between ends which are activities and ends which are products. A chair is an end apart from the activity of carpentering which produced it. Singing is both an activity for making music and music itself. In such cases as the carpentering, Aristotle says, it is the nature of the products to be better than the activity. The skill of the carpenter precedes in time the chair which is produced by that skill. But the chair (and other products of carpentering) are desired before carpentering is desired, and the development of the skill of carpentering (insofar as it is a result of deliberate voluntary action) is a consequence of the desire for its products. It is the utility of such products as chairs which is the final cause of carpentering, even as carpentering is the efficient cause of chairs. Because the chairs stand before carpentering in the order of final causality, they enjoy priority in the order of excellence. Now there are many actions, arts, and sciences, and their ends also are many. Sometimes these ends appear unrelated, but sometimes they are evidently related to each other by their relation to a common end. Bridle-making and the other arts of equipping horses fall under the art of riding; but riding falls under the military art, or strategy. The end of strategy is victory in war, and it is the excellence of this end which is the final cause of the excellence of strategy, and of the lesser excellences of the lesser arts which it has, directly or indirectly, called into existence, and which serve it. The same is true of health in relation to medicine and of medicine in relation to the subordinate arts which serve it. And so with buildings in relation to architecture in relation to, e.g., bricklaying and interior decorating.

Now we see that victory, health, and buildings are final in relation to the arts that serve them. and all are worthy of choice for their own sake: victory for the evils of defeat it averts and for the honor it achieves; health for the evils of disease which it averts and for the healthy activity it engenders; buildings for the discomforts they avert and for the comforts they provide. But victory is valuable not only for the foregoing reasons, but far more because of the activities having nothing to do with war which can be pursued only in peace and freedom. The man would be mad who would go to war for the sake of the honor of victory, if peace and freedom were attainable without war. Peace and freedom are ends more final than victory; the intrinsic value of victory derives from peace and freedom no less than the value of weapons derives from the value of victory. And so the question arises, What is the cause of the value of peace and freedom? Or, to put the question in its most comprehensive form, as Aristotle does, Is there not something always desirable for its own sake and never for the sake of something else? If there is then this must be the thing or, if there be more than one such, these must be the things for the sake of which everything else is done.

Now Aristotle maintains that there is one such thing, which stands in the same relation to all the activities of human life as the target stands in relation to the activity of the archer. It is the mark toward which everything we do is ultimately directed, and only as we can see that mark (or as we are directed by those who do see it) can our lives be said to have direction. The ground of Aristotle's opinion is twofold. First, if there were no absolutely final cause of human action, then everything would be desired for the sake of something else and there would be no term or end of human desire. Each human choice, we recall, initiates a movement to overcome some deficiency in the agent, e.g., eating to overcome hunger, learning to overcome ignorance. It is a movement from incompletion toward completion, from imperfection toward perfection. But if each deliberate action were nothing but the way to another action, the notion of progress from lesser to greater finality would be pure illusion. The only actual finality would be an infinite regress, and life would be essentially purposeless and vain. But human action originates in the human soul, the cause of which is nature. Aristotle holds that nature does nothing in vain, and action originating in the soul would be vain if it could not terminate short of infinity. Therefore there must be a final attainable end of all human action. This argument, it will be perceived, depends upon Aristotle's doctrine of nature. But there is another argument as well, namely, that universal opinion testifies to the existence of such an end. And common opinion, to the extent that it is uncontradicted and internally consistent, is always authoritative for Aristotle.[5] All people speak of happiness and all mean by happiness just such a thing as we have specified as a final end: something for the sake of which every good thing can be chosen—including those good things like honor, virtue, and health which can be chosen for their own sakes—but which is never itself chosen for the

---

[5] Cf. Aristotle *Nicomachean Ethics* 1145ᵇ 1ff.

sake of anything else. To possess happiness means to lack nothing desirable, to be self-sufficient. Self-sufficiency does not imply a solitary condition, but rather whatever a man needs to be happy: parents, children, friends, and fellow citizens. Happiness, unlike other goods, is not to be enumerated *among* good things. To be healthy *and* wealthy *and* wise is better than to be any one or two of these things. But one cannot add wealth or wisdom to happiness to make happiness better, because happiness implies the presence of all other good things in whatever measure is sufficient to define their excellence. Whatever positive measure of goodness can be ascribed to health or wealth or wisdom derives from its ability to contribute to happiness.

We cannot do more here than allude to the substantive meaning of happiness as developed by Aristotle in the ten books of the *Nicomachean Ethics.* The definition given in the first book is that happiness is an activity of soul in accordance with virtue—and if there are many virtues, in accordance with the best and most complete—in a complete life. Virtuous activity is defined as that activity which perfects the specifically human part of the soul, the rational faculty, in the same sense that musical excellence perfects the faculty of music-making in one who has the potentiality to make music. What is crucial in the foregoing for understanding the definition of the *polis* is that the idea of a complete and self-sufficient community, a community that embraces all other communities but is embraced by none, corresponds exactly to the idea of happiness: the human good that embraces and includes within itself as an element of its own definition all other goods, but is itself included in the definition of no other good. Happiness is the term of all human action, and is implicit as the final term of every human action. The *polis* is the term of all human communities, and is the external, organized expression of the unity which governs or ought govern the totality of human actions in all their diversity.

Near the beginning of the *Nicomachean Ethics,* immediately after affirming that there must be one goal for the whole of human life even as there must be a mark for the archer, Aristotle says that of the sciences and faculties the one that would guide us toward this goal or mark would be the most authoritative and the master of all the others. Politics is this supreme discipline, and the language Aristotle uses to describe the relation of politics to all other disciplines corresponds closely to the language used at the beginning of the *Politics* to describe the relation of the *polis* to all other forms of community. Politics determines which of the sciences should be studied in the *polis,* by which of the citizens, and to what degree. Politics alone rules strategy, economics, and rhetoric. For happiness is the end of politics, as victory is of strategy, and wealth of economics. Only the man who understands the requirements of victory can utilize, let us say, a cavalry maneuver, even if he requires a cavalry officer to execute it. And only the one who understands the requirements of happiness can utilize victory, even if he requires a general to secure it. The ultimate end of human life, the good for man, happiness, Aristotle maintains, is one and the same, whether we consider one man or a *polis.* But to attain or preserve it for a *polis* or a nation seems greater or more complete than for one man. The reason why is made clear at the end of the *Nicomachean Ethics,* when the meaning of happiness has been fully elaborated and the transition to the *Politics* is indicated. The conditions of happiness are seldom if ever within the ability of one man to control. Only good men can be happy (although they may not be), but good laws make good men, and good government makes good laws.

Following the definition of the *polis,* the first book of the *Politics* is concerned in the main to establish two things: first, that the unity which constitutes the *polis* is complex rather than simple, that there are several forms of authority within it and not only one; and second, that the *polis* exists by nature and not by law or convention alone, and that the ground of authority in the *polis* is nature and not arbitrary compulsion. Aristotle first attacks "some" (Plato and others) who fail to distinguish between political rule, royal rule, the rule of a household, and the rule of a master, treating them as differing only in the number of those ruling or the number of those ruled. A little later he attacks "others" who maintain that for one man to be master of another is against nature and can be attributed only to unjust force. Those who hold that the distinction between a free man and a slave is altogether artificial maintain as well that all authority is conventional and that there is no nonarbitrary standard by which to distinguish just from unjust compulsion. The Platonic view seems in theory to be the extreme opposite of the conventionalist view, but in practice it appears to have a certain resemblance to it. In the idea of the good, Plato held to an objective standard outside human opinion, and hence outside human convention, which was the ground of all right action, whether by one man or by a *polis.* In the first book of the *Nicomachean Ethics* Aristotle criticizes this doctrine in some detail, the most important result of this criticism, for present purposes, being that such an idea cannot serve as a guide to action. The "good-in-itself" will not serve the weaver, the carpenter, or the doctor, who will not discover from it what is good in cloth, in furniture, or in health. Acting man acts with reference to particulars. The doctor treats not man-in-general, but this man, e.g., Socrates. The doctor must know what health in general is like to treat Socrates, and he does know what such health is like, because he knows what healthy activities of the body are like. But it is these, and not an abstract goodness, that are the tokens of the presence of that good thing, health. The Platonic idea of the good so transcends individual phenomena that it leaves practical life without a guide. Here, we might observe, is also the principle of the criticism of the *Republic* in the second book of the *Politics:* it is an impractical scheme and can no more guide the legislator than the idea of the good can guide the weaver, carpenter, or doctor. The Platonic teaching recognizes an objective standard, but it is impractical; the conventionalists deny that there is an objective standard. Aristotle maintains that we have in nature a standard that is both practical and objective.

Aristotle undertakes to demonstrate both the aforesaid contentions, namely, the differences of the different forms of authority and the naturalness of the *polis,* by tracing the growth of the *polis* from its first beginning and its composition from its elements. Its first beginnings are the coupling together of male and female for the continuation of the species. This clearly is natural and is in accordance with a necessity common to man and all other animals. But the union of male and female for generation is no more intended by nature than the union of ruler and ruled for safety. Foresight of the mind is the basis of ruling the body, as the ability of the body to do what the mind sees is needful is the basis of being ruled. Slave and female are distinct by nature, as the functions of procreation and self-preservation, although intimately connected, are distinct. The right ordering of the family requires recognition of the differences between the two, which the barbarians fail to do by treating women as slaves. The family, arising from natural needs, is a natural community, with a common interest binding its members, male and female, master and slave. Its structuring, in terms of the foregoing distinctions, is not adventitious but is—or should be—rooted in an understanding of nature. The union of several families makes a village, and of several villages a *polis.* When are there enough villages to comprise a *polis?* When the human and nonhuman resources of the several villages, in combination, enable the community to be self-sufficient. What makes a community self-sufficient? When it is able to lead the good life. The distinction between mere life, on the one hand, the consequence of procreation and self-preservation, and the good life, is apparent from the difference between the household and the *polis.*

The union of families into the larger whole is in one sense no less natural than the union of male and female from which the family results. The man who first united villages to form a *polis* was the cause of the greatest goods, says Aristotle, implying that deliberate action, and not the kind of natural necessity that produced the family, is the cause of the political community. But the purpose of the *polis* is no less natural than that of the family, because ultimately they are one and the same. Whether we consider a man, a horse, or a household, the nature of each thing is what it is when it is fully grown and completed. Nature does nothing in vain, and she has endowed man with the faculty of reason and speech. This faculty is not what appears in other animals when they signify pleasure and pain to each other. Nor is the *polis* like the beehive or any other nonhuman community, which carries out the division of tasks by the mechanism of instinct. Reason and speech —not instinct—indicate the useful and the harmful, the just and the unjust. The common burdens and the common advantages must be divided and shared by rules which must themselves be decided upon by the sharers in the common good. What these rules are, and how they are to be applied, is what we mean by the administration of justice in the broadest sense. And it is participation in this which makes a man a citizen, and the partnership in justice is the political community. The family and the village are too narrow for self-sufficiency, and hence too narrow for justice. Hence the *polis,* as the only community adequate for the fulfillment of man's specifically human potentiality, must be *prior* to the family in one of the senses that the oak tree is prior to the acorn. The *polis* is also prior to the family as, in our former analysis, the chair is prior to the carpentering which produces it. That is, it is prior in the order of final causality. The *polis* is also prior to the single human being, as the whole man is prior to the hand or any other organ of the whole. For except as he lives in a *polis* a man cannot live a fully human existence, he cannot function as a man. For man is the rational and political animal.

To comprehend Aristotle's famous discussion of slavery one must remind oneself of the context established by the coincidence of the two contrary theses, Platonic and conventionalist. The latter regards the distinction between master and slave as wholly conventional and as resting upon force. The former, by affirming that there is essentially one science of ruling, and that the variety of forms of rule are differences of degree rather than kind, also affirms by implication that the difference between master and slave except as an example of the distinction between ruler and ruled, is conventional. Aristotle's crucial thesis, which is itself in agreement with Plato, is that the distinction between ruler and ruled, of which master and slave is an example, is a distinction that we find throughout nature. We find in the cause of the difference between man and the lower animals, and even in inanimate things, as for example in the musical scale, a ruling principle. Above all, we find a principle of rule in the difference between body and soul, and within the soul in the difference between reason and desire. The soul rules the body by a despotic rule, and the reasoning part of the soul rules the passions, by a political or royal rule. By this Aristotle means that the faculties of the body, as such, merely experience pleasure and pain, seeking the one and avoiding the other; but the thinking part of man teaches him that he is sometimes preserved by what is painful (e.g., surgery) and destroyed by what is pleasant (e.g., narcotics). That in man which responds merely to the demands of the body, like a child whom one cannot by any possibility persuade to drink bitter medicine, must simply be ruled or overruled, by deception or force. The passions, unlike the demands of the body, are not the response to mere pleasure and pain. Anger, for example, may lead us to seek revenge, however dangerous or painful the occasion. Here reason rules differently, persuading us to seek revenge only when revenge is justified. The passion of anger is clearly capable of receiving instruction; i.e., one can learn not to feel satisfaction in wrongly indulged anger and to feel satisfaction in a rightly indulged anger. One cannot learn to feel bodily pleasure in the surgeon's knife, or to feel bodily pain in a successful sexual act, however illicit. In the latter case one can simply deny the purely physical impulses, and this is the prototype of despotic rule. In the former case one can discipline one's affections to move of themselves in the directions judged good by reason. Trained obedience, as distinct from brute direction, is the characteristic of being ruled politically or royally.

Perhaps the simplest explanation of what Aristotle means by natural slavery is that it is an example of the relation of body and soul, in which the body of one man is related to the soul of another. If there is a man with a mentality like that of the child, who cannot perceive that it is sometimes good to take bitter medicine, then he must be ruled like a child, for his own good. But such a man cannot have a good of his own, as a normal child can have. That is, the child must be ruled by his father in order that he may eventually become a good man, independent of his father's commands. But the natural slave, being a grown man who must be ruled as a child, can never be a complete human being. Properly speaking, he is not a grown man, although he may have the body of one. He is a part, not a whole, and he may become part of a whole only as he belongs to another, in a sense comparable to that in which any grown man's body is part of him, namely, as an instrument of his intelligence. It is in this sense that a natural slave is property, i.e., he is an instrument for action by a soul able to live a good life. He is properly part of the household, because even as an instrument of action he is capable only of the uncomplicated actions which are directly concerned with the business of the household, the business of providing material conditions for the preservation of life. Noble actions are not possible for one who cannot do noble things for their own sake, and a natural slave is bereft of the higher functions of the soul.

That there are natural slaves, in the aforesaid sense, is the universal experience of mankind. Today we call them mental incompetents, among other things. Aristotle is emphatic that those who are called slaves, but who are in fact competent, are not slaves by nature, but by law and convention only, and the slavery of such men does rest, at bottom, upon force. There is a common interest which unites natural slave with natural master, but this is not true when unjust law and force alone are the ground of the relationship. Who is truly a master, and who is truly a slave, depends then upon the intrinsic characteristics of master and slave. The Platonic thesis is wrong in that it makes one man the ruler of another because the former possesses a certain kind of knowledge. Aristotle admits that there may indeed be a science of ruling slaves, but he denies that it is the possession of this science which, in the first instance, entitles a man to be a master. Rather, such a science profits a master in his use of slaves, just as it may profit him to have his slaves instructed in their duties by those who make a study of such things, even as he might employ someone to train his dogs and horses.

The discussion of the relation of master and slave forms the first part of Aristotle's treatment of the household, and the *polis,* as a compound of communities, is essentially a compound of families or households. To understand the genesis of politics means to understand the functions generated by families but incapable of being carried to perfection within the framework of the family. Families consist of freemen and slaves. The relationships of the free members are those of husband and wife, father and children. The rule of the husband is a kind of political rule, in that both husband and wife are rational beings, reason being naturally stronger in the man. The husband is like an official permanently in office, and the wife is like a nonofficial citizen (although Aristotle admits that sometimes, contrary to nature, the wife is more rational than the husband). The rule of the father over his children is more royal than political, in that the distance between them is much greater than between husband and wife, but the kind of direction he gives them is entirely different from that which befits slaves who remain permanently subordinate, while the children eventually become full citizens.

The exact purpose of Aristotle's elaborate discussion of the household in Book I of the *Politics* is the subject of much difference of opinion, and each student can form his own judgment only on the basis of the most detailed consideration. Here we can but set down some guidelines. Clearly, the highest function of the family, like that of the *polis,* is the formation of character. The end of the *Nicomachean Ethics* indicates that the transition from ethics to politics is required by the limitations of the family for the purpose of training. Whether education is public or private, the art of legislating is required for it. That is, not the father as father, but the father who is legislator, can wisely prescribe even to his own son. But in fact it is difficult to have good families in a corrupt *polis,* so for still other reasons legislation is needed. In considering the legislation for the best regime, in Books VII and VIII of the *Politics,* the chief subject is the educational curriculum. But the discussion in Book I is mainly concerned with what we would call economics, or with the provision of the materials by which the bodies of men, rather than their souls, are nourished. Still, the fact that the bodies in question are those of men, and not animals other than man, is the crucial fact when we consider how to provide for their bodies. This may be indicated by considering two texts dealing with the family. In Book VIII of the *Nicomachean Ethics*[6] Aristotle observes that friendship between man and wife seems to exist by nature, since man is more a conjugal than a political animal, and the household prior to and more necessary than the *polis,* as the production of offspring is common to man and the other animals. Yet in the better known passage in the *Politics,* Book I,[7] he says that the *polis* is by nature prior to the household and to each of us. The formal solution of this apparent contradiction is, as we have indicated, in the distinction between what is prior in the order of efficient causality (the household) and what is prior in the order of final causality (the *polis*). However, the question remains as to what are the activities generated by the material requirements of the family, the efficient causes of which are the natural necessities of mere life, necessities consistent with (but not sufficient for) the end of the *polis.*

The analysis consists of two main parts. The basic element of the first part is a comparison of the human family with families of animals other than man. Aristotle had remarked near the beginning of Book I[8] that man in virtue of his rationality was more political than the bee or any other gregarious animal. But the implicit comparison with the beehive was defective in this, that the beehive does not require institution, as does the *polis,* and therefore is in one sense more obviously natural. The comparison of the household with the families of other animals is in one sense more perfect than the comparison of the *polis* with the beehive, since the families of men and of animals other than man are formed in the same way. Deep consideration of similarities and differences of the families of gregarious animals seems to reveal the emergence of the conventional from the natural in the human family by a kind of necessity, and to reveal how nature remains the norm for convention, even as convention replaces nature as the cause of the material conditions of life.

The arts or sciences dealing with the household fall into two classes. First, there are those concerned with household management, which refers to the right use of the goods of the household. Of the goods of the household, there are two kinds: tools or instruments, and materials. A shuttle is an inanimate tool, as a slave is an animate one. Fleece is a material for the weaver, as bronze is for the statuary. Second, there is the

---

[6] Ibid., 1162^a 16-19.
[7] Aristotle *Politics* 1253^a 19.
[8] Ibid., 1253^a 7-9.

art or science of acquisition. Strictly speaking, it is not an art *of* the household, since it is not carried on by the household or in the household, but it provides materials and tools by which the work of the household can be carried on. Of all the goods that must be provided, food of course is the most important. And nature provides not only men, but all animals with food. Some animals are flesh-eating, others grain-eating, and nature points out the proper food to each and provides for each the food for which it has adapted them. The natural modes of acquisition for man— corresponding with the grazing or predatory activities of other animals— are those of pastoral nomads, hunters, farmers. The hunters Aristotle divides into brigands or pirates, fishermen, and the hunters of fowl and game. In a summary statement Aristotle lists nomads, farmers, brigands, fishermen, hunters. Brigands are now separated from other hunters; and still later Aristotle includes the art of war as part of the art of hunting— the hunting of human beings for the purpose of reducing to servitude those who are by nature slaves and who resist enslavement. Brigandage as a natural mode of acquisition, and war for the sake of enslavement as part of the art of acquisition, are the striking features of this analysis. The explanation, whatever it may ultimately be, certainly derives from the idea that nature provides man with the necessaries of life even as she provides the other animals. If plants exist for the support of animal life, then the lower animals exist for the higher, and all animals, or such as are serviceable to him, must then exist for man. Since a slave is something less than a full human being, he, too, is a legitimate object of acquisition.

The second part of acquisition, which is in an especial sense wealth-getting, is acquisition by barter and trade. One part of this is natural, namely, acquisition by simple barter, e.g., the exchange of shoes for grain. The second part is acquisition of money, and this branch, although it is originally merely an extension of barter, becomes something very different, and in this difference is not merely not natural, but is contrary to nature.

Money is invented as a convenience, to facilitate such natural exchanges as shoes for grain, because natural goods are difficult to carry about. Money is a common measure for other goods, with only limited intrinsic value itself. Yet as trade continues, the acquisition of money becomes an end in itself, and what is a measure for wealth is identified with wealth. Finally, money is earned, not only from the exchange of goods other than money, but from the exchanging of money, i.e., from usury. This is wholly unnatural and hence bad.

Why does the human faculty of reason lead to such degeneration, proceeding as it does from the extension of natural barter through the use of money to the final corruption of usury? Natural wealth is limited by the needs of the household, for example, the amount of fleece by the amount of cloth needed for clothing, the amount of food by the hunger of a limited number of stomachs. But every art is unlimited with respect to the good at which it aims: medicine does not aim at a certain amount of health, it aims at as much health as possible. Once wealth becomes an end, as it is the end of what we today call economics, it seeks not the amount of wealth needed by the family, but simply wealth. Yet the connection of economics with the family remains in this fact: the family originates in the need to perpetuate life, and economics seeks to accumulate goods that are serviceable for life. That is, it seeks goods that either support mere life or that gratify the appetites necessary for the preservation of life. The drive for accumulation is rooted in the enjoyable excess of those pleasures which are originally the natural concomitants of the preservation of life. Such excess is the natural enemy, we might say, of the perception of the difference between mere life and the good life, and for this reason Aristotle condemns it categorically.

Still, Aristotle admits that the art of acquisition is part of the art of the statesman, and he nowhere excludes the possibility that even usury may be sometimes useful. The *polis* needs the specialized vocations of the arts of acquisition and of medicine, since the families need the benefits of their skills, and the family as family cannot provide them.

If we compare the two branches of acquisition, we must notice that at the center of one is a species of war and that the other is trade, culminating in usury. Neither war nor trade in their developed forms can be carried on by the family. Thus we see that political activity is generated by the requirements of the human family, even though the human family originates in the same necessities as do the families of beasts. To some extent war and trade are alternative modes of acquisition, and Aristotle seems to praise war, or at least just war, while condemning trade, or at least its extreme form. The root of injustice seems to be the abolition of the limits upon the desires of the body of which man, alone among the animals, is capable. Perhaps the extreme of trade, culminating in usury, is more akin to the abolition of those limits than is war. Whether or not this explains Aristotle's judgment, it is clear that nature has established limits for human life, no less than she has done for the other animals, however much she has left it in the hands of men to enforce those limits.

The second book of the *Politics* consists of these main parts: first, critiques of theories or discourses concerning the best regime by men who did not themselves take part in politics (Plato, Phaleas, and Hippodamus); second, critiques of three well-governed actual regimes (Sparta, Crete, and Carthage); and third, a brief discussion of nine famous lawgivers, men who combined theory with practice by either founding regimes or legislating for existing ones. We might then characterize the order of Book II as theoretical, practical, and practical-theoretical.

Book I established the formal definition of the *polis* as the community of communities and affirmed it to be a complex, natural whole. In tracing its genesis from the family, Aristotle traced the genesis within the elements of which the *polis* is compounded to the distinction between mere life and the good life. The full elaboration of this distinction would provide a description of the best of all possible ways of life; it would describe the best *politeia* or regime. This Aristotle actually does in Books VII and VIII, although he has not completed the task when Book VIII breaks off. It is important to realize, however, that for Aristotle the nature of the *polis,* as of everything that exists by nature, is such that its perfection, which is its nature in the most emphatic sense, is to be sought in the first instance in the manner of its generation. And this in turn is due to the way in which Aristotle conceived the relation of theory and practice, speech and deed, essence and existence.

Every actual *polis* presents itself in the form of some regime: it is either a democracy, an aristocracy, an oligarchy, and so on. Similarly, every man whom we see, apart from having a name like Smith or Jones, is either brave or cowardly, just or unjust, wise or foolish. We never see a *polis* or a man, we only see individual *poleis* or men, and to be man or *polis* is never identical with being the particular being whom we experience with our senses. Further, Smith may be brave, and Athens may be free, but the quality of being a brave man or a free *polis* is never identical with being Smith or Athens. When we reason out what it is that makes a man brave or a *polis* free, we discover that the quality itself implies more than is or can be perceived in any actual *or possible* Smith or Athens. For Plato, the qualities revealed in speech, the qualities which we contemplate with our minds' eyes, hence the qualities which are the objects of theory, always transcend—thus in some sense differ from or contradict—the things of which we have sensible experience. Reality, for Plato, is thus ineluctably paradoxical. Aristotle denies this. Man (like dogs and horses) is generated by man and the sun. The things discovered in speech are reflections of things themselves or, rather, they are more or less adequate reflections depending upon whether the speech about the things is adequately disciplined by a true method or science of the things. The idea of man is in each man and is ultimately identical with the activity in virtue of which human beings generate human beings and not dogs or horses. There is thus no paradox for Aristotle in the unity of man and the plurality of men. The idea of the *polis* is similarly present in the generating factors of the *polis* (similarly, not identically, because the *polis* requires the assistance of art for its generation in a way that generation which is altogether natural does not). Plato's *Politeia* or *Republic* reveals what Plato regards as the nature of justice, but it transcends every actual or possible *politeia* in the way that speech about every idea reveals tendencies in sensible things that sensible things themselves never fully embody.

In approaching Aristotle's critique of the Republic, the dominating topic of Book II, we should consider that Aristotle's demonstration of the impossibility of that regime as a model for political practice (like his demonstration of the impossibility of the idea of the good serving as such a model or guide in Book I of the *Nicomachean Ethics*) is in agreement, rather than disagreement, with Plato. The disagreement lies deeper and concerns whether a model which transcends practice and can never be imitated in practice reveals the nature of practice more truly than a model which lies within the range of what is possible in practice. It is characteristic of the difference between Plato and Aristotle that Plato's quest for the best regime requires a construction in speech (or theory) to which nothing in practice does or can correspond, while Aristotle's quest first takes the form of an inquiry into regimes both of speech and deed, either of which might contain elements of the best regime. The first regime in the *Republic,* the so-called city of pigs, the regime constructed out of the necessities of the bodies of men, revealed nothing of the ultimate demands of justice. For Plato, the generating of living bodies by living bodies does not of itself set in motion the tendencies which culminate in the truly just regime, the regime which can exist only in speech. In Book I of the *Politics* Aristotle contradicts this thesis: the families which result from the generation of the bodies of men evidently require as their complement the *polis.* The justice which makes every *polis* a *polis,* i.e., the form that justice takes in virtue of which this *polis* is a democracy and not an oligarchy, is a variety of the forms of justice. The unity underlying the plurality of the forms of the *polis* is like the unity underlying the variety of individuals of every species. It results from the nature common to all men, who are all political animals. This nature is *in* all men, not beyond them, and the truth about the *polis* like that about all nature is nonparadoxical because it is constituted, not by the duality of form and matter (to which correspond speech and deed, theory and practice), but by their unity.

The first and dominating topic of Book II, as we have noted, is the consideration of Plato's *Republic.* One must attend with utmost care to the manner of its introduction. The *polis* is a community, a having things in common. It is the community of communities, hence it embraces something common to everyone. Aristotle asks, Is its perfection achieved by making common everything that can possibly be common? Or by making some things common and others not? Or by making nothing common? The last appears to be excluded by definition. If nothing were common it would not be a community. In the *Republic* of Plato, observes Aristotle, Socrates says that children and wives and property are to be shared or made common to all the citizens. Which arrangement is preferable, Aristotle asks, that which now obtains or that in the law set forth in the *Republic?*

To facilitate a concise view of a lengthy argument, it may be well to give Aristotle's answer to the foregoing question at the outset. The present system, of private families and private property, if adorned by good morals and by the right laws, would be much superior. Aristotle does not say flatly that the present system is superior because he does not seem to regard the present system (namely, that of Athens, which is not one of those thought by Aristotle to be well governed) as good. But the present system can be made good, whereas that of the *Republic* cannot. Why? The fundamental objection to the communism proposed by Socrates is that it aims to produce the greatest amount of unity in the *polis* but mistakes the nature of political unity. To push unity beyond a certain point, says Aristotle, changes the *polis* into a family, and a family (so far as possible) into one man. But in doing this, he says, you do not unify the *polis* but rather destroy it.

Aristotle now demonstrates how the family, whose growth and proliferation require the institution of the *polis,* is structurally part of the perfected *polis,* because the distinctions which give structure to the family—between husband and wife, father and children—are the foundation of morality within the *polis.* To take the broadest ground, the morality which consists in subordination of private interests to public welfare is impossible if the distinction between private and public is abolished. The *polis,* Aristotle holds, is a heterogeneous, not a homogeneous, unity. It is no more unified by abolishing the distinction between private families than by abolishing the distinction between occupations. That is, you do not make the *polis* more a unity by making every man a shoemaker and every man a carpenter; on the contrary, the *polis* requires division of labor, and by reciprocal equality, which means a fair exchange between artisans like the shoemaker and the carpenter, enables all to enjoy better shoes and better houses. In the isolated family the skills of shoemaker and carpenter may be necessary within the same household, but the institution of the *polis,* in which many specialized skills are available to all, is for this very reason self-sufficient in a way the family by itself is not. If two men call the same woman wife, the result is apt to be, not greater friendship, but conflict. In fact, however, Socrates intended all men to call all women their wives, and all the children collectively their children. Each woman was only a fractional wife of each man, and each child only a fractional child of each father. This, says Aristotle, will not strengthen the social bonds but will dilute them. Better for a man to regard a boy as his own nephew than as his and every other man's son. With the weakening of the strong bonds of private affection and private morality will come a weakening of the moral prohibitions against assaults and injuries against fathers and kinsmen, not to mention the dissolution of restraints against incest and homosexuality. To abolish the private family leads to the abolition of most of the prohibited degrees of sexual intercourse, and in consequence to the introduction of many forms of familiarity which lead to immoral intercourse. The claims of morality cannot thereby be enhanced but are rather dissipated. Aristotle's argument seems to be that the restraints which one learns in the family, e.g., the respect for authority in the person of the father, and the enhancement of an offense of violence if it is against a father, and similarly the horror of incest between parents and children, or between brother and sister, or of homosexuality between brothers, lays a foundation of restraints upon behavior which is then extended to members of different families, and finally to civic morality. Civic morality consists in perfecting the morality whose foundation is the family, at first by giving it an authority greater than the family can achieve, and finally by giving it a purpose which transcends the family.

In addition, Aristotle emphasizes the impossibilities of Socrates' proposal: the resemblances between natural parents and their children will betray themselves, and attachments will accordingly be formed. Public property will not be well cared for, some will be slackers in their work, and quarrels will arise in the distribution of the goods. The reclassing of children, which Socrates says will go on between the guardians and the working class, will betray the origins of some, and even the diluted bonds will be attenuated. Moreover, Socrates leaves a mass of unsolved difficulties: for example, is communism limited to the guardian class, or does it include the farmers and artisans? If there is to be one communist system for them all, so that all are "children" of the same "parents," how can the two classes be separated into menials and guardians? And if communism is limited to the upper class, what will be the political functions and education of the lower class? If they do have private property, it will be very hard to keep them in a subordinate position.

Private property, Aristotle holds, is rooted in human nature. Selfishness is justly condemned; but this does not mean it is wrong to love oneself, only that it is wrong to love oneself in excess. Similarly, love of money is not wrong, but loving it in excess is. The indefeasible roots of private property are the indefeasibly private pleasures of the body. In the *Nicomachean Ethics* Aristotle observes that the pleasures of good food, wine, and sexual intercourse which all men enjoy, pleasures which are natural and necessary, are not bad.[9] Only their excesses are bad. Socratic communism in the *Republic* would, by attempting to abolish the occasions of evil, abolish also many of the occasions of virtue. Even if it prevented some evil, it would also prevent much good. The advantages of communism can be gained by making the use of property common, as in Sparta men freely use each other's slaves and horses and dogs and help themselves to the fruits of each other's fields as they travel. But a man cannot practice liberality if he has nothing of his own to give, or show temperance in relation to women if there is not such a thing as another man's wife. The real cause of evil, says Aristotle, is not the absence of communism, but wickedness. What must be made common is not wives and children and property, but a system of education. The *polis* is no more made one by communism than a harmony is made one by converting it into a unison, or a rhythm made one by converting it to a single beat. It is strange, says Aristotle, that one who, like Socrates in the *Republic,* expects to accomplish excellence by education, should at the same time rely on such institutions, instead of relying on customs, philosophy, and laws.

The *Laws,* says Aristotle, was written later, in an attempt to provide a regime nearer to actual *poleis,* although in fact it leads back little by little to the *Republic.* And so most of the same objections made to the *Republic* apply to it. As a proposal for the regime which is next to the first (or best) it is unacceptable, although as a version of polity, or the mean between democracy and oligarchy adaptable to most *poleis,* it might have something to recommend it.

All other regimes are nearer to actual practice than those of Plato. Phaleas of Chalcedon has made a proposal that resembles Plato's in that it attempts to eliminate the causes of division and strife within the *polis* by the regulation of property. Indeed, Aristotle credits Phaleas with being the first to introduce this notion. Phaleas would make the property of the citizens equal at the foundation of a regime, and in those already established would seek to level inequalities by requiring the rich to give but not receive dowries and the poor to receive but not give them. Aristotle comments, first, that such legislation (as also in the case of Plato's *Laws*) will be ineffectual if the total number of children is not limited in proportion to the total amount of property. Second, not merely equality and inequality must be considered with respect to men's estates, but their size, which must be neither too large nor too small, tending neither to luxury nor penury. Finally, what is needful is not so much to level men's properties but their desires, and this requires education.

Phaleas, it is true, is consistent in providing the same education for

[9] Aristotle *Nicomachean Ethics* 1154ª 15ff.

all. But he does not tell us what that education is to be. But, says Aristotle, dissension is caused not only by inequality of property, but by inequality of honor, the lower classes being concerned primarily with the former, the upper classes with the latter.

According to what Aristotle says here, inequality of property is, relatively speaking, a minor factor in the creation of civil disturbances. This, he maintains, is because it is not so much the avoidance of pain, or the deprivations of the body, which cause trouble as it is the appetites or desires not connected with deprivations. It is not so much to avoid hunger and cold that men steal as to enjoy luxury. That a man's neighbor has a greater estate will not anger him nearly so much as if one he deems his inferior is held in the same honor. There are then three classes of desires which need to be dealt with: those arising from the needs of the body; those arising from the desires of the body in excess of what is necessary; and the desire for pleasures which are not due to pains i.e., as the pleasure of eating depends upon the pain of hunger). For the first kind of desire, a moderate amount of property accompanied by work is needful; for the second, the virtue of temperance or moderation; for the third, the remedy is philosophy, which alone frees us from dependence upon other men.

Phaleas' scheme is directed only to minor evils and fails to take into account that the greatest crimes are not those connected in any way with property. Men do not become tyrants, observes Aristotle, to avoid hunger and cold, nor does one honor a man for killing a thief as one does for killing a tyrant. Leveling estates is not, then, the place to start in the attack upon political evil. The starting point, says Aristotle, is to train those who are by nature superior not to desire to have more than is right, and to prevent the inferior (while not treating them unjustly) from being able to.

Hippodamus was the first man not engaged in politics to speak of the best regime, even as Plato was first to introduce community of wives and children, and Phaleas first to attack the problem of dissension by the regulation of property. Hippodamus was an eccentric, and Aristotle gives a character sketch of him—the original political scientist—that is without parallel in either the *Ethics* or *Politics*. He had long hair (the Spartan style, considered effeminate in Athens), wore the same cheap clothes summer and winter, but with expensive ornaments, and wished to be learned in the whole of natural science. He was also the man, Aristotle tells us, who invented the division of cities and applied it to Piraeus (the port of Athens). He was, we might add, the father of town-planning as well as of political science (in one sense of that term). Perhaps the most revealing brief comment on Hippodamus is one that occurs in Book VII, in the course of Aristotle's thematic discussion of his own best regime. The question concerns the arrangement of streets. The modern fashion introduced by Hippodamus, which is more pleasant and convenient, is for private houses to be laid out along straight lines. But, says Aristotle, the opposite arrangement of olden times was much safer, for it was harder for foreign troops to find their way into the city or make their way through it. Aristotle's own solution, characteristically, is to combine the two kinds of plans, designing certain parts of the *polis* for comfort and beauty and others for security. Hippodamus was, then, a theorist in the modern sense, i.e., one who approached politics as an abstract problem in design, without regard for the problems that statesmen as practical men faced. He was also like certain twentieth-century political scientists in his attempt to assimilate the science of politics to a mathematically oriented natural science. Hippodamus' scheme has a certain resemblance to Plato's in that it appears to be an attempt to impose mathematical harmony upon the *polis.* His best regime had a population of ten thousand and was divided into artisans, farmers, and warriors. The land he also divided into three parts: one sacred, one public, one private. The law, too, he found fell into three categories: outrage, damage, and homicide. He established one supreme court of appeal for all cases, to consist of selected elders. He thought that jurors should not give simple verdicts of guilty or not guilty, according to the indictment as drawn (the current practice), but should give qualified verdicts finding guilt on some counts but not others—if this was the individual juror's belief—and assessing damages according to the juror's judgment in damage suits. For Hippodamus thought that the practice of finding a man guilty or not guilty, when the juror believed him to be guilty of some things but not of others in the indictment, forced the juror to commit perjury. Finally, Hippodamus proposed a law which would honor anyone who discovered anything new for the advantage of the *polis,* as well as one that would provide public support for war orphans. Aristotle dryly observes that Hippodamus apparently thought this last was a new suggestion, but in fact such a law already exists in Athens and other *poleis.* [10]

The last observation sets the tone of the critique of Hippodamus: a man who wants to institute systematic search for political novelty ought to be better acquainted with what already exists. The tripartite division of the *polis* has an air of simplicity which is specious: all three classes are to share in the government, but the farmers have no arms, and the artisans neither arms nor land. The warriors will not tolerate the political equality of those who are thus much weaker than themselves, and the oppression of the warriors will make the other classes enemies of the regime. More trenchant still is Aristotle's criticism of the so-called farming class: on the

---

[10] We cannot help being reminded of present-day investigators who pursue elaborate studies with refined mathematical techniques, which end only in the "scientific" demonstration of what everyone always knew.

face of it, no class would seem more necessary, and yet in fact they farm only for themselves and are politically superfluous. The warriors are to be supported from the public land, which they must either farm themselves (hindering their ability to be soldiers), or there will be yet a fourth class to farm it for them, which in turn will have no political rights. The artisans are self-supporting anyway. Aristotle reveals confusion after confusion beneath the surface of these proposals.

Again, the proposal to reward those who discover advantageous novelties is attractive but unsafe. It may cause malicious prosecutions (either against the innovators or by the innovators) and even revolution. This leads to another, broader question, and it is the fundamental question raised by Hippodamus: Is politics an art or science like the other arts or sciences, in which each new discovery is rightly incorporated into the practice of the art or science? Aristotle's reply is that politics is not like medicine or gymnastics, in which every alteration from traditional practice, in the light of better knowledge, is rightly acceptable. Not that tradition as such is a political norm: on the contrary, the most ancient customs are utterly foolish; and in general what men really seek is not what their fathers had but what is good. The distinction between the good and the ancestral is as fundamental to the art or science of politics as to any other. The possibility of improvement in the political order is in fact twofold: first, because of the progress of general intelligence (including progress in the arts and sciences) from primitive man; and second, because of the necessity of every law to be framed in general terms, while the actions governed by law are always particulars. Experience must always reveal ways in which the laws might be better framed, and therefore how they might be improved. On the other hand, however, much caution must be exercised in making these improvements, says Aristotle. Small improvements would not outweigh the harm done by making changes in the laws, changes which breed distrust in the government. The example of the other arts is false. Politics is not an art like medicine and gymnastics, for the law has no power to persuade other than that derived from custom or habit, and these are formed only over a long period of time. Changing laws weakens their power, it loosens the bonds of the community, and this requires the greatest circumspection. But if changes in the laws are to be made, says Aristotle (and of course they sometimes must and ought to be made, or why write the *Politics*?), does this mean that all laws are open to change in every form of government? To use a modern instance, would we here in the United States today accept proposals for change in the Bill of Rights in the same spirit as changes in the exemptions in the income tax? And again, Aristotle asks, shall anyone propose changes, or only certain people? For example, does it make no difference whether the changes are proposed by a constitutional convention under the presiding genius of a

George Washington, or by anyone anywhere? These things make a difference in politics that they do not make in the practice of the other arts.

After the discussion of the three regimes of speech or theory, we
come to the three actual regimes, which exist in deed. Concerning any
regime, Aristotle says, there are two questions. First, how does it compare
with the best regime? Second, is there anything in its construction
contrary to its hypothesis? The meaning of the second question becomes
clearer from an explanation, at the beginning of the fourth book, of the
different kinds and degrees of political excellence with which the political
philosopher must be concerned. The best regime is such as one ought to
choose if there were no external impediments, either human or nonhuman, to virtue, or virtuous activity, as the end of life in the *polis*. The
hypothesis of the best regime is just this: that virtue is its end and that
there are no external impediments to its attainment. In practice, however,
there almost always will be impediments, both to the choice of the best
end and of the best means. The hypothesis of a regime other than the best
is the assumption (or set of assumptions) by which the controlling aim or
purpose of the regime is qualified in the light of its impediments, as
compared with the best regime.

The analysis of Sparta reveals above all one thing: the inner
connection between the quality of the construction of a regime and the
quality of its hypothesis. Sparta is defective not merely because conditions are less than perfect, but because the legislator mistook a part of
virtue for the whole of virtue, and this intellectual error is the leading
cause of the defects Aristotle discovers.

Aristotle's critique of the legislator's purpose comes almost at the
end of the discussion of Sparta; but as so often happens, the end is in fact
the beginning. The entire ordering of the laws is directed to a part of
virtue, the part which contributes to success in war. The Spartans' warrior
discipline won them safety in war and an empire. But they had no training
in the pursuits of peace and began to go to pieces as soon as they had won
their hegemony. They err also in another respect, according to Aristotle,
and this error is really at the bottom of the other. They rightly think that
the good things won by fighting are the achievements of virtue rather than
of vice. But they wrongly suppose that the external rewards of virtue are
worth more than virtue. The full meaning of this observation is given in
Book VII in the famous discussion of the relative merits of the active and
the contemplative life, as the ultimate goal either for a single man or for a
polis.[11] Sparta is there, too, given as an example of a *polis* devoted wholly
to war, and war is there seen as the goal of those who do not grasp the
ultimate supremacy of thinking over acting, as the basis not only of
thought, but of action.

[11] Aristotle *Politics* 1324^a 5-1325^a 13.

The criticism of Sparta has three main divisions: the last part centers upon the principle or hypothesis of the regime; the first concerns the defects of Spartan economy (slaves, women, property); the second concerns political defects in the narrower sense (the ephors, elders, and kings). We will limit outselves to the first and last and their connection. Aristotle begins his criticism of Sparta by observing that a well-governed *polis* needs leisure, and this can only be provided by slaves. He says little more on the subject here, other than that the helots are like an enemy in the Spartans' midst, waiting only for disaster to strike their masters to rise in revolt. Aristotle does not say here what the remedy for such a situation must be, but the answer has already been made clear: the art of ruling slaves is a part of household management, and the Spartans have not cultivated this art. The reason, too, is clear: household management is an art of peaceful living, and friendship between master and slave, to the extent it is possible, depends upon a common purpose uniting them in such a way that both contribute to it according to their natures. War, or success in war, as an end in itself, means ruling those who are not meant to be ruled and for a purpose for which men are not meant to be ruled. The Spartans' defective relation to foreign *poleis,* in virtue of their policy of conquest, is reflected in their defective internal relation with their slaves and wives. In cruder terms, in their anxiety to rule those abroad whom they ought not to rule, they neglect those at home whom they ought to rule. The same reasoning accounts for the licentiousness of Spartan women, who by reason of the neglect of the men, preoccupied with military pursuits, and because of the addiction of soldiers to the pleasures of love, are self-indulgent and unmanageable. The women tend to get control of the management of affairs as well. What difference does it make, asks Aristotle, whether the women rule, or the rulers are ruled by women? The result is the same. The irony of all this is that the *polis* that identifies the whole of virtue with the supposedly most manly of virtues—courage or fighting—is penalized by being dominated by females. The irony comes full circle when Aristotle points out that, in neglecting to rule their women properly (along with their slaves), both because of their absences on military expeditions and because they had neglected the domestic arts while at home, the Spartans greatly weakened themselves militarily. For during the Theban invasion, the women of Sparta caused more confusion than the enemy. The subordination of the pursuits of war to those of peace is then a necessary condition of a truly successful military policy.

The defects of the system of property are consequences of the condition of women. It is dishonorable in Sparta to sell a family estate but not to give it or bequeath it. The result is that nearly two-fifths of the land is owned by women. Without regulation of inheritances and with the practice of large dowries, the ban upon alienation of estates has proved inconsequential. As a result of the concentration of ownership, there has been a depopulation of the armed class (who need property to furnish the wealth needed for arms), as well as a social division into extremes of wealthy and of poor. Again, we see the attrition of the regime's military strength as an ultimate consequence of its military nature.

The discussion of Crete, which follows that of Sparta, also has three main parts: first, an account of the relationship of Crete and Sparta; second, an account of analogies in the two systems; and third, an evaluation of similarities and differences. Sparta is held to be an improved imitation (on the whole) of Crete, which is the older regime. This raises some subtle and interesting questions as to the possibilities of political progress, a subject first raised in relation to Hippodamus' proposal to reward political novelties. It also involves the question of the relation of Lycurgus, the Spartan lawgiver, to Minos, the Cretan lawgiver, on the one hand, and to Thales, whose pupil Aristotle says Lycurgus is reputed to have been. Minos, son of Zeus and Europa, represents the oldest tradition of Greek law as it ascends to the gods; Thales is the traditional founder of philosophy. The Cretan institution which Aristotle praises most highly is that of the common meals, which are paid for from the public lands and are not a private charge as at Sparta. The legislator, he says, has devised many wise means for securing moderation at table. Also, he has segregated the women from the men in order that they might not bear many children and for the same purpose has instituted homosexual relations among the men. Whether this is good or bad, says Aristotle, there will be another opportunity to inquire. There is, however, no further discussion of this question in any surviving text, and we may observe that this perverse institution does offer one solution to a recurring problem in the *Politics:* how to keep the ratio of population to property constant. Another solution, of course, was emigration. Whether Crete is one of the three best-governed actual regimes because of, or in spite of, this one feature remains speculative. The principal explicit criticism of Crete is that it does not have any constitutional means of reconciling the people to the regime (as at Sparta where the people choose the ephors), so that discontented members of the upper classes combine with the people periodically to make what are in effect revolutions.

The discussion of the Carthaginian regime follows the same pattern as that of Crete. First, some general remarks comparing it to the others; second, the principal points of resemblance to Sparta; third, criticism of the principal features of the regime. The most conspicuous feature of the general remarks is the praise of Carthage. Carthage comes closest to Sparta, which has already been praised as better than Crete. The three regimes, says Aristotle, come closer to each other than any of them do to any other regime, and all are greatly superior to any others. The proof of the excellence of Carthage is the fact that the *dēmos* or common people have remained faithful to it, and that neither civil strife nor tyranny worth mentioning has arisen there. Such remarks go quite beyond what Aristotle has said in praise of Sparta and justify classifying Carthage as the best of all actual regimes. Two further points ought to be made here, although they invite the interpretation of Aristotle's silence rather than his words. Carthage is a non-Greek or, in the technical sense, barbarian *polis;* and we are not given any information by Aristotle concerning the legislator or legislators of Carthage, or their relation, if any, to the famous legislators or teachers of legislators concerning whom he says a great deal elsewhere in the *Politics*.

The three points of resemblance to Sparta are: the common messes of the companions (equivalent to the *phiditia*); the office of the one hundred and four (equivalent to the ephorate); and the kings and council of elders (which correspond to the kings and elders at Sparta). In this context Aristotle mentions that the one hundred and four are chosen for merit, not at random, as in Sparta; and the kings are chosen, not from the same families, but from outstanding ones.

As to political criticism, this falls into three categories: features common to Carthage and the other regimes, which Aristotle has sufficiently spoken of in the case of the other two; and those which depart from aristocracy either toward democracy or toward oligarchy. The democratic deviation is the practice of referring to the popular assembly, not only for approval, but for discussion and for ultimate decision, any question upon which kings and elders cannot agree. The oligarchic deviation is in the manner of choosing the magistrates, which is based upon a kind of electoral college system, comprised of "boards of five" which are co-opted and membership in which is clearly restricted to the wealthy classes (although Aristotle does not explicitly say so). But the chief deviation from aristocracy is in an opinion (rather than an institution), and it is one that is shared by the many (as well as the few). For whatever the ruling class holds in honor, Aristotle says in a memorable phrase, the rest of the citizens are certain to follow. This opinion is that rulers should be chosen not only for their virtues but for their wealth. The Carthaginians think that a poor man lacks the leisure for governing well (in which they are of course right), but the legislator errs in not providing from the outset that the best men have sufficient leisure, whether in or out of office.

This leads us to certain observations concerning Aristotle's procedure with these three regimes: the very first question he took up vis-à-vis

Sparta concerned the provision of leisure, which he said is not easy to provide. He there speaks of the difficulties that Spartans and Thessalians had with their servile classes (and no solution for the problem of leisure is hinted at which does not require a servile class). The Cretans, we are told, have escaped this problem, mainly because of the fortune of geography. The requirement of leisure is clearly correlated with the "hypothesis" or principle of the regime, and Sparta we saw was severely criticized for mistaking the nature of virtue. In the treatment of Crete, much is made of the advantages they enjoy from geography. They are evidently less warlike than the Spartans, but in this they are weak rather than wiser. Aristotle says remarkably little about the principle or hypothesis of the Cretan regime. With Carthage, he returns somewhat obliquely to the question of the principle of the regime. Carthage is the only regime of the three that he plainly calls aristocratic, although he does so only in pointing out how it deviates from aristocracy. But as Sparta confuses a part of virtue—courage or military valor—with the whole of virtue, so Carthage confuses a condition of virtue—leisure and the wealth required for it—with virtue. In doing so, the legislator has made the whole *polis* avaricious. It is significant how the criticism of Sparta and Carthage, which Aristotle has already said are closest to each other, here coincides: the consequence of Sparta's devotion to war was also to cause a deviation mainly to oligarchy.

We now come to the last of the three main subdivisions of Book II. This section—dealing with lawgivers—is frequently regarded as consisting of "jottings" or "rough notes" either by Aristotle or a later hand. This view fails to consider, however, the way in which this section seems to fulfill a plan in Book II, moving as it does from the "theoretical" to the "practical" to the "practical-theoretical," i.e., from those who took no part in politics but wrote on the best regime, to good regimes of practice, to the views of those who both held opinions concerning the best regime and took part in politics. Moreover, while there are three regimes of "theory" and three of "practice," there are nine legislators mentioned by Aristotle. The central one of these is Onomacritus (whose name means "name-judge"), who was a Locrian who traveled in Crete, where he practiced soothsaying. According to a tradition (in which Aristotle himself places little credence), he was the first man who became skillful in legislation (as Plato was first to introduce community of wives and children, Phaleas first to equalize property, and Hippodamus first, not a politician, to speak of the best regime). Apparently, however, he did not have any pupils, but had as a companion Thales, who in turn had Lycurgus and Zaleucus for pupils. The whole subject of the relation of tradition to the arts (as of Minos to Thales) and the nature of the relation of progress in the one to progress in the other, is certainly involved here, as it is in the great thematic passage on Hippodamus. But only a comprehensive analysis of the admittedly episodic passages in this section, in their relation to similar passages elsewhere in the *Politics,* could establish their meaning.

Book III begins as follows: "To the one inquiring concerning the regime, what each is and of what sort, almost the first inquiry to make is about the *polis,* whatever is the *polis.*"

Aristotle says he must discover "what and what sort" each regime is. There is, then, a variety of regimes. We must try to understand what that variety is by again trying to understand what the *polis* is. But have we not already had the *polis* defined for us? Aristotle carefully says that "almost" the first question is, Whatever is the *polis?* The first question was answered by the definition with which the *Politics* began, a definition elaborated and defended in the remainder of Book I. The opening definition establishes the relation of the *polis* to other species of human community on the one hand, and to the genus "communities of gregarious animals" on the other. In Book I Aristotle established the definition of the *polis* as the community of communities, originating in the need to preserve life, but continuing for the sake of the self-sufficient or good life. The analysis of the household, and the sciences arising from its needs, establishes the necessity of a separate science of the *polis,* as it established the specific differences of *polis* and household. Book II demonstrated the need for a new inquiry into the best regime. Book III supplies us with the science of the *polis* and the leading feature of that science: an adequate inquiry into the principles of regimes, and in particular of the best regime.

In Book I Aristotle controverted two scientific or philosophic doctrines, those of Platonism and conventionalism, to establish the doctrine that the *polis* was a complex natural whole. In doing this, he pursues methods concerning which he makes two remarks near the beginning of Book I. It is his accustomed method, he says, to analyze a compound whole into its simplest, uncompounded elements. What he actually does, however, as he indicates, is rather to trace the genesis of the compound whole from the genesis of the elements of which it is compounded.[12] These two methods are not, of course, exclusive. Both speak of the whole and of the parts, but one begins from the parts and discovers from the parts that they must be compounded into a larger whole to fulfill their function as parts. The other begins with the whole, and discovers from the whole that it is resolved into parts whose functioning makes the whole. The parts discussed in Book I, however, are households or families; in Book III, citizens.

Aristotle's point of view in Book I is one of radical detachment from political life. He observes the *polis* as one among the number of

[12] Ibid., 1252ᵃ 18; 1252ᵃ 24.

forms of community which are the result of the gregarious natures of animals, and he wishes to classify it accurately in relation to the genera and sub-genera of which it is a species. In Book II he dissects the various specimens proposed as possessing the perfections upon which the most accurate classification might be based. In Book III, however, when he no longer treats of the opinions of others concerning the regime, but begins to present his own doctrine, he appears not as an external observer but as someone within the *polis*. The conflicts of opinions with which we are immediately confronted are no longer the conflicts between observers of political life, they are the conflicts among participants, among men who differ as to how the burdens and advantages of political life should be divided and shared. What is most significant about Aristotle's method in Book III is not so much that it is analytical in the sense indicated, but that it draws philosophic conclusions from the opinions of men who are neither philosophers nor legislators, but men who are contending for political advantages in political life.

The subdivisions of Book III are not marked in the same manner as those of Book II. This is Aristotle's exposition of his own doctrine and not the critique of other regimes; and there is a continuity in the argument, and a recurrence of themes, which it is not easy to anatomize. Some division of Book III, however provisional, is necessary for an orderly presentation. To begin with, Book III may be divided by the transition from the answer to the opening question, "Whatever is the *polis*?" to the question, "Is there one regime only, or many?"[13] It is a matter of speculation whether we should consider the discussion of monarchy as a third major subsection, or whether this continues and completes the discussion of regimes.[14] The discussion of monarchy begins by recalling that it is one of the "correct" regimes, but the form of monarchy which emerges as the most important topic of discussion is *"pambasileia."* This is a kind of absolute rule, in which the king is to the *polis* as the head of the household to the household. It is thus called a kind of "economic" rule. But, since economic rule is fundamentally different from political rule, according to the general doctrine of the *Politics,* it cannot be assumed that this fifth form of monarchy is a form of regime properly so called. Therefore it is at least doubtful whether the discussion of monarchy, which culminates in the consideration of *pambasileia* or absolute monarchy, forms part of the discussion of the regime, or is a third major subsection of Book III.

The first subsection may be conveniently (although perhaps not definitively) divided into three subsections. First, the definition of the citizen (*politēs*) and therewith the *polis*. Second, the inquiry as to who is a

[13] Ibid., 1278^b 6.

[14] The discussion of monarchy begins at ibid., 1284^b 35.

citizen and what makes the *polis* the same (or different) when the regime changes because of revolution. Third, the first of the great disputations of Book III, Is the virtue of a good man and of a good citizen the same or different?

The definition of the citizen is required because it is a matter of dispute what the *polis* is. Some say that an action is an action of the *polis,* others that it is an action not of the *polis* but of the oligarchy or tyrant. Who are they who thus deny that an action is that of the *polis,* and what is that action? In considering the problem of revolution,[15] Aristotle makes explicit what is implicit at the beginning of Book III. When the regime changes from oligarchy or tyranny to democracy, the people may repudiate the public debt on the ground that the money was borrowed, not by the *polis,* but by the oligarchic clique or the tyrant. Hence the denial is a democratic denial of a financial obligation (and the action is the one of incurring debt). It is well to remember this when we discover that the first or "absolute" definition of citizenship applies more particularly to democracies than to other forms.

The absolute or unqualified definition of citizenship is that it is nothing other than a sharing in the administration of justice and in office. This means participating in what we would call legislation and adjudication, with these two "powers" being sufficiently broad to assimilate what we would understand by administration or execution of the laws. Indeed, Aristotle generalizes from this first definition, saying that what he really means is participation in "indefinite office." This definition, he then observes, fits democracy particularly well, but not necessarily other regimes. The idea of "indefinite office" fits democracy because there all free men constitute a body from whom officeholders are drawn, and nearly all free men participate in some offices (particularly those of jurymen, who had a wide variety of functions in ancient democracy, beyond those we assign to jurymen). But such a definition does not fit regimes such as Sparta or Carthage where political participation is narrowly limited and defined, that is, where few people hold any offices, and only some people can hold some offices. Nevertheless, the definition holds if we say that citizenship means participation in the deliberative and judicial functions of the *polis,* and that he is a citizen who can and does so participate. And, finally a *polis* is a collection of citizens numerous enough to lead a self-sufficient life.

Aristotle next considers the phenomenon we call "naturalization," which in turn leads us to the topic of revolution. In practice, he observes, they are called citizens who are born of citizen parents, but this is obviously inadequate, because the first citizens could not have had citizen parents. The question who, in fact, is a citizen is answered differently

[15] Ibid., 1276ᵃ 9 ff.

after a revolution, when different people exercise the powers by which citizen is properly defined. A regime which excludes many who formerly were citizens will regard those excluded as not having been rightly citizens. Conversely, those included by a new regime will regard the regime which formerly excluded them as not a regime, but a rule of force in contravention of law and justice. This, of course, is the view of a democracy which has overthrown a tyranny and repudiates the tyrant's debts. But, says Aristotle, if an action is repudiated on the ground that it is an act of force and not for the common good, then similar acts of democracies can also be repudiated as not truly being acts of the *polis*. The source of authority does not of itself indicate whether actions are impositions of mere force or are actions taken for the common good. In the opening passage of the inquiry as to where the ruling power should be, Aristotle is still more explicit on this point, as we shall see.[16]

When the *polis* changes in the manner just contemplated, what is it that enables us to say that it is the same *polis* or a different one? We have seen that a *polis* is a collection of citizens, but a revolutionary change will result in a different collection constituting the citizen body. Is it then a different *polis* or not? Aristotle first says what does not identify a *polis*. It is not a place, not even a place enclosed with a wall, for a wall around the Peloponnesus would not make those within the wall fellow citizens. Nor is it population, for the people of a *polis* are always dying and being born, like the water in a river which is ever changing, while the river itself remains the same. The *polis* is a community, a community constituted by a regime (*politeia*), and when the regime changes the *polis* is no longer the same, just as a tragic chorus is not the same as a comic chorus, although the persons of the two choruses may be identical. It is then *chiefly* (although Aristotle is careful not to say solely or exclusively) with respect to the regime that one must say that the *polis* is the same or different. But whether a *polis* which is a democracy should pay the debts of a tyrant whom the democracy has overthrown is not decided by this conclusion, which requires another argument. Aristotle never presents this argument, at least not overtly. We may perhaps infer it from the distinction which he next forces upon our attention: the distinction between a good man and a good citizen. Obligations which men may not have as citizens they may still have as men. If the citizens of a democracy benefited (whether intentionally or not) from the debts contracted by the tyrant, their obligations *as men* would surely be different from what they would be if the debts had been contracted entirely for the purpose of, let us say, unjustly suppressing the democracy.

We come then to a question for which the way has been prepared by the implicit suggestion that, while man as citizen is essentially a

[16] Ibid., 1281ᵃ 11 ff.

member of a regime, man as man may have obligations which do not arise from, and may not coincide with, those of his citizenship. That question is: Is the virtue of a good man and of a good citizen the same, or is it not the same? This third subsection of the first part of Book III is approximately equal in length to the first two together. Complex as the argument is, here, too, there appear to be three well-defined further subsections. First, there is a definition of the virtue of a citizen, which is not, speaking simply or unqualifiedly, the same as that of a good man. Second, there is the inquiry which reaches the conclusion that, while in general the virtue of good man and good citizen are different, they may coincide in the case of a good ruler. Third, there is an inquiry into whether all those admitted to a share of office—who are perforce citizens by the definition previously accepted—can in fact possess the virtue of citizens. To summarize: Aristotle first establishes the general difference between good man and good citizen; next he specifies the case in which a good citizen may be a good man; third, he specifies the cases in which a man *can* be the good citizen who will be a good man. It is most important for the student here to observe how Aristotle, in taking up a new question, enlarges and refines his answer to an old one. For the results of the inquiry in this subsection into the difference between human and civic goodness or virtue establish grounds for distinguishing different kinds of civic excellence that were not before visible. These, in turn, actually transform the definition of citizenship, while preparing as well for the discussion of regimes which follows.

Aristotle employs the familiar "ship of state" metaphor to explain "in outline" what is the virtue of a citizen. Each citizen is a partner, or sharer in a community, like a sailor on a ship. The sailors differ in their functions—one is an oarsman, another a helmsman, another a lookout—yet all share a common purpose, safety in navigation. So do citizens differ. In Book IV Aristotle lists nine different parts of which the *polis* is composed, beginning with the farming and mechanic classes, on through those who fight, who deliberate, and who judge.[17] Different forms of civic virtue would seem to correspond to the different functions of each of these parts of the *polis,* yet the good performance of the work of each part would have one and the same end: the safety of the regime (*politeia*). If, then, there are many forms of regime, there must be many forms of citizen virtue (in addition to the differences internal to each regime arising from the variety of functions therein), yet there can be only one form of excellence or virtue for man as man. Hence the virtue of a good man and of a good citizen cannot be identical.

Aristotle employs yet another argument to establish this conclusion. Not even the best regime could consist entirely of good men, yet if it were in fact the best regime every citizen would have to perform his duties

[17] Ibid., 1290ᵇ 38 ff.

as well as possible. Hence in the best regime it would appear that there would be some good citizens who were not good men. Still a third argument follows. A *polis* is a compound, even as an animal (of soul and body), a soul (of reason and desire), a household (of man and woman), and property (of master and slave). Every compound has a ruling and ruled elements,[18] and the virtue of ruling is evidently different from that of being ruled. Citizenship requires both forms of virtue, but the form of human goodness is one. Hence the virtue of a good man and of a good citizen cannot be the same.

The third argument of the foregoing series leads naturally to the question whether the virtue of a good man and of a good citizen—although they cannot be simply identical, because the virtue of citizenship is twofold—may not nonetheless coincide in a certain case, that of the good ruler. A statesman is a ruler, and hence must be wise in the sense of possessing a form of practical wisdom. (In the *Nicomachean Ethics,* Book VI, Aristotle distinguishes *phronesis,* practical wisdom, of which the virtue of the *politikos* or statesman is a branch, from *sophia,* or philosophic wisdom, which is concerned exclusively with thinking well and not with acting well.) A citizen, simply as citizen, may be a subject, not a ruler, and hence need not have the practical wisdom of a ruler. In the *Nicomachean Ethics* it is affirmed that the moral virtues, in the strict sense, imply the presence of practical wisdom, as the presence of practical wisdom implies the presence of moral virtue. Hence the citizen who does not have the practical wisdom of a ruler need not be even morally good in the highest sense. Nothing sums up this argument better than Aristotle's own example, given at the end of this discussion in the *Politics.* While other virtues may be common to ruler and ruled, practical wisdom (or one form of it) is the ruler's virtue alone. The subject, the man who is ruled, needs only right opinion. The latter is like the man who makes flutes; the ruler corresponds to the man who plays the flute. The virtue of a good man may then coincide with that of a good citizen in the case of the citizen (*politēs*) who is a statesman (*politikos*), who is a good ruler (*archon spoudaios*).

Next, Aristotle asks, Can anyone who is called a citizen by our previous definition—namely, participating in office—be truly a citizen? To put it slightly differently: Can *any* citizen (so called by us) be a good citizen, capable not only of being ruled, but of ruling, and hence of being a good man? The very intricate discussion of ruling and being ruled in the previous subsection, of which we have summarized only the conclusion, indicated that "ruling" and "being ruled" each has different meanings. Being ruled for certain purposes, for purposes which are in some sense

[18] Cf. ibid., Bk. I, esp. 1254ᵃ 20 ff., and the remark concerning the musical scale.

slavish, disqualifies a man for ruling, just as being ruled in certain other ways is part of the necessary training of a ruler. In some regimes—e.g., extreme democracies—men whose occupations are slavish—the mechanic classes—are admitted to citizenship, and while these men may be good citizens, in the sense that they can perform their civic duties well enough to preserve the democracy, they cannot be good men. The conclusion then follows that only under a regime which admits to citizenship only those men who are capable, by birth and training, of becoming good men, will it happen that any good citizen *can* be a good man. The final and strict conclusion of the entire discussion of good man and good citizen is then as follows: He who is capable of ruling (although he need not be an actual ruler), either alone or in conjunction with others, in a good regime (i.e., one which admits to citizenship only those capable of practical wisdom and moral virtue) is at once a good citizen and a good man.

We come now to the central sequence of topics of Book III. The first was initiated by the question, Whatever is the *polis*? The second, to which we now turn, is initiated by the question, Is there one regime or many? This second main section of Book III is divided as follows. First, an introduction setting forth the thematic question. Second, an answer to the twofold question, What is it for which the *polis* is instituted, and how many forms of rule are there? Third, an answer to the question, Who (or what) ought to be the ruling authority in the *polis*?[19]

The thematic question may be translated in full thus: Is there one regime, or many, and if many, what are they, how many, and what are the differences between them? There follows a brief definition of regime (*politeia*). It is an ordering (*taxis*) of the *polis* in respect of its offices, and chiefly in respect of the supreme office. The word "office" is, however, a narrow rendering, and the neologism "decision-maker" conveys something important that is lacking from that translation. What Aristotle means is that whoever makes the big and vital decisions for the political community thereby gives the community its structure and form. The "decision-makers" in the true political sense, as Aristotle would understand that term, combine what we normally understand by legal authority with the authority of the "establishment," in the currently fashionable sense of that term. They are, in other words, both legal sovereigns and ruling class in the traditional meaning. In a democracy, says Aristotle, the people are supreme, and in an oligarchy the few. The government (*politeuma*) is the regime (*politeia*), meaning that what causes the *polis* to have a certain form *is* the form.

The second subsection is devoted to answering a twofold question. What is it for the sake of which the *polis* is instituted, and how many forms of rule are there of man and of the community? Regimes, we are

[19] Ibid., 1278^b 6-15; 1278^b 15-1281^a 10; 1281^a 11-1284^b 34.

told, are distinguished in two ways: first, by the distinction between rightly constituted regimes and those which are wrongly constituted or deviant. Second, by the enumeration of the principal varieties of both the rightly and wrongly constituted. It is in establishing the basis for the distinction between rightly and wrongly constituted regimes that Aristotle gives the first elements of his answer to the question of the purpose of the *polis*. That purpose arises from the fact that man is, he repeats from Book I, a political animal. Men are drawn together not only by necessity (the main emphasis in Book I), but by a desire for the company of their fellows, without whom they could not live well. The aim of a common life is not the better supplying of necessities, but the good life. Still, they *do* need each other for the sake of mere life which has a sweetness which makes men cling to it as long as hardships are not unbearable. Next, Aristotle reviews the forms of subpolitical authority—master and slave, father and children, husband and wife—and then forms of nonpolitical authority—those of a trainer and of a pilot. He points out that rule is always either for a common good or for the good of the ruled. In the case of master and slave, the good is primarily that of the master, but they *do* have a common good, because the deterioration of the slave will deteriorate the master's good. At the other extreme, the trainer and pilot consider essentially only the advantage of those under their direction and benefit themselves only incidentally: the trainer as he happens to take exercise himself while exercising his pupil, and the pilot as he happens also to travel on the ship he steers. By nature, a man holding office is like the trainer and pilot, as in looking after the welfare of his fellow citizens, he thereby stands in need of assistance from them in his own private affairs, which he neglects while attending to the common or public concerns. In the present corrupt times, says Aristotle, men seek office avidly, as a means of advancing their private welfare rather than that of the public. Here then we see the nerve of the distinction between rightly and wrongly constituted regimes: it lies in the distinction between regimes in which the rulers, like practitioners of the art of gymnastics or of sailing, rule those in their charge solely for the good of the ruled (and hence require some recompense for their neglect of their private good while thus occupied) or, on the contrary, consider their offices as sources of private profit.[20]

Next Aristotle gives the number and names of the varieties of regimes. To name the regime means to name the government, or ruling group, and this must be either one man, or a few, or the many. When these govern toward the common advantage they are rightly constituted, and when not, they are deviations from the right forms. The usual designation for the rule of one when it is for the common advantage is

[20] The student should compare this passage of the *Politics* with the Thrasymachus section of the *Republic* of Plato, Bk I, and in particular 345ª-347ᵉ.

kingship, that of a few aristocracy, that of the many polity (*politeia*), which is also the generic name for all regimes. Deviations are: tyranny corresponding to kingship, oligarchy to aristocracy, and democracy to polity. In the first, the single ruler considers only his own interest; in the second, it is the interest of the rich which governs; and in the third, the interest of the poor. In none of the deviant regimes do the rulers think of a common interest, but only of themselves.

Next Aristotle elaborates upon the foregoing distinctions, with especial reference to the difference between democracy and oligarchy. He introduces this elaboration with the unusual remark—for the *Politics*—that for one who is philosophizing, and not merely looking into a subject with a view to practice, it is proper not to overlook or omit anything, but to set forth the truth. The remark is unusual because of the emphasis, in both the *Ethics* and *Politics*, upon the essentially practical nature of these disciplines.[21] The difference between democracy and oligarchy is then *not* primarily the difference between the rule of the many and of the few, for if there were few poor and many rich the rule of the many would not be democratic nor the rule of the few oligarchic. Democracy is essentially rule of the poor and incidentally rule of the many, and oligarchy is essentially rule of the rich and incidentally rule of the few, although, Aristotle observes, the rich are everywhere few, and the many everywhere poor. The particular importance of this theoretical distinction may lie in the peculiar practical importance of democracy and oligarchy as the two regimes which in practice dominate political struggles. And it is also true that it is from the opinions—the erroneous but complementary opinions—of the partisans of democracy and oligarchy that Aristotle compounds the true opinion which is the basis of his own doctrine concerning distributive justice.

We come now to the exposition of oligarchic and democratic justice, or rather to a discourse nominally devoted to this theme, but actually devoted to extracting from the exposition the answer to the broader question of the true purpose of the *polis*, which is the general topic of the entire section. First, Aristotle explains that all men lay hold of a kind of justice. The one kind of partisan says that it is equality, and so it is, *for equals*. The other kind says that it is inequality, and so it is, *for unequals*. Men are bad judges in their own cases. They state the case only to the point it serves their narrow interest, and not as it stands truly. Justice is a relation between things and persons—e.g., positions of honor and trust on the one hand, and men to fill them on the other—and the partisans see very well what is equal or unequal in the division of such places. But they fail to see what it is that makes the men who are to fill them equal or unequal. Those who are freemen think that if they are

---

[21] Cf. Aristotle *Nicomachean Ethics* 1094ᵇ 11-27, 1198ᵃ 25, and 1103ᵇ 26.

equal as freemen, they are equal in every respect; those who are rich think that if they are unequal in wealth they are unequal in every respect. But the ruling principle, the truly authoritative consideration they never mention.

Next, Aristotle expounds this ruling or sovereign consideration. It is, of course, that the *polis* exists, not for the sake of life, but for the good life. The fallacy of the partisans is that they confuse the necessary conditions of political life with the sufficient conditions. The oligarchic fallacy would appear to consist in mistaking the *polis* for a kind of joint stock company, in which the man who contributed 99 percent of the capital is rightly entitled to a larger share, either of principal or profit, than the man who contributed only 1 percent. On the other hand (and this seems to refer to the democratic partisans), the *polis* is not a military alliance for protection against injury. Mere self-preservation would characterize as well a community of slaves or lower animals. But again, neither is it an association for trade. The Etruscans and Carthaginians have commercial relations, but they are not fellow citizens. Aristotle cites approvingly the Sophist Lycophron, who said that the law is a pledge or surety of men's just claims against each other. [22] Indeed it is, but abstaining from injustice is not sufficient to make men fellow citizens. Men who abstain from injustice are not for that reason good or just. (The man who practices honesty because it is the best policy is not for that reason honest.) Good government implies a concern with political virtue and vice.

Having pointed out that neither the virtues engendered by trade nor those engendered by war are in and of themselves to be equated with political virtue, Aristotle considers locality. Megara and Corinth would not be one city even if enclosed within the same walls, not even if the citizens of each intermarried, although intermarriage is an important element in making a community. Nor, again, if they lived close together and exchanged goods, as do carpenter, farmer, shoemaker, and in addition were in military alliance, and yet abstained from wrongdoing.

The sufficient conditions of political life will not, of course, be realized without the foregoing necessary conditions—in particular inhabiting' the same locality and practicing intermarriage. These conditions are accompanied by the various forms of social life which go beyond mere utility—e.g., fraternal, religious, recreational associations—which, however, arise not from material needs, but from friendship. Friendship—as Aristotle makes clear at great length in Books VIII and IX of the *Nicomachean Ethics*—means active concern for others, a concern with their well-being, which means with their capacity for welldoing. This in turn means a concern with their capacity for virtuous activity, from which happiness

---

[22] This may be the best single approximation to what is understood by the *state*, as distinct from the *polis*. See above, p. 11.

results. And so the political community is above all a community for the sake of acting well (or nobly), or for the sake of happiness. Those who contribute most to enabling friends and fellow citizens to become virtuous and live happily have the larger share in the *polis*. They alone are politically superior, be they never so equal or inferior to others in freedom, birth, or wealth.

Next, Aristotle asks, Who (or what) ought to be the supreme ruling authority in the *polis?* This, we might observe, is the supreme political question, for upon the answer to this question every other political question depends. We have been told that oligarchy and democracy are defective regimes, because they mistake contributions to the necessary conditions of the political community's existence for contributions to its true end or purpose; that is, they mistake contributions to the wealth or freedom of the *polis*—things without which there cannot be a *polis,* but which in themselves do not make a *polis*—for contributions to living happily and well. But what weight do we give to the various claims put forward by those who compete for rule? A *polis* is neither a trading community nor a military alliance, but if we reject the claims of the wealthy and the free (those who pay taxes and those who fight), we may not have a *polis* at all. The attempt to realize the higher aims of the *polis* must not be such as to destroy the material conditions which are necessary for the existence of the *polis*, just as the recognition of the material necessities cannot justifiably inhibit the attainment of happiness and a good life.

The subsection we are about to examine is by far the longest of Book III, and in a sense the culminating theoretical analysis of the entire book, and of the entire *Politics*. Let us then describe the topography of this subsection, however provisional the grounds of our distinctions may seem. First, there is an introduction, setting forth the main question, and the other questions into which this main one resolves itself. Second, there is an inquiry into and partial vindication of the claim of the many to rule, as opposed to that of the few best. Third, there is the inquiry into the question into which the opening question is now seen to resolve itself.[23] Justice is the political good, and justice means equality for equals and inequality for unequals, but Equality and Inequality in What?

Turning now to the introductory subsection, we meet the thematic question, What ought to be the ruling authority in the *polis?* The claimants are: the many, the rich, the good, the one best of all, and the tyrant. These correspond to the six regimes enumerated earlier, with the notable difference that "the many" is the numerical and thus ambiguous ground for both democracy and polity. "The many" as such is neither rich nor poor nor, presumably, good nor bad. This is, of course, only ab-

---

[23] Aristotle *Politics* 1281^a 11-39; 1281^a 39-1282^b 13 and 1282^b 14-1284^b 34.

WHAT IS POLITICS? 49

stractly or theoretically true, and Aristotle characteristically proceeds in a "practical" vernacular. The recognition of the claim to supreme authority by any of these claimants, Aristotle says, appears to have disagreeable consequences. Suppose, for example, the poor divide up the property of the rich. Is this not the extreme of injustice? "By Zeus, it was justly passed by the ruling authority." Thus the response of the partisans of the many, i.e., of the poor and of democracy. It is one of two oaths in the *Politics,* and that it justifies what is characterized as extreme injustice is not without ironical significance. Also, we must recall that the definition of the *polis* called for at the beginning of Book III was required because of the democratic (and possibly unjust) repudiation of the debts of the oligarchy or of the tyrant. That the many identify their authority with their manyness (instead of with their poverty, which is the real reason they seize the wealth of the few) is shown next by the identification of their authority with majority rule. Suppose then, Aristotle asks, the majority again expropriates the minority? Clearly, the principle which justifies expropriation on the ground that the many are the *polis* is a monster which eventually devours even itself. But justice is not a destructive principle, and therefore the rule of the many, as such, cannot be a principle of justice. Similar considerations rule out the authority of the rich as rich, or of a tyrant.

But what about the claims of the good? Now Aristotle introduces a still greater perplexity. That neither the poor nor the rich have an unfettered right to rule is clear. But this does not mean they have no claims upon authority whatever. Offices are honors, and to be excluded from office is to be excluded from honor. The unqualified rule of the good would seem unjustly to dishonor classes which do contribute to the common good, by contributing to the necessities without which the *polis* cannot be. And the rule of the one best man would seem to carry the foregoing "oligarchical" tendency to a further extreme. But there are those who say that the law should rule. Yet the law itself can be democratic or oligarchic, so that the same difficulty recurs. Here, then, we have the formulation of the problem of this subsection, and the indication as well that there is no solution in terms of any of the regimes mentioned. However, we already noticed that neither democracy nor polity has been explicitly mentioned in the beginning of this introduction, only the many, who are as such the numerical ground for either democracy or polity. In the difficulties presented by the different kinds of claims, we saw the many referred to in the practical terms of their antagonism to the rich. That their claims need not rest upon their poverty, however, and that a regime of the many need not be identical with democracy, it is Aristotle's immediate concern to demonstrate.

In Book IV Aristotle defines polity as a mixture of two "deviant" regimes, democracy and oligarchy.[24] Here, however, he presents the claims of the many as corresponding nevertheless to the claims of virtue. The claims of virtue would appear to be the only intrinsically valid claims, but the recognition of the claims of virtue is not identical with the recognition of the claims of the virtuous. In the first place, the virtuous are somewhat backward in presenting their claims. Aristotle has indicated,[25] in agreement with Socrates in the *Republic,* that the good man will regard office as at best a kind of duty which he must perform in neglect of his own private interests. Another way of putting this is to say that there is a kind of selfishness in the good which causes them to draw back from, if not to turn away from, political competition as insufficiently rewarding. Illustrative of this is the statement in Book V[26] that those who excel in virtue are the ones who might most justly make a revolution (when others with inferior claims are preferred to them), but that they are the ones least likely to do so. To some extent the political problem is one of compounding the simulacra of virtue in the nonvirtuous, as a device rendered necessary by the withdrawal of the virtuous from active contention. To some extent it arises from a different inadequacy of true virtue. First, there are not likely to be enough virtuous men to constitute a *polis.*[27] Next is the fact that virtue is related to the sufficient rather than the necessary conditions of political life. But virtue as productive of sufficient conditions is not necessarily productive of necessary conditions. There is a kind of disproportion between the necessary and sufficient conditions of political life which makes a genuine equation between political honors and political contributions peculiarly difficult, perhaps impossible. *Political virtue,* as we shall see, is a kind of facsimile of true virtue,[28] a facsimile which compounds certain resemblances to virtue in nonvirtue, to give greater dignity to nonvirtue, and which compounds certain resemblances to nonvirtue in virtue, to give greater political effectiveness to virtue. We now witness Aristotle's laborious attempt, in principle, to achieve such a compound. We say "in principle," because it is in Books IV, V, and VI that he does so in any detail. To some extent, the obscurity which surrounds much of the ensuing argument arises from the danger to political life of expounding too openly the indirectness whereby virtue can become politically effective. That is to say, political virtue which is not confused with strict virtue will not be politically effective, and hence will not be political virtue!

[24] Ibid., 1293^b 29.
[25] Ibid., 1279a 8 ff.
[26] Ibid., 1301^b 1.
[27] Ibid., 1283^b 10.
[28] Cf. Aristotle *Nicomachean Ethics* 1162^a 17, on the distinction between genuine courage and political.

The claim of the many to rule in a good regime is recognized as follows: the many, while individually not good men, may be collectively better than those who are superior to each of them separately. Aristotle gives three analogical examples. A feast to which many contribute is better than a feast supplied at one man's cost. The many judge works of music and poetry better, for one man judges one part of a work, another another, and together they judge the whole with superior judgment. The superiority of the painter's art over reality lies in this: he can select the beautiful eyes of this one, some other superior feature from someone else, and so on, so that the painted figure combines the excellences which in nature are scattered among many. The first example corresponds to the refutation of the claims of the rich: the many poor may yet be collectively wealthier than the wealthy few. The second example, involving deliberation and judgment, refutes the claims of the few good. The third example deals with the claims of the one best man: the many may equal or excel him, not individually but collectively. The argument derived from these examples requires the qualification Aristotle promptly adds: it may justify the popular claims to a share in the regime of *some* multitude (or *dēmos*), but not of any and every one. We have already seen the many characterized by the extreme of injustice, as in the passage in which the people swear by Zeus to justify expropriation, believing it right simply because they have decreed it. We must again recall that the question of what the *polis* is arose because of the democratic denial of a debt. Whether this argument (namely, of collective virtue in the many) applies to every people and every multitude, Aristotle says, is unclear, or, rather, he says, "perhaps, by Zeus, concerning every one it is clearly impossible, because the same argument could apply to beasts; and how, so to speak, do some multitudes differ from beasts?" Thus does Aristotle, in the second (and final) oath employed in the *Politics,* balance the emphatic speech of the many in justifying the extreme of injustice with an oath which insists that they are sometimes bestial. At the same time, we are warned of the limitations of an argument which, explicitly deriving from analogies, justifies no more than an analogical virtue.[29]

The argument from collective virtue is next used to decide what offices may, and what may not, be safely entrusted to a *qualified* multitude. They must not participate in the highest offices. By this Aristotle here means those offices for which collective virtue manifestly cannot be a substitute for the virtue of a single man, as would be the case of such modern offices as president, prime minister, cabinet officers, supreme court justices, or speakers and leaders of legislative assemblies. But offices which contribute to collective deliberation and judgment—e.g., voters,

[29] Cf. the resemblance of bestial courage to true courage, in ibid., 1116[b] 10ff.

members of legislative assemblies, juries petty and grand, and so on—could be filled by and from the many.

Finally, there is a discussion of whether the idea of collective virtue of a lay public does not contradict the experience of the other arts. Aristotle considers the case of medicine, as he had earlier compared politics to the art of the trainer and pilot. The demand for trained intelligence does not, he concludes rule out the general public, for even in medicine there are qualified nonexperts who can judge the work of experts. The argument from the arts further rules out a brutalized public, but not every public. It leads to Aristotle's final conclusion in this context: the possibility of utilizing collective virtue in a properly circum-scribed role demonstrates nothing so much as the need for good laws. For, he implies, the circumscription of the people to their proper functions, and of the higher officials to theirs, as well as the education of both in the requisite virtues, is the work of good laws.

We come now to the third and final subsection of the subsection addressed to the question, Who (or what) ought to be the supreme authority in the *polis?* The problem has been stated, and the claims of the many (under the conditions favorable to those claims) have received their due. Even under favorable conditions, those claims are met without admitting the many to the *supreme* offices. Justice is the political good, and justice is a kind of equality. Common opinion agrees with philosophy in this, that justice is a relation of things and persons, and that to equal persons equal things are due. Offices are honors, and justice demands therefore that for men who are equal there should be equal honors, and for men who are unequal, unequal honors. There is generally no difficulty in discerning whether offices and honors are equal or unequal. But in what is it that men are to be held to be either equal or unequal? This problem, Aristotle says, calls for political philosophy.

In thus defining this supreme political problem, Aristotle twice uses the word "philosophy" as in the foregoing paraphrase. These are the second and third (and last) times the word occurs in Book III. The first time, we recall, was when Aristotle said that for one "philosophizing" (the verb rather than the noun was used) nothing ought to be overlooked or omitted, whether of practical significance or not.[30] What was inquired into then was the essential difference between oligarchy and democracy. That was found to consist in a difference in quality which had no necessary connection with the *numerical* difference between the many and the few. This rejection of a numerical distinction corresponded with Aristotle's opening polemic in Book I against the reduction of the differ-ent forms of rule to differences in the *number* of those ruling or ruled.

[30] Aristotle *Politics* 1279^b 12.

Now, in seeking the thing whose proportions in different men determine the proportions according to which political honors and offices ought to be awarded, we are again concerned with relationships between quantities and qualities.

This becomes more evident when we turn to the thesis which Aristotle now investigates with a view to deciding the matter. "Perhaps someone would say that offices should be distributed unequally according to every excess of a good." According to this thesis, if men are in other respects alike, yet one is taller or has a better complexion, then he should be awarded the office. The fallacy of this thesis, says Aristotle, is evident if we compare the awarding of offices to the awarding of flutes. Among flute-players equally good at playing the flute, we do not give better flutes to the better born. Let us digress, however, and ask whether the idea that a superiority in birth or beauty can contribute to superiority in flute-playing is simply absurd or whether, like many other opinions, it merely requires correction. Good birth is called virtue of race by Aristotle, which also means inherited virtue. Strictly speaking, of course, virtue cannot be inherited, because it is the result of habituation (moral virtue) or teaching (intellectual virtue). Yet there is a kind of virtue[31] which is really an aptitude for virtue, called by Aristotle natural virtue. No one is, strictly speaking, a born musician or mathematician, although we call someone a born musician or mathematician if he becomes one with very little teaching. Similarly, some are born with an aptitude for courage or temperance if, with very little moral education, they become brave or self-controlled. Such aptitudes, or natural virtues, can be inherited. Aristotle says in Book I that nature intends to make the bodies of freemen as different from those of slaves as the statues of the gods differ from those of men.[32] In the same way that nature fails to make freemen visibly different from slaves, she fails to make the sons of good men good. If nature succeeded, however, the ordering of society would be relatively simple.[33] As superior bodies and superior minds would go together, the different kinds of education appropriate to the different kinds of souls would be indicated by the different shapes of their bodies. And the different offices would be allocated by the different virtues resulting from the different kinds of education. Hence good birth, beauty, and virtue would be found together in the regime which was thus truly according to nature. Good birth and beauty would not literally contribute to flute-playing, but aptitude in flute-playing would very likely be found among those who were well-born and beautiful. More important, political virtue would certainly be found

[31] Cf. Aristotle *Nicomachean Ethics* 1144[b] 3ff.
[32] Aristotle *Politics* 1254[b] 26ff.
[33] Cf. ibid., Bk. VII, 1332[b] 17ff.

among the well-born and beautiful and never among the ill-born and ugly. That we picture the gods as superior in beauty no less than in wisdom is itself far from being politically irrelevant.

In this connection we should consider again Aristotle's example of the painter who collects from many their individual points of perfection—e.g., nose, eyes, foot, hand—to produce a portrait of a perfection surpassing that of any one human being. The painter, in combining these many perfections, achieves what nature intended but failed to achieve. Art thus perfects nature in one sense, while in another sense it is nature which perfects art. For in the latter sense it is nature which enables the artist to achieve perfection by teaching him what he must do to achieve perfection. The political philosopher might then be thought of as the artist of the *polis.*

Suppose, Aristotle continues, someone superior in flute-playing, yet inferior in birth and beauty. Suppose, moreover, that good birth and beauty surpass flute-playing more than the best flute-player can surpass all other flute-players. Even so, says Aristotle, we would award the superior flute to the superior flute-player, be he never so inferior in birth and beauty. To suppose that any superiority in birth and beauty could compensate for an inferiority in flute-playing, when it came to a distribution of flutes, would imply that birth and beauty could in some way contribute to flute-playing, which they cannot. The argument Aristotle here controverts implies, he says, the commensurability of every good with every other good. We cannot help being reminded by this observation of the critique of the Platonic idea of the good in Book I of the *Nicomachean Ethics.* According to the Platonic doctrine, as there presented by Aristotle, there is one idea or form of goodness, which is the cause of what is good in every good thing. It would follow from this doctrine that the intrinsic goodness in every good thing is identical with the goodness in every other good thing. From this it would follow that, with respect only to their goodness, they could differ only as more and less, and to such differences numerical values could be assigned.

Why does Aristotle recur to this abstruse metaphysical issue? If the argument from flutes were not sufficient, does not his further example suffice: that athletic prowess is properly rewarded, not by political office, but by athletic prizes? The difficulty here, it seems, lies in the inner inconsistency in the two kinds of opinions upon which Aristotle draws for his conception of distributive justice. On the one hand, opinion says that justice is equality for equals and inequality for unequals. Birth, wealth, and freedom are qualities needed for the existence of the *polis,* hence they and not flute-playing or speed of foot are properly considered with a view to political honors. The same is true of justice and political virtue. The difference between flute-playing and wealth is a difference between non-political and political goods. The difference between wealth and political virtue is a difference between what contributes to the existence and what contributes to the good government of the *polis*. If no amount of a nonpolitical good can equal a political good, can any amount of a necessary good, e.g., wealth, equal any amount of a sufficient good, e.g., virtue? If it cannot, how can the equation of honors or offices with merit be true? In Book V of the *Nicomachean Ethics* we find the formula for distributive justice.[34] It is, says Aristotle, a species of the proportionate, and the proportionate is equality of ratios. In a just distribution, as A is to B, so C is to D. That is, as the merit of A is to the merit of B, so is the honor C (awarded to A) to the honor D (awarded to B). Now if these are genuine ratios, the terms must be commutable. Thus, not only will A/B equal C/D, but A/C will equal B/D. Furthermore, AD will equal CB. But, and here is the crux of the entire matter, if AD equals CB, then *some* multiple of A's excellence equals *some* multiple of B's excellence. But if this is true—as, strictly speaking, it must be—then we are confronted with a dilemma. Either the excellences to be rewarded—namely, A's and B's—must be homogeneous, of one kind, or excellences different in kind are commensurable.

Let us be absolutely clear as to the nature of the foregoing dilemma, for it appears to be the central theoretical problem of the *Politics*. The dilemma stems from the two opinions whose combination yields the formula for distributive justice. One of those opinions is that justice is an equality of ratios. This opinion is itself a philosophic refinement of the nonphilosophic opinions which are the defining characteristics of oligarchic and democratic justice, the former holding that justice is inequality, the latter that it is equality. Combining the two, Aristotle holds that justice is equality for equals, and inequality for unequals, and hence equality of ratios. The other opinion, besides that which holds justice to be equality of ratios, is the one that holds that goods different in kind are incommensurable. But how can one find a set of ratios that will justly relate the claims of wealth and/or freedom, on the one hand, and virtue on the other, unless some amount of wealth and/or freedom will equal some amount of virtue? Or, conversely, how can we deny that some amount of wealth and/or freedom will equal some amount of virtue, unless we deny that justice is an equality of ratios which comprehend the *different* contributions to the common good? We must again recall that the first two books of the *Politics* are pre-eminently devoted to demonstrating that the *polis* is a compound of elements different in kind, to

---

[34] Aristotle *Nicomachean Ethics* 1131^a 10-1131^b 24.

which there correspond virtues or excellences different in kind. In the light of this analysis we can regard the *Republic* of Plato as an attempt to resolve this dilemma by the hypothesis that justice is one and the same in a single man and in a *polis*. The unity sought by Socrates in the *Republic* seemed, however, to reduce the *polis* to a family and the family to one man. This, Aristotle said, does not unify the *polis* but destroys it. Since justice is the preservative, not the destroyer, of political life, this cannot be in accordance with justice. However, we may consider whether Plato took but one horn of the dilemma. If justice demands an equality of ratios, and if such equality cannot be realized unless the different qualities which contribute to the common good are somehow rendered commensurate, then to insist upon the incommensurability of different qualities may also lead to the denial of the possibility of justice.

Aristotle will not sacrifice heterogeneity to homogeneity, nor homogeneity to heterogeneity. His argument seems to turn from the critique of each of these conflicting theses to the critique of the other. And his solution to the problem seems thereby to bear a striking resemblance to the problem itself. We may barely hazard the opinion that the theoretical dilemma which appears to lie at the heart of the analysis of the constituent elements of distributive justice may constitute a ground for rejecting pure theory as a ground for a practical discipline. It may be observed that the doctrine of virtue as the mean, as the right intermediate point between two vicious extremes, in the *Nicomachean Ethics,* is a seemingly mathematical formulation, which proves to be true only in an analogical sense. Virtue is an intermediate point between two extremes, but not a point whose distance from other points can be measured. Something similar is true of Aristotle's solution to the problem of distributive justice, a solution which reflects the theoretical understanding implicit in the grasping of the aforesaid dilemma, but reflects it rather in its negation of the necessity which constitutes the dilemma.

What then is Aristotle's emphatically practical solution? Its principle may be found in the recognition of the claims of the many, which now appears not so much as the recognition of these claims per se as the formula for the commensuration of excellences different in kind. The claims of the many, as they themselves understand those claims, are based upon the freedom of the many. The many think that because they are equal to the rich in freedom they ought to be equal in everything. Aristotle, however, finds a ratio between the claims of the many, on the one hand, and those of the rich and the good, on the other, not by comparing freedom with wealth and virtue, but by comparing the collective wealth and the collective virtue of the many with the collective wealth and virtue of the few. Again, the rich need not only be rich, but may be free and virtuous. And the good may possess not only virtue, but wealth and freedom. In short, each class of claimant can be compared with every other in respect of the claim of the *other*, and in *this* way, heterogeneity can *practically* be homogenized. It may be observed that the class with the intrinsically best claim, that of virtue, is least convincingly collectivized, in respect of the claims of the other classes, and the class with the intrinsically poorest claim, the poor, is most convincingly collectivized. Yet the practical problem is to bring together the extremes, to give the many a claim which will elevate them, and yet restrain them by the very thing that gives them dignity. The many, to repeat, may be lacking in any example of outstanding excellence yet collectively may—in a certain sense—equal or excel in virtue the few, just as they may equal or excel the few in wealth. By teaching the many that the ground of their recognition is not their collective strength, their weight in numbers as freemen, but their collective virtue, a bond is formed between them and the higher classes, in consequence of which the poor gain the respect of the upper classes while gaining as well a motive to earn that respect.

The wealthy, as we also saw, tend to identify political superiority with wealth alone. But as the wealthy see that the poor may collectively make a considerable claim upon the ground of wealth, they will be less inclined to push the argument from wealth, and more inclined to recognize virtue and freedom. Again, the wealthy may also be brought to see that one of their own number may be wealthier than all of the rest of them together. But the wealthy are not likely to wish to be subordinated absolutely to one of their own class either: they are more apt to be inclined to moderate their demands as a class, and rather seek security in a balancing of the different claims of the different classes. The same argument can be applied to the claims of virtue: the advocates of aristocracy do not really wish to yield their claims to virtue alone, when such a claim would result in one man rule; nor, again, would they yield it to the many, if and as the many could prove the superiority of their collective virtue. We can then sum up Aristotle's resolution of the problem of distributive justice as follows. The *polis* is a compound, which requires men who are well born (of good stock) and hence capable of assuming the responsibilities of free citizens; it requires as well men who are wealthy; it requires also men who are good. It requires all these things, in a certain proportion, a proportion which cannot be decided by abstract reasoning alone, but finally only by perception of the facts in each individual case. Those who are wealthy can rightly demand recognition of their claims, a recognition which will neither overbear, nor be overborne by, the claims of others. Since the wealthy, as wealthy, will not be virtuous, it may be pointed out to them, if they try to absolutize their claims, that the many or the one may be collectively wealthier than they are. Similarly, if the aristocrats absolutize their claims, it can be pointed out to them that either the one or the many may be more virtuous than they. The case of the many differs slightly: the argument from their freedom Aristotle at the end resolves into an argument from good birth (for what distinguishes a freeman from a slave is a good nature), and here again it can be maintained that one or a few may be better born than many. The argument for good birth is at bottom but an attenuated version of the argument for virtue, because a good nature is one with a capacity for virtue. Thus the argument for the many is at bottom an argument for virtue which is fully recognized in the argument for collective virtue. And this, to bring the wheel full circle again, means an argument which, if pushed too far, will justify the claims of the few or the one against the many no less than it will justify the argument for the many. As each rival claimant moderates his claim, in the light of the awareness that it can be turned against him the idea of a common good in which the rival claims are harmonized emerges. And the idea of the common good necessarily implies both a limitation upon the absolutized claims of each party—including that of virtue—and a priority of the claims of virtue. Here, then, is Aristotle's resolution of the problem of distributive justice, the just decision of the rival claims to supreme authority in the *polis*.

There is, however, a corollary to the foregoing solution of the problem of distributive justice, and this corollary supplies as well the transition to the subject of monarchy and from monarchy to the other regimes, the regimes which are more important for political practice than those treated in Book III. The quasi-mathematical formula for distributive justice is a means of reconciling the competing claims for political supremacy. In it virtue itself appears as merely one of a number of such claims, although we must recognize a paradox in the play upon different meanings of virtue. Virtue is always directed toward the support of the common good, and yet the common good means a good in which the claims of virtue are moderated to accommodate other claims. What, however, does one do if there is someone whose virtue is so great that no "proportion" is possible between his virtue and the virtue of others?

Let us illustrate the problem by taking wealth, rather than virtue, as the quality to be "proportioned." In so far as wealth is a claim to political office, a rich man who is twice as wealthy as another rich man deserves an office that is twice as important. It would be plausible, for example, to say that the office of secretary of the Treasury of the United States is twice as important as the office of undersecretary. But if there is a man who is a thousand, or ten thousand, times as rich as his next richest fellow citizen, then obviously no such plausible proportion can be imagined, for it is not possible to imagine one office that is one ten-thousandth that of another. Any actual allocation of offices will then either overvalue the inferior claimant or undervalue the superior. If we think, however, not of the impossibility of adjusting the claims of two rich men, but of rich and poor, we see that the excessively rich man is, in a sense, the common enemy of both the rich and the poor. The only solution, then, for dealing with someone who is so excessively rich or otherwise powerful is to banish or ostracize him, for he destroys the basis of the reconciliation of competing claims, and hence of the common good. Or, to be more precise, one must either banish him or make him the absolute and sole ruler. In the case of the other claims, ostracism is, Aristotle says, politically just. But in the case of the man who is "excessive" in virtue, which now means excessive in his propensity and ability to serve the common good, a good in which the claims of virtue are moderated in so far as they can *be* moderated, given the qualities present in a community for compounding a common good, this would be a contradiction in terms. In such a case, the only just alternative is to make the man absolute and sole monarch. To repeat: the harmonizing of the claims of the rich and the poor depends upon the poor having sufficient wealth, and the rich having sufficient numbers, so that each can make a claim upon the grounds advanced by the other. But if one man is too rich or too popular, so that this moderation of conflicting claims is rendered impracticable, then it becomes just to ostracize him, as one who makes the common good impracticable. But if one man upsets this balance not by his excess of wealth or other forms of political power, but by his virtue, then it is not just to ostracize him, and he must rather be made king.

This leads us to the final problem of Book III. We have seen that the common good normally leads to a balancing and harmonizing of competing claims, but sometimes demands unfettered and unqualified recognition of the claims of virtue alone. Which is better? The unhampered absolute rule of the one best man, or the rule of the best laws? For the rule of harmonized, competing claims must be a rule of laws. As it is a rule which prescribes that different men take turns in ruling, it therefore prescribes boundaries to the power of men who take up and lay down their offices, as they do so not at their own discretion, but at that of the law. Aristotle's arguments, both pro and con, are substantially the same as those in Plato's *Statesman*.[35] The decisive reflection is that politics both resembles and yet differs from the other arts, such as medicine. Certainly the doctor ought not to be restrained by written rules, so that he can only choose among treatments set down in a medical handbook, after having similarly chosen among diagnoses. Yet if the patient suspected the physician of being in league with his enemies, he might well prefer inferior medical treatment, and prefer even to doctor himself "by the book" than

---

[35] See Leo Strauss and Joseph Cropsey (eds.), *History of Political Philosophy*, 2nd ed., (Chicago: Rand McNally & Co., 1972), pp. 48-50.

take a chance that his heirs had made a deal to divide the insurance money with the physician. In the case of politics, we must inevitably suspect of interested motives anyone who puts forward a claim to absolute rule on the ground of superior wisdom and virtue. Still, the intrinsic validity of the claim in the case of *someone*—a someone very unlikely to put the claim forward himself—is not hereby destroyed. Aristotle's final conclusion appears to be that the argument stands as valid, but as the man who could justly make the claim will not do so, the only argument that can and will be validly advanced will be that in favor of the best laws. Still, in the infinite contingencies of political life, a moment might come when, contrary to every normal expectation, the rule of the one best man might have to be advanced in practice as well.

Books IV, V, and VI of the *Politics* are the pre-eminently "practical" books, wherein are applied the principles developed in Books I through III. The opening chapters of Book IV read almost like the beginning of a new treatise. Book III began with a question, Whatever is the *polis*? We were immediately plunged into a controversy, a controversy caused by the repudiation by a victorious democracy of debts contracted by a tyrant. The political philosopher appears in Book III as an arbiter or umpire, finding the element of justice and of injustice in the self-interested assertions and claims of partisans. He alone sees the whole of which the partisans are part. Thus he alone possesses the principle which recognizes the part which each partisan occupies in the whole, and thus can reward him in proportion to the importance of that part. Now the political philosopher appears in a different role, a somewhat less elevated but not less indispensable one. He is likened by Aristotle to the gymnastic or athletic trainer.

A practical program for politics would model itself upon gymnastics. The athletic trainer is not only concerned with the perfect regimen for the perfect physique, but must know how to prescribe for anyone who seeks his assistance. This means knowing what is good for the generality of men no less (in practice, a good deal more) than for the topflight athlete, and not only for the generality but for those with special needs and special handicaps. In like manner, the political teacher must know not only what is the absolutely best regime, but what regime is best for each of the different kinds of political communities. For most, the absolutely best would be as impossible and as undesirable as the training program of an Olympic champion would be for an overweight middle-aged businessman. A political teacher should know of a regime that is not only desirable and possible for most *poleis* but one which they can be easily persuaded to adopt. And for those who cannot adopt this second-best, generally practicable standard, he must have a further range of alternatives: he must know what would be best for each particular community, taking into full account its local peculiarities and shortcomings.

The first requirement for carrying out the foregoing assignment is to have available a full classification of regimes. In Book III Aristotle set out the basic forms of government, the three correct and the three deviant regimes. Now, however, he says that it is as important (perhaps more important in practice) to know the different varieties of each form, e.g., to know the different kinds of democracy and oligarchy, as to know the difference between democracy and oligarchy. For the attempt to establish an aristocracy, let us say, when only a democracy is feasible, may lead to disaster. But the attempt to set up one kind of democracy, when only another kind will work well, may also lead to disaster.

Aristotle now gives as the cause of the variety of regimes the variety of parts from which all *poleis* are compounded. In Book III we saw the variety of regimes as due, in the main, to the different principles by which men justified their claims to supremacy, and in particular wealth, freedom, and virtue. Now we see a still greater variety of regimes due to the variety of functions within the *polis* that must be performed by the rich, the poor, and the good. Aristotle lists these as the parts of the *polis:* farmers, artisans, merchants, unskilled laborers, warriors, judges, councillors, the rich, and magistrates. The many are thus seen to include such different elements as the farmers, the artisans, and the merchants, all of whom may be either rich or poor, as well as common laborers (who may be free or servile). Of crucial significance, however, is this: many of the foregoing can be combined, so that the same men can be farmers and soldiers, or judges and councilors; but the same men cannot be simultaneously rich and poor. And so in an especial sense the *polis* seems to be a compound of rich and poor, and democracy and oligarchy seem to be the two basic regimes, of which all others are variations. In principle, Aristotle denies this view because the distinction between rightly constituted and wrongly constituted regimes is more fundamental for him. Yet in practice he gives the distinction between democracy and oligarchy the major weight in his approach to the problem of ameliorating political life. His best generally practicable regime is polity (*politeia*), which happens also to be the generic name for all regimes. It is no accident that the specific and the generic name should coincide in the case of the regime which is a compound of democracy and oligarchy. For it coincides in the case of the one regime which balances the two elements which alone cannot be combined. Polity is a kind of virtuous mean between the two vicious extremes constituted by the claims of wealth and poverty.

Democracies will vary as the class of the many comprising the ruling class varies, whether farmers, artisans, merchants, sailors, fishermen, or laborers predominate among them; similarly oligarchies will differ according to the relative weight among their ruling classes of wealth, birth, virtue, and education. The different kinds of democracy vary as the principle of democracy is mitigated by the variety of interests within the *dēmos*, and the inclination to give greater protection to the interests of other classes, first by the rule of law, and second by some representation within the government of interests other than that of the dominant class. Thus the worst form of democracy would be simple, unrestrained majoritarianism, which usually means rule by the worst kind of demagogues. Better forms would, besides restraining the government by laws which circumscribed its power, give some recognition to property, either by property qualifications for the holding of some offices, or by giving some weight to property in the voting in the assembly. In Book VI there is a remarkable passage in which the concept of distributive justice, as developed in Book III, is adapted to the specific problem of tempering democracy.[36] There Aristotle proposes the following voting procedure in the assembly: let rich and poor constitute two voting classes, and let any resolution pass which commands a majority of each. But if the majority in each class is different, let the one whose total property assessment is greater prevail. For example, if on a given proposal, the rich vote six to four in favor, and the poor vote fifteen to five against, then the result would be nineteen to eleven against, on a purely majoritarian basis. If however, we assume that each rich man is twice as wealthy as each poor man, and they voted by property assessments, the vote would be twenty three to seventeen against, i.e., the minority viewpoint would increase its percentage of the vote from 37 percent to 43 percent. Aristotle's aim is *not* simply to strengthen the position of the rich by this proposal. Where the poor in a democracy are united in their views, they will prevail. In the foregoing example his proposal strengthens the position of the minority of the poor as well as the majority of the rich. Our numerical values in the examples are unrealistic, in that we supposed, for the sake of convenience, that all the rich would be equally rich and all the poor equally poor, which in practice they would not be. Aristotle's basic aim, of course, is to encourage the combination of the richer of the poor with the poorer of the rich, thus leading the poor from democracy, and the rich from oligarchy, and both into polity.

What, then, is polity, Aristotle's most generally practicable regime, the regime which can solve the fundamental problem of most *poleis?* It is, as has been said, a blend of democracy and oligarchy, and the better the blending, the easier it will be for democrats to confuse it with democracy and oligarchs with oligarchy. Its foundation is the middle class, i.e., the class that is neither very rich nor very poor, and which accordingly has no

---

[36] Aristotle *Politics* 1318ᵃ 30-38.

interest either in equality for unequals or inequality for equals. It does not wish to place property at the mercy of the propertyless, or liberty at the mercy of the propertied. Of the devices for encouraging polity, the one given above must serve as an example of Aristotle's almost limitless resources, resources which manifest themselves not only in the discussion of polity proper, but in the multitudinous ways in which he examines each of the many varieties of democracy, oligarchy, and polity, moderating the two former in the direction of polity, and the last in the direction of aristocracy. Polity, as we have seen, is inherently moderate by the moderation of the interests of the middle class. But this moderation only resembles virtue, it is not virtue itself. It makes men disposed toward virtue, however, and aristocracy can begin to flourish upon the soil of polity.

After demonstrating the variety of regimes, and in particular the varieties of democracy and oligarchy, and how the conflict arising from the irreconcilable antagonism of poor and rich can best be dealt with, Aristotle also points out the appropriateness of one or another regime to one or another people. Although polity is introduced as the generally practicable regime, it depends no less upon fortune than the best regime, in that it depends upon a large middle class, or at least upon a gentle graduation from poor to rich. Yet extremes of wealth or poverty are more the rule. Aristotle recognizes that where such extremes exist only one or another kind of democracy or oligarchy is possible. He lays it down as a principle that the part of the *polis* which wishes the regime to endure must be stronger than the parts which are hostile to it. One must in each case examine the composition of the hostile elements, which must be compounded to produce the regime for the particular *polis*. If the poor have virtuous farmers and degenerate artisans, and if the *polis* must be a democracy, obviously it must be built upon the farming class. If there are degenerate *nouveaux riches,* but there is a public-spirited, educated, old aristocracy, obviously if it is to be an oligarchy it must be constructed around the old families. Where the people are dissolute and the wealthy public-spirited, there one should have an oligarchy, unless the rich are too few and the poor too many, in which case there is no alternative to an inferior democracy. If the people are sober and hard-working and the rich are dissolute, there one should have a democracy, unless the rich are relatively numerous and the poor either relatively few or so situated that they cannot easily combine. These are the kinds of considerations which Aristotle advances for deciding, first, whether a regime should be democratic or oligarchic and, second, what variety of democracy or of oligarchy it should be.

Aristotle concludes Book IV with the first comprehensive account of what we have come to call the three "powers" of government, legislative, executive, and judicial.[37] The concept of a "power" of government is itself, of course, alien to Aristotle, because our use of that expression always implies a delegation of power from a sovereign people to a government which is its instrumentality. For Aristotle, the government (*politeuma*) is the regime (*politeia*), as we cannot too greatly emphasize. The legislative is the deliberating element of the regime, it is not an appointed or elected body deliberating *for* someone else. The idea of representation is nowhere visible in Aristotle's *Politics,* in part because a *polis* so large that it required representation would have seemed to him far too large for political excellence.[38] More important is the fact that what we call the legislative power is only one of a number of elements which in the modern representative democratic state go into the deliberative process. Elections, parties, public opinion polls, and so on, all play a part in this deliberative process. When Aristotle speaks of the deliberative element, he means the element which actually deliberates, not a body to which deliberative functions have been delegated, and which performs these not in its own right, but in virtue of the rights of others.

We cannot say more here of Aristotle's treatment of the three branches of government, other than that it is designed to give the practicing legislator a compendium of all the possible ways in which each of these branches of government can be constructed. The legislator must know not only what are the different regimes, what are their intrinsic merits and demerits, and which kind is suitable for which kind of people. He must know how to construct each regime, and in practice this means knowing how to construct a legislature, a judiciary, and a magistracy suitable to each. This means knowing not only how to construct each of the varieties of the three branches of government, but how to produce each of the varieties of mixtures of each of the branches of government. For example, it means knowing how to add a touch of oligarchy to a democratic legislature, or a touch of aristocracy to an oligarchic judiciary, or a touch of democracy to an oligarchic magistracy (this last being characteristic, for example, of Sparta). Nowhere does the resemblance of the art of the political philosopher and the art of the painter become more patent than in these practical books, wherein the variety of possible forms is seen to be so great that politics becomes as malleable as the forms of nature, when they are reconstructed from the painter's palette. And, yet, in precisely the same sense as the painter imitates nature while perfecting it, so does the political philosopher. The knowledge of nature guides and governs the application of technique at every step.

Of the practical subjects dealt with in Books IV through VI none

[37] Ibid., 1297^b 35ff.
[38] Cf. the criticism of Plato's *Laws,* in ibid., 1265^a 11ff. and the size of the best regime, 1326^a 7-1326^b 26.

are more practical than those of Book V, generally known as the book on revolutions. The word revolution has, however, a connotation for us ("drastic change" would be a better translation of *metabolē*) which is quite alien to Aristotle. When we think of the English, American, French, and Russian revolutions, for example, we usually think of a process by which all *anciens régimes*, all regimes based either upon feudal legitimacy or the prescription of ancient customs, are being caused to disappear from the modern world. We think of the replacement of regimes explicitly based upon one or another principle of inequality by regimes all claiming to be based upon equality.[39] We think of a world in which the dynamism of social change culminating in political revolution is rooted in technological change, itself the by-product of a continually progressing body of what we call scientific knowledge. Aristotle's horizon is one in which man's knowledge of nature does not alter the fundamental character of his relations with nonhuman nature, or his relations with his fellow men. The moral and political alternatives remain basically constant. For Aristotle revolution means primarily the process whereby one regime is replaced by another, as one or another group gains power within the same regime, or as the regime is altered so as no longer to be the same. Aristotle remarks that, in his own time (and he evidently means in Greece), with the growth in the size of the class of the common people, it is hard for any kind of government other than democracy to come into existence.[40] Evidently external conditions may impose sharp limits upon the political choices open at any given time and place. But everything that comes into existence passes out of existence, and although regimes are not strictly speaking mortal, neither are they immortal. External conditions are subject to fortune, and in the fullness of time all possibilities become actualities. Aristotle's horizon envisages as an ultimate possibility the transformation of every regime, through every other regime, into every regime. Book V of the *Politics*, is, then, not a book on revolutions in the sense that Tocqueville's *Democracy in America* is such a book. According to Tocqueville, the progress of the principle of equality, the leveling of all monarchical and aristocratic regimes, is providential and inexorable. The only practical question is whether we adapt ourselves to it in one way or another. For Aristotle there are six principal kinds of regimes, a large number of variants of each, and an almost unlimited number of combinations of variants. The problem of revolution is the problem of knowing what preserves and what destroys each of them.

[39] The National Socialist and Fascist regimes, now happily defunct, are only apparent exceptions. Although reviving a kind of primitive tribalism, their use of the plebiscite to establish legitimacy placed them in fundamental opposition to premodern inegalitarians.

[40] Aristotle *Politics* 1286[b] 20.

Book V is the longest of the entire *Politics,* illustrated as it is with a wealth of detail from the political histories of the Greek world that Aristotle had collected. We can do no more here than indicate the scope of the book, and provide an example of how the political philosopher teaches legislators to preserve the regimes he has taught them to construct. The questions Aristotle takes up are these: what are the numbers and kinds of causes of revolutions in general; what causes are peculiar to each kind of regime; out of what into what do regimes usually change; what are the safeguards of regimes in general and of each kind in particular; how are these safeguards put into effect?

The first and most fundamental cause of revolution is identical with the primary cause of the difference of regimes: namely, the different conceptions men have of justice. Those who are equal in one respect think they are equal in all; those who are unequal in one think they are unequal in all. For this reason democrats are the enemies of oligarchs, and oligarchs of democrats, and each will overthrow the other when he can. Yet within democracy and within oligarchy there are those who think they have not got their fair share according to the principle of the regime. And again, there are those who wish to make the democracy more (or less) democratic, or the oligarchy more (or less) oligarchic.

Revolutions originate often in trivial incidents, but these are only the sparks which set the dry tinder aflame. The sense of oppression of the people by the wealthy few, or the sense of dishonor by the few when they are treated as the equals of those they deem their inferiors, this exemplifies the inflammable material. In democracies, for example, the principal cause of revolution—that is, of the rich banding together to overthrow the democracy—is the insolence of demagogues, who court popularity by instituting malicious prosecutions of the rich and stimulating class hatred. In the case of oligarchies, oppression of the poor by the rich corresponds to demagogy. However, it may be the excessive exclusiveness of the oligarchy that drives some of the notables into rebellion against their own class. Again, oligarchies are ruined by riotous living, driving them into oppression and tyranny because of their extravagance, while making themselves contemptible to their rivals, both in their own class and among the people.

As to the things that tend to secure regimes in general, they are the opposite of the things that tend to their destruction. We saw that differences as to what is just are the most fundamental of all causes of dissension. The fundamental cause of security, to be briefer even than Aristotle in this context, is justice. That is, democracies are preserved by refraining from anything that smacks of expropriation, while oligarchies are preserved by the rulers refraining from insolence and oppression. The legislator must know what institutions in a democracy preserve, and what destroy democracy; and what institutions in an oligarchy preserve, and what destroy oligarchy. For example, it is a legitimate aim of oligarchy that superior men not be governed by inferior, and of democracy that freemen have an equal opportunity to share in offices. The two can often be practically reconciled, Aristotle points out, by scrupulous care that no profit is made from public office. If this is achieved, then the poor will relinquish the offices to the rich, since, being poor, they will prefer to devote themselves to their private affairs so long as they think the public funds are not being plundered. And the rich, while not denying offices to the poor, will actually have the offices to themselves. Every *polis* needs both a free multitude and a wealthy minority, and if the poor destroy the rich, or the rich the poor, they will destroy the basis of the common good. The greatest of all means of securing the stability of regimes, Aristotle says, is education. For there is no use in the best possible laws and institutions if the citizens are not trained in their use. But a good education does not mean one that will please oligarchs in an oligarchy, or democrats in a democracy. It means an education that will produce a ruling class that is self-disciplined in respect to its real interests, and not self-indulgent in respect to its pleasures.

Aristotle has a great deal to say about how polities, aristocracies, monarchies, and tyrannies are both destroyed and preserved. Some of the most startling passages in the *Politics* take the form of advice for preserving tyrannies. Tyranny is in one sense no regime, since it is the negation of justice, and regimes are generally understood in terms of their having an element—however incomplete or partial—of justice. But Aristotle takes it for granted that in some cases nothing but tyranny will be possible, and his advice, while calculated to appeal to a tyrant who is rational enough to consider what is in his interest, is also calculated to introduce, however covertly, an element of justice which makes it bearable to consider the tyranny a regime.

In summary, we can describe the spirit and doctrine of the practical books of the *Politics* as follows. Aristotle envisages each kind of regime as being appropriate to a certain set of circumstances. In the case of a people with a wealthy class of ancient lineage, with a tradition of public service and spirit of *noblesse oblige,* an oligarchy, or perhaps an aristocracy, is indicated. In the case of a people whose rich are mostly *nouveaux,* who lack traditions, and who are held in contempt by the common people, aristocracy is out of the question, and oligarchy is doubtful. The same would be true of an ancient ruling class which had grown effete and luxurious. On the other hand, a common people made up largely of sturdy yeoman farmers is much better material for democracy than a *dēmos* of idle artisans, avidly looking for pay from the public treasury as an excuse to leave their work tables. In each situation we must look first for that class which is naturally strongest. If it is the *dēmos,* we must try to build a democracy; if the wealthy, an oligarchy. And if the class that is between rich and poor is sufficiently numerous, we should try to build a polity. But in enfranchising a ruling class, we must always look for those devices which moderate it in the direction of its natural opposite: that is, devices for admitting the poor to office in an oligarchy, devices for honoring the rich in a democracy; and, in a polity, devices for rewarding virtue, or making virtue honored. For polity, although a balance of two bad principles, secures a moderation which permits the recognition of virtue or merit, and this strengthens the foundation of the regime. But the teaching of these books is alive to the mutability of human things, as well as being encyclopedic. Aristotle warns the legislator to be on the lookout for change, not to oppose change per se, but to prevent evils when they are small and still manageable, and constantly to prepare the regime to assimilate changes worked by fortune which are beyond control.

Nothing better illustrates Aristotle's practical teaching than the contrast between the British and continental European ruling classes in the modern centuries. From the days of Henry VIII, or earlier, the general (if not invariable) practice of the British monarchy and aristocracy has been to co-opt the leading members of the newer classes. Britain has always had a ruling class, and it is scarcely less recognizable today than it was four hundred years ago. Feudal overlords have been replaced by merchant princes, by industrialists and financiers, and by leaders of organized labor, by a process in which the old and new have rarely been out of touch and have rarely ceased to share in power and responsibility. The French and Russian monarchies and aristocracies, on the other hand, would not bend and were compelled instead to break. These *anciens régimes* never learned Aristotle's lesson, that a regime must always be constituted by the strongest element in the *polis,* and that the political strength of an element, whether the people, the rich, the well born, or the good, is a product of its quantity and its quality. This is a nonmathematical product, but the true statesman must nonetheless master this political computation. He must perceive what adjustments must be made in a regime when there is outside the ruling class a quantity so large or a quality so potent that it would ruin if it could not rule. But political computation is not limited to perceiving and judging these invincible products. The introduction of either a new quantity or a new quality into a regime must be done in such wise that the quantity realizes that it becomes a genuine political factor only by its infusion with quality, and quality realizes that it becomes such a factor only as it infuses a quantity.

The common good is always a compound of both, and only as there is a common good is there a regime, and a partnership in the good life.

The last two books of the *Politics*—Book VII, and Book VIII as it has come down to us—are the books par excellence on the best regime. As we have seen, the best regime is the implicit subject of every book. In Book I, the understanding of the generation of the *polis* implied an understanding of its perfection—i.e., the best regime—because to understand the generation of anything that exists by nature means to understand the activity of that thing when it has attained its perfection. And the great thesis of Book I, or one form of it, is that the *polis* exists by nature. Book II examined a number of regimes, both of theory and of practice, and they were found wanting. But the principle in virtue of which Aristotle noted those deficiencies was the principle of the best regime. Book III culminated in the examination of the principal rival claims to supreme power in the *polis,* the claims of the poor, the rich, the well born, and the good. The reconciliation of these claims, their harmonization into a common good, itself constituted the principle of the best regime. Books IV, V, and VI demonstrate the different manners in which this reconciliation or harmonization takes place when external conditions forbid its full implementation. Or, to be more precise, the practical books demonstrate the different forms that justice takes when conditions make the predominant factor in the product of quantity and quality something other than virtue. For example, pure democracy or pure oligarchy are in a sense not viable regimes at all. No *polis* can exist without a freeborn and a wealthy element, and a regime which simply despoiled its rich, or enslaved its free, would cease to exist as a community. Only the moderation of the claims of the rich or the poor enables democracy or oligarchy to be viable, and that moderation is the ground of the intrusion of virtue. But there is a difference between that intrusion of virtue which enables a democracy to exist, and a recognition of virtue as the only cause of that activity for the sake of which every *polis* exists, and which alone can cause it to be, not only a rich or a free *polis,* but a happy one.

The books on the best regime consist in the main of these two subjects: first, what it is that is the cause of happiness, in men and in *poleis;* second, what are the institutions of the best regime. The best regime is one in which the best men rule. Each regime is *just,* let us remember, insofar as it is rightly constituted, insofar as it secures the common good as defined by the greatest product of quality and quantity that fortune permits a given community to enjoy. Where fortune permits the qualitative factor to dominate the quantitative factor, that is, where human excellence dominates civic excellence, there is the best regime.

Aristotle turns aside as practically irrelevant the question of whether that regime is best in which one man so greatly exceeds all others in virtue that no proportional equality is possible.[41] For all practical purposes, the best regime appears to be an aristocracy of a multitude of good men ruled by law. Aristotle discusses the material elements of the best regime, which are its resources of land, its location, access to the sea, market places, and so on, and the human stock from which the legislator must raise up citizens. The formal elements are the classes of farmers, artisans, fighters, the wealthy, those performing civic functions, and those providing the services to the gods. Wealth, military service, civic duty, and religious duty all coincide in a single ruling class. When its members are younger they are soldiers, when in middle age councillors, magistrates, and judges, and when in old age priests. The farm laborers are explicitly servile and the artisans apparently so, although Aristotle does say that all slaves should have freedom set before them as a prize.

Throughout the *Politics* Aristotle usually speaks of virtue in contradistinction to birth, wealth, freedom, and other conditional claims to political preference. Yet fundamental to Aristotle's political teaching is the distinction between the virtue of a citizen and that of a good man, and there is a constant interplay between these two meanings of virtue. The virtue of a citizen relates to the regime, and its purpose will differ from the purpose of true virtue in every regime but the best. For example, in a democracy happiness will appear to be doing as one pleases, in an oligarchy it will appear rather as the gratification of avarice. A happy man *does* do as he pleases, but it pleases him only to do good. A happy man also possesses wealth, but he will desire not an unlimited amount of wealth, but only so much as is needed for good actions. At last, however, we must ask, What limit does the desire of happiness place upon the need or desire of good actions? Good actions require only a limited amount both of wealth and freedom. But there can be no limit upon the desire for good action itself. The final problem of the *Politics* is the problem of establishing clearly that distinction within true virtue itself which throughout the *Politics* remained almost invisible: the distinction between the virtue of action—moral virtue plus practical wisdom—and the virtue of thought—theoretical wisdom. And, corresponding to these two virtues are the two activities, of the active and of the contemplative life. Political virtue, which in the best case appears to coincide with human virtue, is practical: that is, it is concerned with the good things that can be gained, and the bad things that can be avoided, by wise action and the practice of the moral virtues. But there is always a limit to the goodness resulting from good action of this kind. To extend practical activity beyond the

[41] Ibid., 1332^b 16-27.

bounds of this limit is to turn it from good to evil. For example, it is good to be brave and strong, for the weak and cowardly cannot preserve their freedom, and the unfree cannot live good lives. But those who are strong and free, and whose strength and freedom are unchallenged, cannot utilize either their strength or freedom in action. To go into action to dominate others, merely to exercise one's freedom of action and one's bravery, is a perversion of virtue; this was the defect of the Spartan regime. Virtuous activity cannot, then, be truly practical, except as it serves an end which is itself not practical, an activity which is good solely with reference to itself, an activity to which there are no limits because its increase does not extend it beyond itself, an activity which is thus wholly self-contained. This is the activity of thought, the contemplation of the truth, which is the same as the activity of God, or thought thinking itself. It is the only absolutely self-contained, self-sufficient activity in the universe, and for this reason unlimited, while being the cause of those limits which pre-scribe boundaries to every other activity, and in virtue of which every other activity becomes good.[42]

The final cause of excellence, in politics and in human life, as in the universe, is, then, ultimately one and the same. Yet the same man cannot be simply virtuous (which means wise) and politically virtuous, for the same reason that the divine activity is not simultaneously practical and theoretical. The activity of wisdom, pure and simple, is self-regarding and not other-regarding. Yet political rulers must have the spirit and practice of philosophy, which means love of wisdom, as distinct from wisdom itself. The solution of the political problem, in Aristotle no less than in Plato, requires a certain coincidence of philosophy and political power. But for Aristotle, unlike Plato, the activity of wisdom itself issues no commands, although it does always indicate the reason why commands should be issued. There is, then, no such necessary antagonism between philosophy and political life as Plato envisaged. Practical life culminates in the recognition of the activity of wisdom as its final cause.[43]

In the *Nicomachean Ethics* Aristotle expounded the different meanings of virtue, and above all the distinction between the moral and intellectual virtues. In Book X he defended happiness as primarily the activity of theoretical wisdom, and in a secondary sense as the activity of the practical and moral virtues. Finally, he observed that the conditions of happiness, the possibility of the good life, depended upon good laws, and this required the science of politics. At the end of the *Politics* Aristotle

[42] Cf. Aristotle *Metaphysics* 1072^b 13-29, and *Nicomachean Ethics* 1177^a 17-1177^b 26, 1178^b 7-23, with *Politics* 1323^b 23-27, and 1325^b 14-31. Compare also the treatment of self-love in the *Nicomachean Ethics* 1166^a 1ff.

[43] Aristotle *Nicomachean Ethics* 1144^b 30-1145^a 11.

considers how the good men who are to make the good laws of the best regime are themselves to be produced. When the eighth book breaks off, either unfinished or lost, he is still engaged in describing the education which will produce the habits of virtue. Fortunately, we already know what these habits are and how they are produced, in principle if not in detail. The end of the *Politics* leads us back to the beginning of the *Nicomachean Ethics*.

THE LIMITS OF POLITICS
3 An Interpretation of
King Lear, Act I, Scene i

According to that profound student of Shakespeare, Abraham Lincoln, the most difficult task of statesmanship is that of providing, not for the foundation, but for the perpetuation, of political institutions.[1] If the political institutions are the best, to perpetuate them is not only the most difficult, but also the greatest of all the tasks of the statesman.

It is generally agreed that Shakespeare regarded monarchy as the best form of government. It is not generally realized, however, that Lear is the greatest of Shakespeare's kings. For the moment, I submit only this evidence: the supreme object of monarchical policy in the English histories is the unification and pacification of England. Only Henry V even approaches success in this, but, in view of his questionable title to the throne, he is compelled to create a dubious national unity by means of an unjust foreign war. Yet the first scene in *King Lear* shows the old monarch at the head of a united Britain (not merely England) and at peace, not only with all domestic factions, but with the outside world as well. France and Burgundy, who represent this world, are suitors for the hand of Lear's youngest daughter. Never in the histories does Shakespeare represent his native land at such a peak of prestige and political excellence; in *King Lear* alone do we find actualized the consummation devoutly wished by all other good Shakespearean kings.

If Lear is, in fact, Shakespeare's greatest king and if it is true that to perpetuate such a rule is an even greater task than to establish it, then the opening of *King Lear* shows us the old king confronted with the supreme problem of his great career—that of providing for the succession to his throne. The action whereby he provides for this succession should,

Reprinted by the kind permission of the publisher from *American Political Science Review* 51, No. 2 (June 1957): 405-27.

[1] See "The Perpetuation of Our Political Institutions," address before the Young Men's Lyceum of Springfield, Ill., Jan. 27, 1838. Compare Machiavelli, *Discourses on Livy*, I. x, where it is said that, not the founders of republics and monarchies deserve the greatest praise, but the founders of religions. One might paraphrase Machiavelli by saying that the founders of religions are the true founders of civil society; Numa, rather than Romulus, is the founder of Rome. Another expression of the same thought, which is classical as well as Machiavellian, is that to found a state is an act of human virtue, but to perpetuate it requires divine assistance. It is the thesis of this essay that Lear's incomprehension of this truth was his tragic flaw. It might not be irrelevant to add that Lincoln acted the role of high priest in the Civil War, a conflict which he interpreted, in his two most famous utterances, as a divine affliction, designed to transform a merely political union into a sacramental one.

therefore, be his greatest action. Since it would be the greatest action of the greatest king and since monarchy is the best form of government, such an action would be Shakespeare's presentation of the consummation of the political art, of political virtue and therewith of political life altogether. But such a presentation could imply even more than this; for, if Shakespeare, as a Renaissance classicist, regarded man as a political animal, it is possible that he regarded the fulfillment of man's highest political function as identical to the fulfillment of his highest human function. It is not improbable, then, that the stage is set, at the opening of *King Lear,* for Shakespeare's presentation of the ultimate in human existence.

The foregoing will, no doubt, strike many as paradoxical. That *King Lear* contains the fullest demonstration of Shakespeare's creative powers and that these somehow represent the ultimate in man's humanity is a proposition that would be widely concurred in. Yet I believe that this latter proposition is consistent with, if not identical to, the former ones. For, if Shakespeare undertook the fullest revelation of his powers in *King Lear,* then it is entirely probable that the story of the play was selected as the most suitable vehicle for this revelation. In other words, the question why we find in *King Lear* the fullest revelation of Shakespeare's genius may be identical to the question, Why does Shakespeare reveal himself to us most fully in a play in which his greatest king is confronted with the task of perpetuating the perfect political regime?

Although many critics have opined that *King Lear* is Shakespeare's greatest work, few call it their favorite play,[2] and few fail to remark adversely on many of its dramatic properties. I will here quote some remarks of Coleridge, who expresses, in somewhat exaggerated form, perhaps, assumptions which have characterized a great deal of the critical literature dealing with the play in the nineteenth and twentieth centuries. Although Coleridge has been attacked on many grounds by recent critics, I do not believe that these particular assumptions have been sufficiently challenged. As will readily appear, they imply a general conception as to the meaning of the play—a meaning which is, in my judgment, inconsistent with the high estimate in which the play is otherwise held. According to Coleridge, one can "Omit the first scene in *Lear,* and everything will remain"; the first scene is a "nursery tale," "prefixed as the *porch* of the edifice, not laid as its foundation."[3] In *King Lear,* says Coleridge, "the interest and situations . . . are derived from a gross improbability."[4] This

---

[2] Cf. A. C. Bradley, *Shakespearean Tragedy* (London: Macmillan, 1905), p. 243.

[3] Thomas Middleton Raysor (ed.), *Coleridge's Shakespearean Criticism* (Cambridge: Cambridge University Press, 1930), 1: 55, n. 1.

[4] Ibid., p. 59.

is but an application of Coleridge's principle that, in a Shakespearean play, the interest does not derive from, indeed is independent of, interest in plot and story. "Shakespeare did not take the trouble of inventing stories. It was enough for him to select from those that had been invented or recorded such as had one or other, or both, of two recommendations, namely, suitableness to his purposes, and second, their being already parts of popular tradition. . . ."[5] Coleridge thus implies that it was less trouble for Shakespeare to take over tales already told than to invent new ones. Yet, since Coleridge admits that Shakespeare had a purpose in writing a play distinct from that of evoking response to the familiar, his choosing only from the available stock of traditional materials must have imposed greater restrictions on him than if he had felt free to go outside that stock. There certainly is no assurance that Shakespeare was saving himself trouble because he did not invent stories. That he was neither lazy nor indifferent in his attitude toward his stories is obvious from the fact that he frequently and freely altered his source materials. There is, certainly, no a priori reason for assuming that the adaptation of plot and story to Shakespeare's purpose in writing a play were not so deliberate and extensive as in his handling of any other of his materials.

From the view that the story of *King Lear* is an absurd fairy tale, Coleridge infers that none of the action initiated by Lear in scene i is to be taken seriously. Yet Coleridge does not fail to observe one fact inconsistent with this general thesis: "It was not without forethought, and it is not without its due significance, that the triple division is stated here (I. i. 1-6) as already determined and in all its particulars, previously to the trial of professions, as the relative rewards of which the daughters were to be made to consider their several portions."[6] A. C. Bradley, commenting on this observation, says that the love test is a "mere form, devised as a childish scheme to gratify his love of absolute power and his hunger for assurances of devotion." Yet neither Coleridge nor Bradley has reflected on the possibility that, if the love test, the trick whereby Lear makes it appear that he is "dividing his kingdom among his daughters in proportion to the strength of their protestations of love,"[7] is a pretense, then perhaps much more in the scene is also pretense. Coleridge and Bradley rightly assume that to make the division of the kingdom depend on such protestations could only signify insane vanity and folly, but they also assume that Lear is doing no such thing. Why, then, do they insist that he is vain and foolish nonetheless? May not this pretense be part of a larger system of pretenses? How do we know that this alone is a pretense and nothing else?

[5] Ibid., p. 226.
[6] Bradley, *Shakespearean Tragedy*, p. 249.
[7] Ibid.

In truth, we know no such thing. Since Lear in the course of the scene does alter the division of the kingdom to fit the strength of the protestations, one may say that the previously decided division was merely tentative. If we are to maintain the view that the love test was really intended as a sham, we must base our view on other and stronger evidence.

It is impossible to drop Scene i from the play, as Coleridge suggests, for the reason given by Bradley: that "it is essential that Lear's contribution to the action of the drama . . . be remembered; not at all that we may feel that he 'deserved' what he suffered, but because otherwise his fate would appear to us at best pathetic, at worst shocking, but certainly not tragic."[8] It is then equally impossible to impute to Lear a serious intention to make the division of the kingdom depend on his daughters' protestations, since we would thus be forced to regard him as already insane, not morally responsible, and accordingly unable to contribute in any moral or dramatic sense to the action of the play. It would seem that the only tenable hypothesis is that the love test was, from its beginning, a pretense.

But, if Lear's sanity and, with it, his status as a tragic hero depends on the premise that the love test is a pretense, then the whole meaning of the play, i.e., the meaning of Lear's suffering, depends on our making this hypothesis intelligible. We do not know why he must suffer if we do not know why he adopted the pretense which was the efficient cause of that suffering.

The generally accepted explanation is that of Bradley: Lear is a foolish, vain, selfish old man whose wits are beginning to fail. His failings are extenuated by his "long life of absolute power, in which he has been flattered to the top of his bent" and which "has produced in him that blindness to human limitations, and the presumptuous self-will, which in Greek tragedy we have so often seen stumbling against the altar of Nemesis." Yet this extenuation, besides being contradicted by internal evidence—which I shall present shortly—runs athwart the larger bias of the play, for it is widely admitted that the sufferings of Lear are the most terrible in all Shakespeare and, probably, a fortiori, in the whole of the world's literature. But great passion, be it that of Lear, of Oedipus, or of Jesus, implies greatness in the soul of the sufferer. A great passion is always, in some sense, compensation for a great error. As Plato teaches in the *Republic,* great errors are the work of great souls, souls capable of either great good or great evil. A petty soul is one that can accomplish neither great good nor great evil. It seems impossible to suppose that a child, a fool, or a knave would be capable of the passion of a Lear. Is it

---

[8] Ibid., p. 281.

not, then, as impossible to suppose that the error which was, in an important way, the cause of such a passion was childish, foolish, or knavish? It is true that the action which precipitated Lear's passion was a sign of the absence of perfect wisdom. But it seems to me that no consistent view of the play as a whole is possible that does not account for Lear's unwisdom in scene i as a defect such as only the very greatest soul could suffer. Bradley's explanation of Lear's failure in scene i is, I think, clearly deficient, in that it is at least compatible with the view that Lear's error was the error of a petty soul.

I have suggested that the stage is set at the beginning of the play for the supreme action of Lear's long and successful reign, the action whereby he provides for its perpetuation. The consciousness of critics has, I believe, been so dominated by Lear's apparent failure in this scene that they have failed to notice his serious intention. Yet the meaning and extent of Lear's failure can be grasped with precision only in the light of his intentions. We must then try to understand exactly how Lear undertook to solve this paramount political problem. Coleridge, it will be remembered, inferred (rightly, I believe) from Gloucester's first speech that Lear's division of the kingdom was determined "in all its particulars"; but Coleridge says no more about these particulars. Bradley, however, observes that it "seems to have escaped the attention of Coleridge and others"[9] that Lear's original plan was not so absurd as it has been taken to be. For example, Lear never intended to live with his three daughters in turn, but with Cordelia alone. He then concludes that Lear's

> . . . whole original plan, though foolish and rash, was not a "hideous rashness" or incredible folly. If carried out it would have had no such consequences as followed its alteration. It would probably have led quickly to war, but not to the agony which culminated in the storm upon the heath.

Bradley calls our attention to the fact that catastrophe is the consequence, not of Lear's original plan, but of the alteration of that plan. Bradley assumes, without any attempt at proof, that Lear's original plan was also foolish and rash, although not "hideously rash." In a footnote to the latter phrase, he mentions that it is Kent who applies this epithet to the *altered* plan. Yet Bradley does not attempt the possible inference that, if Kent, within the play, was informed concerning the original plan "in all its particulars" and had expressed no objection to it, then perhaps he had approved of it. This is, in fact, a necessary inference, if we are not to suppose that Kent, who does not even express a private doubt to his

[9] Ibid., p. 250.

fellowcouncilor Gloucester was, until the penultimate moment of his public service, a time-serving flatterer. But, if the original plan had Kent's and Gloucester's approval, it may not have been foolish at all. It may, indeed, have been a product of sound principles of statecraft.

The proposition that Kent and Gloucester approved Lear's original plan is a necessary inference for anyone who does not reject the premise that, in general, the relationship of characters in a Shakespearean play is made to appear to flow from their entire lives and not to start up, *de novo*, with the raising of the curtain. Lear, Kent, Gloucester, and the three daughters are supposed to have known one another and to have lived in intimate association for many years. Kent is the king's favorite courtier, as Cordelia is his favorite daughter. Both Kent and Cordelia are, in similar ways, mirrors of the master and father they love. Bradley's statement that Lear has been corrupted by flattery and has a foolish craving for it is contradicted by the fact that Lear prefers above all others the two people in the play who are represented as absolutely incapable of flattery or hypocrisy. We can no more suppose that Kent and Cordelia are blunt and plain-spoken to the king for the first time (or that he loved them for anything but their true qualities) than that they have been petty flatterers until the moment the action of the play begins. The long-standing difference between Cordelia and her sisters is stressed in her farewell to them, and they themselves emphasize their father's preference for Cordelia. Moreover, Lear's preference for Cordelia and Kent is consistent with a widely recognized principle of the soul: the principle that self-love is the basis of friendship and that we prefer as friends those who are most like ourselves.[10] Lear's own nature is not that of a flatterer, and, hence, we would expect him to prefer those who were not flatterers. Lear's political success, moreover, would be difficult to understand if he did not have about him those who would tell him the truth. The truth about Lear himself may be said to be "flattering," in the sense that Lear was an honest and noble-hearted man and evoked the spontaneous loyalty and devotion of such a man as Kent. There are few, if any, characters in Shakespeare who command such unqualified esteem as Kent; yet Kent's life is constituted by his devotion to Lear. But, if Lear were not worthy of this devotion, if, that is to say, Kent's discrimination in choosing an object of devotion were questionable, however unselfish the devotion itself, our admiration for Kent would assuredly be mingled with either pity or contempt. That we do not feel the least pity or contempt for Kent is, I think, a sign of Lear's, as well as of Kent's, true worth.

If Kent knew Lear's original plan in all its particulars, he must have approved it, since he is silent concerning any defects it may have

[10] Cf. Plato *Gorgias* 510^b 2ff.; Aristotle, *Nicomachean Ethics*, 1155^a 33; n. 25, *infra*.

possessed and since we know that he did not hesitate to protest in the most vehement manner when Lear departed from it. If it be objected that Kent may have disapproved the original plan but acceded to it after he had exhausted his influence in having it rectified, there is this reply: someone as loyal and devoted as Kent would surely have been preoccupied with the danger to his master, had he anticipated any. Yet, in the moment before the stage fills with the court, we see him and Gloucester turn lightly from state to personal matters, without any sign of apprehension concerning the former. What, then, was the original plan?

The negative view that Bradley and others have taken of the original plan has centered, as has been said, on the love test. The love test has already been dismissed as a pretense, as far as the original division of the kingdom is concerned. The real objection has always been to the division of the kingdom itself. It has always been thought that, since the supreme object of monarchical policy in Shakespeare is the unification of England, a British king who deliberately divides a united kingdom is committing the supreme act of monarchical folly.

Yet, reflection must make us cautious of accepting this view. First of all, there looms the paradox of imputing the crime of dividing the kingdom to the one Shakespearean king whose ascendancy appears to have united it—a paradox enforced by Kent's apparent acquiescence. Second is the radical difference between dividing the kingdom into two, as distinct from three. The very number two is, traditionally, the number for strife, as the number three is the number for unity. Without pursuing allegorical possibilities, it is clear that a balance of power can be better preserved where there are three distinct forces, no one of which can overmatch the other two, than where there are only two forces, however evenly matched. The most important reflection, however, concerns whether, in dividing the kingdom, Lear was doing, during his lifetime, what in any event was bound to come to pass after his death. That is, how do we know that the unity achieved by Lear was not itself the result of an equipoise of forces, in unstable equilibrium, rather than a simple unity? In order to understand Lear's policy, one must analyze the problem he faced, the problem of the succession, in terms of the political realities which confronted him.

We must observe that Lear's problem is complicated by the fact that he had three daughters but no son. Yet, if Lear had had a son the difficulty would not have been greatly different. Lear would still have had to gain the support of major powers in the kingdom—and abroad—for his settlement. And he had to bind them to that settlement by both pledges and self-interest in order to assure its durability. It is striking that, although Goneril and Regan have been married for some time, they have not yet received dowries.[11] All three daughters must receive their dowries simultaneously. Does this fact not indicate that Lear was thinking in terms of an over-all balance of power, each part of which was needed to ensure the rest? Had Lear's power been as absolute as it has seemed, why should he have hesitated so long to give the elder daughters their dowries? Lear was certainly using the dowries and the marriages as instruments of policy, as was the custom in royal (and not only royal) houses. Burgundy and France have "long" made their amorous sojourn at his court, and presumably it is much longer since Cornwall and Albany first made theirs. Lear has delayed as long as possible making his final disposition of both the hands and fortunes of his daughters. What, then, was Lear's matrimonial policy?

First, we must note that Cornwall and Albany represent the geographical extremities of Britain. Cornwall clearly represents the south. Albany, according to Holinshed, originally was the northern part of the island and included Scotland. At I. iv. 179, the Fool tells Lear: "Thou hast pared thy wit o' both sides, and left nothing i' the middle," indicating that the two extremities (Goneril and Regan) have digested the center portion, which was to have been Cordelia's. Lear had married his two older daughters to two great lords whose estates (and, hence, we may assume, whose power) lay at the opposite poles of the kingdom. Now, anyone who knows only as much of English history as is contained in Shakespeare's histories knows that English kings found it impossible to exercise control in any region very remote from the center of the royal domains without the support of the feudal potentates of those regions.[12] The selection of sons-in-law from the remote portions of his kingdom indicates, I believe, that Lear's unification of the kingdom was in part due to his ability to secure the adhesion of the lords of these outlying districts through marriage to the royal house. But the marriage of a daughter involves a dowry; Cornwall and Albany expected more than brides, and the possibility that a descendant might occupy the throne. What could be more natural than that they expected lands that lay in the neighborhoods of their ancestral estates?

From this it would seem that Lear's action in dividing the kingdom was not arbitrary or foolish; it was an action predestined by the very means required to bring unity to the kingdom. Lear, it appears, delayed the division as long as possible, but he could not put it off indefinitely, any more than he could put off indefinitely his own demise.

In Lear's speech announcing to the court the division of the

---

[11] According to Wilfrid Perrett, *The Story of King Lear from Geoffrey of Monmouth to Shakespeare* (Berlin, 1904), p. 175, no earlier version of the play shows Goneril and Regan married before the love test. This accentuates Shakespeare's emphasis on the king's policy.

kingdom into three parts, he gives two reasons for his action: first, that he wishes to shake all care and business from his age, conferring them on younger strengths; and, second, "that future strife may be prevented now." There is a sense in which these two reasons may be regarded as a single one; that is, by devising a political arrangement whereby the peace of the kingdom could be ensured without the adventitious factor of his personal ascendancy, Lear removed his chief present care by providing against future strife. However, if we view these two reasons more superficially, I think that it would be correct to say that the second reason is the real one and the first primarily an excuse for the latter. It is difficult to believe that failing strength was a pressing motive for Lear's action; the old man was the most prodigious octogenarian on record, still spending his days hunting, and able, as the last act shows, to kill a man single-handed.

The decisive consideration, however, is this: there is no evidence that, in the original plan, Lear intended anything resembling an abdication. On the contrary is the fact that Lear never abandoned the crown. What he divided between his sons-in-law in the flush of his rage against Cordelia, was a coronet.[13] He himself was to retain, even in the altered plan, "The name, and all th' additions to a king." Yet, as long as Lear retained the name of king, a name which he in no way shared with a successor, his delegation of authority to his sons-in-law remained fundamentally distinguished from an abdication.[14] One may ask why Lear held a coronet in his hand at all. The answer is, I believe, that the coronet, the

[12] Cf. Tom Paine, *Rights of Man*, Everyman's Library, p. 51: "William the Conqueror and his descendants parcelled out the country in this manner, and bribed some parts of it by what they called charters to hold the other parts of it the better subjected to their will. This is the reason why so many of those charters abound in Cornwall; the people were averse to the Government established at the conquest, and the towns were garrisoned and bribed to enslave the country. All the old charters are the badges of this conquest, and it is from this source that the capriciousness of elections arises."

[13] Crowns and coronets are distinguished from each other in a number of Shakespearean texts: *Henry V* II. Prologue. 11; *Tempest* I. ii. 133; *Julius Caesar* I. ii. 258. The crown is certainly one of the "additions to a king."

[14] Compare Lear's apparent intention to resign authority to that of Charles V, a comparison that would have occurred readily to an Elizabethan audience. Charles had his son crowned in a great state ceremony, in his own presence, and in that same presence had all the great peers of his numerous realms pledge their fealty to Philip. He himself then retired to a monastery and remained virtually inaccessible to the political world. Lear, on the contrary, was to remain king, the sole bearer of regal authority. Living with Cordelia, he would remain at the center of political life. It is not merely the ancient habit of command that compels him, later in the play, to give orders to his daughters' retainers, but the evident assumption that his orders supersede all others. As I will attempt to show below, this assumption would not have been unreasonable if his *original* plan had been adhered to. In fact, Lear's altered plan ran athwart the whole feudal system, and in this respect his elder daughters had just grievance against him.

symbol of ducal authority, was intended for Cordelia's husband.[15] It must be remembered that the scene was intended to be one in which Cordelia received her husband and dowry. Her husband, whether Burgundy or France, would be a foreigner, whose British dukedom would be conferred along with Cordelia's hand. To sum up: Lear might have delegated much of his "business" to his sons-in-law in the original plan, but there is no sign of anything resembling an abdication. As long as he did not abdicate, he would, as king, remain the only personage capable of deciding the highest political questions. Since there is no explicit mention, anywhere in the scene, of a successor, the implication is left that Lear would retain the power of naming a successor, and this in turn indicates an intention to retain decisive power.

Lear's original plan called, I think, for precisely equal shares to go to Albany and Cornwall, husbands of the two older daughters. But Cordelia was to receive a third "more opulent" than the other two. Lear divided his kingdom into "three," but the parts are not mathematical "thirds." Cordelia was not only to be situated in the middle, but to have the richest portion of the realm. Lear, as Bradley pointed out, intended to live with Cordelia alone. Living on as king with Cordelia, with Albany and Cornwall acting as his deputies in regions which he could not control without their loyalty anyway, does it seem that Lear was giving up anything that he could in any case have kept to himself much longer? Since Cordelia's husband would be a foreigner, living in the midst of Lear's long-time retainers, it is difficult to imagine any such conflict of domestic authority arising, as a result of the original plan, as arose in the altered plan. In the altered plan, the division of Cordelia's inheritance between Goneril and Regan left Lear's original retainers a minority among those owing primary fealty to Albany and Cornwall. But, in the original plan, any retainers the husband of Cordelia brought with him to England would in all likelihood have remained a small minority in comparison to those who had been brought up to regard Lear as their master. All indications within the play are that Lear evoked the strongest loyalty from those who recognized him as their legitimate master.

Concerning the marriage of Cordelia, I think the evidence is overwhelming in favor of the view that she was intended as the bride of Burgundy. First, because Lear offers her to Burgundy, although this is after her disinheritance.[16] Second, because Burgundy has had previous

---

[15] This was pointed out to me by Professor R. S. Milne, Victoria University College, Wellington, New Zealand. Perrett, The Story, p. 153, says that it was for Cordelia. But why would a princess of the blood royal receive a coronet now?

[16] Burgundy's reply to Lear's question as to "What, in the least" Burgundy will require in dowry to take Cordelia, is ambiguous: "Most royal majesty, I crave no more than hath your Highness offered." It is not certain whether Lear has already

knowledge of Cordelia's dowry. But such knowledge implies at the same time that he has been privy to some, if not all, of Lear's intended scheme. Such a confidential position certainly suggests the status of an intended son-in-law. Now, France and Burgundy were traditional enemies. Their presence at Lear's court suggests that Cordelia's dowry would have been an important counter in the balance of power between them.[17] Burgundy is the lesser power, as is shown by Lear's style in addressing him and by the fact that Lear fears insulting France, but not Burgundy. Cordelia's marriage to France would have been a political blunder of the first magnitude, a blunder of which there is no reason to suspect the Lear who drafted the plan approved by Kent and Gloucester. A French marriage would inevitably have given rise to the French claims to the British throne, such as actually led to the French invasion that occurs in the play. Lear would never have intended, nor would Kent have consented, that the king of France or his descendants inherit the throne of Britain. In such a case, there would have been the possibility, at least, that Britain would become the appendage of France. Moreover, such a marriage would have heavily unbalanced the system of powers, as that system is envisaged within the horizon of the play. France, commanding the fairest part of Britain, might easily have overmatched Burgundy, thereafter to hold the remainder of Britain in his power. On the other hand, however, Cordelia's dowry, added to Burgundy, might have aided the balance of power on the Continent.[18] Conversely, Burgundy, added to Cordelia's part of Britain, would have neutralized any combination of the older sisters. A combination of the powers of Albany and Cornwall with France against Cordelia and Burgundy, even apart from its geographical difficulty, would have been unlikely. The victory of Goneril and Regan over Cordelia, if achieved with the aid of France, would in all likelihood leave the elder sisters at the mercy of their great ally, to be overpowered and absorbed in turn. We

---

offered Cordelia herself to be bride to Burgundy, with the dowry of which Burgundy appears to have knowledge, or whether Lear has simply informed Burgundy of the amount and kind of Cordelia's dowry.

[17] There does not seem to be any mention of Burgundy in Shakespeare's sources. He thus appears to be a Shakespearean addition, required to make possible Lear's original plan, as we are reconstructing it.

[18] To an Elizabethan audience, the Burgundian alliance would represent, in principle, the Spanish alliance, since Burgundy (or Franche-Comté) was part of the empire of Charles V and Philip II. A Spanish marriage would be in line with traditional English policy, as indicated by Henry VIII's marriage to a Spanish princess and his daughter Mary's marriage to Philip. Elizabeth, on the other hand, although she conducted a long and maddening flirtation with the Duke d'Alençon, never actually brought herself to a French marriage. Only the threat of a Franco-Spanish alliance against England could have led Elizabeth to indulge in her fabulously insincere and equally artful negotiations to become bride of the heir to the French throne. Eliza-

may, however, ask why France, who was no doubt a political reasoner, wasted his time in a vain suit at Lear's court? The answer is, I think, in the first place, that the marriage was too important for him to be absent from the scene of its negotiation. We must remember that Goneril and Regan must have had an intense interest, not only in their younger sister's dowry, but in her marriage. The moment of Cordelia's betrothal to Burgundy would be the precise moment for France to cultivate good relations with her older sisters. There remained, however, as a remote possibility, what actually came to pass. Just as the first Queen Elizabeth could always flirt with French dukes as a threat to Spain, so could Lear use a French marriage for Cordelia as a threat to Goneril, Regan, and their husbands, should they fail to acquiesce in the preferred treatment given Cordelia in the division of the kingdom.

Although the basic problem facing Lear was that of the succession to the throne, there is no direct reference in the text to the subject of a prospective heir. If Cordelia were married to Burgundy, however, it would seem probable that the crown was intended to pass to Cordelia and her descendants. Burgundy would be elevated in the feudal hierarchy by his marriage to a king's daughter, and his ancestral dukedom might become an appendage to the kingdom of Britain, rather than the reverse. Elements in the English tradition would seem to confirm the soundness of this view. The ascent of a foreign duke, William of Normandy, to the throne of England gave English kings claims on the French throne, but not the reverse. Also, the marriage of Mary Tudor to Philip II was a "Burgundian" marriage. It was unhappy and politically near-disastrous, but principally because of the difficulties flowing from the Reformation. No such religious questions are envisaged within the play's horizon. The relevant point is that Mary, although married to a foreign prince who was nominally king of England, alone exercised the powers of the sovereign. Philip was never more than the consort of the queen, even though he was heir to a throne in his own right. A Burgundian marriage, in short, would have made the succession of Cordelia to the throne a viable political arrangement. Lear's scheme of marrying Cordelia to Burgundy gave good promise of leading to a stable international system and a peaceful acceptance of Lear's will and testament at home.

It is not clear whether Lear intended to make an announcement concerning the succession at the court we witness in scene i. In my judgement, he did not intend to do so. It would have been apparent to

---

bethan principles of power politics are clear enough. A smaller power, such as England, forms an alliance with a great but distant power, such as Spain, to neutralize such a great and near power as France. In like manner, Scotland's traditional ally was France: Scotland was to England as England to France; or, again, France was to Scotland as Spain to England.

everyone, from the preferred treatment of Cordelia, that he intended the crown to pass to her. Yet the precise terms of the inheritance of the crown itself would have left some scope for diplomacy. The absence of evidence on which to decide what these terms might have been suggests that Lear himself was not yet in a position to fix them. The evidence I have cited suggests that Lear, being truly wise in the ways of politics, was not a man to force premature decisions and that he was in no hurry to give up any more of his authority than necessary. But the announcement of the succession would have involved some further sacrifice of authority. Like any outgoing officeholder, Lear's authority would be diminished the moment his successor was known. Those who would be reluctant to oppose the king openly, as long as they had hopes of influencing him in their favor, would lose some of that reluctance the moment they were certain that his decision was against them. The succession of Cordelia to the throne had to be accomplished in a succession of steps, each of which required something of a pause in order to test its firmness. The first step was to be the granting of the dowries, simultaneously with the announcement of the marriage. Why these had to be done in one step has been indicated; only in virtue of a foreign marriage, in which a foreign force would be united to Cordelia's native strength, could she defend her inheritance from her sisters. The realignment of power resulting from the dowries and the marriage would be the essential basis of the future succession. But in a feudal system in which power depended heavily on personal loyalties, public pledges would not be a negligible factor in guaranteeing the success of Lear's arrangements.[19] How to secure those pledges was a consideration prior to any plan to announce the succession itself. In my judgment, the love test was, in one of its meanings, a part of Lear's deliberate system of policy. Its purpose was to supply, at least

[19] The legitimacy of Lear's rule, in the feudal sense of that term, is shrouded in the mist of the antiquity which surrounds the setting of the entire play. That the contemporary Elizabethan view of primogeniture is somehow present in Lear's legendary kingdom is indicated by Edmund's famous soliloquy in scene ii and its sequel. All that need be said at the moment is that Lear is very old himself, his rule very successful, and his personal authority apparently unchallenged. But the obscurity of the legal foundation of the monarchy accentuates the political problem of the succession. Under traditional English rules, the eldest daughter would succeed in the absence of a male heir. Lear seems to be reversing that rule in making his youngest daughter his heir. But, if Lear's rule is just (until the fatal explosion), then it must be just in an extralegal sense, since he does not seem to be hampered—or guided—by any legal rules in deciding what is best. Lear's decision (as I believe) to make Cordelia his successor certainly seems right, since she alone of the daughters appears to inherit her father's regal qualities. Lear thus seems to act in the light of the truth—the truth that Cordelia is the best qualified—instead of in the conventional or legal expectation that the eldest should inherit. But a decision based on truth will be politically wise or truthful only if it is supported by public opinion. Lear's design—according to my

inferentially, pledges of support for the division of the kingdom which he was in process of announcing. As I shall shortly demonstrate, these pledges were demanded only from Goneril and Regan, not from Cordelia. They were, that is, demanded only from those who might have motives to repudiate his division.

Certainly, Lear did not have any practical doubt concerning the nature of his daughters' love for him. He had already arranged things to favor Cordelia as much as possible. Not only was the kingdom divided on the map before the start of the court scene, but Lear gave Goneril and then Regan their shares after each had spoken, without hearing the other. Thus, Cordelia's "more opulent" third was awaiting her, as the remainder, before she spoke a word. Clearly, Lear's intention was not to weigh the speeches against the shares in any manner or sense. Yet his shrewd knowledge of his elder daughters put them in a position in which it would have been ludicrous for them to repudiate their father's judgment after their fulsome speeches of devotion.

We do not know whether Kent, Gloucester, Burgundy, or anyone else knew of the king's plan to administer the test. There was great need for secrecy. Many commentators have noted that Goneril and Regan were taken by surprise. It was absolutely necessary that they should have been. If they had had any inkling of the test, they would have sought means other than protestations to increase their bargaining power.[20] They would have quickly guessed that speeches could give them no advantage, that the advantage already lay with Cordelia.[21] The least they might have done was to boycott the court. Had they done this, for however specious a reason, they could have held up the settlements. If these were made in

_____

interpretation—to cultivate the conditions for a public opinion favorable to his settlement is tantamount, then, to a design to provide a legal or conventional foundation for an arrangement which is, in its origin, essentially extralegal.

One might object, however, that public pledges without an underlying favorable distribution of power would be worthless, whereas, if such a distribution existed, the pledges would be superfluous. As suggested above, the pledges might themselves be an ingredient in the distribution of power. For example, consider such public pledges as Magna Carta. Magna Carta only affirmed what the barons present at Runnymede believed that they and the king already knew to be the law of the realm. Despite the fact that all must have believed that the king would in future, when he had power to do so, violate rights which he had disregarded in the past, it must also have been believed that his solemn public pledge would lessen his future power to do so. In like manner, we may suppose it possible that the pledges of Goneril and Regan may have served to minimize the opinion, particularly among their own followers, which might have been favorable to any attempt to upset Lear's will and testament.

[20] They might have threatened Lear with a French alliance, just as Lear could threaten them with a French marriage for Cordelia.

[21] Goneril: ' He always loved our sister most" (I. i. 288). All citations are to the Furness variorum edition (Philadelphia: J. B. Lippincott Co., 1880).

their absence and in the teeth of their objections, they might have challenged the legitimacy of their father's will. Thus, their power to absent themselves from the court might itself have become a bargaining counter, with which they might have exacted a forfeit. The love test, taking them by surprise, trapped them into professions which they otherwise might never have made. Commentators have long noted the swiftness of the action in scene i,[22] and, in the case of the love test, have taken it as additional evidence of Lear's rashness. Yet a sufficient reason for Lear's haste would be his anxiety to have his plan consummated before Goneril and Regan could recover poise enough to object to it. Lear's very haste may be regarded as craftiness. We know that the professions were not intended to determine the shares, but Goneril and Regan could not know that. As far as Goneril knew, her fortune might depend on the effect of her speech. Regan may have suspected that this was not the case, but, with more than two-thirds of the kingdom remaining, she would take no chance. Cordelia alone of the three, seeing the remainder plainly before her on the map, knew in advance precisely what her share was to be. Cordelia alone, therefore, knew that her speech was not needed to establish her share. To Cordelia, it must have been apparent that the test was a trick devised in her interest and that Lear, far from demanding that she heave her heart into her mouth, was making his own protestation of love to her. In truth, Lear was not asking Cordelia to flatter him. Lear rightly counted on the hypocrisy of the elder daughters betraying them. But, when he turns to Cordelia, he seems rather to say, "See how I have turned their greed against them and reserved the fairest portion for you, whose love I have never doubted."

This analysis is now exposed to a grave objection. If Lear has, all along, judged correctly the characters of his daughters, as I have maintained, and, if the love test is meant to exploit the hypocrisy of Goneril and Regan in the interest of Cordelia's truth, why does Lear react so violently to that very truth? If his affection for Cordelia is due to the very qualities she here displays in so transcendent a manner, why, then, does he not place the same interpretation on her behavior that Kent does and that we do and tell the court that he sees in her blunt refusal to compete with her sisters the virtue that he all along wished to reward with the greatest share? Would not this have been hailed as a vindication of the old King's judgment, just as Bassanio's choice of the leaden casket vindicated the judgment of Portia's father in *The Merchant of Venice?*

The answer to this difficulty must be in terms both of the conscious motivation which we can ascribe to Lear and of an unconscious

---

[22] E.G., Raysor (ed.), *Coleridge's Shakespearean Criticism*, 1, 54.

motivation. Before attempting this analysis of motives, however, it is desirable to restate the general thesis maintained concerning the play as a whole. I have said that the subject of the play is monarchy and that it represents the supreme action of the greatest king. The first and most obvious objection to this thesis was the assertion that the king we see in action in scene i is a foolish, vain old man and not a great king at all. Our reconstruction of Lear's statecraft should make it possible now to waive that objection. But the subsequent apparent failure of that statecraft, far from refuting the claims concerning its merits, is actually necessary in order to vindicate those claims.

In order that Shakespeare may make us understand what the greatest action of the greatest king is, it is necessary that he present us with an action that "fails." If the action succeeded, we could not identify it as the greatest action, for then we could not know that the difficulty of the action was such as to require the utmost in human virtue. In determining the tensile strength of a cord, it is necessary to find the least weight that will *break* the cord in order to find the greatest weight the cord will support. So it was necessary for Shakespeare to show us the point at which the most skillful policy of his most successful king *broke* in order to point out, and thus define for us, the limits of kingly virtue. And if, as suggested above, Shakespeare regarded kingly virtue as the highest human virtue, he would thereby mark out for us the limits of human life, distinguishing it both from the life that is more than human and from the life that is less than human.[23]

Let us return now to our difficulty. In brief, it is my thesis that Lear is, on the conscious level, outraged by the injustice of Cordelia's refusal to permit the consummation of his carefully contrived plan. But the violence of his outrage is due to an unconscious sense that that very consummation, which he thinks he desired, would have violated and forever frustrated a passion far more profound than the passion for political success. For Lear, in striking at Cordelia, strikes also at his own handiwork. To understand the violence of Lear's eruption, we must understand the unconscious necessity he was under to destroy that political edifice which it had been his life's work to construct.

Starting from Lear's conscious motivation, we can answer the objection we have posed by observing that Lear certainly did not want the love test to *appear* as a trick. To have done so would have run counter to a host of the political considerations we have advanced. Albany and Corn-

---

[23] We are here concerned primarily with the way in which Lear marks the limits of human life by transcending them in the direction of the divine in his relationship with Cordelia. A full interpretation of the play would explain fully how Goneril and Regan mark the lower limits of humanity, passing beyond them into bestiality.

wall were not to be insulted. Lear wanted the entire scene to be a public "love feast." In this, Lear was acting the role of a hypocrite, we might say, but his hypocrisy was only a concession to his sense of justice. He had devised the best plan for the kingdom, for the common good, and any compromise that he had made with truth was made for the sake of justice. Cordelia's uncompromising, intransigent truthfulness contrasted, then, with his own willingness to sacrifice for the common good.[24] If we remember the key part that Cordelia was to play in the entire plan, we can begin to understand the sense of outrage, even betrayal, that the old man must have felt.

Although the mere fact of Lear's rage can be accounted for by this surface explanation, its violence and its tragic consequences are intelligible only if we relate what occurred on the surface to what occurred beneath it. What occurred beneath the surface may be summarized by saying that, when Cordelia jarred her father by her unexpected response, she upset not only his political plan, but his personal plan, which was to express his love of Cordelia. We must grasp the nature of Lear's need to express this love if we are to understand the passion loosed when that need was frustrated.

Let us turn again to the love test, a dramatic device brilliantly adapted to Shakespeare's multiple purpose in scene i. Its function on the level of mere policy has been sketched. Lear asks his daughters to tell him how much they love him. In effect, he commands their love. Yet, love cannot be commanded; only professions of love can be. By the love test, Shakespeare establishes one precise limit of Lear's power to command and, thereby, one limit of kingly power and virtue. But Lear asks his daughters to tell him how much they love him that he may proportion his bounty to their merit. He thus proclaims a kingly desire to proceed on the rules of distributive justice while also implying that love for himself is a proper test of merit in others. This latter implication is not mere vanity, if Lear is the great ruler we have said he is, for the daughter who loves him most will in all likelihood be the most meritorious, since she will most nearly resemble her father.[25] Yet, in proclaiming his desire to make a just distribution, Lear tacitly admits the necessity he is under to know the

[24] We must also give due weight to Lear's genuine paternal attachment to Goneril and Regan. It has been the thesis from the beginning that Lear was a political realist and estimated his daughters' merits without sentimentality. This does not mean, however, that he wished to think ill of any of them or that he had any inkling of the depths of baseness of Goneril and Regan. Lear's outburst against Cordelia was undoubtedly motivated, to some extent, by an instinctive awareness that Cordelia was tearing a veil that covered all their relationships, a veil on which were painted some pleasing illusions, illusions to which he was deeply attached even when not quite believing in them.

[25] The tacit premise of this assertion is that we tend to resemble what we love. Cf. Plato *Gorgias* 510[b] 2ff. The principle is as follows: when we love someone,

truth concerning his daughters' love for him. But what the love test discloses is the impossibility that Lear can ever have such knowledge as long as he remains on his throne.

If it is true that love cannot be commanded, then he who possesses the power to command professions of love must be at a particular disadvantage in distinguishing genuine from spurious manifestations of love. Because Lear could, as king, command professions of love, it was impossible for him ever to be certain that an expression of love for him, whether by Cordelia or another, was not in fact a response to his power of command.[26] Lear thought that Cordelia loved him most because he saw in her the reflection of his own kingliness. But, if imitation is the sincerest kind of flattery, how could Lear ever distinguish the imitation of flattery from that generated by his virtue in the souls of those who really loved him? Cordelia's defiance in the love test only brought into the open the king's essential impotence, for it is not impossible to ascribe to Cordelia a very shrewd selfishness in scene i. Consider the consequences of her boldness: she was the intended bride of the "waterish" Burgundy; but, losing her dowry she loses a poor lover and gains a superior one, France. Not only does France exhibit a nobility of character that makes him seem worthy of his bride, but he is a king in his own right and, as we quickly learn, one who has no intention of abandoning his bride's claims.[27] Accordingly, Cordelia's course could be interpreted, not only as a sacrifice of public interest to private happiness, but as a clever scheme to become queen of France and England, thus defeating Lear's just policy, which is national and patriotic. Goneril and Regan were shallow hypocrites; but how could Lear know that Cordelia was not a clever one?

Lear, I have said, implies that love of himself is a test of merit in others. To assume the validity of such a test is, we might say, of the essence of monarchy. Love of justice, in a monarchy, is thought to be identical, in essence, to love of the monarch, because he is thought to

---

we praise what he praises and blame what he blames. But character is formed by responding to praise and blame, as a shoe is shaped on its last.

[26] Compare the loveless plight of the tyrant in Xenophon's *Hiero* and the interpretation thereof in Leo Strauss's *On Tyranny* (New York: The Free Press of Glencoe, 1963).

[27] We must not be blinded, by France's beautiful speech accepting Cordelia, to the prudential considerations which supported his action. To France, a claim on Cordelia's dowry, not to mention a claim on the British throne, was worth a good deal, whether acknowledged by Lear or not. France had forces to make good his claims, which Burgundy did not have. Hence, France could affect a generosity which Burgundy could not afford. Note that France parted from Lear "in choler," which is hardly the state of mind of a successful lover who owes the success of his suit to the very temper of the old king which he now resents.

incorporate justice.[28] Lear, I have said, is a great king. A great king must have great power, for, without such power, he would not be obeyed, and, if he were not obeyed, he would not be a great king. Lear, then, must have great power or, what comes to the same thing, the illusion of great power.[29] The root of Lear's power is the conviction, in the hearts of both king and subjects, that he is justice incarnate. Yet the absoluteness of Lear's power, founded on this conviction, shuts him off from the very knowledge on which that justice would have to be based if it were what it seems to be, for a spontaneous show of love cannot be distinguished from a clever imitation, except by a god who can search men's hearts. Humanly speaking, the power to discern disinterested motives, however limited in the best case, exists in inverse ratio to the power to command.[30] In proclaiming love of himself as the principle of distributive justice, Lear proclaimed, as the basis of his justice, a godlike knowledge. Lear, we

[28] This does not mean that, in a monarchy, one cannot obey the monarch and love justice without loving the monarch. One might regard the monarch's commands, as just because they happen to conform to a nonmonarchical standard. Or one might recognize the monarchical principle as the highest one while holding the existing incumbent to be deficient in the qualities of a monarch. The second condition is not a genuine exception, because the regime would then not be monarchical in an unqualified sense. The fact that all actual monarchies may be nominal rather than real does not affect the argument. If, however, we consider the essence of monarchy, I believe the necessity for the statement in the text will appear. Monarchy is a political regime, consisting of a true king and true subjects. The true king is such by his pre-eminence in what his monarchical subjects recognize as virtue, as the true subjects are so by their obedience to the pre-eminent virtue of their ruler. But one cannot recognize virtue without loving it. Thus, the necessary and sufficient condition of the obedience of a *monarchical* subject is the love of the personage who embodies the ruling virtue. It is this kind of obedience alone which makes the regime essentially monarchical, and distinguishes it from other kinds of regimes.

[29] As long as his subjects believe that he has power, this belief is sufficient to produce the obedience which constitutes that power.

[30] Compare Lear with the good Duke Vincentio in *Measure for Measure*. The duke, in order to discover the truth about his subjects' characters, pretends to go on a long journey, delegating authority to some of those he wishes to test. He then returns disguised as a friar and becomes the confessor and spiritual adviser of several of the principals. This course is not open to Lear, for, among other things, he is king of a pre-Christian Britain. Another such comparison would be with Prospero in the *Tempest*. Prospero, however, has Ariel, and Ariel's power to produce illusions (according to Prospero's directions) makes the malefactors helpless to conceal their motives from the man who controls their access to reality. Neither Prospero nor Vincentio, however, although apparently exempted from Lear's "human" limitation of being unable to search men's hearts for their motives, is regal in the sense that Lear is. Both love "the life removed" and "the liberal arts"; neither is a truly political man. Neither, in fact, is a success as a ruler, because both neglect the duties of office for something they care for more.

might say, is compelled by the nature of his situation to pretend to a perfection he does not possess in order to actualize a perfection he does possess.

But what meaning are we to ascribe to the expression, "perfection he does possess"? Lear, I have said, is a great ruler. The unity and amity of the kingdom, although seen for the most part retrospectively and through the attachment to him of all the "good" characters, are witness to this. Yet, granting Lear this superiority, we can still say that Lear never had more than an opinion of his own justice.[31] If we were to assume that such a regime is the best of which human life admits, we would, nonetheless, have to say that the best is, in a decisive sense, an illusion.[32] We would be further driven to conclude that Lear's greatness as a king is an illusion. Lear's supposed knowledge of his daughters' love of him, which was to have been the basis of his greatest and ostensibly most just political action, is of the essence of the illusion.

The crux of the situation is this: that the illusion which is the basis of Lear's policy, though adequate for all the purposes of political life, becomes intolerable at the decisive moment in the love test. The old king has need of genuine love. The entire scene, we must remember, is due to his mortality, to the fact that he must provide for a successor. The very insufficiency which necessitates a succession necessitates love. A god could be loved without loving, but a man cannot. If Lear possessed the perfection which, as king, he pretends to, he would be capable of being loved without loving. But Lear lacks such perfection. His need of love is radical. In pretending to the attributes of divinity, a pretense necessary to the operation of his seemingly most just rule, Lear has had to deny the claims of his humanity. As king, he has denied humanity to serve humanity.[33] Cordelia, however, by her action, destroys the possibility of consummating that self-denial.

[31] Lear's later sense of the limitations of his former justice is shown in the famous lines on the heath:

> Take physic, pomp.
> Expose thyself to feel what wretches feel,
> That thou mayst shake the superflux to them
> And show the Heavens more just.
>   III. iv. 33-36.

[32] The best is an illusion because the virtue on which it is founded is an illusion. The tacit premise is, of course, that virtue is knowledge, but that Lear, deficient in the self-knowledge which the action of the tragedy alone could remove, did not achieve genuine knowledge and hence virtue until after he had ceased ruling. If the regime was constituted by the virtue of the ruler, ruling not only his subjects' actions but their hearts, then the regime, too, was, in this sense, an illusion.

[33] Compare *The Second Part of King Henry the Fourth* III. i. 6-33, the speech ending, "Uneasy lies the head that wears a crown," but especially Henry the Fifth's speech, in the play of that name, IV. i. 246-301:

We must now analyze the precise impact that Cordelia's refusal had on her father and attempt to comprehend the interaction of his conscious and unconscious motivation. At the moment Lear rejects Cordelia, calls her stranger, and dowers her with his curse, she has in fact become a stranger to him. For Lear, in attempting to carry out the well-contrived pretense or deception of the love test, had not hesitated to compromise with truth, albeit for the sake of justice. Cordelia, in refusing to make any such compromise, showed herself in her intransigence unlike her father. But it is this appearance of unlikeness, rather than the appearance of disobedience, that made a mockery of his plan, for the plan was founded on the assumption of such a likeness. But Lear's assumption that Cordelia loved him and that she was like him involved even more than the question of whether he was sound in his intention to make her his successor, for Lear had seen what he thought was the image of his own soul in Cordelia. His passion for Cordelia was his self-love transfigured; in his identification with her, he saw his monarchy perpetuated beyond the grave. His faith in the truth of that image caused him to place faith in the bearer of the image. But, bewildered by the sudden strangeness of the bearer, Lear could no longer recognize the image, and with this he lost the sheet anchor of what had hitherto been his existence. A colloquy in *Julius Caesar* may help to clarify what is here intended:

CASSIUS   Tell me, good Brutus, can you see your face?
BRUTUS   No, Cassius, for the eye sees not itself
               But by reflection, by some other things.

    .   .   .   .

CASSIUS   Therefore, good Brutus, be prepared to hear.
               And since you know you cannot see yourself
               So well as by reflection, I your glass
               Will modestly discover to yourself
               That of yourself which you yet know not of.
                         Julius Caesar I. ii. 60-82.

Lear's alienation from Cordelia involved his alienation from the basis of such self-knowledge as he believed himself to possess. He became alienated not only from her, but from himself and from the world within which he had seen himself in his own mind's eye.[34] Lear's original,

---

            What infinite heartsease
      Must kings neglect that private men enjoy!
      And what have kings that privates have not too,
      Save ceremony, save general ceremony?

That is, kings are paid with an illusory good that their subjects may enjoy a real one.
[34] The connection between Lear's image of the world in which he is king and his image of the world in which he is no longer king is indicated in many ways, including the following. In Lear's curse, disinheriting Cordelia, as in his oath affirming

conventional kingliness was intrinsic to the world implied by the image of himself which he saw reflected in Cordelia. The strange image which Cordelia now reflected separated Lear from this world, the world in which he had been king. He could not continue as king, as his original plan required, when he no longer had a basis for faith in that world. Yet some part of the passion of the outburst against Cordelia, like that against his other daughters later in the play, is due to his attachment to that lost world, an attachment not to be overcome lightly or in a moment. His

---

the banishment of Kent, Lear thinks of the order of the universe as the work of living gods who are concerned with justice and injustice in the same sense in which he is concerned with them. When cursing Cordelia, he calls the light, the darkness, and "the orbs" from whose operation we both exist and cease to be to witness his disclaimer of "paternal care, propinquity and property of blood." But, if it is the operation of the divine order that is the cause of both our existence and nonexistence, Lear's belief that he could disclaim a connection determined by that order must mean that Lear believed that Cordelia, in offending her father, had offended that divine order and, in breaking links that connected her with her father in the local moral order, had broken the links connecting him with her in the supramundane, cosmic order. Similarly, Lear confirms the banishment of Kent with an oath "by Jupiter." The reference is to the king of the Olympian gods, Homer's father of gods and men, who is invoked as the substance of what is shadowy in Lear's authority.

If we now turn from scene i to the great passion on the heath, we observe that Lear's consciousness of himself as a member of the imagined world he has until then inhabited culminates in his tearing off his clothes. The clothes, of course, represent the conventions which have hitherto concealed his true self from himself. Lear's next words after the "divesting" are in response to Kent's "How fares your Grace?" "What's he?" replies Lear, now unable or unwilling to recognize the conventional distinction implicit in the salutation. And Lear's very next words indicate how little of intentional irony there is in these lines. Gloucester is pleading with him to go in out of the storm. Lear demurs. "First let me talk with this philosopher." The person referred to is Edgar, disguised as a madman. "What is the cause of thunder?" demands Lear of the philosopher. Thus Lear, finally gone mad, as madness is understood in the world he has rejected, can no longer recognize the distinction of "grace," by which kings are kings, nor can he recognize in thunder the sign of Jupiter's authority, the authority which reinforces and guarantees the moral order represented in this world by kings. The thunderbolt, symbol of the power of Jupiter, has become a question of theoretical philosophy.

Finally, it is worth noting that Lear, alone of those present on the heath, penetrates Edgar's disguise, for Edgar is the philosopher who, at the last, provides the moral of the play. "Men must endure their going hence, even as their coming hither; ripeness is all" (V. ii. 9). Even this supreme insight has its irony, in that it is a truth conveyed by a son, Edgar, to his father, Gloucester. The catastrophe of the tragedy, its only catastrophe, is the catastrophe of that moral order to which Lear and Gloucester belonged when the play began—the moral order in which kings and fathers command, the moral order which is part of a larger order or cosmos, whose hierarchy maintains and is maintained by the kind of subordination and superordination implicit in the relationship of kings and subjects, fathers and sons. That the moral of the tragedy is expressed by Edgar and that his father must become his pupil to grow wiser is as much a part of the moral of the play as is the moral itself.

attachment to justice was at the root of his attachment to that world, and the tragedy of *King Lear* lies in the necessity of Lear to abandon even his attachment to justice when the claims of love and truth are brought to bear in all their uncompromising imperiousness.

The deeper meaning of the love test was foreshadowed when we observed that Cordelia, alone of the three sisters, knew in advance of her speech what her share of the kingdom was to be. Cordelia, I said, knew that her father, far from demanding a profession of love from her, was making a profession of love to her. In the test, Lear becomes the lover, and Cordelia the beloved. But the relation of beloved to lover is that of cause to effect, of superior to inferior. When Lear, responding to Cordelia's "Nothing," tells her that nothing comes of nothing, he expresses the axiom on which all understanding of causality is founded. He tells her that there is no effect without a cause. He implies that she cannot cause him to be bountiful without obeying him. He does not know, however, that, by becoming the lover, the only bounty he has to offer is his love and that Cordelia, as beloved, can only cause his love by refusing to surrender the sovereignty which he has himself now thrust on her. Ironically, Lear is attempting to command Cordelia at precisely the moment and in the very situation in which his relation to her has been reversed, and she has become the commanding one, for, when Lear turned to Cordelia to hear her profession, she had already ascended a throne. It was not the throne of Britain, but rather the invisible throne prepared by nature for those of surpassing virtue.

We have noted above that Lear's choice of Cordelia as his successor was based on a translegal conception of political right, in that he did not proceed on the legal or conventional rule in accordance with which the eldest, as distinct from the best qualified, inherits. Yet we can now distinguish between the direct rule of political wisdom, which is what we may call Lear's rule before the great eruption, and natural right proper. Lear's wise rule was still founded on opinion, as distinct from knowledge, and to that extent represented a kind of conventional right, albeit the best kind. We now see that Cordelia's precedence over her sisters is also a matter of natural right. But Cordelia's natural right to rule is not an element of political right. It follows, not from the wisdom of her father's choice, but from her intransigence in regard to truth.[35] Cordelia's natural right, far from being an element of political right, is destructive of

---

[35] In short, Shakespeare would not accept Aristotle's formulation that natural right is a *part* of political right; *Nichomachean Ethics* 1134^b 18ff. For Shakespeare, as for Plato, the highest form of political right reflects rather than embodies pure natural right. Natural right is distinguished from political right. It is a transcendental cause of political right, rather than an element in it. Cf. Leo Strauss, *Natural Right and History* (Chicago: University of Chicago Press, 1953), pp. 151-53.

political right. Lear's policy, which I have shown to be both wise and just, depends on a small hypocrisy, a relatively slight pretense. Cordelia's nature, refusing to make the concession that policy called for, reveals, at one and the same moment, its transcendent beauty and its superiority to, if not its contempt for, justice.[36]

It was Lear's intention that Cordelia become sovereign. That intention is fulfilled within the love test itself, but in a way that Lear did not anticipate. Nevertheless, we maintain, Cordelia does do what her father wishes her to do, but it is his unconscious wish that she fulfills. It requires the five acts of the tragedy for Lear to fully realize what that true wish was. Strangely enough, Lear, in his outburst against Cordelia, also acts in obedience to her, who is now his sovereign. In the region beyond that of the political, to which their relationship has now been transferred,

[36] We may here venture a hypothesis concerning one of the most difficult problems in the interpretation of *King Lear*, albeit one that goes beyond the proper scope of this essay. This is the problem of the ending—the apparent wantonness of the gods in permitting the deaths of Cordelia and Lear. It has been cited as a fundamental defect of the dramatic structure that these deaths do not follow as a result of the necessities of the action, as in the cases of Macbeth, Othello, Hamlet, Brutus, and other tragic heroes. It has been held that the poet's theme became too gigantic even for his colossal powers and that, although dramatic fitness required the deaths of the hero and heroine, he knew no way of effecting these deaths but by chance. I believe that there is another explanation.

One of the puzzles of the last scene is the apparently inexplicable delay of the dying Edmund, from line 200, where he promises to "do good," until line 245, where he finally tells of his order for the death of Cordelia. The delay might even conceivably be traced back to line 163, where Edmund already appears to show remorse. The question is, Why, if Edmund's repentance is genuine, does he delay so long to tell of his order? The murder of Cordelia is the greatest of his crimes, and yet it lay within his power to stay the hand whose blow would put more guilt on him than any he had yet struck.

The solution, I believe, is this. The deaths of Lear and Cordelia were not matters of mere dramatic fitness. They were required as retribution for the transgressions against justice that both had committed. Both had sided with France against Britain. Lear's rejection of Cordelia was a blow at his own justice as king. Cordelia's invasion with French forces was not an act of public redress; it was motivated by love of her father, who was no longer the true king, because he had shown himself no longer capable of ruling. The defeat of the French forces and the unification of the kingdom under Albany is, we must observe, a political consummation which achieves all the just purposes of Lear's original plan. The survival of Lear and/or Cordelia would throw all this once more into confusion. Above all would this be true if Cordelia lived, for it would continue the French claims, the excuse for foreign intrusion. The dying Edmund means to do some good yet. What good, in the sense of justice, could he do better than to let the order against Cordelia's life run? It is necessary that Edmund remand the order as a way of showing his repentance for the merely malicious action he had heretofore done, but the silent delay shows a deeper understanding of the demands of justice, the demands that Cordelia, too, had rejected, in favor of something celestial, just as he had rejected them in favor of something infernal.

the act of obedience, the act of the true subject, is the act of love. To command love in this nonpolitical sense means to cause loving in the soul of another. Cordelia can be the cause of that love which Lear's great soul needs only if Lear removes himself from, or removes from himself, every vestige of his monarchy in this world. We may summarize the ironies of scene i by saying that the love test, which at first glance appears to be a straightforward demand for protestations of love, turns out to be an elaborately contrived deception; but the supreme deception is that of the deceiver himself, who really acts, in the final analysis, albeit unwittingly, for the very purpose for which he says he is acting. Lear, acting to discover the truth about his daughters' love, does what would have been foolish as a political action if it were not a pretense; yet it is not foolish in its deeper, nonpretending meaning, because it is no longer a political action, for Lear's action, but not Lear himself, is thoroughly rational in the rejection of Cordelia. Reason could not have devised a more straightforward way than that actually taken by Lear to divest himself of all the attributes of worldly monarchy.[37]

I have said that Cordelia's intransigent truthfulness showed her superiority, even to justice. It did, indeed, show that, on the level of political action, there need be no distinguishable difference between superiority to the claims of justice and rank injustice. This paradox, far from being merely apparent, is at the core of the tragedy of *King Lear* and lies in Shakespeare's vision of a universe in which the demands of justice are in an insoluble conflict with the demands of that truth which is, in its turn, the only unconditional motive for justice. The proposition that truth is the motive for justice is symbolized by the fact that Lear's entire policy—his wise and just policy—has as its foundation his conviction in regard to Cordelia. Yet it was impossible for Lear's conviction to be more than a mere opinion within the framework of that policy. Cordelia, responding to Lear's unconscious demand for truth, as distinct from mere opinion, compels him to act in the most unjust manner possible in order to discover that truth. Thus does the uncompromising quest for truth and love, which can be ultimately understood as different names for the same thing, destroy justice; even as the successful completion of Lear's original plan—while doing justice, that is, serving the common good—would forever have denied him that love and knowledge which alone could link his mighty soul to its source in eternity.

In this incomplete and inadequate analysis of a single scene of a single play, I have attempted only a few hints at the range and precision of

---

[37] The word "divest" is used advisedly. See n. 34, *supra*. When Lear re-awakens, after the "divesting" in the storm scene, he is in Cordelia's arms, wearing different clothes, clothes that he does not recognize.

Shakespeare's analysis of the problematic character of the ultimate in human and political existence. No argument would have been needed to convince anyone of the breadth of the poet's vision of the human scene, but I think it indispensable to realize that there is a no less impressive intellectual precision underlying the amazing sweep. That precision is, I think, not an adventitious factor in the breadth, but its very condition. If there is a single philosophic doctrine which we may, without hesitation, ascribe to Shakespeare, it is that intellectual beauty is the condition of the existence of the beauty we apprehend with our senses. It would be an absurdity unworthy of his greatness to suppose that, though it was given him to move us with the images of the senses, as it has perhaps been given no other man to do, he was for this reason less concerned with the intellectual beauty which was its cause. This essay is intended to suggest that the vividness of the sensual world presented to us by Shakespeare is a pallid thing compared to that other world which was his ultimate concern.

In conclusion, I would apply this generalization to the political problem presented at the outset: the problem of the perpetuation of the perfect regime. Human life, we might say, is set in motion by the demands of human virtue. These demands require political life. But the full demands of virtue transcend political life. In a sense, they transcend human life. Lear, who is, after all, a mythical king of Britain, brought political life in the poet's own land to a peak that no actual king did. But the dynamism of Lear's soul, which drew the kingdom to this pitch, could not rest there. I said before that, according to Shakespeare, monarchy is the best form of government. This may now be qualified by saying that it is best only in a theoretical sense and, rather, that the understanding of monarchy, as the indispensable condition of the understanding of political life, is the condition of such actual perfection as may fall within our human compass. The understanding of monarchy is the condition of the understanding of the true relation of the political to the human and of the human to the divine. Surely, such knowledge was never more needful.

4 | THE VIRTUE OF A NATION OF CITIES
On the Jeffersonian Paradoxes

What *is* a "nation of cities?" That of course depends upon what a nation is, and what a city is. Generally, we associate two groups of ideas with this phrase. First, we think of our continuing population growth, and the continuing concentration of that growing population, under the whip-lash of technology, into fewer and vaster metropolitan areas. Second, we think of the related transformation of our federal system, as the expanding partnership of the national government and the governments of the great metropolitan agglomerations by-passes the states, or at best treats them as administrative devices without important discretion.

A vagrant fact, related to the foregoing, is that only about 6 percent of those now gainfully employed in the United States are directly engaged in farming. Considering how many of those comprehended by this percentage are essentially industrial managers and workers in large, ranch-style operations, we can say that the family farm, as the socio-economic heart of the American polity, now belongs wholly to history and legend. What the division should be between history and legend, we shall not attempt to say; but it is certainly true that the legendary proportion has been as potent in its influence upon American politics as the historical. "Those who labor in the earth," wrote Jefferson in his *Notes on the State of Virginia,* "are the chosen people of God, if ever He had a chosen people, whose breasts He has made His peculiar deposit for substantial and genuine virtue. It is the focus in which He keeps alive that sacred fire, which otherwise might escape from the earth."[1] And again, " . . . generally speaking, the proportion which the aggregate of the other classes of citizens bears in any State to that of its husbandmen, is the proportion of its unsound to its healthy parts."[2] And finally, "the mobs of great cities add just so much to the support of pure government, as sores do to the strength of the human body."[3]

I think it would be difficult to overestimate the influence of these sentiments upon the rhetoric of American politics. They express a connection between virtue and agriculture, a connection that is matched, in other

Reprinted by the kind permission of the publisher from Robert A. Goldwin (ed.), *A Nation of Cities,* Rand McNally Public Affairs Series (Chicago, 1966).

[1] Saul K. Padover (comp.), *The Complete Jefferson* (New York: Tudor Publishing Company, 1943), query 14, p. 678.
[2] Ibid.
[3] Ibid., p. 679.

contexts, by that between virtue and republicanism. And to the leaders of the Revolution, the term *republicanism* came to comprehend all of the politically good, all of what is implied in the statements of purpose in the Declaration of Independence and in the Constitution.

In 1782 Jefferson could write, "Let our workshops remain in Europe"[4]; but thirty years later, with the wars of the French Revolution and of Napoleon added to his experience, as well as our own war with Great Britain in 1812, he had changed his opinions on economic policy. The virtue of the farmer was rooted in his personal independence of the "casualties and caprice of customers." The dependence of artisans and traders "begets subservience and venality, suffocates the germ of virtue, and prepares fit tools for the designs of ambition."[5] But the virtue of the whole nation is similarly undermined if it becomes dependent upon foreigners for manufactured goods, particularly for the manufactured sinews of war, and if it shows a cringing acquiescence in the abuse of its peaceful commerce on the high seas. So Jefferson concluded that there was no prudent alternative to making the country economically sufficient to itself. But he never ceased to regret the necessity that made it wise for Americans to encourage manufacturing. In 1814 he wrote "Our enemy has indeed the consolation of Satan, on removing our first parents from Paradise: from a peaceful agricultural nation he makes us a military and manufacturing one."[6]

Jefferson was the greatest contributor to that vision of a virtuous republic which has from time to time dominated the political imagination of the American people. It is the vision of a republic of free and equal yeoman farmers, who look only "up to heaven" and to "their own soil and industry"[7] for their livelihood, and who can participate equally with friends and fellow citizens in the tasks of self-government because they see them as just that, and not as instruments of profit, or as the source of preferment, favor, and influence.

Yet there was always something anomalous about Jefferson's agrarianism. In the same paragraph of the *Notes* from which we have quoted above, he wrote, "While we have land to labor, then, let us never wish to see our citizens occupied at a work bench or twirling a distaff." And in 1816, although resigned to an expanding industrial sector of the economy, he asked, "Will our *surplus* labor be then most beneficially employed in the culture of the earth, or in the fabrications of art?"[8] By

[4] Ibid.

[5] Ibid. p. 678.

[6] Letter to William Short, Nov. 28, 1814, in H. A. Washington (ed.), *The Writings of Thomas Jefferson* (Washington, D.C.: Taylor & Maury, 1854), 6: 400.

[7] Padover (comp.), *The Complete Jefferson*, p. 678.

[8] Letter to Benjamin Austin, in Washington (ed.), *Writings*, 6: 523.

this he meant to inquire whether, when all our own needs for manufactured goods had been met, the excess productive power of the people should be employed in growing or in making the commodities with which we would trade upon the market of the world. That is to say, Jefferson indicates, by the first of the two passages just cited, his awareness that the availability of cheap land was a temporary condition that could not last indefinitely in the United States. By the second he indicates that the expanding productive powers of a people as enlightened and energetic as the Americans would some day surely require new outlets for investment, and that neither agriculture, nor strictly necessary manufactures, would provide such outlets. Supposing it true that "corruption of morals in the mass of cultivators is a phenomenon of which no age or nation has furnished an example," yet is it also true "the natural progress and consequence of the arts" is precisely that it increases the proportion of the unsound to the healthy classes of the people.

As the patron of the virtuous republic, Jefferson wrote, in 1785, that he considered "the class of artificers as the panders of vice, and the instruments by which the liberties of a country are generally overturned."[9] So did he loathe banks and banking. In 1816 he wrote, "Like a dropsical man calling out for water, water, our deluded citizens are clamoring for more banks, more banks. . . .We are now taught to believe that legerdemain tricks upon paper can produce as solid wealth as hard labor in the earth. It is vain for common sense to urge that *nothing* can produce but *nothing;* that it is an idle dream to believe in a philosopher's stone which is to turn everything into gold, and to redeem man from the original sentence of his Maker, 'in the sweat of his brow shall he eat his bread.' "[10]

Yet this same Jefferson was the supreme American patron of that veritable philosopher's stone, Science, which was, then as surely as now, relieving man's estate of the primeval sentence to hard labor. It is uncommon irony that Jefferson, in this condemnation of banks, and the modern system of credit, should invoke maxims of Greek metaphysics and of Hebrew ethics, for he was an inveterate denier of both the old rationalism and the old revelation. "When I contemplate the immense advances in science and discoveries in the arts which have been made within the period of my life," he wrote in 1818, "I look forward with confidence to equal advances by the present generation, and have no doubt they will consequently be as much wiser than we have been as we than our fathers were, and they than the burners of witches."[11] That is, because of the necessary

[9] Letter to John Jay, Aug. 23, 1785, in ibid., 1: 404.
[10] Letter to Colonel Yancey, Jan. 6, 1816, in ibid., 6: 515.
[11] Letter to Dr. Benjamin Waterhouse, in ibid., 7: 101.

progress of science and the arts, men will become far wiser than they are now and—since Jefferson often affirms this equation—more virtuous. But the same causes will increase the proportion of the unsound to the sound classes of the people, and pile men upon each other in large cities, as in Europe, where they will be as corrupt as they are in Europe! In short, the identical causes would, simultaneously, produce both virtue and vice, and both liberty and despotism. When Jefferson thought simply of science, he thought of the release of men's souls from degrading superstitions, from fear of the "raw heads and bloody bones" by which kings and priests duped the people to accept their fraudulent regimes, as he also thought of the things useful to human life which the method of science was constantly spawning. But when he thought of urbanization, industrialism, and the capitalist economy that accompanied the effects of science, he saw in the future only corruption and the decline of the regime of liberty.

What Marvin Meyers has called the "Jacksonian Persuasion" in a brilliant book by that name [12] is, I believe, essentially nothing more than the Jeffersonian persuasion, as characterized above. "The wealth and strength of a country are its population," declared Jackson, "and the best part of that population are the cultivators of the soil. Independent farmers are everywhere, the basis of society, and the true friend of liberty." Nevertheless, the Jacksonians enlarged the occupational basis of the virtuous majority to include the new working classes and small businessmen, who were growing with the growth of the cities along the eastern seaboard. Jefferson himself, when he had advocated leaving the factories to Europe, had admitted that the manufactured goods needed by the farmers ought to be made at home, so that American agriculture should not have to import its own instruments of production. Thus the mantle of virtue was only extended a little further when the Jacksonians included all those who applied their brains and bones and sinews directly to the production of tangibly useful implements of life. Yet the implication always remained that anyone of sufficient character, although earning his living in a workshop, or by that frugal commerce of small tradesmen which served the marginal needs of a farming community, would sooner or later invest in landed property.

According to Meyers, the Jacksonian movement found its true character and mission in the war against the second Bank of the United States. Disagreement as to the constitutionality of the chartering of the first Bank by Congress was, of course, the pristine issue which divided Jefferson from Hamilton in Washington's first administration. Jefferson and his friends had seen in Hamilton's policy of paying off the Revolutionary debt without discrimination between its original holders and those

[12] Marvin Meyers, *The Jacksonian Persuasion* (New York: Vintage Books, 1960).

who had bought it up on speculation, joined to the assumption of the state debts, and capped by the chartering of the bank, as the groundwork of a massive system of corruption. It could lead and, in their view, did lead to the creation of a corps of American "King's men" in the Congress, that is, congressmen voting as a bloc in accordance with instructions from the Treasury, thus undermining the constitutional separation of powers. Indeed, after Hamilton's leadership in suppressing the Whisky Rebellion, it appeared to be a joining of purse and sword which partook of the essence of despotism. However, the basic point made by the enemies of Hamilton's Bank was that, by its ability to expand or contract the circulating medium, and to expand or contract the flow of credit, it placed too arbitrary a power in hands too remote from the people, and in fact created a large element of government unknown to the Constitution. The warfare between federalists and republicans reached a climax long after Hamilton had left office, but to the followers of Jefferson the Alien and Sedition Acts were only an open move to accomplish by force—by deportation and imprisonment—the ends first sought by the financial policies of Hamilton. That the whole stock in trade of Jacksonian rhetoric was taken from the earlier Jeffersonians is shown by this passage from Jackson's bank message:

> The bank is, in fact, but one of the fruits of a system at war with the genius of our institutions—a system founded upon a creed the fundamental principle of which is a distrust of the popular will as a safe regulator of political power, and whose ultimate object and inevitable result, should it prevail, is the consolidation of all power in our system in one central government. Lavish public disbursements and corporations with exclusive privileges would be its substitutes for the original and as yet sound checks and balances of the Constitution—the means by whose silent and secret operation a control would be exercised by the few over the political conduct of the many by first acquiring that control over the labor and earnings of the great body of the people. Wherever this spirit has effected an alliance with political power, tyranny and despotism have been the fruit.[13]

Historians are in general agreement that neither the first nor second Banks of the United States abused their privileges in the manner charged by their accusers or, indeed, were ever in a position to do the things they were suspected of doing. Although Nicholas Biddle may have done some foolish things during the Bank War itself, the notion that he had it in his power to convert the Bank's franchise into an invisible government, more potent than the legal government, is disproved by the result of the Bank War. Yet the absence of evidence of the Bank's misdeeds became a kind of evidence against it: after all, was not banking a mystery, which worked its will by invisible ways? Did it not intrude upon

[13] Quoted in ibid., pp. 20-21.

the real world, of real goods, honestly produced and exchanged, "a mysterious, swaying web of speculative credit," designed not to reward "industry, economy and virtue," but "fixed to pay off the insider and the gambler?"[14] The Jacksonians who protested the existence of the second Bank of the United States were, by and large—like farmers everywhere— the same ones who wished for easier and looser credit, something they presently enjoyed when Jackson transferred the government funds from the Bank of the United States to favored state banks, with a wild speculative boom ensuing, ending in the crash of 1837. That is to say, while the Jacksonian rhetoric was directed against banking per se, its practical effect was to cast off the shackles of the relatively conservative central banking policies of Biddle's Bank. The typical Jacksonian was a small entrepreneur, either artisan or farmer, but in either case a man striving to improve his economic position in life. He resented old and large fortunes, and his conscience felt better when he denounced any power or position which, from his perspective, appeared unearned. It took hard work, thrift, and an ability to forego present for future pleasures to scrape together that little capital with which he could buy a farm or a shop, or a few more acres or a few more tools. He resented bitterly those who enjoyed the advantages of capital without, as it seemed, making sacrifices for it, and it galled him when one of them—as, for example, Biddle—could deny him the easy credit wherewith to buy those added acres or tools. At the same time, he saw in the whole society around him the corrosion, by the spirit of acquisitiveness, of the heroic virtues of the Revolutionary generation, the men of the Old Republic, the men of the classic Revolutionary mold. But he could not see in that corrosion the effects of his own acquisitiveness. He denounced the system of credit, and professed to believe in hard money as in hard work. In truth, while praising hard work as being the essence of virtue, he resented having to work hard, and often seemed to have no higher end than the ease which wealth provided, even as he hated those who, as it seemed to him, being without merit, already enjoyed it.

Opposition to banking, industrialism, and cities is one of the oldest unifying themes in the rhetoric of great popular reform movements in the United States. Jefferson's success established the pattern, and Jackson's made it a tradition. That it has survived at least until recently is illustrated by the early New Deal. Franklin D. Roosevelt, in his first inaugural address, denounced the moneychangers in the temple, who had betrayed their trust. But he also expressed the opinion that the terrible plight of the unemployed urban workers indicated that we had become too heavily concentrated in big cities, that too many people were depen-

[14] Ibid., p. 26.

dent upon others for the necessities of life, particularly food. And the Resettlement Administration was established with the view of facilitating a movement "back to the land." We may assume, however, that there will be no more such movements, short of another such depression. The kind of protest expressed by the great agrarian-oriented political revolutions of our past was, however, one of the largest elements behind the recent candidacy of Senator Goldwater. Distrust of the power of the central government, distrust of the influence of the big-city states and the big-city political machines and the federal power built upon alliance with those machines were all strongly evident. The role of the great, eastern "establishment," in the rhetoric of the Goldwater movement, with the special place in it for the Rockefeller family and the Chase-Manhattan Bank, could easily have been paraphrased from the Jacksonians and their denunciation of the Bank of the United States. (I cannot forebear the parenthetic remark that Jackson was sufficiently astute to effect a political alliance with New York City in his warfare against Philadelphia. Van Buren, who was one of Jackson's chief lieutenants and who became his successor, had a large interest in the Bank of New York, a sharp competitor of the Bank of the United States, whose main offices were in Philadelphia. New York State, having completed the Erie Canal out of its own resources, could comfortably oppose the use of national financing to assist internal improvements in other states, and therefore could support Jackson's strict constructionism with as good a will as any southern or western states. Senator Goldwater had no such prudent alliances to the rear of his enemies!)

The tradition which associates the virtuous republic with a fundamentally agrarian life goes back at least as far as Plato's *Republic*. In the second book of that notable work, Socrates constructs the first, or healthy city, the true city. It is not simply agrarian, but is based upon the most elementary division of labor, arising from the needs of men's bodies. And the first and greatest of our needs, Socrates says, is for food. So, although there will be carpenters and weavers and cobblers in this first city, as well as a number of other crafts, with a market place and traders to run it in order that the various products be exchanged in the right proportions and amounts, farming will clearly be the dominant occupation. There will be herders for the oxen that the farmers will need for ploughing and drawing heavy burdens, and for the goats and sheep who will supply the fleece for the weaving of woolen garments. But there is no mention of cattle for any other purpose, and it can be assumed that the diet will be a vegetarian one.

This first or healthy city is described as being not only without meat, but without anything else that can possibly be thought of as a luxury. Recreation consisted of reclining on rustic beds, "feasting" on cakes made of wheat or barley, drinking wine, and singing hymns to the gods. In this way the citizens would, Socrates presumes, live healthy lives to ripe old ages, taking care not to beget children beyond their means, lest they fall into either poverty or war. Besides the absence of meat or any other luxury, there is no mention of any institutions of government. Presumably, as the division of labor is so evidently motivated by mutual need, and as there are no goods whose presence can stimulate avarice, so is there no evident need for coercive authority.

There is no call to question whether such a city could actually exist to see that the proposition upon which Jeffersonian agrarianism rests is here present: viz., that in the morally healthiest city there will be the least need for political authority. That such a city is one with the least development of the complex or fine arts is also a common premise of Plato and Jefferson. The latter wrote to Benjamin Rush in 1800 as follows: "I view great cities as pestilential to the morals, the health, and the liberties of man. True, they nourish some of the elegant arts, but the useful ones can thrive elsewhere, and less perfection in the others, with more health, virtue, and freedom, would be my choice."[15] Despite Jefferson's antagonism to the *Republic,* one can almost hear in his remarks the accents of Plato's Socrates, replying to Glaucon's demand for a luxurious city that the true and healthy city is the one already described, the one with nothing but the most necessary arts, with a way of life dominated by the soil and the seasons and the simple rhythms of nature.

It has been well said of innocence that, notwithstanding its charm, it has the great disadvantage of being easily lost. In the *Republic,* Socrates yields his innocent city with scarcely a protest to the demand of Glaucon that it be replaced by a luxurious one, observing that perhaps this will have the advantage of revealing the origin both of justice and injustice. The inference is that the healthy city revealed nothing of the latter, although in truth it does not seem to have revealed anything certain about the former, since innocence is not the same thing as virtue. It is the development of the arts which makes both virtue and vice possible. The demand for luxury in the *Republic* leads to the development of the arts, and to war. One can describe the transition from the first city in Book II of the *Republic* almost in Jefferson's words: from a peaceful and agricultural city it becomes a military and manufacturing one. But at this point the development of Plato's imaginary republic and Jefferson's real one diverge. Plato's is purged of all luxury by a discipline of almost unimaginable severity; the natural consequence of the arts, in pandering to vice, is

---

[15] Washington (ed.), *Writings,* 4: 335.

prevented by the ascetic communism of the guardian class. There is no possibility of vice destroying liberty; liberty has already been destroyed by virtue. The reign of virtue is, moreover, enforced through the medium of a "noble lie," a species of fraud that Jefferson detested.

The teaching of Plato's *Republic* seems to be that the problem created by vice—by the unbridled bodily passions in men—can be avoided by men living the life of the healthy city, called by Glaucon the city of pigs. It is a way of life which avoids the evils of the cities: poverty, disease, and war. But in such a community there will be no Socrates; if there is no luxury, neither is there philosophy. Nothing but chance and the absence of any genuine civilization prevents such men from turning to vice. Philosophy, the art of the soul, only arises from the same circumstances that produce the arts of the body. Only by purging the luxurious city can the city of virtue—as distinct from the city of innocence—be brought into existence. But the purging of a luxurious city will not result in a return to simple, innocent liberty. Given the actual presence of the arts, or the knowledge of the arts, a whole community living on the level of Socratic abstemiousness is possible only under the stifling regime of the armed camp.

In classical political philosophy, it appears that the emancipation of the citizen from coercive authority in a civilized society—that is, one in which the arts are considerably developed—is possible to any extent only in a democracy. It is possible only where the principle of equality treats a variety of ways and styles of life on an equal footing, at least as far as the authority of the regime is concerned. It is possible, that is, only where virtue is not held in too high esteem. Modern republicanism, most particularly of the Jeffersonian variety, was conceived with a view to dissolving, if not transcending, the tension between liberty and virtue. It does so by conceiving of virtue mainly in terms of preserving the principle of equality itself.

Virtue, in classical terms, is what makes a man capable of good and noble actions. It is a necessary means to the good life, but it is, at the same time, intrinsic to the good life. As an element of human perfection, or happiness, it is not merely instrumental. "Virtue," Jefferson wrote to Adams in 1816,

does not consist in the act we do, but in the end it is to effect. If it is to effect the happiness of him to whom it is directed, it is virtuous, while in a society under different circumstances and opinions, the same act might produce pain, and would be vicious. The essence of virtue is in doing good to others, while what is good may be one thing in one society, and its contrary in another.[16]

[16] Ibid., 7: 40.

Virtue, according to Jefferson, is essentially instrumental, and is defined solely with reference to its ability to produce happiness. But happiness itself emerges as a surplus of pleasure over pain, and virtue becomes entirely relative to the circumstances which may cause pleasure or pain. Jefferson once wrote to Adams, in a famous letter, "I, too, am an Epicurean." But he was no more genuine an Epicurean than the tough old Puritan. True Epicureanism would have dictated an avoidance of great seas of political troubles; it would have been wholly inconsistent with the nobly venturesome, stormy careers of both men.

Jefferson's was a political hedonism, that defined one's own happiness in terms of the pleasures that could be enjoyed by others. To be a cause of pleasure in others was itself a greater pleasure than merely self-regarding enjoyment. Not self-perfection, but augmenting the equal rights of others is the end of virtue. But the greatest act of virtue is that which is joined to such supreme acts of benevolence and beneficence as Jefferson caused to be inscribed as a memorial to himself on his own tombstone. To help found a state upon the principle of the equal rights of all, to assist in bringing civil and religious liberty to a people, and to lay the foundations for their enlightenment—such is the greatest work of man. Only one glory would be greater than that which Jefferson assuredly aimed at for himself. Bacon, Locke, and Newton were the three greatest men who ever lived, said Jefferson. They were his teachers, and to be the teacher of such a doer as Jefferson is alone a greater glory. But to be conscious of such well doing, and to be conscious of deserving the fame appropriate to such well doing, is the supreme pleasure and the greatest happiness.

The classical city, the *polis* or political community, was conceived as a partnership in justice. But it was an inward, rather than an expansive, cosmopolitan-tending justice, such as Jefferson espoused. Justice was conceived as something inferior to friendship, as dependent upon it. Friendship, wrote Aristotle, seems to hold political communities together more than justice, and legislators seem to care for it more than justice. For when men are friends they have no need of justice, but when they are just they still have need of friends. The highest reason for political activity is found in the bonds which unite men engaged in shared activities, activities which could not be engaged in at all, or so well, unless they were done together. The pleasure in such activities must be found in their excellence, in their being worth doing for their own sake, and not their excellence in their pleasantness. Such activities need not be benevolent, in the sense that they move outward to enlarge the sphere of participants in a common good. The *polis,* as distinct from the modern state, is therefore a small society. Its size is such that there is virtually no one among the citizens who cannot be a friend, or a friend of a friend, of every other citizen. For this reason the ultimate sanctions for justice are not the penalties that can be exacted in the law courts, but ostracism, formal or informal, from the fellowship in which alone the good citizen feels he can lead the good life. That, at least, is implied in Socrates' apparent preference for death to exile in the *Crito* of Plato.

The modern state, erected upon the doctrine of the equal natural rights of all, is in principle a large and expanding society. We might contrast the common good in the modern state with that in the ancient *polis* by comparing the one to a feast that each man enjoys in his own home, and the other to a public festival enjoyed by all the citizens together. Nothing is more characteristic of this difference than the absence of the theory or practice of modern representation in the ancient world. Jefferson himself never ceased to wonder at the fact. Speaking of classical political philosophers, he wrote:

> They knew no medium between a democracy (the only pure republic, but impracticable beyond the limits of a town) and an abandonment of themselves to an aristocracy, or a tyranny independent of the people. It seems not to have occurred to them that where the citizens can not meet to transact their business in person, they alone have the right to choose agents who shall transact it; and that in this way a republican, or popular government, of the second grade of purity, may be exercised over any extent of country. . . . The introduction of this new principle of representative democracy has rendered almost useless everything written before on the structure of government.[17]

But the principle of representative democracy was the end result, not the originating cause, of the vast difference between the modern democratic state, and "everything written before." In the *Notes on the State of Virginia*, Jefferson wrote:

> From the conclusion of this war we shall be going down hill. It will not then be necessary to resort every moment to the people for support. They will be forgotten, therefore, and their rights disregarded. They will forget themselves, but in the sole faculty of making money, and will never think of uniting to effect a due respect for their rights.[18]

When Jefferson thought of the rights of the people, he thought of something infinitely lofty, infinitely worthy of respect. It did not seem to occur to him that the effect of the recognition of their rights was precisely that it left them free to think much of money, and little of virtue.

[17] Letter to Isaac H. Tiffany, Aug. 26, 1816, in ibid., 7: 32.
[18] Padover (comp.), *The Complete Jefferson*, query 17, p. 676.

For the great spirits, for the Jeffersons of the world, the honor of securing the rights of the people transcends, as a motive, the merely selfish exercise of those rights. But what could the millions whom Jefferson provided for, in this vast new nation, do with their rights, once provided? In perhaps the greatest example of unconscious humor in any state paper, President Jefferson wrote in his first annual message to Congress, December 8, 1801, as follows:

> The bravery exhibited by our citizens on that element [i.e., on the sea, in a naval engagement with the Tripolitan pirates] will, I trust, be a testimony to the world that it is not the want of that virtue which makes us seek their peace, but a conscientious desire to direct the energies of our nation to the multiplication of the human race, and not its destruction.[19]

To say that quantity had replaced quality as a standard of political excellence would hardly do justice to the intrinsic excellence of civil and religious liberty, and to the nobility of the men and the regime that has enshrined them. The problems of nations of cities that are now with us must be faced with something of Jefferson's intrepidity of spirit, and with the same willingness to rethink his principles that he displayed in dealing with his own inheritance from the past.

[19] Ibid., p. 388.

5 | POLITICAL OBLIGATION AND THE AMERICAN POLITICAL TRADITION

In the third book of Aristotle's *Politics* the question is raised, "Whatever is the *polis* (or political community)?" But this question, it turns out, is not altogether abstract or theoretical. It is in fact a political question, and political questions, properly so called, are concrete and practical rather than abstract or theoretical. Indeed, one might contend that it is essential to the understanding both of the question and its possible answers to understand the political context within which the question of what the political community is becomes necessary.

A certain action, says Aristotle, is said not to be an action of the *polis,* but of the oligarchy or the tyrant. Who says this? We soon learn that it is a democracy, a democracy that has overthrown a pre-existing tyranny or oligarchy. The democracy then denies the public debts of the predecessor regime. By saying that they are not debts of the *polis* but of the oligarchy or the tyrant, it denies in effect that the previous regimes were regimes; that is to say, it asserts that the debts contracted were in effect the private debts of the rulers, not obligations of the citizens as such, since the governments in question were not agents of the citizens, or were not representatives of the citizens.

As to the merits of this democratic contention, we must all be struck by the reasonableness of the stricture against oligarchy and tyranny. But we must also have an uneasy feeling that, in so speaking, the democracy is doing so out of a selfish interest that may not be altogether just. For example, if the creditors of the old regime had loaned the money to pay the salaries of a secret police force, to help suppress political opposition, that is one thing. If the money had been borrowed to pay the salaries of professors in a university whose autonomy had been scrupulously respected, that is surely something else. Moreover, it certainly makes a difference whether the money had been borrowed from a neighboring tyrant or oligarchy, or from banks holding the savings of innocent citizens.

The elementary division of regimes, according to Aristotle, is that of the one, the few, and the many. This then is subdivided into those that aim at the common advantage, and those that aim perversely at the advantage of the rulers. Now Aristotle himself regarded democracy, along

Paper presented at the 66th Annual Meeting of the American Political Science Association, Los Angeles, Calif., Sept. 11, 1970. Printed by the kind permission of the Association.

with oligarchy and tyranny, as among the perverse regimes. An example of democratic perversity would be an act of expropriation which did not consider whether the property confiscated was itself acquired justly or unjustly. As we have seen, the repudiation of the debts of the previous regime might be an instance of just such perversity. Nevertheless, a prima-facie case does lie in the identification of democracy with the *polis*. Whether the one or the few aim at the advantage of all is of necessity more problematical than whether the many do. Suppose for example that a democracy had been overthrown by an oligarchy or a tyranny. Would a tyrant, for example, ever declare the debts of the democracy to be invalid, because they were not debts of the *polis?* Whatever argument the tyrant might use—and I see no reason why tyrants or oligarchies would not be as likely as democracies to repudiate debts, unless there would be a greater oligarchic sympathy with private property—it is not apt to be the democratic one. Democracy is always plausible, if not always honest, when it declares that the debts contracted by its antagonists are essentially private, and not political. No oligarchy or tyranny would be plausible in saying that democratic debts, however repugnant, are not political in character. But to say that the debts of a democracy are evidently political is to say that they evidently have something of justice about them. For is not the selfish advantage of the many, merely because they are many, more just than the selfish advantage of the one or the few? Indeed, it is by reflecting upon the relative superiority of democracy to its typical competitors—oligarchy and tyranny—that we come to realize that democratic justice is not synonymous with justice; by itself it is imperfect or incomplete.

It is no accident that classical or Socratic political philosophy came to light in a democracy. For it is democracy that compels the raising of the question, "Whatever is the *polis?*" Classical political philosophy cannot be simply democratic, however, because consciousness of the reason for the question involves consciousness of the questionable motives for causing it to be asked. Democracy appears nonetheless not only as the best of the bad regimes, but as the best of the regimes actually in contention whenever the question of the identify of the *polis* is raised, as in the third book of the *Politics*. While it may be essential to the understanding of political life to know the difference between king and tyrant, and between aristocracy and oligarchy, it is not equally pertinent to the practice of political life. Genuine monarchies and aristocracies—in truth as well as in name—are invariably traditional societies, belonging to the ages before democratic revolutions. These are as well the ages before the critical consciousness congenial to political philosophy. The age of political philosophy, both in the ancient and modern worlds, has been the age of democratic revolutions.

Whether the fundamental intention of modern political philosophy, in all its forms, is democratic, we need not here inquire. Certainly modern political philosophy entered the political arena in the most emphatic way in the American and French revolutions. In them the sovereignty of the people, and the necessary legitimacy of popular government, was vehemently affirmed. The United States, in virtue of its appeal to the laws of nature and of nature's God, was the first government in the history of the world explicitly to ground its right upon a teaching of political philosophy. When Thomas Jefferson wrote that certain truths were self-evident, he did not mean that they were known to all, or recognized by all. He meant that the evidence for them was contained within the propositions affirming them, and known therefore to any who grasped the meaning of the propositions. Like Thomas Aquinas he would have conceded that what is self-evident to the wise is not so to all men. However, the propositions of the Declaration of Independence required, not wisdom, but enlightenment, for their proper apprehension. Wisdom is always the preserve of the few, but enlightenment is possible for the many.

To speak of the debts of a regime refers ordinarily to its fiscal obligations. The national debt of the United States is so many billions of dollars. Yet in a more fundamental sense the government's debts to its citizens are all those things for the sake of which the government is conceived to exist. Among these are life, liberty, and the pursuit of happiness. These rights, with which the Creator is said to have endowed all men, become duties on the part of legitimate governments, entrusted by the citizens with the task of securing them. Of course, governments cannot secure the rights of the citizens, it cannot perform its duties to them, unless the citizens in turn perform their duties to the government. The duties of the citizens are implicit in the duties of the government. The latter cannot be performed unless the former are. The primary and most elementary duty of any government is to provide security from violence. To provide such security requires police, to deal with domestic violence, and national armed forces, to deal with foreign violence. But clearly, the citizens must be willing to serve in the police and in the armed services, and to pay taxes for their support. To withhold the personal service or the financial obligation is to fail in their duty and to dissolve in turn the duty of the government to protect them. Of course, the further inferences are, that where there is no personal security, there is no personal liberty, and where no liberty, no pursuit of happiness. The dissolution of the reciprocal obligations of citizen and government would dissolve both the conditions which make the preserving of life possible, and which make life itself worth living. The self-interest of everyone should prevent that from happening. Recognizing that this is everyone's self-interest is what once was understood to be enlightenment.

The United States is a popular regime, because all the authority of its government rests upon an acknowledgment of prior rights invested in all the people. The exercise of these rights—but not the rights themselves, which are held to be unalienable—has been transferred to government, for the evident reason that solitary men, or small groups, are incapable of exercising them advantageously in their own behalf. The consent to government that is given through elections is a small and derivative part of the fundamental consent. In the Declaration of Independence there is a certain presumption in favor of democracy, since all political power is originally in the hands of the people, whatever they afterward consent to have done with it. However, the Declaration also contemplates nondemocratic forms, to which consent may reasonably be given. Hence the consent resulting from continuing, democratic elections must be regarded as instrumentalizing consent, rather than legitimating consent. Legitimating consent arises, first of all, from recognition by the consenting citizen that the government recognizes his natural rights, that its own sphere is defined with reference to them, and that it acts in a manner that can reasonably be construed as calculated to implement them. Of course, if the form of government consented to is a democracy, then the observation of democratic forms becomes part of the just expectations of the citizen. Were he to see elections arbitrarily suspended, he might have just reason to suspect a tyrannical intention, although the absence of elections in a nondemocratic regime might not reasonably engender such suspicions.

We live today in a period when these principles of political right are either denied, disputed, or ignored. Yet Jefferson regarded them as so elementary that they would be recognized, understood, and acknowledged by all enlightened citizens. "I believe this," he declared in his first inaugural address, "[to be] the strongest government on earth. I believe it is the only one where every man, at the call of the laws, would fly to the standard of the law, and meet invasions of the public order as his own personal concern."[1] Yet in anticipation of our own time, Abraham Lincoln, in 1838, could deplore and denounce "the mobocratic spirit, which all must admit, is now abroad in the land."[2] Yet Lincoln had noted that the American people then found themselves in peaceful possession of the most desirable physical resources on the face of the earth, and "under the government of a system of political institutions, conducing more essentially to the ends of civil and religious liberty, than any of which the history of former times tells us."[3] But Lincoln tacitly diagnosed the evils

---

[1] Saul K. Padover (comp.), *The Complete Jefferson* (New York: Tudor Publishing Company, 1943), p. 385.
[2] Roy P. Basler (ed.), *The Collected Works of Abraham Lincoln* (New Brunswick, N.J.: Rutgers University Press, 1953), 1: 111.
[3] Ibid., 1: 108.

which had befallen these institutions as he continued to describe them. "We toiled not in the acquirement or establishment of them—they are a legacy bequeathed to us, by a *once* hardy, brave, and patriotic, but *now* lamented and departed race of ancestors."[4] Thus a main theme of Lincoln's Lyceum speech is the difficulty of estimating the value of inherited blessings, and the danger to inherited institutions of the passions of men for whom the establishment of new regimes is alone a sufficient outlet for their ambitions. Such ambition, however, only becomes dangerous amid the turbulence which weakens the average decent citizens' attachment to the government. When such men see "their property destroyed; their families insulted, and their lives endangered; their persons injured; [and when they see] nothing in prospect that forebodes a change for the better; [they] become tired of, and disgusted with, a government that offers them no protection; and are not much averse to a change in which they imagine they have nothing to lose."[5]

Certainly the government of the United States has been structured in the light of the founding principles, to which we have adverted. Certainly it has, at moments of crisis, displayed the strength that Jefferson believed it possessed. Yet it has also displayed a curious susceptibility to a lack of confidence, such as Lincoln bore witness to in 1838, an unwillingness to accept the rule of the majority under the Constitution, and the consequent withdrawal by an alienated minority of its allegiance to the Constitution and the laws. This proved true to a degree as early as 1798, when Jefferson himself drafted the Kentucky Resolutions. It proved true at the time of the Hartford Convention, at the time of the nullification crisis of 1832, at the time of the Mexican War, and above all at the time of the Civil War. In his first inaugural address Jefferson also declared, that "If there be any among us who would wish to dissolve this Union or to change its republican form, let them stand undisturbed as monuments of the safety with which error of opinion may be tolerated where reason is left free to combat it."[6] But where the spirit of the mob rules, where men fear for their lives if they openly declare their opinions, there is safety neither for truth nor for error. Where this is the case, the tolerance of which Jefferson spoke cannot live.

For some perspective on our own time, let us therefore turn to that most famous and most massive of all cases of civil disobedience in American history: the Civil War. And let us review the arguments presented to deal with that case by the man who above all others had to deal with it, in deed no less than in speech, Abraham Lincoln. Before turning to 1861, we must again remind ourselves of 1838, and of the solemn

[4] Ibid.
[5] Ibid., 1: 111.
[6] Padover (comp.), *The Complete Jefferson*, p. 385.

warning against the effect of civil disobedience that was there delivered. For Lincoln had there warned, not merely of the possibility of a lawless reaction to lawlessness, but that demagogues, arising amidst the turbulence of decadent democracy, were the traditional destroyers of popular government. He warned against the danger of Caesarism, so recently impressed upon the minds of his generation by the phenomenon of Napoleon. The soul of such a man, said Lincoln, "thirsts and burns for distinction; and, if possible, it will have it, whether at the expense of emancipating slaves, or enslaving freemen."[7] Thus was Lincoln aware, twenty-five years before Gettysburg, that the relation of law to freedom under the American Constitution presented a dilemma. He was perfectly aware that the man who would emancipate the slaves some day might do so, or be thought to do so, not as the preserver, but as the destroyer, of the American republic. Thus when John Wilkes Booth cried, "*Sic semper tyrannis!*" on the stage of Ford's theater, he was in a sense speaking lines which had long since been written for him by the man he had mortally assailed.

No understanding of the American Civil War is possible, nor is any appreciation of the problem of law in today's United States possible, unless one appreciates the elements of right and justice on both sides of the ancient struggle. The United States Constitution, as it came from the hands of its framers, and still more after it had adopted the first ten amendments, was a fundamentally ambiguous document. In both the first and fourth articles, Negroes are referred to as "persons," and in the fifth amendment it is declared that "No person shall be . . . deprived of life, liberty, or property, without due process of law." But the fourth article of the Constitution, by declaring that "no person held to service or labor in one State, under the laws thereof, escaping into another, shall, in consequence of any laws or regulations therein, be discharged from such service or labor," incorporated certain state laws by reference into federal constitutional law. And by those state laws, Negro slaves were chattels, mere movable property, rather than the human persons they were otherwise (sometimes by these same laws) recognized to be.

It is a fair summary of vast volumes of controversy to say that there was no consistent way in which the rights of persons could be assimilated to those of chattels, nor in which chattels could be conceived as having the rights of persons. This same anomaly occurred within the public law of the slave states themselves, where slaves were in varying degrees held liable under the criminal law. But a chattel, by definition, lacks a will of its own; its movements depend upon the will of its master.

[7] Basler (ed.), *Abraham Lincoln,* 1: 114.

A slave considered as a chattel is no more than an ox or a hog, whose acts are legally the responsibility of the owner alone. Conversely, a being possessed of a will of its own, capable of voluntary actions for which it can be held responsible in its own right, and therefore justly punishable for them, cannot be dependent upon the will of another as a chattel is presumed to be. No great political questions became involved in this anomaly at the state level. However, at the federal level it became directly involved in the greatest political question the American government has ever faced.

The Declaration of Independence, as we have seen, invoked the laws of nature and of nature's God, which it believed to be self-evident to all enlightened men, as the moral ground of all political obligation. And according to these laws, which were antecedent to, and superior to, all human laws, all men had an equal right to life and to liberty. As the nation expanded, first by the Louisiana Purchase, and then by the Mexican conquest, the question of the terms upon which new states, carved out of the new territories, would be admitted to the Union became acute. This involved two separate stages: first, the status of slavery during the period of territorial government and, second, the status of slavery in the new states. Everything depended upon the first stage, since it was conceded by all that if slavery could be kept out of the territories during the phase of territorial government, it would be excluded by the settlers when they came to form state constitutions, preparatory to admission to the Union.

Now the free state opinion, as it came to be on the eve of the Civil War, and as it was represented in the person of Lincoln, held that the federal government had no authority to intervene in any way to disturb the "domestic institutions" of any of the states. In his inaugural address Lincoln read the resolution from the Republican platform that "the maintenance inviolate of the rights of the States, and especially the right of each state to order and control its own domestic institutions according to its own judgment exclusively, is essential to that balance of power on which the perfection and endurance of our political fabric depend . . . "[8] He reaffirmed those sentiments, not only as those of his party, to which he found himself morally bound, but as his personal views. "I have no purpose, directly or indirectly, to interfere with the institution of slavery in the states where it exists. I believe I have no lawful right to do so, and I have no inclination to do so."[9] Thus did he try to reassure his disaffected fellow citizens on March 4, 1861.

But Lincoln also held the opinion, now also the ruling opinion of

[8] Ibid., 4: 263.
[9] Ibid.

the free states, that the federal government had the power, coupled with the duty, absolutely to exclude slavery from every federal territory. Of course, this power could only be exercised, under the Constitution, through the instrumentality of a constitutional majority. We will return to the meaning of constitutional majoritarianism. First let us look at the slave states' right to the security of their domestic institution from the slave states' perspective. We must recognize that the right of each state "to order and control its own domestic institutions according to its own judgment exclusively," was also a necessary inference from the laws of nature and of nature's God. If the citizens of the southern states believed that the presence of the Negro population amongst them was incompatible with their safety and happiness on any basis other than slavery, then they had the right to continue the institution of slavery among themselves. This inference may sound harsh to us, and very different in purport from the resounding declaration of human equality in the Declaration. But consider that the right to life and liberty, which each man possesses by nature, makes him the indefeasible judge of what is necessary to secure that right. If he judges another man or men dangerous to him, then he may rightfully take action against that man or men and, when he has formed civil societies, to have his representatives take action for him. Let us be clear, that this is not a right which white men have to enslave black men, more than black men—or any men—to enslave any other. It is simply the natural right to self-defense in one of its practical applications. It is the same right which entitles civil society to kill or imprison those it judges to be criminals, or to sequester those whom it regards as mentally defective. Chattel slavery is simply one of the many ways in which civil societies have dealt with the problem of civil danger.

Now it is quite true that, from our prospective, the slave population of the antebellum South was not dangerous to the white citizens in the way they thought it was. However, it was probably true that a large majority of the free states *agreed* with antebellum southern whites, that the abolition of slavery would have been dangerous. No politically considerable number of whites anywhere in the United States ever sought the abolition of slavery, at least until the Civil War had gone on for some time. This of course raises the question of whether government by the consent of the governed is in fact a sufficient principle of political right. Certainly no majority opinion favorable to the full recognition of the Negro's humanity ever existed before the Civil War. But neither was there ever any possibility of denying the right of white men to live by the principle which demanded their consent, without denying the only ground upon which Negro Americans' emancipation and ultimate enfranchisement was possible.

In short, "all men are created equal" certainly meant that Negroes no less than whites could not justly be governed without their consent, nor by rules different from those by which white men governed themselves. But it also meant that, as an indefeasible right of self-government, the citizens of each state had the right to decide how the police powers emanating from their right of self-government were to be exercised. That the exercise of the right of the one resulted in the violation of the rights of the other created a dilemma. But nothing in the Declaration of Independence, notwithstanding its nobility, justified the assumption that the laws of nature and of nature's God may not result in genuine dilemmas. Or perhaps we should say that if they could not issue in dilemmas it would be due to the fact that all men had become perfectly enlightened.

The southerners were justified then in demanding security for the institution of slavery in the states that possessed that institution. Indeed, there was no way that the antagonists of slavery could deny to southerners that right, without denying the title deeds to all self-government among themselves, nor without denying the principle in virtue of which they would be obliged to work for the eventual abolition of slavery! However, the question of extending slavery was, as we shall see, a very different matter.

Southern opinion on slavery extension was vitally influenced by the presence in the free states of a strong abolitionist movement, a movement that certainly never attained majority status, and became potent only as it merged into the far more moderate antislavery movement of the Republican Party. Southerners had heard the intemperate denunciation of the peculiar institution over many years, and were goaded into the fatal mistake of turning from a defense of slavery as a necessary evil to its justification as a positive good. From that they proceeded to demand what they considered equal access to the territories. To them, that meant, not an equal right to go themselves to the territories, but a right to carry slaves there. Of course, "equal right" was impossible in such a case. To carry slaves to the territories meant, a fortiori, to make them slave territories and, thereafter, slave states. Where would the right of the free-staters to have free states be then? The extension of slavery was one of those issues which, like the two men on a raft that will only support one, admits of no compromise, and no harmony of the demands of the parties in conflict.

Why was the slavery extension controversy taken with such deadly seriousness by the South, and why did they not accept Lincoln's assurances of not interfering with the peculiar institution where it already existed? Among the pretexts put forward was that concerning the fugitive slaves. The complaint was made that the free states did not properly assist in the rendition of fugitives. That was probably true, but it was insignificant, in terms of the numbers or value of the runaway slaves. Besides, southerners consistently refused any measures that would have indemnified them at federal expense for their losses by this means. The underlying conviction of the southerners, that ultimately made compromise of the territorial issue impossible, was the conviction that in process of time, as the free states increased in number, while the slave states remained constant, opinion in the free states would turn ever more abolitionist. If three-fourths of the states ever became free, then slavery could be abolished by constitutional amendment. Long before that time, however, ever larger majorities in the free states, becoming ever more hostile, would ever more harass the slave states. Lincoln's assurances in his inaugural address that he would enforce the fugitive slave law were not believed in the South in 1861. But far more was it doubted that presidents elected eight, twelve, or sixteen years hence, with a constituency far larger in free states, would make such a pledge, or honor it if they did. In short, it seemed that preservation of the institution of slavery demanded that slavery expand. But such expansion within the Union was no longer possible, with the election of a president by a party dedicated to prevent another foot of slave territory under the flag of the Union.

One complaint that the southerners made was peculiarly aggravating. In the words of Jefferson Davis in 1861, commenting on the changing relationship of slavery to the Union:

> The climate and soil of the Northern States soon proved unpropitious to the continuance of slave labor, whilst the converse was the case at the South. Under the unrestricted free intercourse between the two sections, the Northern States consulted their own interests by selling their slaves to the South and prohibiting slavery within their limits. The South were willing purchasers of property suitable to their wants, and paid the price of the acquisition without harboring a suspicion that their quiet possession was to be disturbed by those who were inhibited not only by want of constitutional authority, but by good faith as vendors, from disquieting a title emanating from themselves.[10]

No one, as the course of the Civil War was to demonstrate, was more sensitive to this charge than was Lincoln himself. Indeed, we may see within it the kernel of the argument he must have made out to himself in 1838, that the man who freed the slaves might be a destroyer of the republic. For within that charge is the classic reproach of democracy, celebrated in the *Politics,* that the power of the majority may be used to

---

[10] Dunbar Rowland (ed.), *Jefferson Davis—Constitutionalist: His Letters, Papers, and Speeches* (Jefferson, Miss.: Mississippi Department of Archives and History, 1923), 5:70.

expropriate the minority. Davis, in this same message of 1861, accuses Lincoln of having proclaimed in his inaugural address "that the theory of the Constitution requires that in all cases the majority shall govern," implying that Lincoln believed in unrestrained majority rule. In point of fact, it was Jefferson's words that echoed in Davis' mind. For Jefferson had declared in his inaugural that "the will of the majority is in all cases to prevail."[11] But Jefferson had immediately added those qualifications which were Lincoln's as well, "that the minority possess their equal rights, which equal law must protect, and to violate would be oppression."[12] Lincoln had said, "A majority, held in restraint by constitutional checks and limitations, and always changing easily with deliberate changes of popular opinions and sentiments, is the only true sovereign of a free people."[13] Uncompensated abolition, whether of the direct species, or as the indirect consequence of economic strangulation, was a violation of the Fifth Amendment's guarantee against arbitrary deprivation of property, in Lincoln's view no less than Davis'. In the course of the Civil War, the institution of slavery was destroyed without compensation of any kind either to loyal or to rebel slave-holders. By this time, however, destruction of life and property by the process of war dwarfed any particular injustices connected with the destruction of slavery. Both sides, and every section of the Union, shared willy-nilly in the cost of abolishing slavery. Lincoln's own plan of gradual, compensated emancipation at federal expense would have provided a political solution. But the plan was not politically acceptable because the community for which it was framed no longer formed a community. No solution was possible which did not recognize that the Negro's humanity entitled him, no less than the white, to the liberty which the Constitution was established to secure. Neither was any solution possible which did not recognize that all lawful titles to property, acquired in good faith, deserved the same constitutional protection. But the consent of the governed would not be yielded to a solution fully consistent with those principles in virtue of which that consent was required!

Lincoln's 1861 plea to abide by the decision of the constitutional majority must be viewed against this background—a background of imperfect understanding of why constitutional majorities should rule. His arguments are not the less forceful for the reason that they fell on deaf ears. He pointed out that no express constitutional right of a minority had been violated, and he declared that no such violation was contemplated. But there were differences as to implied constitutional rights. On such ques-

---

[11] Padover (comp.). *The Complete Jefferson*, p. 384.
[12] Ibid.
[13] Basler (ed.), *Abraham Lincoln*, 4: 268.

tions, we must divide into majorities and minorities. Not mere numerical majorities, he made plain, but majorities "held in restraint by constitutional checks and limitations." "Plainly," he maintained, "the central idea of secession is the essence of anarchy."[14] Just as plainly, must we maintain, is the idea of selective obedience (and disobedience) to law which we find current today. "If a minority," said Lincoln, "will secede rather than acquiesce, they make a precedent which, in turn, will divide and ruin then; for a minority of their own will secede from them whenever a majority refuses to be controlled by such minority."[15] We today should remember that the word "Bolshevik" means majority. Where minorities and majorities are no longer bound by the rule of law—by acquiescence in constitutional majoritarianism—despotism must result. And whoever rejects that "does, of necessity, fly to anarchy or to despotism. Unanimity is impossible; the rule of a minority, as a permanent arrangement, is wholly inadmissible; so that rejecting the majority principle, anarchy or despotism in some form is all that is left."[16] Once dissenting minorities abandon the rule of law which governs their own pursuit of majority status, when they employ direct action, whether violent or nonviolent, to gain their ends, they make the same mistake that both the abolitionists and the partisans of slavery extension made in 1861. Once men think they are no less entitled to win an election than to participate in it, or refuse to participate except on assurance that they will win, then the crisis of the Civil War, in greater or less degree, is with us again.

The problem of political government, as has often been observed, is the problem of securing consent to wise decisions. Representative, constitutional government is surely the best device known to wise men for infusing wisdom, and securing consent, that the modern world knows. In a nation of philosophers, to paraphrase James Madison, there would be no tension between wisdom and consent, or between self-interest and the common good. Among the key decisions of the wise men who devised representative constitutional government, was the decision to give wisdom no especial status in the regime. For they believed that the institutionalization of the claims of wisdom invariably resulted, not in wisdom, but in special privileges masquerading as the prerogatives of wisdom. The rule of law was to be the form in which wisdom would be institutionalized. The Founders were as hostile to what Lincoln called "mobocracy," as to tyranny or oligarchy. And "mobocracy" could refer to the mob in the streets or to the "mob" of votes in a system in which equal law did not protect the equal rights of minorities. But law itself is not a mere device

14 Ibid.
15 Ibid., 4: 267.
16 Ibid., 4: 268.

for decision-making. The wisdom of government does not consist in rules that facilitate a game that men may or may not wish to play. Our form of government may properly be described as government of, by, and for the people. But the laws of nature and of nature's God are made for, but not by, these same people. Indeed, they *are* a people (as distinct from a mere number of individuals—or a mob) only insofar as they are dedicated to a proposition emanating from such law. In short, the law must make a people, before the people can make law. And the law that makes a people, does so, not by the force of arms, but by the force of education, education in the laws of nature.

6 | REFLECTIONS ON THOREAU and LINCOLN Civil Disobedience and the American Tradition

Thoreau is the patron saint of the American tradition of civil disobedience. I speak of an American tradition because this nation was born in virtue of what we all hold to be a legitimate rebellion against established authority—a rebellion legitimate according to the "laws of Nature and of Nature's God." "They only can force me," wrote Thoreau—referring to moral force as distinct from physical force—"who obey a higher law than I." So saying, he invoked a tradition older even than the American, calling to mind the words of Socrates to the court of Athens, in Plato's *Apology of Socrates*.

> I should have done something terrible, O men of Athens, if when the commanders whom you chose to command me, both at Potidaea and at Amphipolis and at Delium, had stationed me, and I remained there like anybody else, and ran the risk of death, but when the God gave me a station, as I believed and supposed, commanding me to spend my life philosophizing, and examining myself and others, then I were to desert my post, whether through fear of death or anything else whatever.[1]

Political philosophy, from Socrates to Jefferson, had taught that there is a principle of obligation higher than that of the human authorities of the political communities, and that in a conflict between the higher and the lower, the higher takes precedence. The American Revolution was fought on the premise that such a precedence dissolved the obligations which the rebellious colonists once owed to the British crown, and that the very right by which they withdrew their allegiance enfranchised them to institute new government, such as "to them shall seem most likely to effect their safety and happiness." But is not the same dissatisfaction which the Founding Fathers of the American government felt with the British crown a source of legitimacy for revolt against the government they founded, when dissatisfaction against it shall burgeon? Thoreau, like Socrates, confronted what he believed to be an unjust democracy. Those who would abolish slavery ought not, he said, to "wait till they constitute a majority of one. . . . I think it is enough if they have God on their side, without waiting for that other one."

Reprinted by the kind permission of the publisher from *On Civil Disobedience: American Essays, Old and New*, Rand McNally Public Affairs Series (Chicago, 1969).

[1] Plato *Apology of Socrates* 28d 10 ff. (trans. HVJ).

124

Many Americans today take pride in the fact that Thoreau was the acknowledged teacher of Gandhi, and that the lessons learned by Martin Luther King from Gandhi are in a sense lessons come home to the land of their birth. Thoreau wrote:

> Cast your whole vote, not a strip of paper merely, but your whole influence. A minority is powerless when it conforms to the majority; it is not even a minority then; but it is irresistible when it clogs by its whole weight. If the alternative is to keep all just men in prison, or give up war and slavery, the State will not hesitate which to choose.[2]

It is not difficult to discern in these words the inspiration of Montgomery and Birmingham, and ultimately of the Civil Rights Acts of the last decade. Nor is it unlikely that these same words have recently inspired many of the protesters against the Vietnam war. Thoreau has contributed phrases of undying eloquence to the cause of resistance to oppression, and a device of immeasurable political power in the technique of passive resistance. It will be the work of this essay to examine the import of some of these phrases, and of the technique, within the context of Thoreau's thought. We shall also attempt to deepen our understanding of that thought by seeing it within the context of the American political tradition from which it derives so much of its meaning. Is "resistance to civil government," as Thoreau propounds it, an instrument more likely to be serviceable to good causes than to bad? There is no good thing that cannot be misused, but how good a thing is Thoreau's teaching in *Civil Disobedience?*

The essay begins by Thoreau "heartily" accepting the motto, "That government is best which governs least." "Carried out," he continues, "it finally amounts to this, which also I believe,—'That government is best which governs not at all.' "[3] But a little later, Thoreau says he speaks "practically, and as a citizen, unlike those who call themselves no-government men." In that capacity he asks for, "not at once no government, but *at once* a better government." "Let every man," he continues, "make known what kind of government would command his respect, and that will be one step toward obtaining it."[4] Was Thoreau an anarchist? If so, in what sense? Did he think of anarchy as the best condition of human society, but to be obtained only at the end of a kind of evolutionary process, as did many other nineteenth-century thinkers, including Karl Marx? Or did he think of anarchy as an ever-present

[2] Thoreau, *Walden and Civil Disobedience,* ed. Owen Thomas, Norton Critical Edition (New York: W.W. Norton & Company, Inc., 1966), p. 233.
[3] Ibid., p. 224.
[4] Ibid., p. 225.

positive force, always existing side by side with government, and from time to time so interfering with government as to compel the abandonment of some of its evils? There can be no question but that the best human condition, according to Thoreau, is one in which there is no coercive power of man over man, and the work of society is carried on by voluntary cooperation. That is the kind of "government" men will have "when they are prepared for it."

There is a similarity between Thoreau's attitude toward government and St. Paul's toward marriage: both institutions are seen as lesser evils necessitated by the blind strength of the human passions. (Thoreau, incidentally, remained celibate throughout his life; one wonders whether the views expressed in *Walden* could have been held by a man for whom the married state was a vocation.) One might address a similar question to Paul and Thoreau: is the Kingdom of Heaven—or the best government which governs not at all—only within each man, as a higher standard by which the superior are to govern themselves, and judge and admonish others? Or is it something objectively to be fulfilled here, in a Messianic era yet to come?

In the peroration of the Temperance Address, by Abraham Lincoln, on Washington's birthday, 1842, we can see the extent to which the Pauline conception of the Kingdom of Heaven had entered the utopian thought of the time, and had made utopian ends the direct aim of political reform movements:

> And what a noble ally is this [i.e., the temperance revolution], to the cause of political freedom. With such an aid, its march cannot fail to be on and on, till every son of earth shall drink in rich fruition, the sorrow-quenching draughts of perfect liberty. Happy day, when, all appetites controlled, all passions subdued, all matters subjected, *mind*, all conquering *mind*, shall live and move the monarch of the world.[5]

Lincoln himself privately mocked this utopianism, and was distressed at the fanaticism it implied. But there can be no doubt that such utopianism and fanaticism motivated much of the nineteenth-century reform movements, radical abolitionism and temperance prominent among them. Nor can there be much doubt that Thoreau was among those who believed that such a vision of the absolutely best human condition constituted the true principle of political action. *Walden* is above all a political work—devoted to showing how the life according to nature is a life of emancipation from superfluous desires (and hence from govern-

[5] Roy P. Basler (ed.), *The Collected Works of Abraham Lincoln* (New Brunswick, N.J.: Rutgers University Press, 1953), 1: 279.

ment), and therefore one which eliminates the causes both of war and of slavery.

James Madison, in *The Federalist* No. 51, when he considers that such constitutional devices as separation of powers rely upon base human motives, observes:

> It may be a reflection on human nature, that such devices should be necessary to control the abuses of government. But what is government itself, but the greatest of all reflections on human nature? If men were angels, no government would be necessary. If angels were to govern men, neither external nor internal controls on government would be necessary.[6]

We thus see a kind of agreement between Thoreau and Madison (as well as with Karl Marx) that government is an evil. But for Madison it must always be a necessary evil, while for Thoreau (as for Marx) it is an evil which the progress of mankind must eventually make superfluous. Thoreau's man of conscience leads the way toward "no government" no less than Marx's proletariat leads the way toward the classless society and the withering away of the state.

Having exhorted every man to make known what kind of government would command his respect—a strange exhortation considering the high respect in which slavery was held by so many of his fellow citizens— Thoreau proceeds to let it be known that the government commanding his respect is one in which not majorities but conscience decides. "Can there not," he asks, "be a government in which majorities do not virtually decide right and wrong, but conscience? . . . Must the citizen ever for a moment . . . resign his conscience to the legislator?" Thoreau here strangely confuses acceptance of majority rule with abdication of conscience; a confusion made plausible by his belief that it is the function of majorities (or, a fortiori, any government) to decide right and wrong. But the function of government, in the American political tradition has always been that of deciding how to secure (or implement) certain rights—to life, liberty, and the pursuit of happiness. The existence of these rights, as we all know, was regarded as a self-evident truth, so that there could be no question whether one was conscientious in seeking their fulfillment.

It was widely held, moreover, that matters of conscience, properly so called, were beyond the province of government. Jefferson, in Query XVII of the *Notes on Virginia*, wrote as follows:

> The error seems not sufficiently eradicated, that the operations of the mind, as well as the acts of the body, are subject to the coercion of the laws. But our

[6] Modern Library Edition, p. 337.

rulers can have no authority over such natural rights, only as we have submitted to them. The rights of conscience we have never submitted, we could not submit. We are answerable for them to our God. The legitimate powers of government extend to such acts only as are injurious to others.[7]

Thus the traditional understanding of conscience referred primarily, though not exclusively, to opinions as distinct from actions, and to our relations with God rather than with men. Government, from this perspective, was first of all a means whereby we provide ourselves with security against injury, whether from enemies abroad or criminals at home. For this there must be collective action and, therefore, government.

The anarchist, of course, denies that collective self-defense is a true necessity of human life. For him, the motives which cause men to commit aggression against other men are themselves caused, directly or indirectly, by government. To abolish the need for police and armed forces, one must abolish police and armed forces. This certainly is the inference to be drawn from the famous lines on soldiers in *Civil Disobedience:*

> Now what are they? Men at all? or small moveable forts and magazines, at the service of some unscrupulous man in power? ... Such command no more respect than men of straw, or a lump of dirt. They have the same sort of worth only as horses and dogs.[8]

There is here no suggestion that armed force is sometimes necessary to protect the innocent from malefactors. The view that government—and its ultimate expression in armed force—is dehumanizing, has as its corollary the view that man by nature, man apart from government, is good. But for those who believe that the requirement of armed protection is a consequence of human nature, the adoption of such protection cannot be intrinsically hostile to the demands of conscience, however grave the problems of conscience may be that arise because of it.

To abide by majority rule does not mean resigning our consciences. It means rather that we have, as citizens, surrendered our natural freedom to act independently, in order that we may have the cooperation of other men who have equally surrendered their natural freedom to act independently. We have made a bargain with others, and as honest men we have a duty to keep that bargain—so long, at least, as good faith is kept with us. Jefferson, in the Declaration of Independence, in his indictment of the British crown, gives a detailed argument as to why the American people are conscientious in dissolving their political bonds with Great

---

[7] Saul K. Padover (comp.), *The Complete Jefferson* (New York: Tudor Publishing Company, 1943), p. 675.

[8] Thoreau, *Walden and Civil Disobedience*, p. 226.

Britain. Whether good faith is indeed being kept with us—whether the "us" be a majority or a minority—seems a large enough political sphere for conscience without conscience usurping the whole province of law and government, as Thoreau demands.

But why, it may be asked, should the majority principle be the one to decide the common concerns of fellow citizens? The answer is that unanimity is impossible, and the majority principle is the only direct reflection of the original equality of natural rights of the members of the political association. It is *not* the case that the majority are permitted to rule because, as Thoreau says, "they are physically the strongest." That would be necessarily true only if all men were equal in physical strength, which they are not. It is the equality of natural *right* which supplies the moral ground of the majority principle. In the last paragraph of the essay, Thoreau says, "There will never be a really free and enlightened State, until the State comes to recognize the individual as a higher and independent power, from which all its own power and authority are derived, and treats him accordingly." *But the principle of the equality of all men, and its corollary, the requirement of the consent of the governed, affirmed in the Declaration of Independence, mean precisely that.* However imperfectly the United States may have implemented these principles, their recognition constituted an epoch in the history of the world, and Thoreau seems not to have appreciated the fact at all. What Thoreau seems to want is a "State" in which nothing is ever done without the concurrence of every single member. But were such a state possible, it would seem to be unnecessary. Such agreement could prevail only among angels—and were men angels, government would be unnecessary.

Majority rule is a necessary substitute, but by no means a sufficient substitute for unanimity: the Constitution is a massive device for instilling qualitative safeguards into the practical operation of the quantitative rule of the majority. Thoreau's strictures against majority rule are related to his still greater scorn for the Constitution.

Thoreau denies that there is any general duty to obey law. "The only obligation which I have a right to assume," he says, "is to do at any time what I think right." In one sense, of course, that is a mere truism. But *most* of us think it is *usually* right to obey the law, without considering in *every* instance whether the law squares with the dictates of conscience apart from law. For example, one might read the transcript of a criminal trial, and conscientiously disagree with the verdict of the jury; but this does not impose a duty to do violence to that verdict, or to overthrow the jury system. One might still think, as most of us do, that the jury system, with all its faults, is the best system possible, in an imperfect world, for administering criminal justice. Moreover, the view that there is a general obligation of obedience to law does not forbid us ever to participate in revolution against an established government, nor does it forbid us ever to disobey a particular lawful enactment even in a regime we regard as just. According to Thoreau, however, the very presence of conscience requires the disavowal of every presumption in favor of law as a guide to human behavior. Conscience and law, as used by Thoreau, are simply incompatible.

"It is truly enough said," declares Thoreau, "that a corporation has no conscience; but a corporation of conscientious men is a corporation *with* a conscience. Law never made men a whit more just; and, by means of their respect for it, even the well disposed are daily made agents of injustice."[9] In his desire to have conscience abolish both law and government from a good society, Thoreau distinguishes a corporation of conscientious men, a corporation *with* a conscience, from a corporate conscience. But is it a distinction that corresponds with any real difference? For example, if men engage their faith to each other—as fellow citizens are supposed to do—that if one is attacked the others will come to his defense, do they not, for certain purposes, thereby constitute a corporation? And is it not a sufficiently conscientious corporation by the mere fact that it exists (if it really does) to implement the natural right of every man to defend himself? Do we not properly distinguish the principle of such a corporation from that of one like a pirate ship, or a pirate nation, which associates for the sake of collective aggression upon the rights of others? Does not respect for law, in the first instance, imply respect for civil society, properly so called, as distinct from a band of robbers? However much we may call by the name of "law" the collective rules of any regime, it belongs of right to those regimes which are directed, however imperfectly, to lawful ends. Thoreau's characterization of the "State" as a kind of abstract entity, indifferent to the difference of ends among men, and among collectivities of men, is an unreal abstraction from political life as we know it.

If there may be men who are conscientious, in the sense of being committed to each other for the lawful end of mutual protection, must they not have means to implement their agreement? How shall they decide the contributions each shall make in money and personal service to the cause of their common defense? Let us suppose their government is, for reasons already suggested, based upon majority rule. Would it not be wrong to decide separately what each man—for example, Henry David Thoreau—should pay? Might not even conscientious men, in an assembly, be influenced by Thoreau's eccentricities to assess him more than his fair share? Is it not better to employ *laws* rather than *decrees* to levy taxes upon *classes* rather than *persons*? Is it not better, for example to levy a

[9] Ibid., p. 225.

sales tax, to be paid by anyone who purchases, or an income tax, to be paid at preestablished rates by anyone with taxable income? Similarly, is it not better that men be drafted into the armed services by rules laid down in advance, so far as possible, rather than at the pleasure even of a majority? Laws may not be perfect, and their practical administration may require some discretionary judgment, but the principle of law is that it is not a respecter of persons, and it thereby takes on an attribute of justice. The rule of the majority by law is better than majority rule by discretion or decree. This connection between law and justice, and hence between law and conscience, seems never to be recognized by Thoreau. Thoreau's doctrine of the supreme right of conscience not only is impractical, but it undermines the morality it purports to invoke.

Thoreau is far from being the isolated individualist his eloquence sometimes conjures. His teaching is, notwithstanding its exaggerations, in the main current of the popular political opinions of his day. The secret of his power may be explored in relation to the motto with which the essay on *Civil Disobedience* begins. "That government is best which governs least" has echoed through the corridors of American history. When President John F. Kennedy, in his inaugural address in 1961, said that we should ask, not what our country can do for us, but what we can do for our country, he was evoking one implication of that aphorism. Richard M. Nixon more evidently evoked another when, in his speech accepting the Republican nomination for the presidency in 1968, he said that America had grown great, not because of what government had done for the people, but because of what people had done for themselves. And so Thoreau wrote:

> ... this government never of itself furthered any enterprise, but by the alacrity with which it got out of its way. *It* does not settle the West. *It* does not educate. The character inherent in the American people has done all that has been accomplished; and it would have done somewhat more, if the government had not sometimes got in its way.... Trade and commerce, if they were not made of India rubber, would never manage to bounce over the obstacles which legislators are continually putting in their way....[10]

Thus we see Thoreau lending authority to those today regarded as on the "right" of the political spectrum in their opposition to government interference with business or education, as we have seen him in a similar relationship to those regarded as being on the "left" in their opposition to the use by government of armed force.

"That government is best which governs least" is commonly

[10] Ibid., pp. 224-25.

thought to have originated with Jefferson, although no one has ever found it among his writings. It seems first to have appeared as the motto of the *United States Magazine and Democratic Review*, a journal founded in 1837 at the very apogee of the Jacksonian movement, and designed to strengthen and perpetuate the fighting faith of the party, now that the retirement of the Hero was at hand. The very first number of the *Review* contains an essay explaining the principles of the editors and incorporating an extended explanation of the famous slogan. The main thrust of the essay is to strengthen faith in the mass of the people for self-government, while acknowledging that minorities have rights which are not always recognized by majorities "flushed with triumph and impelled with strong interests." But the conflict between the majority and minority rights is not, the essayist holds, intrinsic to democracy, but arises from an imperfect understanding of its true theory. Democratic republics have hitherto, he says, been

administered on ideas and in a spirit borrowed from strong governments of the other forms. . . . It is under the word *government* that the subtle danger lurks. Understood as a central consolidated power, managing and directing the various interests of the society, all government is evil, and the parent of evil. A strong and active *government* . . . is an evil, differing only in degree and mode of operation, and not in nature from a strong despotism.[11]

And then he declares, "The best government is that which governs least." The grand reason is, that "no human depositaries can, with safety, be trusted with the power of legislation upon the general interests of society. . . ."[12] But if *no* human depositaries can with safety be so entrusted, how are the general interests of society to be attended to? The solution to this riddle is to be found in a thesis closely resembling that of the famous "invisible hand" of Adam Smith. But now it has been generalized to include not only the market place but society at large. Indeed, the laws governing man in society are now seen as but particular applications of more general, universal laws. The principle of *inertia,* in physics, has its parallel in the *voluntary principle* of society. The sole necessary connection between the internal polity of society and of government is the administration of justice.

Afford but [this] single nucleus . . . and, under the sure operation of this principle, the floating atoms will distribute and combine themselves, as we see in the beautiful natural processes of crystallization, into a far more perfect and

[11] Joseph L. Blau (ed.), *Social Theories of Jacksonian Democracy* (New York: The Liberal Arts Press, 1954), pp. 26-27.
[12] Ibid.

harmonious result than if government, with its "fostering hand" undertake to disturb, under the plea of directing, the process.[13]

It is apparent that Thoreau's belief in the beneficence of human nature apart from government is a particular instance of a widespread nineteenth-century conviction of the beneficence of nature in general, whose laws the progress of science was steadily revealing. The enlightened adaptation of man to nature would result from the diffusion of the knowledge of nature, and this diffusion would explode the superstitions which had so long enslaved men—among them the superstition that government had to organize and direct the general interests of society, and coerce men to do what it was in their interest to do.

The eighteenth-century antecedent of this view may be seen in Thomas Paine's *Rights of Man,* published in 1791 with Jefferson's endorsement. In chapter 1 of book 2, Paine says that

> Great part of that order which reigns among mankind is not the effect of Government, and would exist if the formality of Government was abolished. [It is the] mutual dependence and reciprocal interest which man has upon man, and all the parts of a civilized community upon each other. . . . The landholder, the farmer, the manufacturer, the merchant, the tradesman, and every occupation, prospers by the aid which each receives from the other, and from the whole. . . . In fine, society performs for itself almost everything which is ascribed to Government.[14]

And again, "The more perfect civilization is, the less occasion it has for Government, because the more it does regulate its own affairs and govern itself." One can reformulate Paine's thought into the Jacksonian dogma of Thoreau's day by saying that civilization perfects itself in direct proportion to government's being prevented from interfering with it; that the incentive to perfection is weakened or corrupted by the presence of government, and strengthened in its absence.

The affinity of Paine and Jefferson—at least as far as abstract theories is concerned—is well known. The struggle occasioned by the Alien and Sedition Acts led to the Kentucky and Virginia Resolutions, which laid down the political dogmas that were to dominate American party rhetoric for the next two generations. "It would be a dangerous delusion," wrote Jefferson in the Kentucky Resolutions of 1798, "were a confidence in the men of our choice to silence our fears for the safety of our rights; that confidence is everywhere the parent of despotism—free government is founded in jealousy, and not in confidence; it is jealousy and not confi-

---

[13] Ibid., p. 28.
[14] Everyman's Library Edition, p. 157.

dence which prescribes limited constitutions, to bind down those whom we are obliged to trust with power." With reference to the obnoxious Alien Act, Jefferson declaimed, "Let him say what the government is, if it be not a tyranny, which the men of our choice have conferred on our President, and the President of our choice assented to. . . ."[15] Thus was expressed in its classic form, that Jeffersonian and Jacksonian creed, which combined faith in the people with distrust of their representatives, especially in the government of the United States. After the victory of the republicans in 1800, this was further expressed in the memorable lines of Jefferson's inaugural address, when he said that the "one thing more" necessary to make us a happy and prosperous people, was "a wise and frugal government, which shall restrain men from injuring one another [and] shall leave them otherwise free to regulate their own pursuits of industry and improvement, and shall not take from the mouth of labor the bread it has earned." "This," said Jefferson, "is the sum of good government."[16]

To this point, it might appear that Thoreau merely represented an eccentric radicalization of the Jeffersonian viewpoint, that government was at best a necessary evil, and that it was usually a great deal less necessary than was commonly supposed. But Jefferson, and Jackson after him, saw in the Constitution the great ark of the covenant that restricted government as much as possible to its proper sphere. Thoreau, on the other hand, held the Constitution in contempt, as the very symbol of the law that caused men to abandon conscience. But even this difference is less in substance than in appearance. Jefferson and Jackson expressed their reverence, not for the Constitution simply, but for the Constitution very strictly construed, which meant the Constitution seen as a device for limiting the sphere of government.

Jefferson and Jackson are today reputed strong presidents; but they were strong presidents opposed in principle to active government. They saw themselves as tribunes of the people, protecting the people from the aristocratic corruptions of government. In his purchase of Louisiana, the crowning achievement of his presidency, Jefferson himself believed he had performed an action unauthorized by the Constitution. But he believed it to be something critically necessary to the safety of that severely limited form of government in which he so believed. Thus he confided not in the Constitution but in the people, who would ratify what he had done after the fact.

Similarly, Jackson saw in his vetoes, of bills for internal improvements and of the bill to recharter the Bank of the United States, a

[15] Padover (comp.), *The Complete Jefferson*, p. 133.
[16] Ibid., p. 386.

vindication of the people against those who, equally with himself, were their constitutional representatives. Thus did the tribune, or people's champion, theory of the presidency originate, a conception of an office in some sense outside of the Constitution, whose exercise, even if in conflict with the letter of the Constitution, would enable the true Constitution to prevail.

Thus Thoreau's call to civil disobedience is, at the least, an apolitical, or antipolitical analogue to Jefferson's and Jackson's supra-constitutional constitutionalism. Thoreau summons the phalanxes of the conscientious, enjoining the righteous to clog the machinery of government, to compel the "State" to give up war and slavery, even as Jefferson and Jackson acted in crises *ultra vires,* in defense of, and in the name of the people.

In the secularized radical Protestantism of his day—the quasi-religious Protestantism of Unitarianism and Transcendentalism—Thoreau's individualism, like Emerson's, is a species of antinomianism, seeing the individual under the grace of conscience emancipated from the lower law of the merely political order, and helping to elevate that order by defying it. It is, we have argued, a kind of eccentric coordinate of the Jacksonian hero-worship (Thoreau was himself an admirer of Carlyle), which saw its idol slaying the dragons of oligarchy and aristocracy. It was in full accord with that popular opinion of the day—to the prejudice in favor of which it appealed—which held that government was something evil, while the people were essentially good.

Yet there was—and is—within the American political tradition another opinion, both popular and philosophical, that holds nearly the opposite. It is perhaps an oversimplification to say that the leading doctrines of *The Federalist* papers were governed by the assumption that people were evil and government good. Both Hamilton and Madison saw man apart from government as not in society or civilization but in a state of nature very like that described by Thomas Hobbes. While the government they recommended differed widely from the monarchy preferred by Hobbes, it was nonetheless conceived, like Hobbes's, mainly in terms of overcoming the ills of human nature, for which society, apart from good government, possessed no remedy.

Yet despite the formal opposition of these two great theses—the one insisting upon human depravity by nature, and the goodness of government, the other upon human goodness by nature, and the inherent depravity of government—there is a point of agreement. We have already alluded to it in citing Madison's aphorism that if men were angels no government would be necessary. Notwithstanding the Madisonian assumption that men cannot be angelic, there is a tacit admission that, in the best case imaginable—even if that case be impossible—there is no government. Madison thus makes a concession to human desire or aspiration going back at least as far as Plato's *Republic*. There Socrates, in constructing in speech the perfect city, asks to be excused from proving that what he proposes is possible, and invites his interlocutors to consider at first, only whether it is desirable.

Whether the *Republic* intends to set forth the human condition that is most desirable, even if impossible, or whether it intends to set forth the condition that is both most desirable and possible, we need not here inquire. Suffice it to say that it has been taken in both senses within the tradition of the Christian West, and a form of Platonism has motivated messianic reform movements within that tradition. Lincoln's apocalyptic vision, in the Temperance Address, of the perfect (albeit passionate) conquest of passion by reason, is at once an evocation of the rule of philosopher-kings and of the rule of the Kingdom of God. It is curious that Lincoln refers to this perfect regime as at once the culmination of the political revolution based upon equal human rights, and as the *monarchy* of all-conquering mind. This monarchy resembles that of the Heavenly City promised by divine revelation, since it implies what is at once the perfection and the extinction of authority. The rule of love or pure reason or both transcends authority because it directs men toward what they above all desire. By abolishing all impediments to consummation, it is the perfection of liberty. But a state of perfect liberty, even if in accord with the dictates of authority, can no longer be understood as a state under authority. Hence it must be a state of "no-government."

In Plato's *Republic* justice is defined as everyone doing only that work for which he is by nature best fitted. By doing that one work, he may carry to perfection the art of doing it well. His capacity for his work and his devotion to his work may then be fully equal to each other. While the guardians, the ruling class, will be set over the shoemakers, they will not tell the shoemakers how to cobble. The *Republic* is essentially a community of craftsmen, in perfect harmony because each craftsman abstains from another's craft. This abstention is assured by the very thing that makes each a craftsman: since the free practice of his own craft is the consuming passion of his soul, perfect cooperation is secured not by coercion, but by the form of consciousness that makes one a craftsman. The harmony of the workman and his work ends the tension between private ends and the common good, and hence ends everything today called "alienation." The *Republic*, in this aspect, is the ultimate source of those anarchist-syndicalist theories of the nineteenth and twentieth centuries which see in the voluntary cooperation of workers (or craftsmen or guilds) the solution to the problem of authority in society. This is the *Republic* as it may indeed be seen, in the perfection of its communism and its egalitarianism of the sexes, prior to the introduction of the philosopher-kings.

But in the *Republic*, one may recall, the rule of philosopher-kings is introduced, not as an end, but as a means, a means of bringing into actual existence the perfect communist regime already sketched. By the nineteenth century, however, it seemed to many who had (however indirectly), accepted Plato's premises as to the desirability of such a regime that its actualization might be easier than he had supposed and that, indeed, the abolition of private property and the introduction of equality of rights would be a sufficient condition for that actualization. Implicit in this judgment, however, was the taking over of the role of philosophy by different aspects of modern science. Modern craftsmanship has scientific know-how infused into it; philosophy in the form of modern science has descended from the clouds of sterile metaphysics and entered the cities as fruitful technology. Craftsmanship has indeed been sub-divided now into capital and labor—capital embodying technology, as distinct from mere tools. The improvement upon Plato concerning the feasibility of the best regime arises from the perception that in the *Republic* the perfect cooperation of the craftsman is assumed rather than demonstrated, and that in point of fact it is not spontaneous because it is not intrinsic to their craftsmanship. That a man's whole soul can by nature be absorbed in cobbling (or restricted to any other single function), is a myth. The shoemakers, and all the other artisans, are in the final analysis kept in their places by lies, noble and not-so-noble.

But the knowledge of nature which informs the modern machinery of shoemaking is the same as that which underlies all other forms of efficient material production, including that in virtue of which the universe itself has come to be. The world is now unmediated by myth, all stand in the same relationship to it; there can be no permanent basis for class distinctions. All may be freed by communism from an invidious alienation from the means of production, all may be freed by technology from an invidious alienation from the means of consumption, all may be freed by science from an invidious alienation from nature. Slavery, intemperance, other-worldly religion, coercive government—all become superfluous when society has become thoroughly rational. This, I believe, conveys the outline of that transformation in the radical political thought of the nineteenth century, in virtue of which Madison's hypothetical preference for a society of "angels" became the nonhypothetical ground for demanding that such a society be made actual. One can easily understand why, once the conviction arose that such a society was possible, there should be a belief in a Categorical Imperative to bring it into actual existence.

The foregoing has been intended not as a characterization of any particular of Thoreau's own thought, but rather of the milieu within which it flourished. It was the milieu within which the numerous communist societies of mid-nineteenth century America flourished, along with the numerous radical reform movements—to abolish slavery, to abolish strong drink, to reform the prison systems, to bring about full equality of rights for women, to abolish war, and many others. No one reading the *Communist Manifesto* of Marx and Engels, together with *Civil Disobedience,* both of them composed at about the same time, can fail to perceive the same temper, a temper which indicates that the total reform of society is, or should be, near at hand. This milieu is still the ground of the politics of the revolutionary "new left" of today, a left which is more than a century old, as we realize when we understand why Thoreau, perhaps even more than Marx and Engels, is one of its authentic heroes.

The tradition of obedience to law in the United States is at best an ambiguous one. The most obvious reason for this we have given at the outset of this essay: the United States annually celebrates its revolutionary origins, its withdrawal of its allegiance from a system of law upon grounds of natural right. These grounds indicate that the laws of nature and nature's God take precedence of any human positive law. The sense of obligation to law has long had its focus upon the Constitution, most obviously because the Constitution is the supreme law of the land, and it invites respect because of this supremacy.

Yet the very circumstance which makes the Constitution supreme encourages certain tendencies toward civil disobedience. The supremacy of the Constitution is a supremacy over all public officials, state or national, legislative, executive, or judicial. In theory, any act in conflict with the Constitution is null and void. To challenge a public act, however, it is frequently necessary to violate it, in order to secure a test of its legality in the courts. Hence disobedience to lawfully constituted authorities may be an act of respect for the Constitution.

The supremacy of the Constitution is a very practical matter: the nature of American federalism is such—the diversity of its political jurisdictions and their overlapping character—that American public law would tend toward chaos if there were no final arbiter, and final authority. The final arbiter of American public law is usually the Supreme Court of the United States. The expression "usually" is in recognition of the fact that questions regarding the law cannot always be tried in the courts. The word "arbiter" is in recognition that, at any given time, the Supreme Court is the deciding body. But the authority of the Court is the authority of the Constitution, and if the sense of the political community of the United States differs with the Supreme Court, as to the meaning of the Constitution, the authority of the Court will not stand, and future Courts will interpret the Constitution in a manner more consistent with the sense of the community.

But suppose the community itself is divided? It is, of course, normal that any community should be divided: divided into majority and minority. However, the acceptance of majority rule by the minority (or minorities), on the one hand, and the acceptance by the majority of the minority's right not to be coerced in certain matters, on the other hand, depend upon a prior understanding of the relationship of majority rule to minority rights. "All too will bear in mind this sacred principle," said Thomas Jefferson in his first inaugural address, "that though the will of the majority is in all cases to prevail, that will, to be rightful must be reasonable; that the minority possess equal rights, which equal laws must protect, and to violate which would be oppression."[17]

The Constitution, as every schoolboy knows, is in certain respects a bundle of compromises. In order to interpret the Constitution, one must make a judgment as to what in the Constitution are mere expedients, and what are dictates of principle. To take a contemporary example, if the Warren Court has been correct in its opinions on the subject of apportionment, then the United States must be the most malapportioned legislative body in the country, whose existence can be justified only as the merest expedient. On the other hand, if one sees the Senate as an institution designed to secure a certain equality of the states within the Union, to the end that national majorities be distributed as well as amassed, then the Senate may at least be viewed as a wise or principled expedient. It may be seen as one of those expedients designed to induce reasonableness in the majority, and to protect those equal rights which the minority possess, and to violate which would be oppression.

The most fundamental of all the compromises which the Constitution of 1787 exhibited, and the source of the most undoubted mere expedients, was that which treated the Negro slaves both as persons and things. The population which determined the representation of each state in the lower house of Congress was arrived at by adding to the whole number of white persons, three-fifths of all others, exclusive of Indians. There is an anomaly in the very idea of a "three-fifths person." But in the so-called fugitive slave clause (the words "slave," or "slavery," or "Negro," do not themselves ever occur in the original Constitution), it is said

[17] Ibid., p. 384.

that all persons held to labor or service under the laws of any of the states, escaping into another state, shall not be discharged from such service or labor, but shall be returned to the person to whom the service or labor is due. By this clause, the government of the United States was committed to assisting in enforcing the laws of the slave states. These laws treated Negro slaves as chattels—that is, mere movable property—although in certain respects, for example, responsibility for most felonies—they were also regarded as human persons. By its indirect incorporation of state law, the United States Constitution undoubtedly treated Negro slaves as both human persons and nonhuman chattels.

When, therefore, the Constitution in Article V of the Bill of Rights commanded that no person should be deprived of life, liberty, or property, except by due process of law, it commanded two absolutely contradictory things: one, that no slaveowner might be arbitrarily deprived of his chattel; and another, that no Negro might be arbitrarily deprived of his liberty. But when conflict arose, which of these two conflicting imperatives represented the "real" Constitution?

It is against this background of difficulty that the problem of respect for law, above all the law of the supreme law, the law of the Constitution, must be examined. Everyone knows that the greatest cause of social and civil conflict, and hence of lawlessness, in the United States, has been racial difference. But it has not been mere racial difference, such as has existed in many times and places. It has been racial difference in the presence of the great commitment to the proposition "that all men are created equal."

Thoreau saw no problem: if the Constitution sanctioned slavery, disobey it. If the Union included slave states, secede. But Abraham Lincoln, in his Springfield Lyceum speech of 1838, saw the matter differently. The turmoil wracking the country was similar to that of today. Then the question concerned the American Negro's transition from slavery to legal freedom. Today it concerns his transition from legal freedom to social and political equality. Lincoln foresaw even then that terrible forfeits might be exacted for the abolition of slavery, even as we must contemplate the price that may yet be exacted from us.

The first quality of the Lyceum speech, that immediately sets it in a different *genre* from Thoreau's essay, is that it is *political*. It is an oration by a rising young Whig member of the Illinois legislature. It deals with a matter deeply agitating the country at large, and it displays a special sensitivity to the impact of that matter upon the south central Illinois city of Springfield. This community, like most others in southern Ohio, Indiana, and Illinois, was formed of families like the Lincolns, who had migrated across the Ohio River from slave states. Such families had usually preferred to live on free soil, to get away from slavery. But it was more often the degrading competition of Negro slave labor, rather than the moral obliquity of slavery itself, to which they objected. Many still had family ties southward, and resented condemnations of slavery that implicated their kinsmen. Moreover, they feared abolitionism as much as they feared the extension of slavery, and for much the same reason: either would bring them into an unwanted contact with Negroes.

The rise of abolitionist agitation in the 1830s had led the Illinois legislature, in January of 1837, just a year before the Lyceum speech, to pass resolutions denouncing abolitionism. Six weeks after these resolutions, a protest against them was spread upon the journal of the House, signed by Dan Stone and A. Lincoln, representatives of Sangamon County, which declared that "the institution of slavery is founded on both injustice and bad policy, but that the promulgation of abolition doctrines tends rather to increase than abate its evils. . . ."[18] It is of some interest that the intervention of six weeks between the time that the majority resolutions passed and the time that Lincoln and Stone entered their dissenting views was the period when the two representatives of Sangamon County brought to a climax their successful maneuvers to remove the state capital from Vandalia to Springfield—a log-rolling operation that was perhaps the high point of Lincoln's career in the state legislature. Politicians are certainly permitted to have convictions of their own, but the expression of those convictions must not be deeply offensive to the people they represent. Lincoln's rhetorical maxim was ever that a drop of honey catches more flies than a gallon of gall. The abolitionists were, certainly at this time, profoundly galling, even to most shades of antislavery opinion.

Some six weeks before the Lyceum speech, on November 7, 1837, there had occurred the lynching, at nearby Alton, Illinois, of the abolitionist editor, Elijah Lovejoy. It is this event that hung like a pall over both Lincoln and his audience. The extraordinary tact with which Lincoln treats his own and his audience's complex reaction to this ambiguous event accounts for much of the complexity of the speech.[19]

Today the tendency is to regard Lovejoy, like John Brown, as a genuine witness to the cause of freedom. Yet Lincoln had no great sympathy with either man. Brown he regarded as a mere fanatic, who brooded over slavery until he became demented with the notion that he had a divine mission to extirpate it. To Lincoln, Brown accomplished little—after the murders of a number of innocents—besides his own de-

[18] Basler (ed.), *Abraham Lincoln*, 1: 75.
[19] I have attempted to give a comprehensive analysis of this masterpiece in chap. 9 of *Crisis of the House Divided* (1959; reprint ed., Seattle, Wash.: University of Washington Press, 1973); here I can only touch on some of its leading features.

struction and that of his followers. To Thoreau, on the other hand, John Brown was an authentic Carlylean hero, a prophet, a martyr, and a saint. An ultimate judgment on the wisdom of Lincoln and Thoreau would require judgments on the respective contributions of Lincoln and John Brown to the ultimate emancipation of the slaves. Lincoln's attitude toward the murder of Lovejoy must have been influenced not only by his belief that Lovejoy's denunciations of slavery and slaveowners were doing more to strengthen proslavery than antislavery feelings, but by the fact that Lovejoy was as violently anti-Catholic as he was antislavery.

The abolitionist movement had its roots in the evangelical Protestantism of the day. In today's parlance, it was emphatically "waspish." The same roots produced the temperance movement, which also was mainly Protestant. The Irish were objects of antagonism both for their supposed addiction to whiskey and to popery (not to mention their tendency to march down the gangplanks directly to the polls, under the guidance of Democratic politicians), and Lovejoy was against them for both reasons. But the Irish were also violently anti-Negro, for they, as the lowest class of white labor, were in competition with Negroes. It was the Negroes who, before the Civil War, built the southern railroads, as it was the Irish who built the railroads of the north. But the problem of civil liberty in the antebellum United States was not the problem of Negro slavery alone—it was the problem of discrimination based upon race, religion, and nationality together.

In the period between 1854 and 1860 the antislavery movement was muddled by the fact that the Know-Nothings flourished side by side with the Republicans, and both movements were, to a great extent, competing for the same votes. In 1856, the anti-Democratic vote was divided between Fremont, the candidate of the Republicans, and Fillmore, who was nominated both by the Know-Nothing (or American) party and by the remnant of the Whig Party. It was this division of the free-soil vote that enabled Buchanan to be elected. In 1855, Lincoln gave his private opinion of the Know-Nothings to his old friend Joshua Speed, who had moved to Kentucky.

I am not a Know-Nothing. That is certain. How could I be? How can any one who abhors the oppression of negroes, be in favor of degrading classes of white people? Our progress in degeneracy appears to me to be pretty rapid. As a nation, we began by declaring that "*all men are created equal.*" We now practically read it "all men are created equal, *except negroes.*" When the Know-Nothings get control, it will read "all men are created equal, except negroes, *and foreigners, and Catholics.*" When it comes to this I should prefer emigrating to some country where they make no pretence of loving liberty—to Russia, for instance, where despotism can be taken pure and without the base alloy of hypocrisy.[20]

[20] Basler (ed.), *Abraham Lincoln,* 2: 323.

Yet in 1860, so important was the Know-Nothing vote to the Republicans, that Lincoln refused to make any public denial of association with them. In considering the letter to Speed, one must be struck, not only by the vehemence of Lincoln's views, but by the fact that he was under a necessity to make such a disavowal. So close was the affinity of Know-Nothingism and the antislavery movement, that even such a close personal friend as Joshua Speed could not be certain as to where Lincoln stood. There is a remarkable resemblance between the political currents which carried the antislavery movement forward in the 1850s—currents which included some of the noblest and some of the basest passions which American politics exhibits—and those which have brought "law and order" to the fore in the latter 1960s. So closely are the good and the bad intertwined politically, and so delicate therefore is the problem of political persuasion.

Lincoln sympathized with Lovejoy's antislavery feelings; but he disagreed strongly with his anti-Catholicism and his antiforeignism. He certainly believed in Lovejoy's constitutional right to freedom of speech; but he did not believe that one could properly claim the protection of the Constitution in one respect, and then disregard the Constitution in other respects. This the abolitionists did, when they denied the validity of the provisions for the rendition of fugitive slaves, or when they denied the limitations upon federal power to interfere with slavery in the states. In the Lyceum speech, Lincoln is not making a bid for partisan electoral support, as he was to do in 1858 and 1860. But he provides a remarkable example of his capacity for leadership, in his diagnosis of a grave problem, and in the manner in which he discriminates the point upon which conscience and prudence might agree.

The Lyceum speech[21] begins by announcing as its subject, "the perpetuation of our political institutions." This was also to be the theme of the Gettysburg Address twenty-five years later. Lincoln then goes on to remind his listeners of their great good fortune to be citizens of the United States: of their material prosperity, of their comparative immunity from foreign dangers, of the fact that they have inherited nearly all these blessings, having "toiled not in the acquirement or establishment of them." At the heart of our blessings, however, is a "government . . . conducing more essentially to the ends of civil and religious liberty, than any of which the history of former times tells us." Thus whereas Thoreau looks forward to an apocalyptic vision of uncoerced men of conscience freely associating in a regime of pure virtue, Lincoln looks back toward the despotism and religious persecution from which "a political edifice of liberty and equal rights" has freed us, and rejoices. While Thoreau feels the intolerableness of a system which permits slavery and unjust war,

[21] Ibid., 1: 108-15.

Lincoln warns against the spirit of lawlessness abroad in the land, a spirit which may in time lead to the overthrow of these free institutions. As we have seen, Lincoln is keenly aware of the fact that the fear and hatred engendered by slavery and racial difference is the principal cause of the mob violence sweeping the land, but he makes little direct reference to the fact, preferring to find that neutral ground upon which he can unite his audience in the contemplation of the dangers into which their own conflicting passions might be leading them. After reviewing the terrible scenes of mob violence, Lincoln comments, "Its direct consequences are, comparatively speaking, but a small evil; and much of its danger consists, in the proneness of our minds, to regard its direct, as its only consequences." The lynching of gamblers, or of murderers, is in itself no matter of necessary regret. But once the habit of taking the direct way with the guilty is adopted, what is to prevent its being extended to the innocent? Presently, the lawless in spirit, encouraged by the example of those who smugly believe they can dispense with the forms of law in dealing with malefactors, "make a jubilee" of the suspension of the operations of legal government.

Lincoln deals subtly and elaborately with the distinction between the direct and indirect consequences of what might, somewhat inaccurately, be called "innocuous lawlessness." There is the obvious point that those who in their self-righteous indignation lynch undoubted malefactors, cannot easily be brought to believe that they are endangering the innocent. To persuade the individuals in a lynch mob (whether at the moment they form part of the mob or at other times) that they might be mistaken in their victims is not easy. Lincoln makes this point, but lays more stress upon the next one, namely, that toleration of "justifiable" lynchings supplies the pretext eventually for general assaults upon personal safety and property. The distance from this to the death of constitutional liberty is not so great as may be supposed, and it is to a warning against this danger that most of the Lyceum speech is directed. When "good men . . . who love tranquility, who desire to abide by the laws, and enjoy their benefits . . . seeing their property destroyed; their families insulted . . . become tired of, and disgusted with, a Government that offers them no protection . . . ," the turning point is at hand. It is at this juncture that the danger of the demagogue becomes acute.

Lincoln cites the three great destroyers of republics according to the tradition of his day: Alexander, Caesar, and Napoleon. But we cannot help thinking also of Hitler and Mussolini, both of whom induced street rioting to precipitate the crises that brought them to power. In the crunch, they used the middle-class fear of lawlessness as a means of installing regimes from which the very idea of law was rooted out in favor of the iron first of dictatorship. And this fist was presently brought down without discrimination upon erstwhile supporters as well as former foes. Lincoln, it seems, anticipated with something like clairvoyancy, the typology of the process by which twentieth-century dictatorships have been established upon the ruins of constitutional government.

Lincoln is, in the Lyceum speech, directly addressing the very people whose unwitting defection from the forms of law might bring about the constitutional crisis. In the most remarkable passage of the Lyceum speech, he warns that the demagogic destroyer who "thirsts and burns for distinction . . . will have it, whether at the expense of emancipating slaves, or enslaving freemen." Lincoln here, as elsewhere, appears to display a curious neutrality between proslavery and antislavery positions. In part, this reflects the ambiguity in the feelings of his audience. Yet the select committee of the Illinois legislature which had reported the resolutions of the year before denouncing abolitionism, had also deeply deplored "the unfortunate condition of our fellow-men, whose lots are cast in thraldom in a land of liberty and peace." But it is also the case that, throughout his life, and until the very moment that he issued the final Emancipation Proclamation, Lincoln was profoundly opposed to the uncompensated emancipation of the slaves. And that is what the abolitionists (as distinct from free-soilers) stood for—Thoreau among them.

Abolition at a stroke would destroy a vast body of invested capital. It would throw the economic cost of emancipating the slaves entirely upon those who, by the accident of the moment, held the title to the slaves. It would unnecessarily exacerbate the feelings of those whose good will and assistance would, of necessity, be integral to the process of social reconstruction which would follow emancipation. Slavery was woven into the economic life of the entire nation, and the guilt for its presence must be allocated among all, north and south, who were implicated in it. That was always Lincoln's conviction. Northern shipowners had made fortunes by the foreign slave trade before 1809. Their descendants were carrying slave-produced cotton to Europe now. The mills of the north were spinning it and weaving it. Railroads were moving it; banks were financing it; stores were selling it; and every household in the land was consuming it. Many a northern free state, when it had arranged for emancipation of the slaves within its boundaries, had allowed owners to sell their slaves in the south, rather than actually emancipate them. Were those who bought always so much more guilty than those who sold that the entire burden should fall on the buyers alone? Not a man, woman, and child who was free in the antebellum United States did not share in the product of the unrequited toil of the slaves. The injustice of uncompensated emancipation, Lincoln thought, was of the kind practiced throughout history by designing demagogues, who would set class against class, by offering to despoil one for the benefit of the other, and end by destroying the liberties of all. The zeal of the reformer may well be indistinguishable from that of the would-be tyrant. It is Lincoln's thesis that it is the proneness of our minds to regard direct consequences as if they were the only consequences that provides the tyranny both of the mob and of the demagogue with opportunity.

The Lyceum speech does not, in any programmatic sense, provide a solution to the problem it describes. The only solution mentioned by Lincoln is that reverence for the Constitution and the laws become the political religion of the nation. Lincoln is well aware of the defects in the American political system, above all those connected with slavery and the Negro. He is careful to mention that bad laws may exist, and that grievances may be intolerable. Yet the alternative to the constitutional means for rectifying evils is unconstitutional. This is to adopt a remedy which may in the end be as bad, if not worse, than the disease. A free society which tolerates slavery is under a reproach from its own principles and may undertake to make freemen of slaves. A society in which no man is free, and from which the principle of freedom has been banished, offers no reproach to slavery and has no principle of reform.

Thoreau and Lincoln both consider the question of unjust laws. Lincoln says that they should be obeyed until they can be changed by legal means, "if not too intolerable." With this exception, Lincoln's argument touches Thoreau's thesis. However, Lincoln continues, "There is no grievance that is a fit object of mob law." The question then arises, does the justification for civil disobedience that might arise in extreme cases justify as well organizing a minority to clog, by its whole weight, and force the majority to bow to its will?

Thoreau calls upon the government—which means the constitutional majority—to "cherish its wise minority." Of course, this in substance is what representative government, as distinct from direct democracy, is supposed to do. But why should a self-appointed "wise minority," outside of government, be entitled to an obedience denied by Thoreau to the minority chosen constitutionally by the majority? As for the ways provided by law, says Thoreau, "They take too much time, and a man's life will be gone." But the time required for constitutional decisions reflects the inborn difficulty of infusing rationality into political decisions, and then of securing widespread consent. Thoreau wishes, on the one hand, to have no decisions by society to which everyone has not consented—that is of the essence of his anarchism—but, on the other hand, he demands that society bow to its wise minority.

Lincoln's call for a "political religion" is a recognition that law, of itself, as Aristotle says, has no power to persuade other than the power of habit. It is habit that forms character, and the rule of law presupposes the character of law-abidingness. A regime in which law rules becomes more lawful by reason of its legality; this may have the sound of a tautology, but it is founded upon the perception that every habit grows by the repetition of the activity from which the habit first arose. Lincoln recognizes the possibility of intolerable grievances even under a good government. But he believes that the more the rule of law takes effect, the less the possibility becomes of such grievances existing, because the more people will respect the processes by which reform takes place. Thoreau's approach, setting conscience against law, rather than enlisting it on the side of law, corrupts the very process by which reason replaces force in arbitrating human differences.

Lincoln's call to make reverence for the Constitution and the laws the political religion of the nation is a recognition that a merely utilitarian view of the value of freedom and free institutions can never induce the sacrifices necessary for their preservation. The crucial sacrifices are not those required by war—of blood and treasure. The dearest sacrifices are those of self-love and obstinate opinion, which tend to dominate a free society at peace. Lincoln began the Lyceum speech by indicating the relationship between a relative immunity to foreign danger, and the violence sweeping the country in 1838. He was aware, as was Madison in *The Federalist* No. 10, that human nature embodies a propensity to violent faction, which is particularly manifest when that nature is emancipated from arbitrary government and from myths which induce in everyone the same opinions and passions. Lincoln agreed with Aristotle (as did Madison), that man when separated from law is not divine, but bestial. Yet he disagreed with the opinion to which Madison gives countenance, that government is a reproach to human nature. For government, as Aristotle and Lincoln see it, is required not only to overcome the ills of human nature, but to give scope to the good. However rhetorical Madison's concession to the superiority of a state of anarchy, he does imply that there is a human condition imaginable better than that of the best regime imaginable. But government is needed not only to prevent harm, but to achieve good. Friendship, says Aristotle, is better than justice. But friendship does not arise in a vacuum. The conditions under which men become friends are those which the political community has provided. Outside the political community there is neither the leisure nor the activity in which men discover friendship.

Thoreau demands life according to principle. But principle, as he speaks of it, is something asocial, as inconsistent with friendship as with justice under law. "Action from principle . . . changes things and relations," he writes, "it is essentially revolutionary, and does not consist wholly with any thing which was. It not only divides states and churches, it divides families; aye, it divides the *individual*, separating the diabolical in him from the divine."[22]

But the question must be asked, does the separation of the diabolical from the divine send the diabolical or the divine forth to rule the world? Thoreau's strictures against law and constitutional majority rule can only lead not to rule by a "wise minority" but to lawless tyranny. Lincoln's solution is to subject the diabolical to the divine, by moral education and the rule of law, in a regime dedicated not to any minority, wise or unwise, but to the proposition that all men are created equal.

[22] Thoreau, *Walden and Civil Disobedience*, pp. 230-31.

7 | WHAT IS EQUALITY? The Declaration of Independence Revisited

Equality is the well-nigh irresistible principle of authority in the modern world, as Alexis de Tocqueville observed so well so long ago. The concessions to slavery that formed part of the compromises of the original Constitution may once have cast doubt upon that authority here in the United States. But the Civil War, the Civil War amendments to the Constitution, and the implementing of those amendments in recent years should have gone far to remove any ground for such doubt. Nor should we forget the Nineteenth Amendment, the culmination of nearly a century of agitation, reminding us how early in our history the ferment of equality reached the distinction of the sexes no less than that of the races. In the second half of the twentieth century equality seems to have made its presence felt most powerfully within the Constitution in the words of the Fourteenth Amendment wherein it is provided that "No State shall . . . . deny to any person within its jurisdiction the equal protection of the laws." Under the aegis of this clause the Supreme Court of the United States has engineered a vast social revolution. Any deliberate separation of tax-supported facilities by race—whether these be swimming pools, golf courses, public transportation systems, colleges and universities, or elementary and secondary schools—has been forbidden as a violation of the Constitution. An amendment to the Constitution is now before the states, guaranteeing equal rights (other than voting) to women. It is difficult to imagine what the rights are for which guarantees are sought, and which cannot find protection within the existing scope of the Fourteenth Amendment. Inequality because of race and sex has been assailed in the most sweeping terms by the great series of civil rights acts, culminating in those of 1964 and 1965. It is hardly too much to say that the imagination has been exhausted in the search for new demands for equality. Perhaps no assault upon the alleged citadel of inequality has been more potent than that made in the field of representation. The reapportionment revolution, with its slogan, "one man, one vote," has nearly unhinged some of our most settled, or archaic, constitutional arrangements, particularly in the field of state government.

There was a time, a very short time ago, when equality was held to entail an absence of invidious discrimination. For example, it was said that

Paper presented to the Center for Constructive Alternatives, Hillsdale College, Hillsdale, Mich., 1972. Printed by the kind permission of Hillsdale College.

the Constitution must be color blind. Thus it came to be forbidden to require people to attend or use different schools, golf courses, bus seats, etc., because of their different race or color. But now something euphemistically called "affirmative action" is required instead. Such action is demanded, to be sure, in the name of equality. But we may be permitted to wonder by what strange alchemy equality may be defined in terms so nearly opposite to each other. Where once it was said to be unequal, and therefore unconstitutional, to send certain children to certain schools, solely because of their race or color, it is now held to be a requirement, an "affirmative" requirement, of that same equality. Where once it was held to be unequal, and therefore unconstitutional, to prefer one applicant to another, whether for a job or a place in a college, university, or professional school, because of his race or color (or her sex), it is now held to be an "affirmative" requirement of equality to do just that.

In the field of representation, we find that former Chief Justice Warren, has made the discovery that what is represented in virtue of the principle of equality in the American Constitution, is people, and not stones or trees or acres. Exactly how Mr. Warren was vouchsafed this mighty revelation, it is no part of our purpose to inquire. Yet Mr. Warren might have pondered that older wisdom which found it desirable, in the ordering of equal governments, that such governments be able to control, not only the governed, but themselves. To this end, it was once found that "dependence on the people is, no doubt, the primary control," but that experience had also "taught mankind the necessity of auxiliary precautions." Mr. Warren might have reflected that reasonable men have held that an appointive Supreme Court, holding office for life, was such a wise precaution. And other reasonable men have seen in a principled bicameralism, such as that represented by the United States Senate, another such wise precaution. He might then have been spared the absurdity of calling unconstitutional a state constitution that was approved, not only by a majority of all the people of that state, but by a majority of the people of every county in it. The ground of this absurdity was that the districts from which the members of the upper house were to be chosen had unequal numbers of people. Clearly we have reached a state of affairs where, as the demand for equality becomes ever more intense, its meaning becomes ever more indistinct, if not absolutely incoherent.

Any inquiry into the meaning of equality begins properly with the Declaration of Independence. And let us first take note of the unique character of the Declaration, and of the event it celebrates. It marks the first time in the history of the world that a nation proclaimed its independence, not in virtue of some particular attribute or superior mission, but because of rights which it shared with all men everywhere. Of course, it soon fell to the United States to demonstrate to all the world the feasibility of a government based upon the recognition of such rights, and such a demonstration became the special mission of this people. Yet these rights—whose feasibility as a ground for just government they were to demonstrate—remained the rights of all mankind.

Today the sonorous phrases of Jefferson may seem to have taken on some of the qualities of cliches; even in his own time it was alleged that the ideas had become hackneyed. Yet however widespread at that time may have been the sentiments to which Jefferson gave expression—and of course they could not have furnished forth the testament of a people if they had not been widespread—we must not lose sight of the fact that to employ them as he did had then no precedent. The only similar event we recall in the history of the world is the promulgation of the Ten Commandments, and the assertion therein that God is One. Although there may have been monotheists before Moses—as there assuredly were prohibitions against murder, theft, adultery, and false witnessing—the public affirmation of the unity of God as the foundation of the law of a people was itself unique and unprecedented. Familiarity with the Declaration—as with the Ten Commandments—deprives us of the sense of its novelty, and with it some of our capacity to understand. It may be as difficult to articulate the meaning of equality as of monotheism today, since both depend to a degree for their intelligibility upon a contrast with their opposites, a contrast altogether lacking from our horizons. We may even wonder whether they may not both be disintegrating into their opposites, because of a lack of opposition.

The Declaration begins with an appeal to "the Laws of Nature and of Nature's God," and it is held to be a self-evident truth "that all men are created equal." It is said that all men are endowed by their Creator with certain unalienable rights, among them "Life, Liberty, and the pursuit of Happiness." To secure these rights, "Governments are instituted . . . deriving their just powers from the consent of the governed." What a mass of concepts is here! Law nature, nature's God, self-evident truth, unalienable rights, just powers of government, and the consent of the governed. Many years later Jefferson was to assert that he had aimed "to place before mankind the common sense of the subject, in terms so plain and firm as to command their assent."[1] He claimed no "originality of principle or sentiment," for the Declaration was intended to be "an expression of the American mind." That the language drawn from books of the political philosophers should have seemed to be no more than

[1] Letter to Henry Lee, May 8, 1825, quoted in Robert Ginsberg (ed.), *A Casebook on the Declaration of Independence* (New York: Crowell, 1967).

common sense to the American mind is but another of the extraordinary features of that amazing episode. Yet let us try to understand why it should have been so.

First, let us consider that troublesome expression, "self-evident truth." This is a concept borrowed from geometry, although nothing in it limits it to such a subject matter. A self-evident truth is one which. is evident to anyone who grasps the terms of the proposition in which the truth is expressed. That "things equal to the same things are equal to each other," is self-evident to anyone who understands the meaning of "same" and "other." For no one, comprehending these terms, can fail simultaneously to comprehend the meaning of "equal." But there is no necessity that a self-evident truth will carry its evidence to everyone. Some men are readier at grasping certain concepts than others, and some concepts are more difficult to grasp; and so, as Thomas Aquinas observes, what is evident to the wise is not such to all men. Moreover, obstructions to the grasping of evidence may come, not only from native intelligence (or the lack thereof), but from the presence in the mind of false doctrines. The proposition of human equality is, first and foremost, an assertion that all men share a common *nature,* an assertion that depends upon the prior recognition of nature in general, of which human nature forms a part. Yet many people have no idea whatever of nature, and see the effects to which we give this comprehensive name, whether it be the wind, the stars, trees, or tigers, as the manifestations of gods or demons. And to those possessed of such a false consciousness, other men, of other races or tribes or classes, may seem to differ as much from themselves as if they had been trees or tigers. We might add, at this point, that the false consciousness that sees other men primarily as non-Aryans, or as bourgeoisie, is just as corrupting (if not more corrupting) than the absence of any idea of nature from the minds of primitive peoples.

Now the proposition that all men are created equal means that all are the *same* in *some* respect. It does not mean that they are the same in every respect. As Lincoln once observed, it does not mean that all were the same, or equal, in "color, size, intellect, moral development, or social capacity." Men might indeed be unequal in these respects yet be equal— the same—in respect to certain unalienable rights. Now what is this sameness—equality—in respect to certain rights? The unalienable *rights* mentioned in the Declaration are those from which *obligations* can be inferred or deduced. For the Declaration is a statement of when some men might, and when they might not, be rightfully regarded as the rulers of other men. I suggest that we begin to try to understand the *sameness* of all men in regard to these unalienable rights, by understanding a corresponding *otherness.* We understand man, and his rights, as much by understanding what he is *not,* as by understanding what he *is.* In fact, we understand the latter only by understanding the former. And man is not either beast or God. Whether the God whom the Signers assume to exist can be proved to exist is not necessary to the argument of the Declaration. What can be proved is that a divine nature is of a certain sort. Such a nature would carry to absolute perfection those partially existing perfections perceivable in man (such as reason, justice, mercy), without the corresponding imperfections (above all, the passionate self-love that corrupts the perfections). Men form the idea of such a perfect being, as much to understand the limits of their own humanity, as to decide objectively of that superior being's existence. Aristotle defines law in the *Politics* as "reason unaffected by desire." And God appears first in the Declaration as a legislator. The conception of a being in whom reason is not, or cannot be, affected by desire is the conception of a being in whom just power naturally resides. It is the conception of a being in whom the different powers of government can safely be united. And the God of the Declaration appears in three roles (besides Creator): first, as noted, that of legislator; second, that of "Supreme Judge of the World"; and finally, that of "Divine Providence," or that executive power, upon whom the Signers place a "firm reliance" for their protection.[2] It is an absolutely necessary condition of the rule of law that these three powers of government never be united in the same *human* hands. For them to be so united, whether in a singular or in a collective body, is the very definition of tyranny, as the Founding Fathers never cease to repeat. For the equality of mankind is an equality of defect, as well as an equality of rights: no man in civil society may be permitted therefore to be a judge in his own cause. That such a rule does not apply to God is but another way of saying that it must apply to all men.

But if man is not God, neither is he a beast. If man cannot justly rule man, except by law, nevertheless he can, indeed must, rule beasts despotically. We do not expect a man to ask his dog's consent to be governed. In fact, the dog is incapable of giving that consent, for consent implies a rationality lacking in the dog's nature. In short, as men are neither beasts nor gods, they ought not to play God to other men, nor ought they to treat other men as beasts. Here is the elementary ground, not only of political, but of moral obligation. Thus it is that the starting-point for the comprehension of the source of the just powers of government lies in the proposition that all men are created equal.

[2] That the "three persons" of the God of the Declaration correspond to the three powers into which constitutional government is divided was first pointed out to me by Professor George Anastaplo. See his essay, "The Declaration of Independence," *St. Louis University Law Journal* 9 (1965): 390.

But the equality of all men is in one sense hypothetical. It is an assertion concerning human nature. Yet we never actually see human nature, except as it has been modified by human laws or customs. We see some men in an improved or perfected condition; often we see them in a corrupted or depraved condition. Toward the end of the Declaration, Jefferson inveighs against the King for "works of death, desolation and tyranny . . . scarcely paralleled in the most barbarous ages, and totally unworthy the Head of a civilized nation." Later he denounces the King for exciting "domestic insurrection amongst us," and for endeavoring "to bring on the inhabitants of our frontiers, the merciless Indian savages, whose known rule of warfare, is an undistinguished destruction of all ages, sexes, and conditions." The distinction between civilization, on the one hand, and "barbarous ages," or "savagery," on the other, is not one of natures, but of laws, customs, or individual states of character. The infirmity or vice which infects the King, making him unworthy to be head of a civilized nation, discharges these subjects from their obligation to the laws over which the King presides.

Let us now turn to the much misunderstood concept, "the consent of the governed." While the consent of the governed and the opinion of the governed may coincide and, in a well-ordered democracy they do coincide, the two are not necessarily identical. Clearly, neither children, savages, nor felons need be governed in accordance with anything denominated as their consent. We had best approach the meaning of consent by seeing it first as the reciprocal of equality. Consent becomes necessary to the just powers of government because men are equal. That is, because men are not unequal, as are man and God, or man and beast, nature by itself does not decide the question of who is to rule. Consent comes to light in the Declaration as the alternative to nature, as a source of the just powers of government. But consent does not, cannot, reside in mere will or willingness. Nothing can be further from the true meaning of consent than the notion currently fashionable that consent may be withdrawn by anyone who fancies himself "alienated," particularly if what he is alienated from is the "establishment." Indeed, the Declaration points to a particular deference due to "Governments long established." Mere willingness to be governed does not give rise to the just powers of government, nor does mere unwillingness deprive a government of these powers. The proof of this is simple. Most of the governments by which men have been governed since the world began have been founded upon some combination of force and fraud; most have, in short, been illegitimate from the point of view of the Declaration. Yet their subjects have, for the most part, yielded willing obedience to them. That some men regard other men as Gods, or that they are willing to be governed like beasts, does not change nature; and the opinion derived from such errors does not result in that consent contemplated by the Declaration of Independence as the source of just powers.

Only that opinion may rightly be denominated consent that distinguishes men from beasts and gods; only that may be denominated consent which is, in the decisive respect, *enlightened*. For only enlightened human beings recognize other human beings for what they are, namely, persons with rights which they must respect, in order to have their own rights recognized and respected. Governments, says the Declaration, are "instituted." What this means is well expressed in the Massachusetts Constitution of 1780, which states that "The body politic is formed by a voluntary association of individuals; it is a social compact by which the whole people covenants with each citizen and each citizen with the whole people that all shall be governed by certain laws for the common good." Now it is clear that such covenants are not made by savages with savages, nor by civilized men with savages. Nor is the definition of savage limited to those we may denominate as "primitives." Those anywhere who see other men merely as means to their own ends, and who cannot see the reciprocal obligations that flow from the act of agreement to have a common good, are deficient in that enlightenment which is a necessary condition of true consent.

We have said that enlightenment is necessary to the just powers of government, and we have contrasted enlightenment and civilization, with barbarism and savagery. But enlightenment must be contrasted with something else. Just as equality represents the middle rank in the order of nature occupied by mankind, between beast and God, so does enlightenment represent a middle state between a defective human condition, and that perfection we call wisdom. And it is as important to understand that consent does not require wisdom, as to understand that it does require enlightenment. Still more, one must understand that the enlightenment necessary to consent becomes then an element of the government consented to; but that the wisdom which transcends consent, cannot be demanded of the government based upon it. Had the king of Great Britain been merely unwise, as distinct from tyrannical, his subjects would not have had the same right that they did have to throw off their allegiance to him.

Let us reflect further upon this distinction. Wisdom, we say, is the greatest of human needs, whether as a good itself, or as the condition for the gaining of the highest good. But to know what wisdom is, and how to obtain it, has puzzled the minds of men—including the wisest men—for time out of mind. The dilemma of political life consists above all in this: how to obtain an appropriate recognition of wisdom among the unwise, among those whose very unwisdom creates the need for wisdom in political affairs. The difficulty is not so much that the unwise always reject the claims of wisdom; on the contrary, they have sometimes been too prone to give power to those who advance those claims. The difficulty stems from the fact that it is not the wise who advance under the banners of wisdom, but that it is pretenders to wisdom, who unscrupulously exploit the need for wisdom of the unwise. Here is the source of the unjust privileges, and of the tyrannical power, of the kings, priests, and aristocracies of the past, as it is of the leaders of the allegedly master races, and of the dictatorships of the proletariat, of more recent times. The people have, through the ages, repeatedly enslaved themselves to those who have offered them not equal justice under law, but messianic promises of "final solutions" to the problems of the human condition. But the prophets of such salvation have been false, and the claims they have made have been spurious. It is a dispensation of wisdom, from the perspective of the Declaration, that consent replace wisdom, as the ground upon which rule can be legitimated. The substitution of consent for wisdom has meant a lowering, in a certain way, of the ends of government. It has, for example, led to the exclusion of eternal salvation from among those ends and, therefore, to the separation of church from state. That is also why it is not happiness, but the pursuit of happiness, that Jefferson lists among the rights to be secured by government. It is not for government to see that men become happy, any more than that they are secured for the throne of grace. All that government may rightfully do is to secure, so far as possible, an equal opportunity for each citizen to pursue what he regards as happiness. And it may bar him only from those pursuits which are inconsistent with the equal rights in his fellow citizens. The widespread dissatisfaction we have witnessed in recent times, with the extraordinary freedom and material well-being of American life, on the ground that it does not touch our higher nature, and our higher needs, is in some respects justified. Those whose task it should be to point out the ways of salvation, whether they be the representatives of revealed religion, or the teachers of the arts of the mind in the universities, have abandoned their proper vocations. But it is utterly destructive of a healthy political life to expect the salvation of souls from political activity as such. To try to satisfy these unreasonable utopian expectations by bringing them "within the system" can lead only to disillusionment or to despotism—or both. The rule of law, as envisioned by the Signers and Framers, involved a tempering of the expectations of the governed, even as it involved the governed themselves in the process of government, by requiring their consent.

Let us again consider what this consent is which enfranchises the government. When every citizen covenants with every other to have a body politic, he creates an artificial person. The rights which each individual possesses naturally—above all the right to life—are such that they cannot be well protected by those bodies we inhabit naturally. Although each individual, being by nature equal in authority to every other, has a perfect right to do everything he thinks necessary to protect his life, yet that right is ineffectual. By creating a body politic he may be protected by a body far more powerful than any that exists by nature, and one that never sleeps. But the power of that body becomes useful only if it can act. And it can act only if a part can decide for the whole. Unanimity is impossible. Indeed, had it been possible government would not have been necessary. A part must then decide for the whole, and everyone included in the whole must recognize and accept that decision as his own, whether or not he personally had endorsed it. Here is where the idea of representation enters modern political thought: it is first of all the idea of the part that decides for the whole. Had Chief Justice Warren understood this, he might not have attempted to reduce representation to the pretentious oversimplification of "one man, one vote." He might even have recognized that the Supreme Court of the United States might reasonably be regarded as a representative institution because, for certain carefully specified purposes, a majority of the people of the United States unquestionably regarded it as such.

In order for there to be a body politic, and majority rule, and representation, there must first be unanimous agreement, or common consent, to have the body politic. Unanimity is a self-evident necessity; it is no more than a matter of definition. All who consent are members, all who do not consent are no part of the body, and are not counted either in the majority or minority that appears thereafter. The Tories of the American Revolution were no part of the "one people" who declared independence; and most of them eventually emigrated. Second, a part that is less than the whole decides for the whole; and that part, to repeat, is the majority. Why? Because the majority is that part of the whole that most nearly resembles the whole. But why not three-fourths, or four-fifths? It is because these larger proportions imply, not nearer approximations to unity, but rather vetoes by a minority upon decision by the majority. And for a whole to be decided by a minority, either affirmatively or negatively is, at this level, to imply some inequality among the original contracting members of the body politic. It implies some reservation of right by some members, as against their original equality with other members. Any such reservation would void the social compact and nullify the obligations of the others.

But let us understand what it is that we say the majority, and the majority alone, has the right to do at this point. It is not to govern, but to institute or establish government. It is what the Declaration has in mind when it speaks of "the Right of the People . . . to institute new Government." And this means the people deciding by the majority. It does not, for example, imply that every American personally favored independence on July 4, 1776. Many did not. We may here distinguish two kinds of "minorities." The first, which is not a minority properly so called, retained their allegiance to the British crown. The second, who may have opposed independence, nevertheless felt bound by the decision of what they regarded or accepted as the majority. These became part of the American people, whose decision they accepted as their own, even as they were opposing it. A similar situation arose in a later generation, when some Unionists in the seceding states of the Confederacy accepted secession as binding upon them, even after they had opposed it, while others retained their loyalty to the Union.

Now the doctrine of human equality leads necessarily to a simple majoritarianism only at the level of instituting government. It does not specify the form of government to be established, other than that it must be nondespotic. The purpose of government, the Declaration teaches, is "to secure these rights," the unalienable rights possessed equally by all men, but which no man without government can adequately secure. But beyond that the Declaration cannot go. It says merely that such government shall lay its foundation "on such principles and [organize] its powers in such form, as to them [viz., the people, acting through the majority] shall seem most likely to effect their Safety and Happiness." The Virginia Bill of Rights of 1776 merely says that "of all the various modes and forms of government, that is best which is capable of producing the greatest degree of happiness and safety, and is most effectually secured against the danger of maladministration." And the Massachusetts Bill of Rights of 1780 is equally indeterminate, stating only that "It is the duty of the people . . . in framing a constitution of government, to provide for an equitable mode of making laws, as well as for an impartial interpretation and a faithful execution of them." Now the reason for this openness, or vagueness, concerning the desirable kind of government, is as follows: The primitive majority, which acts for the whole, following the incorporation of naturally discrete individuals into a body politic, possesses the same kind of authority that those individuals formerly possessed. That is to say, the people collectively have the same freedom to choose the means for securing their rights that individuals had in the state of nature. The people are not even obliged to set up popular governments, although we can see why they would think it safer to keep the government close to themselves. Certainly they may now require special majorities of three-fourths, or four-fifths, for certain purposes; although such requirements always rest at bottom, upon the underlying majority. If the majority may establish a Supreme Court, holding office for life, why may it not establish an upper house of the legislature, also holding office for life? Such decisions may or may not be prudent, but in themselves they need not be unequal. What form of government best represents the people's need to be properly represented cannot be determined in the abstract. From this we can see the absurdity of the holding of the Warren Court, that numerical equality of electoral districts is the only legitimate consideration in designing a system of representation.

In reflecting upon the considerations that ought to inform the people's judgment, when choosing a form of government to represent them, let us remind ourselves what it is that we seek when we choose representatives in other relations of life. When we choose a lawyer, a physician, an architect, or a bargaining agent, we also choose someone to act for us, and in place of ourselves. We choose someone else, not merely because we cannot be in the place or at the time of the action called for. We choose someone whom we believe able to act more competently than we ourselves can act, in the matter in question. In short, we choose someone wiser in a certain kind of wisdom. Although we think the physician or the lawyer wiser than we in medical or legal matters, and although we might consult other lawyers or physicians in making our choice, yet we keep the right of choosing firmly in our own hands. In short, we make the distinction between enlightenment and wisdom which underlies the whole Declaration. For we believe that our enlightenment, although it falls short of the excellence represented by wisdom, yet is so firmly wedded to our self-interest, that it is a better source of authority for our lives than the utmost wisdom unalloyed by self-interest. Thus we prefer to choose our own lawyers and physicians, rather than have the assignment of all such in the hands of self-appointed boards of physicians and lawyers. Moreover, it is an element of that same enlightenment to realize that it is better that we pay the lawyers and physicians ourselves, for we want their wisdom to have the wholehearted motivation of self-interest, to make sure that their skill will in fact serve us. The idea of representation, as it applies to the business of government, as distinct from the establishment of government, involves the same idea of competence or wisdom, on the part of the representatives, combined with the idea of attachment to the interests of those they represent. An incompetent devotion to our interests, and a skillful self-serving, are equally repugnant.

The problem of government is much more complicated than the one we face in these nonpolitical forms of representation. The Founders recognized a rich body of constitutional experience available to them both in British and colonial history. The separation of powers supplies the leading example, although it is a question whether this example comes primarily from theory or from practice. It is a device which is effective when supplemented by a system of checks and balances. The effect of these instruments is, as *The Federalist* assures us, to make the interest of the man coincide with the duties of his place. But separation of the powers of government would be meaningless if it did not rest upon the vast institution of private property, for where there is no separation of political from economic power, there can be none of political powers. Moreover, the multiplication of factions which, *The Federalist* also tells us, is the best security for political liberty, rests upon that diffusion of economic power that flows only from a system of economic liberty, in which neither private nor public monopolies dominate. All systems either of socialism or so-called state capitalism approximate that condition that would obtain if doctors or lawyers assigned themselves to their clients and patients, and were paid by someone who took no personal interest in the outcome of their cases.

As the examples of private representation suggest, the enlightenment of the governed is of decisive importance in a free society. It is always possible, but extremely difficult, for a government to rise much above the intelligence of its citizens. While the government ought to be more competent than those it serves, it may not be. Just as some lawyers and doctors are more skillful in persuading their clients and patients that they are benefiting them, than in actually doing so, so representatives in a democracy may be better in flattering their constituents than in serving them. To detect political quacks and shysters is not so easy.

In the crisis of 1860 the South believed that they were to be governed without their consent in the matter that concerned them most deeply. The North believed that the South had turned its back upon that idea of equality which alone made consent reasonable and society civilized. Equality and consent are theoretically always in harmony, because logically they are two aspects of the same common denominator. Yet in the passionate pursuit of incomplete opinions they, like the nation, may be torn asunder. To prevent this we need opinion informed as was that upon which the Founders relied for the "common sense of the subject." We need the opinion of those uncommon men who are not only enlightened, but wise.

8 | PARTLY FEDERAL, PARTLY NATIONAL On the Political Theory of the American Civil War

> Sir, I know that the discussion of the elementary principles of government is dry and uninteresting; indeed, all abstract discussion is so ... [but] I think it is greatly to be regretted that the true principles of our free institutions have not been more frequently the subject of discussion. The clear comprehension and maintenance of them is essential to the liberty of the people. To obliterate or obscure them will always be, as it always has been, the purpose of those who would misrule and oppress the people.
>
> Senator Rowan of Kentucky,
> in the Debate on Foot's Resolution,
> February 8, 1830

When in 1964 Governor George Wallace vainly attempted to interpose the authority of the state of Alabama to prevent the carrying into effect of a federal court order for the enrollment of Negroes in the University of Alabama, the doctrine of state rights, founded upon the doctrine of state sovereignty, may have reached its end as an effective force within American politics. Yet the ambiguity in the American regime, in virtue of which these doctrines came to life, remains. Still more, the problem which caused the ambiguity, being itself endemic to modern politics, if not to politics simply, also remains. In attempting to understand the dispute concerning sovereignty—or supremacy—within the American regime, we attempt to understand, at its deepest level, this ambiguity and this problem.

In his message to Congress on July 4, 1861, Abraham Lincoln declared that the people of the South would never have rebelled against the national authority had they not been first convinced that to do so was in fact, not rebellion at all, but the exercise of a lawful right under the Constitution.

> It might seem, at first thought, to be of little difference, [Lincoln wrote] whether the present movement at the South be called "secession" or "rebellion." The movers, however, well understood the difference. At the beginning they knew they could never raise their treason to any respectable magnitude by any name which implies *violation* of law. They knew that their people possessed as much moral sense, as much devotion to law and order, and as much pride in, and reverence for, the history and Government of their common country, as any

Reprinted by the kind permission of the publisher from Robert A. Goldwin (ed.), *A Nation of States: Essays on the American Federal System,* 2d ed., Rand McNally Public Affairs Series (Chicago, 1974).

other civilized and patriotic people. . . . Accordingly . . . they invented an ingenious sophism, which, if conceded, was followed by perfectly logical steps . . . to the complete destruction of the Union. The sophism itself is, that any State of the Union may, *consistently* with the national Constitution, and therefore *lawfully* and *peacefully*, withdraw from the Union without the consent of the Union or of any other State. . . . With rebellion thus sugar-coated they have been drugging the public mind of their section for more than thirty years, and until at length they have brought many good men to a willingness to take up arms against the Government the day *after* some assemblage of men have enacted the farcical pretense of taking their State out of the Union, who could have been brought to no such thing the day before.[1]

We can understand the anguish that impelled Lincoln to speak so harshly of the "movers" of the rebellion, as the crisis of the Union broke upon him. Yet there is little reason to believe that, if there had been deception, the movers were less deceived than the moved. Lincoln's assertion that the public mind of the South had been drugged for more than thirty years is itself a confession of the depth and pervasiveness of that "ingenious sophism." This ill accords with the hypothesis of a conspiracy of clever bad men misleading simple good ones. Nor does it tell us why such a sophism should originally have been conceded.

The time span indicated by Lincoln takes us back to the nullification crisis. This began with the publication by the South Carolina legislature of the "Exposition and Protest" of 1828, which had been secretly drafted by John C. Calhoun, then vice-president of the United States. Calhoun followed the example (as he thought) of Thomas Jefferson, who had secretly drafted the Kentucky Resolutions of 1798 when he was the vice-president. The precedent is not merely fortuitous. Throughout the five years of intense controversy that followed the South Carolina Exposition, climaxed by the Ordinance of Nullification of November 24, 1832, the nullifiers always based their constitutional arguments squarely upon the doctrines they alleged to have been set forth in the Kentucky and Virginia Resolutions of 1798, and in Madison's Report of 1800, adopted by the Virginia legislature in that year. If the nullifiers' contentions were correct, the "ingenious sophism" had its origin with Jefferson and Madison, rather than with Calhoun and his associates, and it would have been proper to say that the public mind had been drugged, not for thirty, but for sixty years.

Obviously, such a view of our history is inconsistent with that of Abraham Lincoln. Yet surprisingly enough, Professor Berns endorses it, not less than Mr. Kilpatrick.[2] We should hasten to add, however, that

[1] Roy P. Basler (ed.), *The Collected Works of Abraham Lincoln* (New Brunswick, N.J.: Rutgers University Press, 1953), 4: 432.

[2] Walter Berns, "The Meaning of the Tenth Amendment," and James Jackson

most modern authorities seem to concur in the view that the Kentucky and Virginia Resolutions did in fact supply the premises, if not the detailed reasoning, from which the doctrines of nullification and secession might properly be drawn. Yet there is one earlier authority who warns us against these later ones. This is no less a personage than James Madison, who was alive and full of vigor throughout the nullification controversy, and who was relentless and indefatigable in his opposition to the South Carolina doctrines. He repeatedly and elaborately denied any validity to the arguments purporting to ground those doctrines upon what he and Jefferson had written and done thirty years before. While historians have generally noted this fact, no one has, so far as I know weighed Madison's contentions—or South Carolina's rebuttals—by the theoretical standards to which they themselves appeal.

In his essay on "What the Framers Meant by Federalism," Professor Diamond points out that federalism, prior to the Constitution of 1787, referred to a "voluntary association of states," for purposes of common advantage, in which no powers of government properly so called, were surrendered to the association.[3] The term "federal government" would have been a solecism, since to be federal meant by definition to be a league resting ultimately on the good faith of the associates, while to be a government meant to have powers of lawful coercion. The government created by the Constitution, by being "partly federal and partly national," as Madison says in The Federalist No. 39, corresponded to no prior theoretical understanding of what either the federal or the national was. It is not surprising that in controversies concerning the nature of the regime, the partisans should choose between its federalism and its nationalism, and interpret the one in the light of the other. In the nullification crisis, South Carolina made a resolute attempt systematically to reduce the national features to the federal. It is our thesis that the Carolinians failed in their attempt; yet we would have to admit an equal doubt that the pure nationalists succeed better in their opposite attempt. Both sides appeared to concede that, as Calhoun was reputed to have said, sovereignty was like chastity, and that it could not be surrendered in part. To call the Constitution of the United States partly national, and partly federal, was very much like saying that in the new Union, the states were neither maids nor matrons, but that their status was nevertheless legitimate. Clearly there was a new and imperfectly understood "family" relationship in this Union. The rights of the respective parties were far from settled by the Founding Fathers; and yet, as Lincoln declared in 1861:

Kilpatrick, "The Case for 'States' Rights,' " in Robert A. Goldwin (ed.), *A Nation of States: Essays on the American Federal System*, 2d ed., Rand McNally Public Affairs Series (Chicago, 1974).

[3] Diamond, "What the Framers Meant by Federalism," in ibid.

> A husband and wife may be divorced, and go out of the presence, and beyond the reach of each other; but the different parts of our country cannot do this. They cannot but remain face to face; and intercourse, either amicable or hostile, must continue between them.[4]

Let us now turn to South Carolina which, in its attempt to annul its relationship with the other states in 1832, addressed these words, among others, to them.

> We hold, then, that, on their separation from the Crown of Britain, the several colonies became free and independent States, each enjoying the separate and independent right of self-government; and that no authority can be exercised over them, or within their limits, but by their consent, respectively given as States.[5]

That is to say, South Carolina believed that in declaring independence of Great Britain, each of the thirteen states was, at the same time, declaring its *de jure* independence of each other. Of course, at the moment of independence the new states were not *de facto* independent of each other, since they were jointly conducting a war against Great Britain, upon the success of which their actual independence was contingent. By this view of the Revolution, the United States was then in much the same political condition as the United Nations in World War II. Moreover the Articles of Confederation do affirm that "Each State retains its sovereignty, freedom, and independence, and every power, jurisdiction, and right, which is not by this Confederation expressly delegated to the United States in Congress assembled." It is of the highest importance to notice that, while "power, jurisdiction, and right" are delegated, "sovereignty, freedom, and independence" are retained. Accordingly, the United States may today submit to the jurisdiction of, let us say, the World Court, without abandoning in the smallest degree its sovereignty or freedom.

But the position adopted by South Carolina in 1832, allegedly upon the authority of Jefferson and Madison, maintained that the Constitution did not differ in the decisive respect from the Confederation. While more powers may have been delegated, and while these powers may have been permitted to operate directly upon the citizens of the several states, yet sovereignty, they said, remained where it had been. Because it did so remain, each state retained among its reserved powers the power to prevent the operation of these delegated powers within its borders and upon its citizens. Whether this preventive power was called interposition or nullification, its essence was the power to suspend one or more of the

---

[4] Basler, *Abraham Lincoln*, 4:269.
[5] "Address to the People of the United States," Appendix to Gales and Seaton's *Register*, 22d Cong., 2d Sess., p. 169 (hereafter cited as *Register*).

powers it had delegated to the United States in the Constitution. In the Address of the Convention to the people of South Carolina, it was further argued that

> The constitution of the United States, as is admitted by cotemporaneous writers, is a compact between sovereign States. Though the subject-matter of that compact was a Government, the powers of which Government were to operate to a certain extent upon the people of those sovereign States aggregately, and not upon the State authorities, as is usual in confederacies, still the constitution is a confederacy. First. It is a confederacy, because, in its foundations, it possesses not one single feature of nationality. The people of the separate States, as distinct political communities, ratified the Constitution, each State acting for itself, and binding its own citizens, and not those of any other State. The act of ratifying declares it "to be binding on the States so ratifying."[6]

It should be observed that Article VII of the Constitution declares that "The ratification of the conventions of nine States shall be sufficient for the establishment of this Constitution between the States so ratifying." Moreover, James Madison, in *The Federalist,* in examining the question of what the relation would be between the nine or more states ratifying, and those failing to do so, concluded that "no political relation [could] subsist between the assenting and the dissenting States." This would seem to bear out the Carolina contention that the acts of ratification alone made the states members of the Union. It would appear to be in massive contradiction to the position taken by Webster and Jackson in 1832, and by Lincoln in 1861, that the Union was older than and prior to the states, and that the states had no political existence outside the Union.[7] As we shall see, the meaning of the Tenth Amendment turns this prior and independent existence. In the speeches and letters of the time, we find it endlessly repeated, as Madison says in a letter of 1833 to Daniel Webster, "that compact, express or implied, is the vital principle of decisively upon the question of whether the states are conceived to have

[6] Ibid., p. 163.

[7] "In our colonial state, although dependent on another power, we very early considered ourselves as connected by common interest with each other. Leagues were formed for common defence, and, before the declaration of independence, we were known in our aggregate character as the United Colonies of America. That decisive and important step was taken jointly. We declared ourselves a nation by a joint, not by several acts, and ... agreed ... [to] form one nation for the purposes of conducting some certain domestic concerns and all foreign relations." Andrew Jackson, Proclamation, Dec. 10, 1832, *Register*, p. 186.

"The original [states] passed into the Union even *before* they cast off their British colonial dependence; and the new ones each came into the Union directly from a condition of dependence, excepting Texas. And even Texas, in its temporary independence, was never designated a State." Abraham Lincoln, Message to Congress, July 4, 1861. [Basler (ed.), *Abraham Lincoln,* 4: 433.]

free governments as contradistinguished from governments not free; and that a revolt against this principle leaves no choice but between anarchy and despotism." Now if the states are the communities created by the original social compact, the compact which took their citizens out of the state of nature, and if this compact has never been dissolved or modified in any authoritative manner, then it would appear that the states must have created the Constitution. And while it would be true to say that they have a legal status *in* the Constitution, it would not follow that they have their legal status *from* the Constitution. South Carolina claimed a lawful right, both to nullify federal laws and to secede. Yet South Carolina did not say that the right to secede was a right granted *by* the Constitution. Rather did it hold that the rights in question were rights which it had reserved, rights which had not been delegated, and which were necessary incidents of the sovereignty which had been vested in the state by the social compact of its citizens.[8] And let us repeat, that it was conceded on all sides that the social compact was the vital principle of free government, and that such compact was the origin both of sovereignty and of political obligation. Thus, the Carolinians continue,

> The States are [the] authors [of the Constitution]; their power created it; their voice clothed it with authority; the Government it formed is in reality their Government; and the Union, of which it is the bond, is a Union of States, and not of individuals.[9]

In the same letter to Daniel Webster, Madison distinguished the pure nationalist theory of the Constitution, according to which the Union is a compact of the American people taken as an aggregate of individuals, from that theory which holds that the social compact was made solely at the level of the states. In the former case, he observes, the dissolution of

[8] "If we are asked upon what ground we place the right to resist a particular law of Congress, and yet regard ourselves as a constituent member of the Union, we answer, the ground of the compact. [Note this refers to the constitutional compact between the states, not the social compact proper.] We do not choose . . . to recur to what are called our natural rights, or the right of revolution. We claim to nullify by a more imposing title. We claim it as a constitutional right, not meaning, as some have imagined, that we derive the right from the constitution . . . it being distinctly understood, at the time of ratifying the constitution, that the exercise of all sovereign rights, not agreed to be had conjointly, were to be exerted separately by the States. Though it be true that the provision in favor of what we call the reserved rights of the States was not necessary to secure to the States such reserved rights, yet the mere circumstance of its insertion in the instrument makes it as clear a constitutional provision as that of the Congress to raise armies or declare war. Any exercise of a right in conformity with a constitutional provision, we conceive to be a constitutional right, whether it be founded on an express grant of the right, or be included in a general reservation of undefined powers."

[9] *Register*, p. 169.

the Union would return every man to the state of nature; in the latter, each individual would still live under the protection of the government of his state. Yet Madison does not hesitate to say that the dissolution of the Union would leave the states intact.

> Secondly. It is a confederacy, because the extent of the powers of the Government depends not upon the people of the United States collectively, but upon the State Legislatures, or on the people of the separate States acting in their State conventions, each State being represented by a single vote.[10]

Here the Carolinians refer to the amending power, which they treat as the ultimate power, not merely of changing, but of expounding the Constitution. The amending power represents the ultimate constituent power of the people of all the states, as it is found within the framework of the Constitution. And this power, they point out, is not exercised by any majority of all the people collectively, as an aggregate of individuals, but by the people of the states, acting through the states, whether by the regular state legislatures or by conventions.

> It must never be forgotten that it is to the creating and to the controlling power that we are to look for the true character of the Federal Government, for the present controversy is not as to the sources from which the ordinary powers of government are drawn: these are partly federal and partly national. Nor is it relevant to consider upon whom these powers operate. In this last view, the Government, for limited purposes, is entirely national. The true question is, who are the parties to the compact? Who created it, and who can alter and destroy it? . . . We repeat that, as regards the foundation and extent of its powers, the Government of the United States is . . . a league between several sovereigns. . . .[11]

The foregoing clearly echoes Madison's summary view of the Constitution at the end of the The Federalist No. 39. But where Madison says that the Constitution is "in strictness, neither a national nor a federal Constitution, but a composition of both," the Carolinians say that it must, in strictness, be one or the other. And they say it is federal. The meaning that Professor Diamond says belonged to federalism before the new Constitution was drawn up is still the only meaning recognized by South Carolina in 1832. Their only visible concession to novelty is in their combining the word "federal" with the word "government." To what an extent this is a concession which undermines the integrity of their entire position remains to be seen.

Professor Berns, in his essay on "The Meaning of the Tenth Amendment," argues that this amendment did nothing to alter the distri-

[10] Ibid., p. 169.
[11] Ibid., p. 170.

bution of power already provided, nor did it do more than declare that all the powers not delegated had been reserved—a tautology or, at best, a truism. Yet Mr. Kilpatrick calls the Tenth Amendment "the key that unlocks every mystery of our form of government," and "the polar star of our fundamental charter." But Mr. Kilpatrick only echoes Jefferson who, in his opinion on the constitutionality of the first Bank of the United States, had declared that he considered "the foundation of the Constitution as laid on this ground—that all powers not delegated to the United States by the Constitution, nor prohibited by it to the States, are reserved to the States, or to the people." Later, in the Kentucky Resolutions, Jefferson again repeats the language of the Tenth Amendment—three times—in magisterial cadences that recall the opening paragraphs of the Declaration of Independence. It is difficult to reconcile this almost liturgical symbolism with the view of the Amendment as a mere truism, eminent as the authorities are who take this view. Yet Jefferson himself, in the Kentucky Resolutions, prefaces each recitation of the Amendment by saying that it is "true as a general principle" and yet that it must be "expressly declared." Thus Jefferson anticipates the South Carolina Convention's assertion that, on the one hand, the Amendment was not needed to establish the reserved powers of the states, and yet that by doing so, it made such powers "express," and therefore as unquestionable as the expressly enumerated powers. The Kentucky Resolutions seem to have planted in the political consciousness of the nation—or of a large part of it—the proposition that the Constitution *expressly* declares that all powers not delegated have been reserved. This in turn has led some commentators to read the Amendment *as if* it had said that all powers not *expressly* delegated had been reserved.

Yet there is an ambiguity concerning "the people" both in the Preamble and in the Tenth Amendment which lends a certain plausibility if not authority to such an error. We must recall that by the social compact theory *all* the "just powers" of government are delegated, those of the states no less than those of the United States. There are, in the Tenth Amendment, two reservations of powers: the first is "to the States respectively," and the second is "to the people." Thus the people have delegated some governmental powers to the United States, and some to the states, and those they have delegated to neither they have retained. But who are the people? The difficulty in answering this question is the greater because the word itself may take the same form, whether in the singular or the plural. If the "people" of the United States are conceived as united by the social compact only on the level of the individual states, then it is the combined "peoples" of the different states to whom we are referring. But then the Tenth Amendment should have read that the powers not delegated are reserved "to the States, or to the people of the

States respectively." Such a reading of the Tenth Amendment is, we maintain, plausible. And we should observe that it is no less a truism than that of Chief Justice Marshall or Justice Story—but it is an entirely different truism. And it is this truism which appears to be favored by Jefferson in the Kentucky Resolutions, when he wrote that the several states had constituted "a general government for special purposes . . . reserving each State to itself, the residuary mass of right to their own self-government." The phrase "each State . . . itself" seems to imply that sovereignty is reserved "to the people of each state."

The tension between the two alternative conceptions of the people of the United States may be seen by a backward look at the struggle over ratification of the Constitution. The opponents, known paradoxically as the antifederalists, had charged that the Constitution was designed to destroy the states, and to establish one "consolidated" government. For example, Robert Yates of New York, under the pseudonym of "Brutus," had declared in 1788 that

> . . . this Constitution, if it is ratified, will not be a compact entered into by the States, in their corporate capacities, but an agreement of the people of the United States, as one great body politic. . . .

And again:

> The first object declared to be in view is, "To form a perfect union." It is to be observed, it is not an union of states of bodies corporate; had this been the case the existence of the state governments, might have been secured. But it is a union of the people of the United States considered as one body, who are to ratify this constitution, if it is adopted.[12]

Thus Yates in 1788 gives the Constitution an interpretation exactly opposite to that given it by the South Carolina Convention in 1832. Of course, in the debate over ratification it was the interest of the opponents of the Constitution thus to characterize it, just as it was the interest of the advocates to deny this characterization. After ratification, these positions were in a certain sense reversed. Yet it was James Madison, as the leading nationalist in the Constitutional Convention, and the leading advocate of ratification in Virginia, who took the initiative in the First Congress to produce in the Bill of Rights such a statement as finally appeared as the Tenth Amendment. He did so largely to persuade the antifederalists that such fears as those expressed by Yates were unfounded, and that the delegated powers of the general government would not swallow up the functions of the governments of the states.

[12] Cecilia Kenyon (ed.), *The Antifederalists* (Indianapolis: The Bobbs-Merrill Company, Inc., 1966). p. 345.

It is of some interest to observe an error that Yates appears to make in his paraphrase of the Preamble. He cites its purpose "to form a perfect Union." Yet in the logic of the social compact theory, a "perfect union" differed from a "more perfect union" as much as "powers not delegated" differed from "powers not expressly delegated." Men in a state of nature, agreeing to form that union which is the body politic or civil society, do these two things. First, they agree unanimously to have such a body politic. This unanimity is necessary, because whoever does not agree is no part of the body; and whoever does agree is henceforward part of the body, and bound by its decisions. Second, in agreeing to be part of the body politic, each consents that the exercise of the executive power of the law of nature—the right to be judge in his own cause—is entirely or perfectly surrendered. It is this unanimous consent, and the concomitant surrender of the executive power of the law of nature, which is the vital principle of free society. It is this which makes civil society a voluntary association which yet may lawfully coerce. It is this which makes every civil society properly a "perfect union."

We see then that Yates's error was necessary to his thesis: namely, that the Constitution abolished the social compact, in virtue of which the states possessed the sovereignty which was reserved to them in the Articles of Confederation. At the same time, we must observe it *is* an error. A "more perfect union" can only be one in which a perfecting process is applied to a preexisting union. And that preexisting union was assuredly one, not of individuals, but of states. The ambiguity, the mystery, of the Tenth Amendment, and of the reserved powers of "the people" remains.

To the South Carolina Convention of 1832, the rights of nullification and secession were necessary to secure the right of the people to be governed only by those just powers to which they had consented, a right which had been solemnly declared on July 4, 1776. They were *lawful* as distinct from *revolutionary* safeguards, because they could be asserted by the people of the state, acting in accordance with the same peaceful and lawful procedures by which the state had ratified the Constitution. Yet the Carolinians were faced with their own admission that "the subject-matter of that compact [viz., the Constitution] was a Government." And if that government was the mere agent of sovereign states, with no inherent powers of its own, it was nonetheless the agent of *all* the states. An unqualified unilateral veto by one state upon the action of the agent of all, not only contradicted the idea inherent in government, it contradicted the right even of sovereign states to form a league with such an agent as South Carolina proclaimed the government of the United States to be. Under the guidance of John C. Calhoun, South Carolina adopted the theory of the concurrent majority, which was an attempt to strike some kind of a balance, between the idea of a mere league, and that of a national government representing "one people." The nullification of an act of the general government which was declared by a sovereign state to be the exercise of a power not delegated, was not in fact said to be absolute and unconditional. It was a suspensory rather than a final veto. If a constitutional convention were to propose the power under which the challenged act had been passed, and if such a proposal were to be adopted as an amendment by three-fourths of the states, by any of the procedures described in Article V of the Constitution, South Carolina would recede from its position. Or, rather, it would accept the power as being now authorized by the sovereign powers of the states.[13]

Yet this led to a difficulty hardly less than that for which it offered a solution. The Constitution had been adopted by *all* the states. And the South Carolina Convention had declared that this unanimous consent, and the provision in the Constitution that it was to be established only "between the States so ratifying" it, was evidence of the strongest character, that sovereignty remained in the states. It was this seventh article of the original Constitution, more than anything else in that document which justified them, in their own eyes, in asserting that the Tenth Amendment was not strictly necessary for securing the reserved rights of the states. Yet amendments might be made by three-fourths of the states. By what right might *three-fourths* now do what hitherto could rightfully be done only by *all?* In the state of nature, all must consent to form civil society; but from this unanimous consent arises the sovereign authority of the *majority.* The only way in which the social compact might authorize government other than that of the majority is by delegation from the sovereign majority. We may observe the difficulty faced by South Carolina, in maintaining the idea of state sovereignty, in the presence of the idea of the concurrent majority, in the following passage from Calhoun's draft of the South Carolina Exposition of 1828. This is the composition which contains the seminal ideas informing the work of the South Carolina Convention of 1832. The emphasis has been supplied to two crucial passages.

> ... by an express provision of the Constitution, it may be amended by three-fourths of the States; and thus each State, by assenting to the Constitution with this provision, *has modified its original right as a sovereign,* of making its individual consent necessary to any change in its political condition; and, by becoming a member of the Union, has placed this important power in the hands of three-fourths of the States—*in whom the highest power known to the Constitution actually resides.*

[13] *Register,* p. 167.

Professor Freehling has pointed out that the South Carolina legislature changed Calhoun's draft, so that in the published version "has modified its original right as a sovereign" became "has surrendered its original right as a sovereign"; and "in whom the highest power known to the Constitution actually resides" became "in which the sovereignty of the Union . . . does now actually reside."[14]

Now if sovereignty is indivisible, as the Convention of 1832 also declared (in accordance with what Calhoun had elsewhere maintained), then Calhoun's "modified" sovereignty had to become the "surrendered" sovereignty of the South Carolina legislature. Yet by the logic of the same theory, in virtue of which sovereignty is indivisible, it could not be given up to three-fourths of the states. If sovereignty had been surrendered, it must have been surrendered to the one people of the entire United States, who, by the consent, implicit or express, of the numerical majority might have authorized the three-fourths of the states to exercise the amending power.

But if sovereignty had been surrendered to the Union, then the sovereign power of the Union might be exercised "in all cases whatsoever." That is to say, three-fourths of the states, exercising the sovereignty residing in the majority of the people of the United States and embracing all their "reserved powers," might do anything which "to them shall seem most likely to effect their Safety and Happiness." A sovereign is by definition a source and not a subject of law. Yet we find it stipulated in Article V, as part of the amending power itself, "that no State, without its Consent, shall be deprived of its equal suffrage in the Senate." Given the presence of this stipulation within the amending article, equal force would seem to attach as well to the provision, in Article IV, that no new states might be formed by the junction of two or more states, without the consent of the states involved, as well as of the Congress. This of course would be necessary to prevent subdivisions or mergers from circumventing the guarantee of equal representation. There are many other features of the Constitution which might profitably be examined to see whether, either independently or as inferences from the ones just mentioned, they might be considered unamendable. Such would certainly include the declaration that "no religious test shall *ever* be required" as a qualification for office under the United States (emphasis supplied); as well as the guarantee by the United States to every state of "a Republican Form of Government." One might ask, of course, whether the concept of un-amendable provisions could stand in the face of a determination by three-fourths of the states to abolish them. But would it not violate every

---

[14] *Prelude to Civil War: The Nullification Controversy in South Carolina, 1816–1836* (New York: Harper and Row, 1965), pp. 167-68.

PARTLY FEDERAL, PARTLY NATIONAL 173

sense of constitutional propriety to amend the amending procedure itself, by anything less than unanimous consent? To suggest that an amendment might abolish the states is only to say that revolutionary changes might take place under the forms of the Constitution. But the Constitution as originally ratified and subsequently amended seems to have pledged, even against the constituent power of the people, as embodied in the amending article, to maintain the states in their prescribed constitutional role, as indestructible components of the Union. However flexibly this role might be interpreted, there would appear to be a design in the Constitution destined forever to prevent the people of the United States from becoming a mere numerical aggregate. It would prevent that people ever from becoming a mere number of individuals, as distinct from an organic composite of individuals in states. We would consider then that Vice-President Calhoun in 1828 was wiser than his revisers. He may indeed have been wiser than he himself was elsewhere, when he insisted more inflexibly upon the indivisibility of sovereignty. But he was not wiser than James Madison, the Father of the Constitution, who had seen since 1787 that the new government, although a composite of the federal and the national, was yet not reducible to either of these elements. The compact theory of the Constitution, as first set forth in the Kentucky and Virginia Resolutions, and appealed to so confidently by the nullifiers of 1832, did *not*, according to Madison, provide any authority for the concept of individual or separate state sovereignty.

In the following passage from his Proclamation against the nullifiers, President Jackson indicates something of the agreement as well as the difference between the positions then in conflict.

> It is true that the Governor of the State speaks of the submission of their grievances to a convention of all the States, which, he says, they "sincerely and anxiously seek and desire." Yet this obvious and constitutional mode of obtaining the sense of the other States on the construction of the federal compact, and amending it, if necessary, has never been attempted by those who have urged the State on to this destructive measure.[15]

Thus Jackson and the nullifiers *agreed* that a convention of all the states represented an authoritative mode of determining controverted points of constitutional construction. They *differed* concerning the lawfulness of nullification, as a device to compel the states to deliver their judgment in this mode. Yet in their agreement lay a recognition *both* of state sovereignty *and* of national supremacy. Neither side could escape from the implications of the other's position, because it was always, in some sense,

[15] *Register*, p. 185.

an element of their own. Jackson had imbibed, according to his own understanding, the doctrine of the Virginia and Kentucky Resolutions; and it is well to remember that he combined an ardent strict construc- tionism with the most thoroughgoing nationalism. Although Lincoln's career as a party politician prior to the repeal of the Missouri Compromise had been that of a Whig, it was the precedents established by Jackson, both of word and of deed, that he followed most closely in the secession crisis. And both Jackson and Lincoln were supported by Madison, in their denial that any ground whatever was to be found, for that "ingenious sophism" that led logically both in 1832 and 1861, to the destruction of the Union.

We have already seen that the idea of the concurrent majority implied a decisive modification of the idea of state sovereignty from its original purity. Nullification was, in fact, claimed as an inference from the sovereign right of three-fourths of the states to amend the Constitution, a right which itself was, at best, a kind of quasi-sovereignty. And secession, far from being the direct manifestation of unqualified state sovereignty, was itself a sanction for nullification, and therefore an inference from this inference. Every attempt by the Carolinians, whether in 1832 or 1860, to present the right of secession as a constitutional right, standing squarely on its own feet, rather than an indirect consequence of other rights, was hopelessly entangled in self-contradiction.

On the other hand, however, Jackson's reference to the Constitu- tion as "our social compact," if it were taken in the usual sense of that term, implying sovereignty in a numerical majority of the American people would equally lend itself to self-contradiction. As Madison was to point out to Edward Everett, in the letter that was published in the *North American Review* in 1832,[16] the government of the United States re- quired the active cooperation of the state governments, in the election or selection of all its branches, while the general government plays no role whatever in the selection of the state governments. Moreover, the states have a crucial role, by means of the federal Congress, in the impeachment, and the trial for impeachment, of the federal executive and judiciary, while the general government has no role in the removal of state officers. As long as the constitutional existence of the states is guaranteed, a considerable measure of state sovereignty necessarily accompanies it. Yet Madison denied, in 1830 and thereafter, that such sovereignty ever im- plied a right such as South Carolina attempted to assert, of a *single* state, to nullify the action of the government of the United States, unless reversed by the action of three-fourths of the states.

[16] Gaillard Hunt (ed.), *The Writings of James Madison* (New York: Putnam, 1910), 9: 383-403.

Madison was confronted, throughout the nullification crisis, with the language which he had used in 1798 and 1800, and which had been widely if erroneously regarded as supplying justification both for nullification and secession. Let us examine some of that language, and its bearing upon the controversy. The compact theory of the Constitution, which has been held to contain the essence of the doctrine of state sovereignty, appears in the Virginia Resolutions of 1798 as follows:

> That this Assembly doth explicitly and peremptorily declare that it views the powers of the Federal Government as resulting from the compact to which the states are parties, as limited by the plain sense and intention of the instrument constituting that compact; as no further valid than they are authorized by the grants enumerated in that compact, the states, who are parties thereto, have the right and are in duty bound to interpose for arresting the progress of the evil, and for maintaining within their respective limits the authorities, rights, and liberties appertaining to them.

In order to judge fairly what Madison meant by saying that the *states* were the parties to the federal compact, let us listen to the following account of the ambiguities of the word "state" in the Report of 1800.

> It is indeed true that the term "States" is sometimes used in a vague sense, and sometimes in different senses. . . .Thus it sometimes means the separate sections of territory occupied by the political societies within each; sometimes the particular governments established by those societies; sometimes those societies as organized into those particular governments; and, lastly, it means the people composing those political societies in their highest sovereign capacity.[17]

It is only in this *last* of the four enumerated senses that the word "state" has been used in the Virginia Resolutions. And as Madison then and thereafter argued, the *states* in their highest sovereign capacity are identical with the *people of the United States* in their highest sovereign capacity. For this people has no political existence, except as people of the respective states.

Madison argued in 1830 and thereafter that the Virginia Resolutions, in calling upon "the states . . . to interpose," had reference only to the states collectively. But that the states in their sovereign capacity constitute the highest tribunal known to the Constitution is at least as much a truism, as the proposition that all powers not delegated are reserved. Some difficulty may, however, attach to the use here of the word "tribunal." It may be objected that the states in their sovereign capacity do not constitute a tribunal, a term which ought to be reserved for such a body as the Supreme Court. Yet any doubts we might have on

[17] Ibid., 6: 348.

this point are resolved by Abraham Lincoln when, in his first inaugural address, he pronounced these magisterial lines:

> Why should there not be a patient confidence in the ultimate justice of the people? Is there any better, or equal hope, in the world? In our present differences, is either party without faith of being in the right? If the Almighty Ruler of nations, with his eternal truth and justice, be on your side of the North, or on yours of the South, that truth, and that justice, will surely prevail, by the judgment of this great tribunal, the American people.[18]

That the "American people" is the highest of all tribunals known to the Constitution, was then Lincoln's conviction no less than Madison's, notwithstanding the fact that Madison referred to this people, in its highest sovereign capacity, as "the states." It should be also borne in mind that Lincoln, no less than Madison in 1800, rejected the thesis that the Supreme Court was the tribunal in which questions of conflicting jurisdictions should have their final resolution. Madison put it thus in his Report.

> However true, therefore, it may be that the judicial department is, in all questions submitted to it by the forms of the Constitution, to decide in the last resort, this resort must necessarily be deemed the last in relation to the authorities of the other departments of the Government; not in relation to the rights of the parties to the constitutional compact, from which the judicial as well as the other departments hold their delegated trusts. On any other hypothesis, the delegation of judicial power would annul the authority delegating it; and the concurrence of this department with the others in usurped powers might subvert forever and beyond the possible reach of any rightful remedy, the very Constitution which all were instituted to preserve.[19]

This denial of the political, as distinct from the legal supremacy of the Court, was later expressed by Lincoln thus:

> I do not forget the position assumed by some, that constitutional questions are to be decided by the Supreme Court; nor do I deny that such decisions must be binding in any case. . . . At the same time the candid citizen must confess that if the policy of the government, upon vital questions, affecting the whole people, is to be irrevocably fixed by decisions of the Supreme Court, the instant they are made, in ordinary litigation between parties, in personal actions, the people will have ceased, to be their own rulers, having, to that extent, practically resigned their government, into the hands of that eminent tribunal.[20]

We must recall here that, in 1861, it was the seceding states of the South that had demanded that the opinion of the Supreme Court, delivered by

[18] Basler (ed.), *Abraham Lincoln*, 4: 270.
[19] Hunt (ed.), *James Madison*, 6:352.
[20] Basler (ed.), *Abraham Lincoln*, 4: 268.

Chief Justice Taney in the case of Dred Scott, be accepted as a final judgment as to the true meaning of the Constitution, and binding as such upon the states and upon the people. In their view, the states that had cast their votes for Abraham Lincoln in 1860, had by this fact manifested a determination not to be bound by the Constitution. For Lincoln had been elected upon a platform pledged to the federal prohibition of slavery in the territories, after the Court had declared that legislation to this end was unconstitutional.

Madison, Jackson, and Lincoln all held to the position that the primary remedy for real or alleged usurpations by governments, whether state or federal, was in changing the officers of those governments by free elections. Although the principal charge made against the Sedition Act, especially in Madison's Report, was that it undermined the integrity of the electoral process, yet in the end Madison declared that the Resolutions were "expressions of opinion, unaccompanied with any other effect than what they may produce on opinion by exciting reflection." He contrasted them with the "expositions of the judiciary" which "are carried into immediate effect by force." If the "interposition" referred to in the Resolutions could not be carried into effect by any legal compulsion, then they could have had nothing in common with the nullification declared by South Carolina in 1832. The purpose of the Virginia Resolutions was to excite those reflections that might result either in the political defeat of the authors of the offending acts, or in amendments to the Constitution. We may note that Lincoln, in 1861, besides defending the sovereign right of the people, by the electoral process, to overrule the Supreme Court's opinions, also endorsed the idea of a constitutional amendment—or amendments—to clarify points of disputed construction. And he preferred, he said, the convention mode,

in that it allows amendments to originate with the people themselves, instead of only permitting them to take or reject propositions originated by others, not especially chosen for the purpose. . . .[21]

We would particularly call attention to the expression "the people themselves" in a context unmistakably similar to, if not identical with, that in which Madison elsewhere refers to the states in their sovereign capacity.

Throughout American history—at least since July 4, 1776—it has been conceded that all people everywhere have the right to resist intolerable oppression. This is a right which belongs not only to the people of a state, but of any part of a state. Indeed, it belongs to each individual, although it is a right which is seldom valuable to individuals, since they seldom have the power to make resistance effective. But this right—the

[21] Ibid., 4: 270.

right of revolution—is a right paramount to the Constitution, and to all positive laws whatever. It is a natural right. In his inaugural address Lincoln said that

> If, by the mere force of numbers, a majority should deprive a minority of any clearly written constitutional right, it might, in a moral point of view, justify revolution—certainly would, if such a right were a vital one.[22]

As James Madison put it in a paper he wrote on sovereignty,[23] a majority may do anything that could *rightfully* be done by the unanimous concurrence of all the members of a civil society. The rule of the majority being a substitute for unanimity, although itself arising from unanimity, requires that it be exercised only for ends to which all have consented. Clearly, the degradation of the minority cannot be one of those ends. Majority rule itself then cannot be understood as the rule of mere numbers; it must be the rule of numbers for certain ends. And numbers must then be assembled in a certain way, if they are to be presumed restrained by the ends for which majority rule was instituted. It was then not a majority simply, whose rule Lincoln endorsed in 1861, but one

> held in restraint by constitutional checks and limitations, and always changing easily, with deliberate changes of popular opinions and sentiments. . . .[24]

Such a majority is "the only sovereign of a free people." State rights, as one of the devices to qualify the "mere force of numbers," were, to Lincoln no less than to Madison, an essential feature of that constitutional majority which made the voice of the American people in some sense the voice of God.

The Kentucky Resolutions differ from those of Virginia in an important respect, from which many consequences have followed. Much of the confusion, both as to their meaning, and that of Virginia's, are due to this difference. While Madison took great pains, in the great Report of 1800, to clarify Virginia's resolves of 1798, prudence forbade that he comment openly upon the differences that we know he perceived between the resolutions he had drawn, and those that Jefferson had secretly drawn for Kentucky. Since the Kentucky Resolutions were published first (November 16, 1798), there has been a tendency then and since to read Virginia's (December 24, 1798) as if they expressed identical views. According to the resolutions drawn by Madison, the Constitution is a compact "to which the States are parties." That is, the states have entered

[22] Ibid., 4: 267.
[23] Hunt (ed.), *James Madison*, 9: 570.
[24] Basler (ed.), *Abraham Lincoln*, 4: 268.

a compact analogous to that entered into by individuals in a state of nature. As the subject of the agreement is a *government*, the states are bound by the *lex majoris partis*, as the *pars major* is defined in the instrument.[25] If the government established by the states—that is, by the people of the states in their highest sovereign capacity—usurps powers not delegated to it, then recourse to the sovereign is possible under the Constitution by any of the modes prescribed therein. But any attempt by one state, or even the people of one state in their highest sovereign capacity, to decide for all, is itself an act of usurpation. As Madison points out, over and over again, by adopting the Constitution of the United States, the people of each state formed part of a single nation, as they formed part of a single government, for the purposes specified—or enumerated—in the compact uniting them. The very equality of rights of the states, both as contracting parties whose unanimous consent was required to bring the Constitution into operation, and whose continuous cooperation was necessary to keep the government in operation under the Constitution, made it inadmissible either that one or one-fourth plus one decide for all. The doctrine of the concurrent majority, Madison noted, reverses the logic of the amending clause. Instead of three-fourths deciding for all, one-fourth plus one finally decides, *after* one has completely arrested the motion of the government. But no free government can recognize the permanent rule of the minority. And the right of secession, Madison noted long before Lincoln, leads to the destruction of the rights, not only of the majority, but of the minority as well. "An inference from the doctrine that a single State has the right to secede at will from the rest," he wrote in 1833,

> is that the rest would have an equal right to secede from it; in other words, to turn it, against its will, out of its union with them. Such a doctrine would not, till of late, have been palatable anywhere, and nowhere less so than where it is now most contended for.[26]

These words have a powerful echo in Lincoln's message to Congress of July 4, 1861.

> If all the States, save one, should assert the power to *drive* that one out of the Union, it is presumed that the whole class of seceder politicians would at once deny the power, and denounce the act as the greatest outrage upon State rights. But suppose that precisely the same act, instead of being called "driving the one out," should be called "the seceding of the others from that one," it would be exactly what the seceders claim to do.[27]

[25] Cf. Hunt (ed.), *James Madison*, 9: 570.
[26] Ibid., 9: 497.
[27] Basler (ed.), *Abraham Lincoln*, 4: 436.

In the Kentucky Resolutions, the role of an individual state, as a member of the Union, is presented differently. As in the Virginia Resolutions, the Constitution is a compact, but it is a compact to which

> each state acceded as a State, and is an integral party, its co-States forming, as to itself, the other party. . . .

Whereas Madison conceived each state, by adopting the Constitution, to place itself under the rule of the majority—as majority rule was defined in the Constitution—Jefferson conceived of each state as one of two parties, the other states collectively forming the other party. And of course, where there are only two parties, majority rule is impossible. In fact, the parties remain, in the decisive sense, in the state of nature. As Jefferson puts it,

> . . . the government created by this compact was not made the exclusive or final judge of the extent of the powers delegated to itself; since that would have made its discretion, and not the Constitution, the measure of its powers. . . .[28]

Jefferson here lays a foundation for South Carolina's errors, by calling the creation of the compact a "government," while leaving the "final judge" of its powers in a state of nature, as he does when he declares

> . . . that as in all other cases of compact among parties having no common Judge, *each party has an equal right to judge for itself, as well of infractions as of the mode and measure of redress.*[29]

There is a relationship of ideas here which is not easy to reconcile within a framework of consistency. Jefferson conceives of a relationship between states and government, which is that of principal and agent. But there can be no adversary relationship between principal and agent, since there is no equality, such as is presupposed in an adversary relationship. The only adversary relationship conceivable is between the individual state and its "co-states." Yet the co-states are presented by Jefferson, not as adversaries, but as partners necessarily having the same interest in retaining all powers not delegated to their common agent. In the ninth resolution, Jefferson had Kentucky declare that

> this commonwealth is determined, as it doubts not its co-States are, tamely to submit to undelegated and consequently unlimited powers in no man or body of men on earth. . . .[30]

[28] Henry S. Commager (ed.), *Documents of American History* (New York: Appleton, 1963), 1: 178.
[29] Ibid., 1: 179.
[30] Ibid.

Now of course the very idea of government based upon the consent of the governed at once excludes the idea of submission to powers not delegated—that is, not consented to—and to the idea of having "no common judge." Jefferson seems to believe that while the states have created a government for certain enumerated purposes, that in all "cases not made federal" the states remain in a state of nature. In these cases not made federal, the same ninth resolution declares, the states have a "natural right" to declare the acts of their common government "void and of no force." But neither in the resolutions of 1798 or those of 1799, which employed the fatal word "nullification," did Kentucky assert unequivocally, a right to *act* upon its declaration. The 1798 resolutions arrive finally at what must have been a lame conclusion to the nullifiers, for they ask at the end only that the co-states "unite with this Commonwealth in requesting . . . the repeal at the next session of Congress" of the offending acts. While those of 1799, even while asserting nullification—which is nowhere defined—as a "rightful remedy," continue by declaring that Kentucky will nonetheless "bow to the laws of the Union."

The mystery of Jefferson's doctrine in the Kentucky Resolutions may perhaps be rendered somewhat less obscure by a reference provided by Madison in one of his letters, written in 1832. In this letter Madison is emphatic upon the point to which we have already referred, namely, that "In the Virginia Resolutions and Report, the *plural* number, *States,* is in *every* instance used where reference is made to the authority which presided over the Government." The Kentucky Resolutions, however, "being less guarded have been more easily perverted."

> It is remarkable how closely the nullifiers who make the name of Mr. Jefferson the pedestal for their colossal heresy, shut their eyes and lips, whenever his authority is ever so clearly and emphatically against them. You have noticed what he says in his letters to Monroe and Carrington. . . .[31]

We give the references in Jefferson's own words, instead of Madison's summary. To Carrington, Jefferson wrote from Paris, in 1787, in defense of the Articles of Confederation.

> But with all the imperfections of our present government, it is, without comparison, the best existing, or that ever did exist. . . . It has so often been said, as to be generally believed, that Congress have no power by the Confederation, to enforce anything: for example, contributions of money. It was not necessary to give them that power expressly; they have it by a law of nature. When two parties make a compact, there results to each a power of compelling the other to execute it. Compulsion was never so easy as in our case, where a single frigate

[31] Hunt (ed.), *James Madison,* 9: 491.

would soon levy on the commerce of any State the deficiency of its contributions. . . .[32]

Earlier, Jefferson had written to Monroe in a similar vein.

The States must see the rod; perhaps it must be felt by some one of them. . . . Every rational citizen must wish to see an effective instrument of coercion. . . .[33]

A fair conclusion from these letters—certainly the one drawn by Madison—is that Jefferson, while seeing both the Constitution and the earlier confederation as a compact in which there were but two parties, saw also a right of compulsion of the weaker by the stronger party, a right which it possessed by the law of nature. The natural right referred to in the Kentucky Resolutions becomes then a *reminder* to the co-states of their common interest in keeping the common government within the boundaries of its delegated powers, and of preserving the states in the possession of all their reserved powers. Yet if the co-states refuse to concur with the protesting state, that the common government has usurped powers not delegated, the protesting state has no further recourse except revolution. And if it chooses to exercise this ultimate right, the co-states assuredly have an equal right under the law of nature to coerce it. The differences between Jefferson and Madison in 1798 are at bottom the same as their differences in 1787. Jefferson saw the law of nature as impliedly giving powers to the Congress of the Confederation, which made the revision or replacement of the Articles less urgent—to put it mildly— than Madison believed it to be. The appeal to the law of nature, as an element in the continuous implementation of the law of the Constitution, was a constant feature of Jefferson's thought. The difference between the Virginia and Kentucky Resolutions can, perhaps, be best seen by considering Madison's critique of Jefferson's 1783 draft of a constitution for Virginia, as Madison set it forth in *The Federalist* No. 49. It would take us beyond our present purpose to consider this here, except to note that Madison thought the constant appeal to the natural rights of the people dangerous to the stability of civil society. Yet there can be no doubt that Jackson and Lincoln had as much sanction for using force against South Carolina in 1833 and in 1861 from the Jeffersonian as from the Madisonian standpoint.

[32] Julian P. Boyd (ed.), *The Papers of Thomas Jefferson* (Princeton, N.J.: Princeton University Press, 1950–), 11: 678.

[33] Ibid., 10: 225. The Boyd edition reads "national" instead of "rational," as in the older editions. It seems certain to us that Jefferson wrote "rational," although the context does suggest that a "rational" citizen would take a "national" point of view.

It was Jefferson, not Madison, who had recourse to the law of nature, as a power necessarily implied—even if not expressly mentioned—in constitutions. Nevertheless, Madison had no less keen an appreciation than Jefferson of the importance of the law of nature in the foundation of constitutions and of governments. It is instructive therefore to consider once more that section of the Constitution to which South Carolina appealed, as the most incontrovertible evidence of state sovereignty. We refer of course, to Article VII, which declares that it requires the ratifications of nine states "for the establishment of this Constitution between the States so ratifying the same." It is a Constitution between *states,* not between *individuals,* and the states have not expressly divested themselves of their sovereignty, so that their sovereignty must remain among their reserved powers—thus ran the most fundamental of all South Carolina's theses. How did James Madison regard this evidence in 1787? We have already noted that he agreed with South Carolina, to the extent that he conceded that "no political relation" could "subsist between the assenting and dissenting States." Yet, he continued, in *The Federalist* No. 43, "The claims of justice, both on one side and on the other, will be in force, and must be fulfilled." How the claims of justice are to be regarded in this context, Madison had suggested earlier in the same number, by referring "to the great principle of self-preservation . . . to the transcendent law of nature and of nature's God. . . ." More explicit information on the practical conclusions to be drawn from the existence of a transcendent law of nature must be referred to the whole body of argument in *The Federalist* concerning, not merely the utility, but the absolute necessity of a firm Union, to the safety, no less than the happiness, of the United States. While it was true, therefore, that during the interval between the time that the new government went into operation, and the time the Constitution was ratified by Rhode Island and North Carolina, the latter were, in a certain sense, foreign states, this was more a formal than a substantive truth. For Rhode Island and North Carolina could never have acted upon their hypothetical independence. The question of what would have happened to them if they had not ratified the Constitution is, in fact, identical with the question of what would have happened had they attempted to form alliances with European powers. Three times, in *The Federalist* No. 43, Madison refers to this question as a "delicate" one, of which "the flattering prospect of its being merely hypothetical forbids an over-curious discussion." When the question ceased to be hypothetical in 1861, Lincoln only followed the dictates of Madison and of Jackson when he declared, "I hold, that in contemplation of universal law, and of the Constitution, the Union of these states is perpetual." And that law, a law at once that of the Constitution and of nature, a law upon which the safety and happiness of the entire United States depended, was enforced.

9 | CRISIS OF THE HOUSE DIVIDED
A New Introduction

Crisis of the House Divided was completed in the spring of 1958, on the eve of the centennial of the Lincoln-Douglas debates. Among the purposes of the book was a demonstration of the vitality of the issues with which the debaters were concerned. It is certainly worth more than a passing observation that the revolution in the status of Negro Americans in the years following the centennial, and following the first publication of this book, has been less drastic only than that which occurred in the years following the original debates. Perhaps, however, it would be better to refer to the changes in American citizenship rather than to the change in the status of a particular group. Such drastic alterations as occurred either in the 1860s or in the 1960s affect, of necessity, all the citizens and the nature of their citizenship. It is hoped that a book such as this might assist in the understanding of the purport of the changes that occurred after, as well as before, it was written.

Crisis of the House Divided was received, on the whole, with a gratifying acceptance of its interpretation of the political thought both of Lincoln and of Douglas. My attacks upon some members of the historians' guild—in which I made no claim to membership—was regarded by some of them as unnecessarily acerb. Rereading some of these pages a decade and a half after they were written, I find myself in occasional agreement with my critics. Yet I thought—and think—it was necessary to make it clear that the issues at stake in the Lincoln-Douglas debates were still the fundamental issues in American politics, and that they underlay the interpretation of the debates themselves. I felt, with Lord Charnwood, that I should not "shrink too timidly from the display of a partisanship which, on one side or the other, it would be insensate not to feel." With him, I felt, "the true obligation of impartiality is that [one] should conceal no fact which, in [one's] own mind, tells against his views."[1]

Upon one point, I believe, the issues that divided me from the historical revisionists transcended the division within the debates themselves. They had maintained that the debates were not a serious effort to come to grips with a serious problem. Yet Lincoln and Douglas had taken

Reprinted by the kind permission of the publisher from Harry Jaffa, *Crisis of the House Divided* (1959; reprinted., Seattle, Wash.: University of Washington Press, 1973).

[1] Godfrey Rathbone Benson (Lord Charnwood), *Abraham Lincoln*, Pocket Books Edition, p. 2.

each other with the utmost seriousness, and notwithstanding the cut and thrust of the debates, had treated each other's policies and arguments with respect. The revisionist thesis treated the entire antebellum controversy over the territories, within the Democratic Party no less than between Democrats and Republicans, as a debate over "an imaginary Negro in an impossible place." This implied a radical depreciation of the politics of popular government altogether, as it involved a condemnation of the political perceptions of every important segment of political opinion of the generation that had, as these historians thought, blundered into civil war.

To condemn a "blundering generation" implies, of course, a possibility of not blundering. Neither he who gives judgment in the courtroom nor he who sits in judgment for posterity presumes to condemn for what it was not in the power of the accused to avoid. Yet I did not think that these historical judges had understood the jurisprudence of their judgments. They had adopted a facile superiority to their subject that, when examined, turned out to be little more than the advantage of hindsight. They believed that slavery would not go into the territories because it did not go there, and they implied that the men of the 1850s should have known as much. Had they been wiser members of their own guild, they would have known that it was their responsibility to understand the past, as nearly as possible, exactly as it understood itself, before attempting to understand it differently or better. By following the logic of Lincoln and Douglas as they confronted an undetermined and therefore unknowable future, I believe I was able to demonstrate how patriotic and moderate men could still disagree and how they could, from good motives and with sober judgment, yet lead the nation down a road upon which war might become the only means of honorable resolution.

It seemed to me that the proper way to explicate a debate was to adopt, however provisionally, the viewpoint of the debaters themselves. And it seemed that the Socratic method—and in particular its medieval form, the disputed question—was an apt model for this purpose. In the *Summa Theologica,* Thomas Aquinas asks a question, proposes an answer, and then gives both the objections to that answer and the replies to the objections. In each case Thomas gives a response drawn from authority and then his own argument in support of that response. Yet the objections elaborate the contentions on the other side, usually with such fullness that the attentive scholar may perceive stronger ground than that occupied by Thomas himself. At any rate, I found in this procedure an openness to conflicting opinions for which I could find few, if any, analogues in our own more liberal age.

But Thomas Aquinas differed from contemporary authorities not only in the habit of stating the arguments on both sides of every question. He had done so in the conviction that there was a possibility of reaching reasonable opinions as to where the truth lay in most cases if the arguments on the contrary were set forth with sufficient fullness and perspicacity. It was above all this belief in the power of reason to guide judgment, and therefore to guide human life, not only concerning the true and the false, but concerning the good and the bad, and the just and the unjust, that distinguished his scholarship and the tradition it represented. It also occurred to me that Thomas Aquinas and Thomas Jefferson, whatever their differences, shared a belief concerning the relationship of political philosophy to political authority that neither shared with, let us say, the last ten presidents of the American Political Science Association. It seemed to me that both believed it was the task of political philosophy to articulate the principles of political right, and therefore to teach the teachers of legislators, of citizens, and of statesmen the principles in virtue of which political power becomes political authority.

The Lincoln-Douglas debates are concerned, in the main, with one great practical and one great theoretical question. The practical question was resolved into the constitutional issue of whether federal authority may, and the political issue of whether it should, be employed to keep slavery out of the organized federal territories. The theoretical question was whether slavery was or was not inconsistent with the nature of republican government; that is, whether it was or was not destructive of their own rights for any people to vote in favor of establishing slavery as one of their domestic institutions. In examining these questions within this book, I was of course interested in discovering the truth as to what exactly Lincoln and Douglas, as well as their eminent contemporaries, had said and thought about them. But I did so not as one interested primarily in the past, but as one interested in political truth. I was interested in the political truth partly for its own sake, but also because I wished myself to know, and to teach others, the principles of just government. Lincoln had said that, in a government like ours, public sentiment was everything and that he who could change public sentiment could change the government, practically speaking, just so much. I was aware that I was a member of that comparatively small class, the university professoriate, that today is the decisive source of the ruling opinions in our country. Primary and secondary teachers, the mass media, and the elected officials are usually the retailers of ideas that come in the first place from the universities, and in particular from the graduate schools. Here is where the teachers of the teachers are taught. We have become the ultimate source of change in the regime. I might perhaps have rejoiced somewhat more than I did in the contemplation of this power had it seemed that its exercise had been salutary. But changes generated by this class have been in the direction of denying the existence of any objective standards whatever. This meant denying that the exercise of political power might be, and therefore that it ought to be, governed by any truths external to the will of those who wielded power. In short, the traditional idea that political power is to be distinguished from political authority, by the light of the distinction between force and right, had come to be regarded within the academy as obsolete.

In the discipline of political science, a distinction was made between normative theory, which dealt with "values," and empirical theory, which dealt with "facts." Distinctions such as "the just powers of government," like the rights to "life, liberty, and the pursuit of happiness," were "values." That is to say, they were the preferences of those who had established this government, and to refer them to the "laws of Nature and of Nature's God" was a rhetorical redundancy adding only emphasis to a preference. It was thought to be a delusion, however, to believe that one might actually arrive at a judgment as to whether a government was or was not legitimate by examining whether that government was or was not in accordance with the laws of nature. As far as I know, *Crisis of the House Divided* is the first book to take seriously the question of whether the laws of nature mentioned in the Declaration did in fact exist, and therefore whether Lincoln or Douglas was correct in asserting that his policy, and not his opponent's, squared with the teaching of that Declaration.

Modern social science appears to know neither God nor nature. The articulation of the world, in virtue of which it is a world and not an undifferentiated substratum, has disappeared from its view. The abolition of God and nature has therefore been accompanied by the abolition of that correlative concept, man, from this same world. The only apparent link between the blankly unarticulated universe—or multiverse—which has become the ground of the scientific outlook, and the stately, ordered universe of the Founders seems to lie in the word "equality." Modern social science, at least in its American variant, finds itself committed to equality. The civil rights revolution, to which we have made reference, was largely inspired by this commitment. Evidence from a test devised by a social psychologist concerning how children reacted in play to white and black dolls was an important factor in convincing the Supreme Court of the United States in 1954 that separate schools could not be equal. Certainly the schools in question *were* unequal, and the decision of the court was right. But the opinion of the court was most unwise, because it gave credit to the opinion that the *feeling* of equality was identical to equality itself. The radical subjectivity of the social sciences with respect to what it called "values" had crept into the law, and into the opinion upon which the law rested. For this reason the civil rights revolution, which was for the most part a proper implementation of the Fourteenth and Fifteenth Amendments, quickly passed over into a revolution of black power. The demands of this new revolution often went far beyond the scope of law, and sometimes were in flat contradiction to the principles of the earlier demands for full equality under law. But the feeling of inequality had become a well-nigh irresistible principle of ultimate appeal. The utopianism and the intolerance of the new politics—the success of which would surely spell the end of constitutional democracy—was rooted in the social scientism of the academy.

In his speech on the Dred Scott decision Lincoln said, in opposition to Chief Justice Taney, that the rights enunciated in the Declaration of Independence were understood by its authors to apply to all men, Negroes included. That Negroes in the United States were not then enjoying the rights with which they had been endowed by God and nature did not mean therefore that they were not understood to possess them. If equal rights were not then enjoyed by Negroes, said Lincoln, neither were they enjoyed by all whites. The Declaration, said Lincoln, meant to declare the *right* so that *enforcement* might follow, as fast as circumstances should permit. It seemed not to have occurred to the Supreme Court in 1954, or to the lawyers who prepared the briefs upon which the court relied, that changing circumstances might reasonably elicit constructive interpretations of old principles. By failing to recognize that a change in circumstances does not of necessity imply a change in the principle applied to the circumstances, the court gave credit to the opinion that the Constitution is not in fact based upon any unchanging principles at all. The great Civil Rights Acts of 1964 and 1965 were then seen by contemporary social science merely as registers of the pressures generated by the protest movements, including those arising from civil disobedience. And the protest movements were seen simply as the friction of oppressive social conditions.

Of course, no sensible observer failed to see these causes at work; but neither could he fail to see a successful appeal to the conscience of the nation. The social scientists did not assist the observer in explaining why similar protests, at about the same time, in eastern Europe and in the Soviet Union resulted in brutal repression. It was therefore not surprising, however tragic the error, that the fulfillment in law of so much of the original promise of equality should have been followed not by a strengthened belief in the rule of law, but by a widespread tendency to regard the distinction between law and force as a myth. This tendency reached a kind of climax in 1968 in the report of the President's Commission on Crime and Civil Disorder, when chief blame for the urban rioting was placed upon white racism, and the endemic character of that racism was held to be exhibited above all in the fact that the Declaration of Independence had failed to include within its scope the members of the Negro race! Taney's opinion in the case of Dred Scott—that the Founders believed that Negroes had no rights which white men were bound to respect—had now become the hallmark of official liberalism. Nowhere in the report is there any awareness that Lincoln had opposed both Taney and Douglas (among others) in this reading of the Declaration. The experts upon whom the commission confidently relied were too committed to the subjectivity of all values to bother with the historical debate.

It is a striking fact that the proponents of black power in the 1960s and 1970s rely upon the same evidence for their view of the Founders as did Taney and Douglas. That is, they argue that the authors of the Declaration could not have meant what they said and still have continued to hold slaves or have failed to promote political and social equality for free Negroes. On one level Lincoln's rebuttal was sufficient— that the enjoyment of rights enunciated in the Declaration was a goal to be pursued and not a fact to be assumed. It is certainly true that racial prejudice—not, incidentally, "white racism"—has always constituted an obstacle here to equal justice under law. Indeed, prejudices come to enjoy authority in a free society precisely because the government of such a society does rest upon the opinion of the governed. *Crisis of the House Divided* is, I believe, the first study to point to the comprehensive character of Lincoln's understanding of the teaching of the Declaration and to the presence therein of a tension between equality and consent. This tension must perforce engender conflicts among those whose understanding was less capacious than Lincoln's. But free government would be an absurdity did it require citizens all like Abraham Lincoln; yet it would be an impossibility if it could not from time to time find leaders with something of his understanding. Lincoln demonstrates that the obstacles to the fulfillment of the promise contained in the Declaration do not detract from the validity of that promise: those obstacles are elements of the same nature which pronounces men to be equal in their rights. We could not wish away the nature without wishing away the rights.

The Declaration not only implies what are the goals to be sought with the consent of the governed in a free society; it also states a theory of political obligation. Indeed, that is the immediate purpose of the document. Yet it is fair to test the authors of the Declaration by this very theory. We would be right to condemn them for inconsistency, or for not meaning (or understanding) what they said, if they failed this test. But let us be clear as to what the test is. In the Declaration, the Continental Congress says that their political bands with Great Britain and the British Crown are dissolved because of evidence of an intention to establish despotic rule over the colonies. In other words, political obligation is at an end where despotism—that is, slavery—begins. But did any of those who held the doctrines of the Declaration ever maintain that their slaves had a duty to be slaves and to serve as slaves? That some may have found it convenient to keep slaves, or that they may have known no way to emancipate their slaves, except at a loss or risk they did not feel obliged to pay, is nothing to the purpose. Statesmen of the Confederacy in 1861 declared slavery and the theory of racial inequality to be the "cornerstone" of their regime. But when the cornerstone theory was enunciated, it was done with the explicit rejection of the teaching of Jefferson and the doctrine of the Revolution. But I know of no evidence yet brought forward by anyone to show that Jefferson or Adams or Franklin or any other subscriber among the Founders to the doctrine of universal human rights thought either that the Negro was not a man or that, being human, there was any argument which ought to have persuaded him to be a slave. In a passage that Lincoln loved to quote, Jefferson wrote, "Indeed I tremble for my country when I reflect that God is just." And in considering a possible slave revolt, Jefferson declared that "the Almighty has no attribute which can take side with us in such a contest."[2]

The Civil War of 1861–65 had its roots in many things. Paramount, however, was the attenuation of the convictions with respect to a human freedom, rooted in the laws of nature and of nature's God, that had inspired the Revolution. Since *Crisis of The House Divided* was first written, we have witnessed great constructive steps carrying forward the impulse of the "new birth of freedom" declared at Gettysburg. Let us hope that the solid progress toward fulfilling the original promise of "freedom to all" may not be undone by reason of the rejection once again of those convictions which are their only sure foundation. Let us recall that it was the *cognoscenti* of the last century who were so confident that the progress of science had rendered obsolete the original teachings of equality.

[2] Saul K. Padover (comp.), *The Complete Jefferson* (New York: Tudor Publishing Company, 1943), query 18, p. 677.

10 | TOM SAWYER
Hero of Middle America

In the last chapter of *Tom Sawyer* Becky tells her father, in strict confidence, how Tom had taken her whipping in school: " . . . the Judge was visibly moved; and when she pleaded grace for the mighty lie which Tom had told in order to shift that whipping from her shoulders to his own, the Judge said with a fine outburst that it was a noble, a generous, a magnanimous lie—a lie that was worthy to hold up its head and march down through history breast to breast with George Washington's lauded Truth about the hatchet."

Tom Sawyer, master of the noble lie, is the master figure of American literature, the character in whom, more than in any other, Americans fancy themselves to be reflected and idealized. Not Captain Ahab, pursuing the great white whale, or Walter Mitty at the bridge of the destroyer, but Tom Sawyer playing hooky comes closest to our aspirations for glory. To be described as having a "Tom Sawyer grin" is an accolade of immeasurable value to any rising politician. In recent years the man to whom this epithet was most frequently applied was the late president, General of the Army Dwight D. Eisenhower. It is a curious revelation of the American soul that the reflection of his Kansas childhood in his boyish smile and wave of the arms conveyed more of the reassurance the republic sought from his leadership than any specific achievement of his later life. We are a democratic people, and democracies love equality above all else, as Alexis de Tocqueville so forcefully pointed out so long ago. We tend to equalize the distinctions based upon wealth and birth, but we tend also to equalize those based upon age. Where else is it considered an achievement not to be able to tell the mother from the daughter—or the grandmother from the granddaughter? It is nature's way of providing immortality that a father should find in his son signs of his own qualities and characteristics. But it is part of democracy's quest for immortality to seek signs of its childhood in its elders. The ancients celebrated the strength that comes with maturity and the wisdom that comes with age. But we moderns turn instead to the cleverness and charm—if not the innocence—of the young. In part this follows from our belief in science and progress. "When I contemplate the immense advances in science and discoveries in the arts which have been made within the

Reprinted by the kind permission of the publisher from *Interpretation* 2, no. 3 (Spring 1972): 194-226.

period of my life," wrote Jefferson in 1818, "I look forward with confidence to equal advances by the present generation, and have no doubt they will consequently be as much wiser than we have been as we than our fathers were, and they than the burners of witches."[1] As a nation we seem early to have been committed to a depreciation of ancestral wisdom and to an elevation of the young that reverses the order of nature. Tom Sawyer had no father. Aunt Polly tells us that he is her dead sister's son; but no allusion of any kind is ever made to his paternity. Even Huck Finn had a father, albeit the town drunk. Tom is the new boy, if not the new man, par excellence. "Tom Sawyer's Gang," whose formation is the culminating event, or conclusion, of the novel, is in fact the United States, whose founding or refounding is described symbolically within the framework of the plot. The democratization of the republic requires a juvenile hero to replace the father figure of Washington. We know of course that the "lauded Truth about the hatchet" was Parson Weems's invention, just as we know that Judge Thatcher is utterly deceived as to the generosity of Tom's lie. But Judge Thatcher's declared intention, to send Tom first to the National Military Academy and then to the best law school in the country, indicates that even he comprehends somehow that Tom's destiny is that of a guardian of the democratic republic. What Judge Thatcher fails to realize is that Tom's education is already complete, that in the new order, of which Tom is a new prince, the boy is father of the man, and the old are ruled by the young.

In the third chapter we find that the small fry of St. Petersburg meet regularly in battle under the rival generalship of Tom and Joe Harper, a bosom friend. The two commanders do not, we are told, condescend to fight in person. Rather do they sit upon an eminence and conduct operations through aides-de-camp. We are not vouchsafed details of the conflict, although we may surmise it is carried on by well-defined rules, by which the advantages of the respective sides are evaluated. We are told that Tom's army won a great victory after a long and hard battle, after which "the dead were counted, prisoners exchanged, the terms of the next disagreement agreed upon, and the day for the necessary battle appointed." All Tom's virtues, we learn, are in a manner arts of war, arts of force and fraud, in which the latter component is predominant. Tom may be said, like the grandfather of Odysseus, to surpass everyone in thievery and perjury. Yet his deceptions are of the grand, not of the petty variety. And they turn out, in the end, to be in the service of the law and justice and piety against which he appears to rebel. Tom's unregenerate

---

[1] Letter to Dr. Benjamin Waterhouse, in H. A. Washington (ed.), *The Writings of Thomas Jefferson* (Washington, D.C.: Taylor & Maury, 1854), 7:101.

individualism, or protestantism, which is the book's never failing source of humor, strikes a deeply sympathetic chord within the sanctuary of the conventions he appears to ridicule. In one of his moments of supreme glory, produced by a most profane deception, he makes the congregation of the little village sing the doxology with a passion and intensity they had not known. In the opening chapter the author tells us that Tom "was not the Model Boy of the village. He knew the model boy very well though— and loathed him." In the end, however, Tom is the Model Boy. Tom, we may say, captures the town by his generalship.

Tom's military skills are displayed in the opening episode, when he is hidden in a cupboard as Aunt Polly seeks him out. As her back is turned, he makes a dash for freedom, only to be caught by the tail of his coat. He stoutly denies all wrongdoing, but the evidence of the jam jar is upon him. "The switch hovered in the air—the peril was desperate—'My! Look behind you, aunt!' " And as the old lady whirls around, Tom is gone in the instant, over the high board fence outside, and is lost to sight.

There follows a long soliloquy in which we learn from Aunt Polly that Tom is always playing such tricks and that she is always being victimized by them. She ought to be on to them now, she says, "But my goodness, he never plays them alike, two days, and how is a body to know what's coming?" Tom is an expert in trickery, not only because of the variety of his tricks, but because he knows how to work on the feelings of his subjects. "He 'pears to know just how long he can torment me before I get my dander up," she observes, "and he knows if he can make out to put me off for a minute or make me laugh, it's all down again and I can't hit him a lick."

The next episode displays still further Tom's resourcefulness—and something of the magnitude of the obstacles it faces. Tom has played hooky, as Aunt Polly expects he has, and at dinner she conducts a guileful (as she in her simplicity thinks) inquisition designed to entrap him. It has been a warm day and she supposes that he has gone swimming. He forestalls her by observing that "Some of us pumped our heads—mine's damp yet. See?" Aunt Polly retorts that he wouldn't have to unbutton his shirt to pump his head and demands that he open his jacket to see whether the collar she had stiched closed is still securely in its place. Tom feels he is safe now, until his half-brother Sid treacherously comments, "Well, now, if I didn't think you sewed his collar with white thread, but it's black." At this, Tom has no recourse but to flight. When alone, he examines the two large needles with black and white thread he carries concealed in his lapels and complains bitterly at his aunt's inconsistency in using now one and now the other. Nevertheless, we must be impressed by the fact that his guile was more than sufficient for dealing with her, had not Sid betrayed him. He vows retribution to Sid, which is not long to come.

Aunt Polly is now determined to punish Tom. She will make him work the next day, which is Saturday, when all the other boys will be having a holiday. Aunt Polly loves Tom, and there is a conflict within her, between a loving heart and a stern Puritan conscience. Her heart is vulnerable to Tom's wiles, which play upon her weakness. Her love for him is not without return, but it is slight beside the great love they share, which is for himself. There is no conflict within Tom between heart and conscience, of the kind that so dramatically preoccupies that other transcendent hero in the later volume, *Huckleberry Finn.* Yet Tom does, as we shall see, have a conscience of a sort. Tom, unlike Huck, is essentially a man (or boy) of the law, who needs only to have it settled that he is the lawgiver.

Or perhaps we should say that he is like Machiavelli's Prince, who knows that good laws require good arms and therefore devotes himself first to attaining eminence in arms. Tom retreats from the dinner table, discomfited. Wandering through the town, he comes upon a stranger, "a boy a shade larger than himself." The stranger is dressed to a degree of fashion that to Tom is astounding, and he "had a citified air about him that ate into Tom's vitals." Later Tom calls him "aristocracy," using the noun as adjective. The necessary outcome of the ensuing confrontation is a fight. It is a bitter one, and results in Tom's victory. Before the fight takes place, however, there is a contest of wills, in which we see both Tom and the other boy resort to every imaginable bluff. They come to force only after the resources of fraud are exhausted. But we see that Tom, although something of a bully, is no coward. Much later, when Tom, along with Joe Harper and Huck Finn, is thought to be dead, the children of the town vie with each other in memories of the departed. "One poor chap," remarks the author, "who had no other grandeur to offer, said with tolerably manifest pride in the remembrance: 'Well, Tom Sawyer he licked me once.' But that bid for glory was a failure. Most of the boys could say that. . . ." We thus see that Tom's democratic leadership among the village boys is founded upon the natural right of the stronger, a right not inconsistent with an aristocratic love of glory.

Tom returned home late, only to find his aunt awaiting him, and "when she saw the state his clothes were in her resolution to turn his Saturday holiday into captivity at hard labor became adamantine in its firmness."

Tom's generalship had enabled him to play hooky. But will it enable him to do so with impunity? He had nearly escaped scot free until Sid's treachery betrayed him. Aunt Polly's heart—before it was hardened—might have rescued him, had not her conscience accused her and him together. "He's full of the Old Scratch," she says, and to allow him to go unpunished is only "a-laying up sin and suffering for us both." She *must* do her duty by punishing him, or she will be his ruination. Thus is he cursed with Adam's curse; and being as full of the Old Adam as of the Old Scratch, "he hates work more than he hates anything else." But Tom's genius does not forsake him. Not only will he escape the fate of Adam, and revenge himself upon Sid, but he will in the end displace Sid and the Model Boy as the paragon of respectability. He will look down upon them, and he will do so *ex cathedra,* from a new seat of authority he will have created for himself. Sid, we are told, "was a quiet boy, and had no adventurous, troublesome ways." Tom will triumph, not only over Sid's person, but over the orthodoxy in Aunt Polly's soul that Sid dutifully accepts. Tom is a hero of the new Calvinism, in which a new wine of worldly glory is poured into the old churchly vessel, and such success will henceforth be regarded as the hallmark of election and salvation.

"Saturday morning was come, and all the summer world was bright and fresh, and brimming with life. . . . Cardiff Hill, beyond the village and above it . . . lay just far enough away to seem a Delectable Land." Thus is the scene set for a most unpromising Christian. Tom is set to work with a bucket of whitewash and a brush. "Life seemed to him hollow, and existence a burden." Tom first attempts to suborn the little Negro boy Jim, who has been sent to pump water. He offers three temptations to Jim to whitewash for him: first, that he will carry the bucket to the well for him; next, that he will give him his white "alley"; and finally, that he will show him his sore toe. After many remonstrances that "Ole missis . . . [will] take an tar de head off'n me," poor Jim succumbs. He is bent over with absorbing interest as the bandage is unwound, but before the stigmata come into view, Aunt Polly descends in force, and Jim is sent "flying down the street with his pail and a tingling rear." Tom, for a moment, whitewashes with vigor. But soon despair settles upon him. He empties his pockets to examine his wealth; but by bartering it all away, he finds that he could not purchase more than half an hour of pure freedom. "At this dark and hopeless moment an inspiration burst upon him! Nothing less than a great, magnificent inspiration."

The effect of this inspiration is to set Tom tranquilly to work. This he could not hitherto do, because his soul within him was troubled. Now it is serene. But what is the work? It is not the work of whitewashing the fence, although that is how it will appear to Ben Rogers, the first of the long series of Tom's victims. The real work is in deceiving Ben into believing that he, Tom, is absorbed in the whitewashing, a work that requires for its consummation that he appear beyond possibility of detection to be so absorbed. The work of whitewashing and the work of deceiving are distinguishable to the mind, but not to the eye. And Tom does enjoy his work and take pride in it. At the end of the chapter the author intrudes the following reflection: "Tom . . . had discovered a great law of human action, without knowing it—namely, that in order to make a man or a boy covet a thing, it is only necessary to make the thing difficult to attain. If he had been a great and wise philosopher like the writer of this book, he would now have comprehended that Work consists of whatever a body is obliged to do, and that Play consists of whatever a body is not obliged to do."

But Mark Twain, that great and wise philosopher, like Tom, is not altogether candid. Tom could not have sold the boys whitewashing privileges, however unconstrained the activity, merely under the aspect of its being play. He had first to create in them the vision of its desirability, and this vision is a work of art. Tom makes Ben believe, first, that he, Tom, is enjoying it; second, that it is something that requires skill in its execution; and last and most important, that to be selected or permitted to do it is to occupy a position of envy and distinction. In a polity whose principle is equality, where the individual feels himself lost in the mass, no passion burns more universally than the passion for distinction, or more precisely, the illusion of distinction. Actual distinctions are of course by their nature rare and difficult, but the illusion of distinction is easy and can be made available to anyone who is gullible and willing to pay for it.

As Ben begs for a chance to take a turn at the whitewashing, Tom cautiously refuses, saying it wouldn't do, since Aunt Polly is so particular about this fence, "right here on the street, you know—but if it was the back fence I wouldn't mind and she wouldn't." Tom says he reckons "there ain't one boy in a thousand, maybe two thousand that can do it the way it's got to be done." And then in the spirit that was to descend upon one hundred, or maybe two hundred thousands of used-car salesmen, whose ancestor Tom is, he goes on in response to Ben's begging, "Ben, I'd like to, honest injun; but Aunt Polly—well, Jim wanted to do it, but she wouldn't let him; Sid wanted to do it, and she wouldn't let Sid. Now don't you see how I'm fixed? If you was to tackle this fence and anything was to happen to it—" Ben's appetite is now whetted, from a faint inclination to a raging desire. He offers Tom the core of his apple; Tom holds out. Then he offers *all* of the apple. "Tom gave up the brush with reluctance in his face, but alacrity in his heart. And while the late steamer *Big Missouri* worked and sweated in the sun, the retired artist sat on a barrel in the shade close by, dangled his legs, and planned the slaughter of more innocents." And, as used-car salesmen have discovered ever since, "There was no lack of material; boys happened along every little while; they came to jeer but remained to whitewash." At the end of the operation Tom "had had a nice, idle time . . . plenty of company—and the fence had three coats of whitewash on it! If he hadn't run out of whitewash, he would have bankrupted every boy in the village."

In that moment of great inspiration, Tom had revealed to him some of the profoundest mysteries of American democratic capitalism. Its essence does not, we see, lie in "the relief of man's estate," if that estate is understood to be merely the estate of nature. Rather does it lie in the relief of an estate the capitalist himself has created, by infusing the desires by whose relief he is to profit. Long after Tom, John Kenneth Galbraith was to make a theory of this fact, and call it the "dependence effect." Tom is the quintessential capitalist, carrying enterprise to that consummation that is every entrepreneur's deepest longing, but which he never hopes to achieve except, no doubt, in that better world to which good capitalists aspire to go. He turns the workers into customers and sells them their own labor. What he realizes is pure profit, purer profit indeed than Karl Marx ever imagined in his wildest polemics against the iniquity of surplus value. He has no overhead, no labor cost, and no cost of material, and he exacts the entire purchasing power of his market, at least until the whitewash runs out. We should, moreover, not omit to notice the twofold nature of the entire transaction. Tom sells not only to the boys but to Aunt Polly, with whom the original "exchange" takes place. He is under a "debt" to her—under what we might call the old, precapitalist order—a debt contracted by playing hooky. This debt too he discharges at no cost to himself. And there is a further bonus. When he reports back to headquarters, and "his" work is inspected, Aunt Polly "was so overcome by the splendor of his achievement that she took him into the closet and selected a choice apple and delivered it to him, along with an improving lecture upon the added value and flavor a treat took to itself when it came without sin through virtuous effort." Tom thereupon doubles his bonus, or, we might say, enlarges upon his state of grace, by "hooking" a doughnut, as Aunt Polly is closing with a happy scriptural flourish.

Tom has imposed his will upon every one of its obstacles; fortune has proved his slave, as it will hereafter. He has played hooky, and far from paying the wages of sin, he has reaped a wonderful bounty of profits from a venture of marvelous enterprise. The inspiration that brings these rewards is founded upon the capitalist discovery that wealth is not to be measured by the work it embodies—the principle of the just price— but by the appetites of those who exchange. By shrewdly rigging the market in his own favor, he exemplifies the new principle, upon which most of the great fortunes of America in the later nineteenth century were based. Tom Sawyer is an exquisite example of the genius of the "robber barons" of the Gilded Age, concealed in the idyllic setting of a Golden Age.

Taking his apple and the "hooked" doughnut, Tom skips off. But in passing out he sees Sid, with whom he still has an account to settle. A storm of clods fills the air; and although Aunt Polly comes to Sid's rescue, it is not before revenge has been exacted. Now Tom's soul is at peace.

The peace however is short-lived. Tom goes off to direct the victory of his army over Joe Harper's. But this is mere epilogue to the victory at the fence. The more important sequel occurs afterward as Tom is passing the house where Jeff Thatcher lives, and where for the first time he catches sight of a "lovely little blue-eyed creature with yellow hair plaited in two long tails," who has just come to town. Mars and Venus are in conjunction, and the "fresh-crowned hero fell without firing a shot." But the hero's affections, we learn, had not been a *tabula rasa*. "A certain Amy Lawrence vanished out of his heart and left not even a memory of herself behind. . . . He had been months winning her; and she had confessed hardly a week ago. . . ." Later we watch the wooing of Becky, and the betrothal ceremony in which she plights her faith to Tom. After the coy denials, the chase, the maidenly blushes, and finally the kiss of surrender, he tells her that now she is never to love or marry anybody but him, "never, never, and forever." She agrees, and demands in return that he never marry anyone but her. Tom's reply is, "Certainly. Of course. That's *part* of it." But his obligations are clearly an afterthought. A moment later he blunders into disclosing the engagement to Amy and that "forever" to him can be a very short time. Tom's conquest of Becky thereupon faces the same kind of complicating circumstances that had previously befallen his hooky playing, when Sid ratted on him. This time he has ratted on himself. But as before, his victory will be all the more astounding. The illusion of virtue that he will conjure before Becky (and her father), which will obscure the memory of his infidelity, is exactly of a piece with that with which he confronts Aunt Polly when he presents her with the thrice-whitewashed fence.

We have followed our hero from Friday to Saturday, and now it is Sunday. Aunt Polly's religion, over which Tom so mightily triumphed at the fence, now assails him with all its multiplied Sabbath-day force. First there is family worship, followed by a drill in the verses he is supposed to have memorized for the Sunday school. Sid, of course, had learned his days before. His cousin Mary tries to help Tom, but "his mind was traversing the whole field of human thought," and the case appears hopeless. In her perplexity, Mary offers him a prize, without telling him what it is. Then, "under the double pressure of curiosity and prospective gain, he did it with such spirit that he accomplished a shining success." And what were the verses? The five lines of the Sermon on the Mount, beginning "Blessed are the poor in spirit, for theirs is the kingdom of heaven." Tom had chosen them "because he could find no verses that were shorter." As we shall see, they constitute the exact point on the moral compass 180 degrees opposite to the principle by which Tom lives. Tom does nothing except for gain, the chiefest gain being the glory that nurtures self-esteem. But memorizing the injunctions to humility and meekness brings him a "sure-enough Barlow" knife, which sends convulsions of delight through his system. It was a good deal.

At the door of the Sunday school Tom drops back a step from the family procession and accosts a Sunday-dressed comrade. The trading for tickets begins, with a "yaller" exchanging for a "piece of lickrish and a fishhook." Each blue ticket, we learn, is payment for memorizing two verses. Ten blue tickets are worth one red one, and ten reds equal one yellow. Ten yellow tickets would bring the scholar who had memorized 2,000 verses a Dore Bible, very plainly bound, and "worth forty cents in those easy times." "Only the older pupils managed to keep their tickets and stick to their tedious work long enough to get a Bible, and so the delivery of one of these prizes was a rare and noteworthy circumstance." We are told that it is doubtful that "Tom's mental stomach" had ever "really hungered for one of those prizes, but unquestionably his entire being had for many a day longed for the glory and éclat that came with it."

This Sunday proves to be different from other Sundays. There are visitors to the school of august presence. The great Judge Thatcher, from Constantinople, the county seat, comes accompanied by his wife and child, she of the yellow hair and blue eyes. Everyone, we are told, from the most restless of the boys to the Sunday school superintendent is, each in his own way, "showing off." "There was only one thing wanting, to make Mr. Walters' ecstasy complete, and that was a chance to deliver a prize and exhibit a prodigy." But no one seemed to have the requisite number of tickets, or so his inquiries among the star pupils had indicated. "And now at this moment, when hope was dead, Tom Sawyer came forward with nine yellow tickets, nine red tickets, and ten blue ones." We are assured that the superintendent had not expected "an application from this source for the next ten years." But the "certified checks . . . were good for their face," and "Tom was therefore elevated to a place with the Judge and the other elect." Too late did the other boys, their vitals "eaten with envy," realize that "they themselves had contributed to this hated splendor by trading tickets to Tom for the wealth he had amassed in selling whitewashing privileges. These despised themselves, as being the dupes of a wily fraud, a guileful snake in the grass." Or perhaps we should say that, like Esau, they found out too late that they had sold their inheritance for a mess of pottage. Certainly Tom here fits the role of the crafty Jacob, and like him will vindicate his character as one chosen of the Lord.

Tom has repeated upon a grander scale the miracle of the fence. As before he had used the labor of the boys, gaining the credit for it himself, so now he has utilized their labor in memorizing Bible verses. In doing so, Tom again demonstrates his superiority. He displays that "rational and industrious" soul that, by its prosperity in this world, came to be regarded as the elect of God, and therefore a proper witness of the true faith. Tom has already shown himself an artisan of belief, when he led the boys to credit something directly opposite to what they had previously supposed to be true. Of the many successors of Ben Rogers, the author had said that "they came to jeer, but remained to whitewash." This paraphrases a familiar line in Goldsmith's *The Deserted Village,* "And fools, who came to scoff, remained to pray," spoken of a gifted divine in a village church. Although Tom's mental stomach may never have hungered for the prize Bible itself, yet he had the vision to see a good connected with its possession that the others—who presumably knew its contents better than he—lacked. Moreover they lacked his entrepreneurial genius, which saw that the assembling of the scattered efforts of many could create a new, capital asset, as distinct from the consumption goods with which he entered the market. Whereas the others sell the testimonials of their faith, he buys them. We see that it is not mere love of ease that drove him to escape work, or an appetite for goods that led him to sell whitewashing privileges. Nor is it love of glory or éclat alone, great as that is, that motivates him now. He displays a shrewdness that transcends these undoubted motives when he exchanges his newly acquired liquid assets for the far more durable capital of a churchly reputation. Tom is acquiring credit with the world, a world represented by the vast dignity of Judge Thatcher—who is, besides all else, *her* father.

Tom's aspiration for the prize Bible may have had little to do with the contents of that book. Or perhaps we should say that it had little to do with such contents, as understood by the old Protestant orthodoxy, if a protesting orthodoxy be not a contradiction. As Tom was introduced to the Judge, "his tongue was tied, his breath would hardly come. . . . He would have liked to fall down and worship him, if it were in the dark." Tom sadly flunks the test of scriptural knowledge, and we are left to wonder, as the "curtain of charity" is drawn, what lies behind. It is our hypothesis that nothing detracts from Tom's essential triumph. As far as the Judge is concerned, Tom's display of genuine feeling, if not his rote learning, testify in his behalf. We must remember that at the end of the book Tom is as much the Judge's hero as the Judge is Tom's upon this occasion. We would surmise that the Judge misconstrues Tom's motives in Tom's favor on each occasion.

Tom is presented to us throughout as a rebel against the constraints of home, church, and school. But in each case his rebellion is the occasion for his becoming a hero, either of the institution, or at least in the institution, against which he rebels. By disobeying Aunt Polly, and grieving her beyond measure, he becomes the beloved prodigal, for whom she rejoices ninety and nine times more than ever she could for Sid. Tom's naming David and Goliath as the first apostles is infinitely funny. Evidently they were the only two Biblical names he could summon from the depths of a highly functional memory. But we should not overlook the significance that the story of David's herosim must have had for Tom. Nor must we forget that, very soon, Tom *does* play David to Injun Joe's Goliath and helps rid the town of a scourge believed to have taken the lives of five of its citizens. In Plato's dialogue on piety, *Euthyphro,* we are presented with these alternative definitions: that piety consists in obeying the gods or that it consists in imitating the gods. In both the Athens of Socrates and Tom Sawyer's America, the conventional wisdom would appear to have been on the side of obeying the gods, of doing what one is told to do, upon divine authority. But both Euthyphro and Tom insist upon the more radical form of piety; both insist upon imitating the gods, or the heroes who represent the divine to them. Euthyphro prosecutes his father for murder, upon the pattern of conduct he believes to be true of Zeus and Kronos; Tom imitates both David and the scion of the house of David.

In the service in the church that followed the Sunday school, Tom was busied in many ways designed to relieve his oppression. "Tom counted the pages of the sermon; after church he always knew how many pages there had been, but he seldom knew anything else about the discourse." This time, we are told, "he was really interested for a little while." The minister had evidently taken as his text the eleventh chapter of Isaiah and "made a grand and moving picture of the assembling together of the world's hosts at the millennium when the lion and the lamb should lie down together and a little child should lead them." But, says the author, "the pathos, the lesson, the moral of the great spectacle were lost upon the boy; he only thought of the conspicuousness of the principal character before the onlooking nations; his face lit with the thought, and he said to himself that he wished he could be that child, if it was a tame lion."

Whether the moral of the spectacle of the prophecy was lost upon the boy depends upon one's point of view as to what that moral was. The author seems to be assuring us that his own understanding is orthodox and that he finds Tom to be amusing but mistaken. We doubt that this is Mark Twain's real intention. Tom wants the glory of the little child of the millennium. Are we to understand that the child himself does not want it? Does God not create man for his own glory? Tom understands that the admiration of the child depends upon a certain kind of belief in that child; and Tom becomes an ever greater expert in compelling wonder, or belief in himself. We believe Tom's enterprise, or the enterprise of which Tom is the vehicle, becomes intelligible in the light of a famous passage in the sixth chapter of Machiavelli's *Prince*. There it is said that all armed prophets have succeeded, and that all unarmed ones have failed. This must be understood in the light of the reflection that both Jesus and Machiavelli were unarmed prophets. Of the unarmed prophets who failed, Machiavelli mentions only Savonarola, "who was destroyed amid his institutions when they were still new, as soon as the multitude ceased to believe him, because he had no way to keep firm those who once believed or to make the unbelieving believe." The art embodied in *Tom Sawyer* demonstrates how without the compulsion of arms men may become firm believers in the principle of a new regime. Tom runs away with Huck and Joe Harper to punish Aunt Polly and Becky by becoming that dread and fearful figure, the Black Avenger of the Spanish Main. But he returns instead as the central figure of that pathos that is his own funeral. He returns to enact his own resurrection! Let us retrace the development of this Machiavellian *Imitatio Christi*.

The evening of the day that Tom had gained his great victory over work, the ancient curse of Adam, he returned home in the best of spirits. He was reproached for clodding Sid, but this he did not at all mind. His knuckles are rapped for stealing sugar, and he complains that Sid is not punished for the same crime. "Well, Sid don't torment a body the way you do. You'd be always into that sugar if I warn't watching you," is the reply. Then Aunt Polly steps into the kitchen and Sid reaches for the sugar. "But Sid's fingers slipped and the bowl dropped and broke." Tom expects that Sid will catch it and adopts an attitude of demure silence on Aunt Polly's return. But just as he expects the thunder of vengeance to fall upon Sid, a potent palm sends him sprawling on the floor. Then Tom speaks up, "Hold on, now, what 'er you belting *me* for? Sid broke it!" Poor Aunt Polly is perplexed, and all she can say is that she is sure that Tom didn't get a lick too many, for all his many transgressions, seen and unseen. Now the situation between Tom and his aunt is the reverse of what we saw in the opening chapter. Her conscience, which then condemned him, now reproaches her. And he in turn is quick to perceive possibilities in the advantage he has gained. "He knew that in her heart his aunt was on her knees to him, and he was morosely gratified by the consciousness of it." But the genius within Tom will have no cheap reward, merely by humbling her. He will die for her sin. "And he pictured himself brought home from the river, dead. . . . How she would throw herself upon him . . . and her lips pray God to give her back her boy. . . . But he would lie there cold and white and make no sign. . . . And such a luxury to him was this petting of his sorrows that he could not bear to have any worldly cheeriness or any grating delight intrude upon it; it was too sacred for such contact. . . ." Then the scene shifts to the "deserted street . . . where the Adored Unknown lived," for this is before the meeting with Becky. He lies on the ground beneath her window, clasping to his bosom the wilted flower that is the memorial of his secret passion. "And thus he would die—out in the cold world, with no shelter over his homeless head, no friendly hand to wipe the death damps from his brow, no loving face to bend pityingly over him when the great agony came." This reenactment of the cross is interrupted when a window is raised and "a maidservant's discordant voice profaned the holy calm, and a deluge of water drenched the prone martyr's remains." The erstwhile "martyr" is now a "strangling hero" who now further profanes what had been a holy calm with a curse, which is quickly followed by the sound of shattering glass. The mysteries of love, war, and religion are in close proximity.

But the mood of martyrdom returns. After wooing, winning, and then losing Becky, he retreats into the woods beyond Cardiff Hill. "The boy's soul was steeped in melancholy. . . . It seemed to him that life was but a trouble, at best, and he more than half envied Jimmy Hodges, so lately released. . . . If he only had a clean Sunday school record he could be willing to go and be done with it all." This latter sentiment is one of the few expressions of what we might call conventional remorse. It should, of course, be taken for what it is, namely, an excuse, since Tom has not the slightest inclination for an early death. "Now as to this girl. What had he done? Nothing." Tom conveniently forgets the infidelity, or perhaps we should say hypothetical bigamy, that had so disturbed Becky. "He had meant the best . . . and been treated like a dog. . . . She would be sorry . . . maybe when it was too late. Ah, if he could only die *temporarily!*" In the earlier scene Tom had wished that he could be drowned, "all at once and unconsciously, without undergoing the uncomfortable routine devised by nature." Tom, we see, is the paradigm of that latter-day Christian, whose passion is the pleasant indulgence of his own self-love, expressed as grief at the neglect of others to take him at his own self-estimate. Or, more precisely, it is the pleasant contemplation of the grief or pain of others, for failing to take him at his own self-estimate. The pleasure that he is to enjoy occurs in virtue of a death that is both painless and temporary! Tom is unmindful that, by the traditional Christian doctrine of the resurrection, all death is temporary, for the faithful. Of course, traditional Christianity also taught that the soul of the individual found its fulfilment by the recognition given it after death, by God in Heaven. Tom demands that recognition, not by God, but by men (and women), not in Heaven, but on earth. Moreover, this is to happen, not in virtue of the grace and power of God, but in virtue of a certain secular skill. The fraud that Tom now perpetrates replaces traditional piety, in the same way that the traded tickets replace the work of memorizing the sacred scriptures, as title deeds to the prize Bible.

Tom's wish for a painless, temporary death is followed by a series of fantasies of self-glorifying revenge. But we should notice that the fear and envy that he inflicts upon others in these fantasies are equivalents of the grief and remorse of earlier fantasies, in which Aunt Polly and Becky weep bitter tears over his poor dead body. They are simply alternative ways of enjoying the pain of others, ways with which he retaliates for his supposed rejection. First, then, an idea he had once had of becoming a clown recurs, to be rejected with disgust. It is entirely out of harmony with his present mood. Next he considers going away to be a soldier, "to return after long years, all warworn and illustrious." Better still, "he would join the Indians . . . and away in the future come back a great chief, bristling with feathers, hideous with paint, and prance into Sunday school, some drowsy summer morning, with a bloodcurdling war whoop, and sear the eyeballs of all his companions with unappeasable envy." This is getting closer to the mark. "But no, there was something gaudier even than this. He would be a pirate!" And the future is now vouchsafed to him in colors of unimaginable splendor. "How his name would fill the world, and make people shudder! . . . And, at the zenith of his fame, how he would suddenly appear at the old village and stalk into church, brown and weather-beaten . . . his crime-rusted cutlass at his side . . . his black flag unfurled, with the skull and crossbones on it, and hear with swelling ecstasy the whisperings, 'It's Tom Sawyer the Pirate!—the Black Avenger of the Spanish Main!' "

And so Tom gathers up Joe Harper, who has had a difference with his mother, similar to Tom's with Aunt Polly, and Huck Finn, who is ready to go anywhere with anybody, and off they go to Jackson's Island to play pirates.

The pirating expedition turns out, in the main, to be no more than skylarking, away from the town, away from all adult supervision or interference. They do steal certain provisions—a boiled ham, a side of bacon, and hooks and lines for fishing. And Tom and Joe have difficulty getting to sleep that night. They remember the stolen meat, and conscience causes trouble. "They tried to argue it away by reminding conscience that they had purloined sweetmeats and apples scores of times; but the conscience was not to be appeased by such thin plausibilities . . . there was no getting around the stubborn fact that taking sweetmeats was only 'hooking,' while taking bacons and hams and such valuables was plain simple *stealing*—and there was a command against that in the Bible." So they inwardly resolve that "their piracies should not again be sullied with the crime of stealing. Then conscience granted a truce, and these curiously inconsistent pirates fell peacefully to sleep." Tom's piracy, as we shall see, is of the grand, not petty variety. He means to capture the town. Why then should he despoil it? That would be to diminish the value of his own. All the laws of property are in his favor—as his commercial genius has already demonstrated. He should be the last one to hold them in disrespect. Mark Twain's interpretation of his leading character is again misleading. These pirates, or at least one of them, are anything but inconsistent.

In the middle of the day, the boys are puzzled to hear a distant booming. Presently they see the village's little steam ferryboat, its decks crowded with people. Then they realize that the booming is a cannon and that the entire town is engaged in a quest for drowned bodies. But it is Tom's mind in which the "revealing thought" flashes. "Boys, I know who's drownded—it's us." "They felt like heroes in an instant. Here was a gorgeous triumph; they were missed; they were mourned; hearts were breaking on their account; tears were being shed . . . the departed were the talk of the whole town, and the envy of all the boys, as far as this dazzling notoriety was concerned. This was fine. It was worthwhile to be a pirate, after all."

But when the excitement subsides, trouble sets in for the pirate chieftain. His crew grows homesick and mutinous, and play loses its savor, reversing the process by which the work of whitewashing had been transmuted into play. After Joe and Huck have drifted off to sleep, the troubled leader steals out of camp and makes his way back to St. Petersburg and to his own home. He creeps unobserved into the sitting room and squeezes under the bed. Aunt Polly, Sid, Mary, and Mrs. Harper are there. It is a kind of wake being held for the lost boys. Tom who is believed—at least by Aunt Polly—to be in a better place, is quite literally beneath them. Now the fantasy that Tom had imagined, of the grief occasioned by his death, is being enacted in his very presence. He is enjoying a "death" that is both painless and temporary!

Tom remains silently beneath the bed until everyone has departed. He joins the heavenly witnesses to Aunt Polly's prayer for him, delivered "with such measureless love" that Tom welters in tears in his hiding place. As she finally falls into a troubled sleep, he steals out and looks down at her, "his heart full of pity." Tom takes from his pocket a sycamore scroll, upon which he had written a message. "But something occurred to him. . . . His face lighted with a happy solution of his thought; he put the bark hastily in his pocket." The light on Tom's face, of course, is the idea of coming and hiding in the church, to provide the tremendous climax to his own funeral. And he couldn't bear to spoil such a gorgeous spectacle. So his love and pity for Aunt Polly do not deter him from making her love and her grief an instrument of his self-glorification.

There is a curious epilogue to the secret visitation of that night. After the funeral is over, and the resurrection has transfigured Tom into unbelievable glory among the smaller fry, and unappeasable envy among the larger, he imposes scandalously upon Aunt Polly's credulity for a further enlargement of his apotheosis. He tells her in complete detail—but with artful hesitations—the story of everything he overheard from beneath the bed, pretending that it came to him in a dream while on the island. Sid overhears this shameless imposture in silence. He is now hopelessly overpowered by Tom's grandeur. He only comments to himself, "Pretty thin—as long a dream as that, without any mistakes in it!" Eventually the hoax is revealed because Joe Harper had told his mother of Tom's having left the camp that Wednesday evening. Poor Aunt Polly, who had rushed to tell Mrs. Harper of Tom's prophetic powers, is subject instead to remarkable embarrassment. Yet Tom has a knack for profiting from the exposure of his deceptions no less than from the deceptions themselves—as we saw in the case of the collar thread, and as we guessed in the case of the "curtain of charity." In the pocket of his old jacket he still had the bark on which he had written, "We ain't dead—we are only off being pirates." When he pleads in extenuation of his fakery that he had come over that night to relieve Aunt Polly's anxieties and not to gloat over them, she says, "Tom, Tom, I would be the thankfullest soul in this world if I could believe you ever had as good a thought as that, but you know you never did, and I know it, Tom." He pleads that this is the truth, and Aunt Polly begs him not to lie, that it only makes things a hundred times worse. Tom insists, against all probability and reason, that this is not a lie. Aunt Polly rejoins that she would "give the whole world to believe that—it would cover up a power of sins." Tom explains that it was only the thought of the funeral that made him change his mind and put the bark back in his pocket. Then he tells her how he kissed her as she slept, to which she responds with infinite pathos. Tom has so wrought upon her that her will to believe in him is equal in full to the great power of faith that is in her. It will require but a single scrap of evidence to make him the complete beneficiary of that faith. When Tom leaves she turns toward the closet with its tattered jacket. Her heart is overwhelmed with its burden of love, and she reasons herself into justifying him, whatever the evidence. "Twice she put out her hand to take the garment . . . and twice she refrained." Finally, "she fortified herself with the thought; 'It's a good lie—it's a good lie—I won't let it grieve me.' . . . A moment later she was reading Tom's piece of bark through flowing tears and saying: 'I could forgive the boy, now, if he'd committed a million sins!' " As far as Aunt Polly is concerned, Tom's redemption and glory are complete.

Before turning to the culminating episode of Tom's piracy, let us consider it against the background of certain alternatives. Tom's favorite game is that of Robin Hood. We see him at it twice, once with Joe Harper and once with Huck Finn. Joe and Tom play at it regularly and store their equipment in the woods beyond Cardiff Hill. What they do is, in fact, to play roles in episodes drawn from the story, just as if it were a stage production. It is not a game, played to win. It is, rather, a dramatic ritual. Here we first see Tom's own kind of scriptural authority. But Huck has never heard of Robin Hood, and Tom tells him, "Why, he was one of the greatest men that was ever in England—and the best. He was a robber." Huck asks who he robbed. "Only sheriffs and bishops and rich people and kings, and such like. But he never bothered the poor. He loved 'em. He always divided up with 'em perfectly square." Huck rejoins, "Well, he must 'a' been a brick." To which Tom replies, "I bet you he was, Huck. Oh, he was the noblest man that ever was. They ain't any such men now, I can tell you." When Tom had played Robin Hood with Joe Harper, the boys had ended "grieving that there were no outlaws any more, and wondering what modern civilization could claim to have done to compensate for their loss. They said they would rather be outlaws a year in Sherwood Forest than President of the United States forever." In the final episode of Tom's and Joe's reenactment, "Tom became Robin Hood again, and was allowed by the treacherous nun to bleed his strength away through his neglected wound." Then Joe, "representing a whole tribe of weeping outlaws, dragged him sadly forth," and put his bow into his hands, that the falling arrow might indicate Robin's place of burial. Tom shot the arrow, "and fell back and would have died, but he lit on a nettle and sprang up too gaily for a corpse." All Tom's deaths are, we see, highly dramatic and extremely temporary. But the story of Robin Hood is the romantic embodiment of that Machiavellian or piratical Christianity that is Tom's religion.

Tom calls Robin "the noblest man that ever was." We can understand why. The people that Robin robbed, "sheriffs and bishops and rich people and kings," are essentially appendages of a feudal regime. He appeals therefore to democratic, Protestant radicalism. In his attack on the privileged orders, Robin represents the egalitarianism of the American Revolution; in his betrayal by the established church, he represents the spirit of the Reformation. But Tom's America, represented by Judge Thatcher, whom Tom would have liked to fall down and worship (if it were dark), is dedicated to that "simpler but wider justice" that Robin Hood robbed to implement. When Robin Hood's principle becomes that of the establishment, noble outlawry is no longer possible. That is why Tom can engage in ritualistic play as Robin Hood, but when it comes to a serious choice of a vocation, it never occurs to him to make Jackson's Island into Sherwood Forest. In the world of American democracy Tom is on the side of property and authority, because that world is itself antagonistic to bishops and kings. Yet that world lives, in its imagination, in the golden glow of its revolutionary past, symbolized by the story of Robin Hood. In a deeper sense, Tom *does* enact Robin Hood, in the same sense that Robin himself enacts the Christ of radical Protestantism. Robin is a robber, and Tom Sawyer's Gang is a robber gang. But it is a robber gang that meets the highest standards of *respectability*. At the end of the novel Tom explains it to Huck in this way: "A robber is more high-toned than what a pirate is—as a general thing. In most countries they're awful high up in the nobility—dukes and such." Robin himself, if memory serves, was an earl. Tom Sawyer's Gang is founded, not only upon the powerful imagination of its leader, but upon his wealth—which is inherited from an earlier nonrespectable gang, Murrel's, whose treasure cache becomes Tom's and Huck's in the end. In other words, Tom ends by despoiling the despoilers, which is exactly what Robin Hood had done; only after the American Revolution, the despoilers can only be enemies of the legal order. Yet nothing prevents the ill-gotten gains from supplying an admirable foundation for the new, respectable gang. In the new legal order the highest and most respectable kind of robber is also the most highly honored. And so the myth of Robin Hood is replaced by, or becomes instrumental to, a new myth—that of Tom Sawyer.

Before piracy is settled upon for the expedition to Jackson's Island, one alternative is briefly considered. When Tom meets Joe as he is on the point of running away and finds that Joe is about to do the same, "they began to lay their plans." "Joe was for being a hermit, and living on crusts in a remote cave, and dying, sometimes, of cold and want and grief; but after listening to Tom, he conceded that there were some conspicuous advantages about a life of crime, and so he consented to be a pirate." We know that Tom's piracy consisted eminently in the appropriation of all those pleasant passions connected in Joe's mind with the spectacle of the unpleasant life of the hermit. Tom has already indulged the fantasy of a lonely death, and his steps are already directed toward enjoying all its advantages without its disadvantages. On Jackson's Island he has some further discussion with Joe and Huck about the comparative merits of hermiting and pirating. A pirate, Tom explains, "don't have to get up mornings, and you don't have to go to school, and wash, and all that blame foolishness. You see a pirate don't have to do *anything*, Joe, when he's ashore, but a hermit *he* has to be praying considerable, and then he don't have any fun, anyway, all by himself that way." Joe assures Tom that, now that he's tried it, he much prefers being a pirate. "You see," Tom continues, "people don't go much on hermits, nowadays, like they used to in old times, but a pirate's always respected." Moreover, Tom continues, "a hermit's got to sleep on the hardest place he can find, and put sackcloth and ashes on his head, and stand out in the rain, and—" This is too much for Huck, who demands to know what they do such things for. Tom says he doesn't know, but they always do these things, and Huck would have to do them too, if he was a hermit. Huck stoutly insists that he would not, upon which Tom demands, "How'd you get around it?" Huck says he wouldn't stand it, that he'd run away. At this Tom exclaims, "Run away! Well, you *would* be a nice old slouch of a hermit. You'd be a disgrace." Tom thus sees quite clearly that hermiting, meaning ascetic Christianity, is out of style. On the other hand, pirating ashore comes close to Marx's vision, in the *German Ideology,* of a communist society in which there is perfect freedom, and all distinction between work and play is abolished. It also resembles the Garden of Eden. The "work" of piracy is said to consist in taking and burning ships, making people (but not women) walk the plank, and burying treasure. But these pirates, we soon learn, do none of these things. Their climactic moment comes not afloat but ashore, and it comes in the church, where they demonstrate the superiority of the piratical to the hermitical, of the comfortable to the uncomfortable brand of Christianity. Yet Tom remains true to his compulsive sense of propriety, which is also an unreasoning sense of authority, even as he rejects hermiting. Whereas Huck would reject the hermit's life because it makes no sense—even though it comes closer to his own style of living than to Tom's—Tom rejects it because it is out of fashion. Yet if it were in fashion, Tom would see no way for departing from the authoritative version of hermiting. Tom cannot conceive of an alteration or variation from an authoritative model except if it be founded upon an equal or superior authority. All Tom's defiances of authority are based, like Euthyphro's, upon a higher and more esoteric version of the authority he seems to defy.

Let us then return to the churchly consummation of Tom's piratical Christianity. "When the Sunday-school hour was finished . . . the bell began to toll, instead of ringing in the usual way." The villagers gathered in the hushed atmosphere induced by the presence of the mystery of death. "None could remember when the little church had been so full before." The congregation rises reverently as the bereaved families enter. Amidst muffled sobs the minister spreads his hands and prays. "A moving hymn was sung, and the text followed: 'I am the Resurrection and the Life.'" Little could the congregation guess that, but a week before, the central figure of the present drama, sitting in their midst, had lusted after the glory of the little child who should lead them. They had seen in the departed only "faults and flaws ... [and episodes] that at the time had seemed rank rascalities, well deserving of the cowhide." These same incidents are now related by the minister in such a way as to illustrate the sweet, generous natures of the departed. And the congregation, conscious that heretofore they had been persistently blinded to the truth about the lost lads, felt the pangs of conscience compounding their grief. "The congregation became more and more moved, as the pathetic tale went on, till at last the whole company broke down," including in the end the preacher himself. At this moment, when the pathos of the occasion has reached its extremity, there is a rustle in the gallery. A moment later the astounding event occurs, as the three boys come up the aisle, Tom in the lead, Joe behind, and Huck in his tattered rags slinking miserably in the rear. In the pandemonium that follows, two incidents are remarkable. As their families throw themselves upon Tom and Joe, Tom laid hold of Huck and said, "Aunt Polly, it ain't fair. Somebody's got to be glad to see Huck." As Aunt Polly responds with her warm humanity, the minister's voice thunders out, "Praise God from whom all blessings flow—SING!—and put your hearts in it!" "And they did. Old Hundred swelled up with a triumphant burst, and while it shook the rafters Tom Sawyer the Pirate looked around upon the envying juveniles about him and confessed in his heart that this was the proudest moment of his life."

We are told by the author that "As the 'sold' congregation trooped out they said they would almost be willing to be made ridiculous again to hear Old Hundred sung like that once more." This puts us in mind of the missionary piracy of the king, as he worked the camp meeting in Pokeville, in *Huckleberry Finn,* as well as reminding us of how the king and the duke "sold" the little Arkansas river town with the "Royal Nonesuch." When Jim is shocked by the rascality of the king, Huck explains that it's "in the breed ... [that] all kings is mostly rapscallions, as fur as I can make out." Later Huck comments to himself, "What was the use to tell Jim that these warn't real kings and dukes? It wouldn't 'a' done no good; and, besides, it was just as I said: you couldn't tell them from the real kind." Kings and dukes are the fraudulent rulers of the *anciens régimes,* who appear as mere frauds, divested of all the aura of rule in this democratic regime. But Tom's fraud is a success. Unlike the gulled townspeople who come back for blood to the third performance of the "Royal Nonesuch," those in the church of St. Petersburg have, in a manner of speaking, got their money's worth. And it was not money but glory that Tom sought. His ambition, unlike the king's and the duke's, is not vulgar. Yet the price that Aunt Polly and the town pay for Tom's ambition—a price exacted not in money but in grief and anguish—is far higher than that taken by the emblems of spurious nobility in the later work.

All Tom's virtues, we have said, are arts of war; yet the consummation of these virtues has been an imitation of the greatest of the unarmed prophets. But the deceptions practiced by Tom have been recognizable *as* deceptions. The fame Tom has achieved in the episodes noted, and the pleasures attendant upon a painless and temporary death, are only stages upon his way to a place and station beyond detection and beyond reproach. We have noted a resemblance in Tom to the patriarch Jacob, who deceived both his brother and his father. But there could be no final recourse to fraud when alone Jacob wrestled with the angel of the Lord. Tom, as he wrestles with his conscience during the trial of Muff Potter and as he faces death in the cave, also demonstrates that his daring and his cleverness are not the full measure of his character.

We have presented Tom's piratical Christianity as animated by a lust for glory in a world still believing itself to believe in the otherworldly religion of humility. Tom's religion appears as a sanctification of that process by which the blessed have their rewards here and now. We should bear in mind that the *ancien régime*—the one plundered by Robin Hood—was characterized by inequality and the postponement of the pleasures of the many to the next world. Modern democracy is characterized by equality and the enjoyment by the many of the pleasures of this world. Tom is a hero of that myth by which religion is transformed to meet the requirements of modern democracy.

Tom has an elaborate set of superstitions, which strike one as having a kind of humorous absurdity, against the background either of staid orthodoxy or of scientific reasoning. However, if we remember the orthodox roots of Tom's piety, in imitating rather than obeying the divine, we can see an equally radical Protestantism in his superstitions. Protestantism was in its origins a movement of religious authority from the established church to the common people. The extension of this movement is shown here when Tom reveals the source of his convictions in regard to the supernatural. Tom, we should remember, always settles disputes by an appeal to authority, never to experience. Usually it is the books he has read, about Robin Hood, hermits, pirates, or robbers, that supply the truth about these things. In *Huckleberry Finn* Tom undergoes a radical extension of his literary authoritarianism. Tom Sawyer's Gang is there conducted upon methods borrowed from Don Quixote. The attack upon the Sunday school picnic is closely modeled upon episodes from Cervantes. The emancipation of Jim, at the end of the latter novel, is based upon borrowed bits and pieces from "Baron Trenck . . . Benvenuto Chelleeny . . . Henry IV" and other of "them heroes," the Count of Monte Cristo chief among them. Tom's Law is derived from the Book, the original being transformed by infusions from such other sources as we have suggested. Accordingly, it is remarkable when, in considering a question in regard to the supernatural—with Huck questioning the authenticity or reliability of the superstition that a stray dog howling in the night is a certain prophecy of death—Tom settles the matter by saying, "That's what the niggers say, and they know all about these kind of things, Huck." Negroes as a source of authority stand outside conventional Christianity in Tom Sawyer's America, much as earlier Protestants were outside the precincts of authority in the Europe from which Tom's ancestors had fled.

Tom is led by his superstitions to a rendezvous with Huck Finn, to test the virtues of a dead cat for the removal of warts. The cure requires going to the graveyard "'long about midnight when somebody that was wicked has been buried," on the assurance that "a devil will come, or maybe two or three" to carry off the deceased. "When they're taking that feller away, you heave your cat after 'em and say 'Devil follow corpse, cat follow devil, warts follow cat, I'm done with ye!' '" We suspect that Huck himself is as much an attraction for Tom at this point—the beginning of their relationship in the novel—as the ritual of the cat. Huck's position outside conventional society, like that of the slaves, promises communion with an esoteric and more genuine reality. But Huck's belief in a devil or devils coming for the corpse has a certain foundation in reality. It is notable that Huck expects the body and not merely the soul of the deceased to be carried off. From the events that follow in the graveyard, culminating in the murder of young Doctor Robinson, we infer that body snatching was practiced by many young medical scholars, who needed cadavers for dissection and who could not get them any other way. The main obstacle to dissection was the traditional religious belief in the bodily resurrection, a belief to which Tom also addresses himself, as we have seen. The doctor, like Huck, Tom, and the Negroes, represented a ground of conviction outside traditional religious views. Huck's superstition was then not random, but arose from the frequency of grave robbing in the early days of modern medicine. Dobbins the schoolmaster is also a secret votary of medicine, and the book he keeps locked in his desk—and which must be kept from the view of children, as Becky discovers, because of its pictures of the naked human body—is a textbook in anatomy.

Huck's and Tom's wart cures have other points of resemblance to modern medicine, and indeed to modern science altogether, in contradistinction to traditional religious beliefs. Getting rid of warts is a catharsis of the body, in contrast with ridding oneself of sin, a catharsis of the soul. In ridding oneself of warts, method is all-important. The devils that carry off Hoss Williams must be approached at the right time, in the right place, and with the right incantation. Earlier, Tom had described two other methods of removing warts. One is with spunk water, the rainwater remaining in the hollow of a tree stump. Bob Tanner is said to have failed with this method. For Huck this is evidence of the inefficacy of the method. Tom, however, insists that Bob had not done it correctly, the proper way being as follows. One must go at midnight to a stump that is in the middle of the woods, and back up to it to immerse one's hand. Then you recite a prescribed verse, take eleven steps with your eyes shut, turn around three times, and walk home without speaking to anyone. "Because if you speak the charm's busted." The other method consists in splitting a bean, drawing blood from the wart and putting it on one half of the bean, and burying that half at midnight at the crossroads in the dark of the moon. Then you burn the rest of the bean. "You see that piece that's got the blood on it will keep drawing and drawing, trying to fetch the other piece to it, and so that helps to draw the wart, and pretty soon off she comes." Implicit in the three wart cures—all of which are performed at midnight—is the belief that the powers of darkness are impersonal forces, like the laws of physics and chemistry, and have no option but to produce the desired results if they are solicited in the proper manner. They differ in this from prayer, to which a personal God may or may not respond, according to the desire of the petitioner. They are also like modern science in that the power in question obeys anyone who discovers the right method, and the possession of this method is independent of the character of the seeker. For one of these superstitions to fail means to Tom only that it has not been performed properly. In fact, we never see Tom verifying any of his wart cures. He claims that he has taken off "thousands" of warts with spunk water and attributes the supposed multiplicity of his warts to the fact that he plays a great deal with frogs. That frogs cause warts is as much a superstition as the idea that spunk water removes them, and we suspect that the cause and the cure are equally imaginary. Neither of the boys exhibits any warts for removal before the trip to the graveyard. All their interest is concentrated upon the ritual and none upon the warts for the sake of which the ritual is ostensibly performed. We observe that, to a devotee of modern science, the failure of science to solve a problem does not mean that science cannot solve the problem. All it means is that the right experiment has not yet been devised or the right formula found. The votary of traditional religion, however, believes that God acts for the best, whether he seems to grant our prayers or not. It is assumed that God knows better than we do what is good for us and that, moreover, his purposes are fulfilled and his goodness made manifest, in the next world as well as in this one. Tom's expectations are confined strictly to this world, and we can see that science and superstition in a kind of fluid mixture are reshaping the traditional beliefs of St. Petersburg. Aunt Polly, although a traditionalist in religion, subscribed to all the new "health" periodicals and "phrenological frauds" and made Tom their victim whenever she deemed his health in need of assistance. Aunt Polly's traditional faith does not protect her from these incursions of pseudoscience, any more than it protects Tom from wart cures. In Aunt Polly's decisions to "cure" Tom with the water treatment, the sitz baths, the blister plasters, and finally the "pain-killer" (which was probably raw whiskey), both the ailment and the cure are probably as imaginary as the warts and the wart cure. In this respect the triumph of imagination over experience is no less in the new than in the old dispensation.

We can see that in Tom Sawyer's St. Petersburg law, religion, science, and superstition are moving in the direction of a new order in which self-preservation in this world replaces salvation in the next as the dominating human concern. All Tom's superstitions are ways of recognizing and evading or controlling threats to his person or his property. Although he believes the devils are coming to take Hoss Williams, there is no mention of the hell or hell-fire awaiting the victim. The only allusion to future punishment—there is none whatever to future reward—is when he contemplates the fate of Jimmy Hodges, "lately released," and thinks he might be willing to go too "if he only had a clean Sunday school record." When the stray dog howls nearby as the boys flee the murder scene, they reckon they're "goners." Again, Tom momentarily regrets his Sunday school record, but only because of the conviction of doom that has seized him. Elements of the old-time religion thus survive in Tom, but only as part of the new religion of self-preservation in this world. That is, they appear, along with his superstitions, as elements of his wariness in dealing with the supernatural as one among the threats to his personal safety.

Tom and Huck are drawn to the graveyard at midnight, ostensibly by the dead-cat wart cure but in fact by the secret exigencies of modern medicine. There they witness the murder of the young doctor. They become the guardians of an important truth, upon which both the justice of the law and (to a degree) the safety of the community depend. Not even Muff Potter knows the facts about the murder, because he was drunk and unconscious when it was committed. The boys are terrified and swear an oath, written out by Tom on a pine shingle, that "they will keep mum about this and they wish they may drop down dead in their tracks if they ever tell and rot." Huck admires Tom's facility in writing and takes a brass pin to prick his flesh. But Tom stops him and insists on using one of the clean needles he carries for the sewing of his shirt collar. There is a danger of poisoning from the pin, he explains to Huck. We can see, in this informative sidelight, the beginning of Tom's transition from superstition to science. Although invoking the powers of darkness by their oath, Tom will take care not to corrupt the blood that invokes those powers by any negligence with respect to natural causality. The oath is required, as Huck puts it, because "that Injun devil wouldn't make any more of drownding us than a couple of cats, if we was to squeak 'bout this and they didn't hang him." The oath then has the purpose of guaranteeing their personal safety by adding a supernatural sanction to the fear already engendered by Injun Joe. It draws a kind of pledge for its enforcement from the blood, which takes the place of God in what we would consider a conventional oath. Of course, it is their lifeblood that they wish to safeguard. Shedding blood makes the oath a kind of homeopathic antitoxin, in which respect it bears a certain resemblance to the wart cures.

Before the night is out the horror of the murder has been augmented by the howling dog. After that omen of death has passed, Tom is convinced that it is Muff Potter who is doomed. He seems unaware that if Muff is doomed, it is because of their own oath to conceal the truth. As we have seen, that oath now stands in the way of truth, justice, and the security of the community. This oath, we see, protects Injun Joe at the inquest, where the boys for the first time feel the pull of sympathy for poor, betrayed Muff Potter. They hear the "stonyhearted liar [Injun Joe] reel off his serene statement" falsely accusing Muff, and they expect "every moment that the clear sky would deliver God's lightnings upon his head." When divine vengeance fails, they conclude that "this miscreant sold himself to Satan and it would be fatal to meddle with the property of such a power as that." Tom's conscience is thus quieted by the opinion that God has abdicated responsibility too. When in the crisis he does the work of God, it will not, however, appear to be God's work. It will be Tom Sawyer's.

It is some weeks later that Muff, who has now been charged with the murder, finally comes to trial. The boys are oppressed by their secret, yet fear dominates guilt. Tom seeks out Huck to find whether the latter's resolve has weakened. Huck seems firm enough. He appears to know Injun Joe better than Tom, and being an outcast himself is less likely to have protection from Joe's vengeance. It is clear that Tom fears his own resolve more than he fears Huck's when he suggests that they swear their oath of secrecy again. Having sworn, the boys relapse into commiseration for Muff. "He ain't no account," says Huck, "but then he hain't ever done anything to hurt anybody. Just fishes a little, to get money to get drunk on. . . ." But it transpires that he also shared food with Huck, when there wasn't enough for two, and that he has mended kites for Tom and knitted hooks to his fishlines. They try to relieve their guilt by doing many small kindnesses for Muff at the village jail, but the pathetic gratitude they receive in return only adds mightily to their inward torture.

The trial comes on, and at the end of the second day, with Injun Joe's evidence unshaken, it appears there can be but one verdict. That night Tom is out late and returns home "in a tremendous state of excitement." The next day three witnesses are called. The first testifies to seeing Muff wash himself at a brook, early in the morning following the murder. A second testifies to the identity of the murder knife. A third attests that the knife in question was Muff's. In each case, Muff's lawyer declines to cross-examine. The courtroom buzzes with dissatisfaction at the lawyer for the defense, who appears to be letting his case go by default. But suddenly the lawyer addresses the court, saying that he has changed his defense from that he had indicated in his opening remarks two days before. Then he had intended to prove only that Muff had committed an involuntary homicide under the influence of drink. Turning to the clerk, he says. "Call Thomas Sawyer!" In an atmosphere electric with puzzled anticipation, the clerk administers the oath, an oath different from that Tom had administered to himself and to Huck. Then Muff's lawyer leads Tom, breathless and almost inaudible at first, through the sensational narrative of the events he and Huck had witnessed from their hiding place that night in the graveyard. "The strain upon pent emotion reached its climax when the boy said: '—and as the doctor fetched around and Muff Potter fell, Injun Joe jumped with the knife and—' Crash! Quick as lightning the half-breed sprang for a window, tore his way through all opposers, and was gone!"

"Tom was a glittering hero once more—the pet of the old, the envy of the young." The heroism is on a more solid basis than before; but Tom now pays a price for his glory. His days, we are told, were "days of splendor and exultation," but his nights "were seasons of horror." "Injun Joe infested all his dreams, and always with doom in his eye." What was it that tempted Tom into this new heroism? All his glory hitherto had been the consequence of tricks played upon others. Fear had dominated him from the moment of the murder. Sympathy for Muff Potter had only led to the precaution of a second oath, until the trial was under way and the tension began to build. The scene in the courtroom certainly was one whose "theatrical gorgeousness" appealed to his nature as strongly as that in which he returned to play the lead at his own funeral. We have no introspective evidence of what it was that led to Tom's great decision to risk Injun Joe's vengeance, or the doom invoked upon himself in his own oaths. In *Huckleberry Finn* we are provided abundant evidence of the hero's inward processes of moral crisis and of the deliberations accompanying their resolution. The Huck of the later novel articulates his private world much as does Hamlet in the great soliloquies. In Tom's case, we are never told in advance how the hero determines upon his great deeds. In the whitewashing episode we are told only that "an inspiration ... a great, magnificent inspiration" had burst upon him. At the Sunday school we saw Tom mysteriously trading for tickets among the boys, but his sudden presentation of himself for the prize Bible, in the presence of Judge Thatcher, is almost as much of a surprise to us as to Mr. Walters, the Sunday school superintendent. Later, in the midst of his pirating expedition, as he stands silently in the night over the troubled sleeping form of Aunt Polly, we only know that "his face lighted with a happy solution of his thought." In each of these cases we only learn what he had decided from the results of his decision. An indication of how Tom decides may be gleaned, however, from the description of how he chooses his runaway vocation. He contemplates the careers of the clown, the soldier, and the Indian chief. Then, as the vision of the Black Avenger of the Spanish Main seizes and convulses his being, it sweeps the field, and his choice is made. It is the workings of Tom's passions, not any inner reflection upon alternative courses or motives, that determine his fate. We venture to suggest, therefore, that fear controlled him from the moment of the murder but that compassion for Muff Potter warred closely with fear until the second oath recorded the ascendancy of the latter.

We recollect but one reference to Tom's conscience in connection with the murder trial. In the twenty-third chapter, in which the case is brought on, we are told that "Every reference to the murder sent a shudder to his heart, for his troubled conscience and fears almost persuaded him that these remarks were put forth in his hearing as 'feelers'; he did not see how he could be suspected of knowing anything about the murder, but he still could not be comfortable in the midst of this gossip." It is not clear from this whether conscience and fears are altogether different things. Tom would like to be "comfortable," even as he earlier had sought a comfortable way of enjoying the advantages of death. He feels threatened by Injun Joe; but he also feels threatened by the community, which could use legal processes to compel him to testify if they suspected what he knew. Yet we know that he is troubled also by his attachment to Muff Potter and by the threat to Muff. It is our judgment that it is, strictly speaking, compassion for Muff, not conscience proper, that motivates Tom in the direction he finally takes. By compassion we mean sympathy arising from a sense of identification with another. We distinguish it from conscience, insofar as the latter implies recognition of a duty or obligation. Tom shows no sense of obligation to Muff, or to either law or justice. But he quite literally *feels* for him, and this feeling, this passion, is at war with the more fundamental passion he has for his own life. In the end, the ascendancy of fear over compassion is reversed, not by the strength of compassion, but by its mighty assistance from Tom's love of glory and éclat. The melodrama of the trial and the vision of himself in the central role—like that of the little child of the millennium—overcome the contrary force of fear. The playing of the heroic role before the entire community, and of the role of personal savior of Muff, presented over-whelming immediate gratifications, which obliterated for the moment the more remote sense of danger from Injun Joe.

But let us understand thoroughly what that love of glory was that seems to have acted so decisively upon Tom. Love of glory has two roots that, strictly understood, differ as much as conscience and compassion. Glory is an intensification of fame, as fame is of honor. We can love honor either from self-knowledge or from self-love. In the former case, what we ultimately seek is a competent assurance of our virtue or excellence. That is to say, we may desire virtue as a means to well-being, and honor as a means to virtue. The quest for honor may then be an element in the quest for self-knowledge in the service of excellence. But the quest for glory rooted in self-love apart from self-knowledge tends to make glory an end in itself. The passion Tom seeks to gratify—clearly of the latter species—thus appears as a passion merely for a name. Perhaps this is not unnatural for a boy who has no father and who must overcome his anonymity by becoming a founder in his own right. We spoke earlier of the love of distinction to which Tom appealed in his sale of whitewashing privileges. Love of fame, in a modern mass democracy, tends to be the passionate negative to the constant threat to the sense of individual identity. At bottom, it is the equivalent upon the human level of the reaction of the organism to the threat of physical extinction, as that threat is seen from the perspective of modern science. From this perspective the individual organism is never more than a hypothetical and temporary sequestration of atoms upon a gravitational field into which, presently, it will dissolve. Radical nominalisms in physics and in ethics parallel each other. Because Tom's glory has no foundation beyond the acclaim he sees and hears—or feels—he is constantly driven to repeat it. He must constantly revive that limelight in which alone he experiences assurances of his own authen-ticity. Whether he is swearing the oath to keep the secret, or revealing the same secret before the astounded court, he is obeying the same law of his nature.

Tom's questionable glory in the church has now been transformed into unquestionable glory in the courtroom, and beyond. Yet Injun Joe remains at liberty. Rewards have been offered, a detective from St. Louis has come and gone, but no Joe. Of course, it is Tom, assisted by Huck, who must prove Joe's nemesis. After the trial had ended so sensationally and Tom had been immortalized by the village newspaper, "There were some that believed he would be President, yet, if he escaped hanging." The humor notwithstanding, it is Tom's quasi criminality that qualifies him as an antagonist of Joe. "Set a thief to catch a thief" is the relevant proverb.

In fact, Tom never sets out to catch Joe. Because of Mark Twain's myth that this is a story of a boy, certain things are ascribed to chance by the art of the novel that otherwise might be ascribed to the art of the protagonist. Tom and Huck discover the secret meeting place of Joe and his confederate as an accidental by-product of a treasure hunt that is presented to us as a development unrelated to the prior action of the plot. In a ruined, abandoned house, they witness the equally accidental discovery by Joe of the long-lost treasure of the Murrel Gang. From their hiding place they watch the criminals cart off the treasure, which they hear is to be hidden in one of Joe's dens, "Number Two—under the cross." At that point the boys set off, not to apprehend Joe, but to steal the treasure for themselves. Their motive is simply to rob the robbers.

It is of some interest to recognize the cause of Joe's undoing. It is not Tom's skill in tracking either him or the treasure. Joe and his companion planned to light out for Texas with their loot; but Joe would not do so until they had done one more "dangerous" job. Had they foregone that final job, they might have taken both their loot and the treasure and departed for a life of ease, and perhaps even respectability. But the job consists, as the confederate himself discovers only at the last moment, in taking revenge upon the Widow Douglas. At a crucial moment, Joe threatens even the confederate with death unless he renders the necessary assistance in carrying the act of vengeance to its conclusion. Joe had murdered young Doctor Robinson as revenge for once having caused him to be jailed for vagrancy. The widow's husband, who had been a justice of the peace, had done the same thing. Moreover, he had once done something infinitely worse; he had had Joe horsewhipped in front of the village jail, "like a nigger!" The insult to Joe's pride had demanded the judge's death, and since the judge had cheated him by dying without Joe's assistance, it now demanded the widow's mutilation. Joe has a brutal and barbaric sense of honor, yet it is a sense of honor nonetheless. It is moreover a sense of honor that has nothing in common with Tom's love of glory and éclat. It causes him to lose both treasure and life. Yet Joe shows, in the dialogue with is confederate, that neither life nor gold count for much with him in comparison with his pride or honor. Mark Twain presents Joe to us as a worthless as well as a dangerous being. Yet except for Aunt Polly's old-fashioned piety, Joe appears to be the sole representative within the novel of devotion to an immaterial good. Joe's pagan pride joins Aunt Polly's Christian humility upon the altar of Tom's materialistic self-glorification.

Tom and Huck trace Injun Joe to his lair in the whisky room of the temperance tavern. They believe the treasure is in the room and that if they can get in there when Joe is away they can make off with it. They are certain he will not leave by day, and agree that Huck will watch every night and come for Tom when Joe has left on the "dangerous" job. Several nights pass without event, and on Saturday Tom goes on the long-heralded picnic that had been planned by Becky. Why Tom risks being away on a night when Injun Joe might emerge from his den is expressed to us as follows. "The sure fun of the evening outweighed the uncertain treasure; and boylike, he determined to yield to the stronger inclination and not allow himself to think of the box of money another time that day." We think the author meant, not that Tom "determined to yield," but that he yielded. The present good of the picnic outweighed the treasure, just as the fear of Injun Joe had been outweighed by the glory in the courtroom.

Before pursuing the dual themes of the treasure and the picnic, we must direct attention to an episode that was a necessary condition of the picnic, namely, the reconciliation of Tom and Becky. Their estrangement, which began with the discovery by Becky that Tom had been engaged to Amy Lawrence, had finally reached an impasse. But one day during the noon recess, Becky passes the schoolmaster's desk and sees the key in the lock. The master keeps a book there, the identity of which is the great and tormenting mystery of the school. Becky turns the key, opens the drawer, and presently is inspecting the anatomy text with its handsomely engraved frontispiece, "a human figure, stark naked." At that moment Tom steps up behind her, Becky starts, and as luck would have it, tears the page, Becky bursts into tears: her terror of discovery and punishment thereupon multiply a thousandfold her grievance against Tom.

What old Dobbins does in such cases is to demand of the class that the guilty party step forward. When no one volunteers, he asks each of the scholars in turn, fixing his gaze full upon him or her, to discover evidences of guilt. Such a procedure might not succeed with such a hardened prevaricator as Tom, but it cannot fail with such an innocent as Becky. Becky might have confessed had she not been so paralyzed by fear. The beating that is the sure punishment for such a crime appears to her in all the lurid light of eternal damnation. But Tom has been licked times without number. We have seen him deliberately court a licking in order to be sent to sit with the girls, the first day Becky had come to the school. He can't understand why Becky is so bitter at the prospect. "That's just like a girl—they're so thin-skinned and chicken-hearted," he comments. But of course we know that that is part of their charm for Tom. At the same time, we know that taking a licking is about the smallest price Tom could possibly pay for any good thing he might desire. At the crucial moment, just as Dobbins reaches Becky in his relentless search for the guilty one, Tom has another of his great inspirations. "He sprang to his feet and shouted—*I done it!*' . . . and when he stepped forward to go to his punishment the surprise, the gratitude, the adoration that shone upon him

out of poor Becky's eyes seemed pay enough for a hundred floggings."
Their reconciliation is complete. Indeed, it should be characterized, not as
a reconciliation, but as a conquest. No knight slaying a dragon had ever
won fair lady by what the lady had perceived as greater valor.

So Tom and Becky are inseparable upon the long-delayed picnic.
In the afternoon the children take to exploring McDougal's cave. There
was a main avenue that was familiar to most. No one, we are told "knew"
the cave, for there were labyrinths beyond labyrinths, and it was not
customary to venture beyond the main avenue and the corridors and
recesses immediately adjacent thereto. "Tom Sawyer knew as much of the
cave as any one."

Tom leads Becky on into the cave, beyond the known portion to
the unknown, until finally they are lost, with no idea, and finally no
rational hope, of emerging alive. Why? At a certain point, "the ambition
to be a discoverer seized him." Tom is a venturer; his is the spirit of
enterprise. But Tom never seeks danger for its own sake; nor does he
willingly face danger except when, as in the courtroom, it is suppressed by
another, more immediate passion. But now Tom is led to unsought and
unnecessary danger. There was no reason for him to venture into the
unknown without marking the pathway by which they might return. But
Tom is under a compulsion to break with the trodden pathways, to go
onward without retracing his steps. There will be either death or salvation,
but no turning back. And so, having lost the way and being driven ever
onward, Tom and Becky are lost.[2]

Their only food is a piece of cake she has "saved . . . from the

---

[2] The exact cause of the break with the return path is not easy to state
precisely. Tom had made two smoke marks for future guidance before they were
attacked by the bats. To escape, Tom leads Becky hastily down a corridor, just as
Becky's candle is put out. The flight continues for some time, down a succession of
corridors entered at random. Is the pathway broken at this point? Tom does not think
of returning for some time, still impelled by his search for novelties to brag about
later. He then tells Becky he reckons he could find the way back, but fears encounter-
ing the bats again. He insists upon searching for a new way. His fear of the bats appears
to govern him at this point, just as his fear of Injun Joe does a little later. But the bats
are a largely imaginary danger. A resolute attempt to protect the candle, at least until
they reached the smoke marks or the staircase might have succeeded. Even if they
failed, they would have remained at a point in the cave where they might easily have
been rescued. In fact, had they remained near the bats, they might have followed them
out of the cave when night came, and the bats emerged in their quest for food. If it is
true, as we are told, that Tom knew the ways of bats, his behavior becomes even more
unreasonable. But Tom is ever dominated by the passion of the moment. He never acts
reasonably. It is in his defiance of reason, and the cunning of his passion, that his *virtu*
consists. His way is irreversibly downwards, and he emerges not from the top, but
from the bottom of the cave. One can hardly imagine a more apt symbol of the
replacement of Platonic by Machiavellian republicanism.

picnic for us to dream on, Tom, the way grown-up people do with wedding cake. . . .'' Tom shows great tenderness for Becky's growing weakness in the cave and reserves the greater part of the cake for her, never eating more than a small part of his own share. Yet he never returns the pledge of her troth. To him, the cake is not consecrated; it is only a means of survival. When they come to a spring, Tom decides that they must make a halt; at least the water will keep them alive longer, while they wait and hope for rescue. Becky becomes very weak; slowly she sinks into "a dreary apathy," and eventually loses all hope. She tells Tom to take his kite line and continue to explore if he chooses; but makes him promise to return from time to time and to hold her hand when the end comes.

During this terrible vigil, Tom makes a discovery—that Injun Joe is in the chamber of the cave next to their own. Fear of Joe overcomes fear of the cave at that moment. It apparently never occurs to Tom to appeal to Joe to rescue them. Yet Joe could have had no grudge against Becky; and it might have been in Joe's interest to have saved both of them. After all, there was already a petition being circulated for Joe's pardon. Rescuing the children after all other hope had gone might have led to the success of the petition. But Tom's future glory brooks no such medium. How then and why does Tom succeed?

There are two conspicuous facts about the vigil in the darkness. First is the apparent absence from Tom of any conception of his own death. Although Tom knows fear—particularly of Injun Joe—there never seems to be the decided equation between hopelessness and death that there is in the case of Becky. Becky feels her growing weakness and accepts death as its inevitable conclusion. But Tom, although aware of the facts of the situation, never resigns himself to it. Second is the absence of any suggestion of prayer, by either Tom or Becky. We recall that only once before did Tom ever pray, when Huck was overcome by fright at the approach of the "devils" in the graveyard. But he broke it off before ever naming the Lord. In his utmost extremity, Tom relies on no other power than himself, whether higher or lower.

Tom then, wasting no time or energy on useless thoughts or actions, extends his kite line, first down one corridor, then down another, and then down still another. Turning back from the third, "he glimpsed a far-off speck that looked like daylight." Dropping the line, he groped toward the light and presently "pushed his head and shoulders through a small hole and saw the broad Mississippi rolling by!" Tom is thus saved, and Becky is saved by Tom, by a light vouchsafed to him far within the innermost recesses of the cave, at a point where the probability of finding light—or of light finding him—was the most remote, if not most unreasonable. Tom thus becomes an authentic hero of that new Calvinism in which grace comes, not by works or faith, but by the spirit of utter and indefeasible self-reliance. Tom, we may say, is saved by the Lord because the Lord finds merit in the fact that it had never occurred to Tom to ask for help. Tom may have appeared as a clever and lucky trickster hitherto. But he will emerge with a new aura of authenticity and legitimacy. The highest principle of the old order has now anointed the leader of the new. Tom's education and the formation of his character have been completed deep within the earth. Tom Sawyer's Gang is now ready for the light of the sun.

Huck meanwhile has kept his own faithful vigil. On the night that Tom and Becky are wandering ever deeper into the cave, Huck follows Joe and his companion as they leave their lair. But they carry a box with them, which Huck mistakenly believes is the treasure. There is no time to go for Tom. The men pursue a course toward the Widow Douglas's, and following closely in the dark, Huck discovers the evil nature of their mission. But the widow has company, and the men lurk under cover waiting for the lights to go out. Then Huck runs for help. The Welshman and his sons arrive with guns. Joe and his confederate are driven off, but not captured. Huck is terrified and is taken into the Welshman's house, where he is seized with a fever and for a long time loses consciousness. When he comes to himself again, he too will taste, but without pleasure, the glory of a hero.

Before Huck recovers, Tom and Becky triumphantly return. Judge Thatcher has the mouth of the cave sealed, not knowing that Joe is within. And Joe dies of thirst and starvation before Tom discovers what the Judge had done. The light that had been vouchsafed to Tom has been denied to Joe.

Now the boys are safe, and when Huck is well enough, Tom takes him aside and imparts his secret. Number Two is in the cave, and Tom knows an easy way to get there. He is sure that that is where the treasure is kept. They gather up provisions and two bags to carry the treasure. Then they head for the secret place five miles below the mouth of the cave from which he and Becky had emerged to safety. Exploring the chamber where Tom had nearly stumbled upon Joe, they discover a cross, done with candle smoke on a big rock. This without doubt is "Number Two," and the treasure must be "under the cross." But Huck is again struck with terror. Injun Joe's ghost must be nearby. Tom remonstrates that the ghost must surely be at the mouth of the cave, where Joe had died, rather than here. But Huck disagrees, "No, Tom, it wouldn't. It would hang around the money. I know the way of ghosts, and so do you." Tom begins to have doubts too. That the ghost would stick to the treasure seemed eminently reasonable. But once more inspiration comes to Tom.

"Looky-here, Huck, what fools we're making of ourselves! Injun Joe's ghost ain't a-going to come around where there's a cross!" And so the sacred symbol performs the function that will now be characteristic in the order over which Tom is to preside. It will point the way to the new salvation and keep the air pure and free of evil spirits for the votaries of the faith.

Huck and Tom return to St. Petersburg. As they enter the town, the Welshman sees them and tells them they are wanted at the Widow Douglas's. Their wagon appears to him to be loaded with old metal. As they reach the widow's it appears that something great is in progress. All the people of consequence in the town are there. The boys are quickly sent aside for scrubbing and dressing. Huck wants to find a rope and drop out the window and escape. But Tom senses another scene of grandeur and won't miss it for anything. The celebration is a setting for the supposed grand revelation by the Welshman of how Huck had risked his life that Saturday night to save the widow. Huck had earlier sworn the Welshman to secrecy, but the death of Injun Joe evidently has convinced the Welshman—but not Huck—that the oath is no longer binding. Huck still feared that Joe might have some friends around. But the secret had already leaked out, and the surprise lacked some of its supposed force. When the widow responded by saying that she meant to give Huck a home, have him educated, and start him in business some day, "Tom's chance was come. He said: 'Huck don't need it, Huck's rich.' "

And so the long trail of successes winds its way to the triumph to end all triumphs. Once more Tom is the little child in a drama that has all the glory of the millennium. The whitewashing of the fence, the prize-winning in the Sunday school, the return from the dead, the revelation in the courtroom, all pale into insignificance beside the twelve thousand dollars in gold coins that now transfix the assembled magnates of St. Petersburg.

Tom's glory will now endure. The Lord has shown him to be truly of the elect. He has shown him the light of salvation in his hour of sorest need. His cross has pointed him the way to the treasure. And the treasure the cross has revealed and protected is such as neither moth nor rust can corrupt, or other thieves can steal. Tom Sawyer's Gang is set upon the path to greatness and immortality such as no faith can assure so well, either in this world or the next, as a large capital.

11 | THE CONDITIONS OF FREEDOM

A recent issue of the Sunday *Los Angeles Times* carried a story[1] about an attractive twenty-three-year-old Radcliffe graduate who had recently joined the Harvard staff as "assistant to the Director of University Health Services." This euphemism, we are told, was translated in the Harvard Bulletin into "Harvard's sex czar—or czarina." The Bulletin went on to give her almost complete credit "for the flowering of the sexual ministry at Harvard." The article gives no details as to how this vocation flourishes, and it is to be hoped that there has been no bowdlerization by a prudish typographer. The sentiments expressed in the interview suggest a general lack of satisfaction to be the order of the day at Harvard, a sort of communal deflourishing, one is tempted to say. Of course, "czar—or czarina" and "ministry" suggest authority and salvation, two things that I thought were in ill repute at Harvard, except for those who think Harvard itself the source of authority and the place of salvation. Perhaps the reappearance of these discredited ideas in the person of an imperial priestess indicates once again that, although nature may be expelled with a pitchfork, it will always return. Without a conception of authority and of salvation, no less than of freedom, human life is intolerable. Curiously enough, that is the main idea to be gathered from the interview with the young lady herself.

Concerning her professional specialty, she remarks, "For the most part the organizations in our society have abnegated any responsibilities to try to help find a new reasonable, workable code of sex ethics." But we are not given any indication what the criteria for discerning such a code might be, should someone discover it. In fact, it was my impression that the problem had arisen because of the rejection of the very idea of a "code" laid down by organizations—any organizations—for individuals, whose freedom was held to be stultified by that very fact. In the assumption that a reasonable code would, perforce, be a new one, we are in the presence of a dogma as unquestionable as the doctrine of the Trinity

Reprinted by permission of the James Madison Society of Claremont Men's College and the *Claremont Journal of Public Affairs* 1 (1972). This is a revised version of the author's inaugural lecture as Henry Salvatori Research Professor of Political Philosophy, Claremont Men's College, Claremont, Calif., Mar. 2, 1972.

[1] Robert J. Donovan, "The New Permissiveness and Students' Old Confusion," *Los Angeles Times*, Feb. 20, 1972, section G, p. 7.

in thirteenth-century Rome. But what if the most reasonable and work-able code were to be an old one, and the failure to find it due to the fact that the searchers are looking in the wrong direction? According to our czarina-priestess, "people are groping desperately for some personal code of ethics. There isn't any good guiding principle to follow now." It is certainly illuminating that, some millenia after the *Old* and *New Testaments,* the *Republic,* and the *Nicomachean Ethics,* not to mention such comparatively recent works as the *Foundation of the Metaphysics of Morals,* or even *Utilitarianism,* Harvard's undergraduate counselors preach the gospel of no gospel.

But this young person, although apparently illiterate, is not un-observant. Concerning the current campus scene, she says, "Young people are turning inward to try to find something they can do free from political manipulations, from financial squabbling. They want to do something that can bring them a sort of inward satisfaction. . . .A lot of people are turning to things that can be done with their hands—pottery, woodwork, weaving, things like that." Well, if they don't read books at Harvard, at least they're not burning them. She goes on to observe that more are turning to law and medicine, not because of any good intrinsic to them, but because they have something of the concreteness of pottery and weaving. The one thing that nobody at Harvard wants now is "success—as measured by money, fame, prestige." They want success, "but not on those terms. They want to find their own terms." Here I think it would be proper to interject that most universal and revealing of contemporary slogans, that what is wanted is success defined as "doing one's own thing." But the great problem is precisely here. What is one's own thing? If one does not know what it is, how can you do it? To Jerry Rubin's famous injunction, "Do it!" the chorus returns, "What?" According to our au-thority, "The most desolate thing is when a person has turned inward after having abandoned those outward values as worthless and then can't find anything inside either." This is the typical predicament of her clients. "They are not worrying about survival, but whether it is worth surviving." This is the fashionable existential crisis of our times. For those to whom it means taking seriously Hamlet's question, "To be or not to be?" it could perhaps prove a blessing. On the other hand, if it is a rhetorical question, assuming a negative answer, the epitaph of Western man might very well come to be: he might have survived but didn't think it worthwhile.

It is the thesis of this essay that the goodness of life has come into question because what once were called "the laws of Nature and of Nature's God" have disappeared from our view. As we approach the bicentennial of the Declaration of Independence, there seems to be hardly a scholar or a statesman in the nation who takes seriously the teaching of which that notable document is an expression. That it represents the ideology—or even the ideals—of the Founders, and that somehow we have benefited from their commitment, might be granted in some loose sense. But that the laws of nature do exist, and that we are bound by them because they are, not the ideals of men, but the reality of a purposeful universe, and that human freedom is a freedom to disregard such laws only at our cost, seems to be taken seriously almost nowhere. The emancipation of Western man by technology from the necessities of nature has led to a loss of consciousness of the goodness that those necessities serve. As the old struggle for survival has, through the equivocal beneficence of technology, receded into the background of daily existence, the uses of leisure have become mysterious. Never has a whole society enjoyed such wealth as has the United States, and this wealth has increasingly become the share of Western Europe, Great Britain and the Commonwealth, Japan, and to a degree even some of the communist states. Wealth, properly understood, is the instrument of freedom and of happiness, and in the past freedom has always been seen as an oasis in the desert of necessity. But as the desert blooms, we do not see the enlargement of the oasis. Instead, as the desert disappears, so does the oasis, and we fail to comprehend the uses of the garden that blooms in their place. Apparently, if you do not worry about surviving, then you do worry about whether it is worth surviving. And so, what is perhaps the most privileged class in the entire history of the human race, that of the Harvard College student, is among the most miserable!

Our Harvard counselor spoke of a turning to handicrafts and to law and medicine, in the current quest for meaningful lives. Certainly the value of hobbies—or pastimes, as they once were called—is not to be depreciated. But professions or hobbies have this in common: they are essentially instrumental, and what is instrumental cannot endure in the absence of that to which it is instrumental. Instrument-making cannot go on indefinitely, if there are no musicians. And health cannot be chosen always for its own sake. Healthy people can be miserable, and they may even commit suicide when they do not think it worth surviving. For someone to pursue medicine as an alternative to suicide may be opportune on occasion; but in the long run helping others to be healthy, any more than being healthy oneself, does not solve the problem of someone who can see no other reason for living than to be healthy. And hobbies in the form of the ornamental arts are equally vain. All such arts are means of adorning, of making beautiful, something useful. But what is useful must be useful in relation to an end which is not itself merely useful. The art of the Parthenon and the art of the Cathedral of Chartres were not in the service of themselves. In each case the artisans gave reverent homage to a purpose and to a design which they believed to be greater than anything of which they conceived themselves to be capable. Without this belief in something greater than their art, their art would not have been possible. But it is precisely disbelief in something greater than themselves which characterizes the spurious inwardness of the apathetic clients of our Harvard counselor. An empty soul turned inward finds: nothing. Turning to the handicrafts or to the professions can for these young persons be little more than a random attempt to relieve their apathy, and likely to last only until they are overcome once again by a new fit of revolutionary nihilism.

What is so strikingly absent from the horizon of our Harvard counselor—and we suppose from the education she had so recently received—was any conception of the liberal arts. In truth, the liberal arts, like the idea of God, seem moribund, if not dead in higher education today. The liberal arts I would define, very briefly, as the arts of free men. And free men I call those who, supplied with the necessities of life, and living only under laws they have given themselves, know how to employ their leisure well. And they only can be said to know how to employ their leisure well, who find a sufficient cause of the good life, in the arts by which the mind articulates its consciousness of the world. As the human mind becomes conscious of itself as a mind, it must ask if there is in fact anything to understand, that is to say, whether there is in fact a world, and whether and in what sense it can be known. Moreover, it must ask whether it is itself equipped to understand that world. If these questions are answered affirmatively, then it must ultimately be with a single answer. For if the mind does find an intelligible universe, it must find in the existence of that universe some ground for the mind's ability to know it. In thus stating the question or questions to which the liberal arts are in their nature addressed, I can state the problem which I believe lies at the heart of the crisis of Western civilization. Modern science is predicated upon the assumption that there are sufficient causes of all events, that is, that when all the causes bearing upon a given event are known, that event will be understood as necessary, as a fully determined outcome of those causes. This hypothesis can be most easily seen in the case of the most powerful doctrines claiming scientific status in our time: Marxism and Freudianism. Freud never wearied of repeating that the greatest of fallacies was to believe that there were any exceptions to the law of universal determinism of psychic phenomena. Psychoanalysis is based absolutely upon the premise that the unconscious determines the conscious. The fundamental energy of the living organism—human or nonhuman—is directed toward self-preservation. The "libido" is the name given by Freud to the primitive form of psychic energy. All higher forms of psychic energy are displacements of the primal form. Consciousness, including its highest form, reason, is itself understood as a displacement of unconscious appetitiveness, by obstacles or frustrations. But it is unconscious desire which is the moving force in human experience. The experiences which decisively determine behavior are those which have been thrust below the level of consciousness by reason of their painfulness; the process of forgetting is held to be one whereby the painful is transformed into the tolerable, if not into the pleasant. It will appear therefore that psychology is seen by Freud—and this is the distinctive character of modern psychology in its many non-Freudian variants as well—as a comprehension of the displacement, and transformation by displacement, of an original, undifferentiated inertial force within the soul. That is, psychology is the physics of living beings. But living beings are said to be understood when the energy within the soul has been comprehended in the same way that the energy of matter in motion has been comprehended by modern physics. In other words, living beings are said to be understood when they can be conceived as if they were dead beings.

The psychoanalytic procedure consists in the attempt to recapture forgotten experiences, and to retranslate the symbolic forms in which they are remembered by the patient into the generic prototypes of human experience recognized by the analyst. Of these, the most famous is the Oedipus complex. The end result of analysis is supposed to be the freeing of the patient from the power of those painfully repressed experiences. When the symbols, particularly those found in dreams, are unmasked, when the patient can be made to see why in a literal sense his behavior is childish, he is supposed to be free to change it. Thus, the conscious behavior of the patient is supposed hitherto to have been a byproduct of unconscious motives derived from repressed experiences; and these repressions in turn to have been caused by obstacles presented to a primal libido. None of the reasons why the patient thinks he does what he does are the real reasons until analysis has revealed the chain of causality to him. After analysis, however, he may choose the things that he wishes—or wills—to do. The chain of determinism is thought to come to an end here. Apart from the inconsistency of so supposing—to which we shall return later—there is the question of what, now that he is "free," the patient ought to do. It is not altogether surprising that we encounter at this point the dilemma of our Harvard counselor. For neither Freud nor any of his epigones have discovered any "code of sex ethics" or, for that matter, any way of life, which they can pronounce to be superior to any other. The neurotic is distinguished from the nonneurotic only by conventions which are themselves intelligible only as long-sustained collective neuroses. In fact, as Freud makes clear in *Civilization and Its Discontents,* civilization itself is one vast neurosis. To be cured means no more than to be in a kind of equilibrium with the prevailing neuroses. But why equilibrium is better than disequilibrium is something for which no reason can be found. It seems to me, at least, that the happy fetishist may be better off than the cured patient, faced with the existential crisis. The only comfort I find in Freudianism is in the fact that no cure is more than partial, and that it is always temporary!

But why is all perception of reality determined by the passions, while what is called scientific reason is exempt from the determination of those same passions? In truth, modern science lives in a dualistic universe, exempting itself from the laws of the phenomena it studies. This is the root of that "multiverse" whose institution is the "multiversity," within which youth, not surprisingly, can find no guidance for their lives.

We may see this same dualism in Marxism, where the laws of historical development are said to be absolutely predetermined, and where all religion, philosophy, art, and even scientific thought are said to be the outcome of a class consciousness, which has been engendered upon the mind by mindless matter. The laws of matter inhere in the matter itself, and are held to be without exception—without, that is to say, any indeterminacy or freedom—in the manner of their causality. In Marxism, revolutionary activity corresponds exactly to the psychoanalytic interview, as a process wherein the maladjustments caused by the conflict between illusion and reality are resolved. In the one case, conscious rationality is the spurious handmaiden of buried, repressed experience, at the bottom of which is the Oedipus complex, and beneath which is the libido, itself only the psychic affection of the body. In the other, class consciousness is the spurious surrogate of the primeval serpent, which in this case is private property. Private property is to Marxism what the Oedipus complex is to Freudianism. But the proletariat, like the patient, can be freed from the contradictions of a false consciousness at the end of a process which is now revolution. In both cases the reason of the scientific analyst is held to be exempt from the determinism characteristic of the human subjects he studies and guides. He claims to be announcing a truth in which his mind conforms to reality, and his passions, unlike those of ordinary humanity follow a course dictated by his reason. Yet there is this further correspondence between Marxism and Freudianism: just as the latter cannot say what the patient ought to do, when he is free to do what he wishes to do, so the former cannot tell what the forms of life either will be, or ought to be, in the classless society of the future. In neither case, that is to say, is there any argument whatever that addresses itself to the uses of freedom, or says why the possession of freedom is not a curse rather than a blessing.

Both Marxism and Freudianism are obsessively atheistic, and fanatically hostile to Biblical theology. Central to that theology is the idea of particular providence; that is, the idea that God can and does interfere with the causality of things that exist apart from God. God, it is held, brings about ends which would be impossible if the sufficient causes of all events were only those powers that inhere in the agents themselves. Yet Marx and Freud—like our contemporary behavioral scientists—reserve to scientific intelligence within the world precisely this power of intervening in what would otherwise be a seamless web of ineluctable necessity. Every schoolboy once knew—at least every schoolboy who had read Milton's *Paradise Lost* once knew—the riddle posed by the simultaneous assertion of God's omnipotence and foreknowledge, on the one hand, and man's freedom on the other. It was enough for the believer that God had vouched for the truth of this teaching, however mysterious that teaching might remain on the level of human intelligence. Marx and Freud, aiming at the demystification of the human phenomena, attack Biblical theology as irrational. Yet there is nothing self-contradictory in a position which, accepting the divine origin of the world, accepts the dualism of God and the world, and ascribes to God a power it denies to the world. Yet to assert an all-comprehensive necessity, springing from the properties of matter, and to see mind itself as one of these properties, and *then* to exempt certain particular minds, is a self-contradictory and utterly unacceptable dualism. Unreason has erected its altar in the temple of Science, and its votaries have in the name of Science, exacted a blinder faith than was ever known in the so-called ages of faith.

The universe observed by modern science is then one from which the mind of the observer himself has been banished. In fact, mind itself has been banished, for what remains are only events, or behavior, from which the decisive element of inwardness or self-consciousness is lacking. That is why behavioral scientists cannot distinguish between cybernetic devices, including computers, and the human brain. For the brain to them is not an instrument of thought, but only of action. Thinking is conceived as the activity of a self-compensating automatic control device, a mechanism by which the organism reacts upon its environment, in order to maintain an equilibrium with and within that environment. Thought about thinking, except of course in the present sense of methodology, is dismissed as illusory, although every scientific doctrine ultimately asserts the truth of such an illusion. But a world without mind is a world without purpose, and a mind conceiving itself to be part of such a world can find no purpose for life, whether it turns inward or outward in its quest.

But is this dilemma consistent with a genuinely empirical view of the world? Everything depends upon how one conceives of the term empirical. This term is derived from the Greek, *empeireia,* which means experience. Modern science, as we have said, believes that every event in the world, when it is fully understood, will be seen to be fully determined, that is to say, to be the necessary outcome of all the causes of which it is the effect. And I cited Freud in particular, to the effect that freedom is a delusion, and determinism the reality, of the world of psychic reality. The quest for reality is the quest for the underlying experience, the true empeireia—the Oedipus complex—and away from the appearances which we mistakenly take for reality. Above all, we are enjoined by modern science never to trust ordinary sense perception, by which we might believe that the earth is the center of the solar system, or the sun is no bigger than a silver dollar, or that light does not travel but is instantaneous. True empiricism is said to dispel these illusions. Scientific empiricism is the necessary corrective, it is said, for the naive, or prescientific forms of understanding of the world. Now let us see. Let us raise a question which is today very fashionable, but let us consider it in a most unfashionable way. That question is, who am I? My reason for raising this question is not to confront you with the cosmic dread of the existential crisis. I mean in fact to show you that the question can be answered, and that it is answered because reason itself is reasonable—contrary to all the things said about reason these days. There will be grave difficulties with our answer; it will, in fact, be an answer that in a decisive sense leaves the question open, while enabling us to live with the self whose identity has been challenged. And I suggest that the answers to many important questions, including most of those that drive them up against the wall at Harvard, may be answered in the same way. Among such questions are, "What is happiness?" and "How shall I live my life?" These may be answered with something of the same degree both of certainty and uncertainty, as the question concerning one's identity. The mark of an educated man, says Aristotle, is that he seeks only such precision in each class of things as the nature of the subject admits. He does not, Aristotle continues, accept probable reasoning from a geometer, nor does he demand mathematical reasoning from an orator. If man is a being wholly determined, the motions of whose soul are to be sought like that of a billiard ball on an inclined plane, then a mathematically precise answer would be proper. But if his nature is not wholly determined, then the very freedom or indeterminacy that belongs to him will forever prevent him from being known in the way in which the motions of mere matter can be known. In short, there will be a variety of good answers to the good questions, none of which are or can be, by mathematical or apodictic demonstration, necessarily and exclusively authoritative. Indeed, the heart of the liberal arts, of the good life for free men, lies precisely in the contemplation of the variety of such questions and answers. For in this variety we contemplate human freedom, which is the indeterminate and inexhaustible cause of that variety. Human freedom is in certain respects necessarily mysterious, and every attempt to end the challenge of that mystery, whether by religious or political fanaticism or by dogmatic scientism is bound to end, both in self-contradiction and despair.

The question of who I am necessarily begins with one's name. I believe that it will end here as well. The objection is obvious: a man can change his name without changing his identity; a name is merely conventional, and we think that a man's identity must somehow be intrinsic to him, that about him in virtue of which he is always the same and in no way other than himself. But how do we know that there is such a thing as identity in this pure and absolute sense of the term? For the moment we put aside names as a ground for identity. Names are words, and words are air, so let us turn from air to earth or, less poetically, from our names to our bodies. Names, like language in general, may be conventional, but our bodies certainly are natural. Yet a man's body, although natural, is always changing; in fact, it changes far more than most names change. With the exception of the DNA molecules, an infinitesimal fraction, all of a human body is in a perpetual state of material exchange. Not only is it either a young body or an old one, moving across the path of a cycle of growth and decay, from birth to death, but it maintains itself upon that path by ingesting and metabolizing alien matter from the external world and discharging waste into the surrounding environment. In fact, a living body never possesses identity of matter, and as soon as the identity of a body and its matter occurs, the body is dead. A living body resembles a river, the water of which is always changing. But it is a river without banks or boundaries, if such a strained metaphor be permitted! Both the form and the matter that make any living body are always changing, are never the same. Where then is its identity? Can it be its fingerprints? Fingerprints identify a body for the purposes of the law (and possibly for other purposes). But those who use fingerprints as a means of identification assume the existence of an identity different from the fingerprints. That is, what the fingerprints identify is itself not fingerprints. And we are asking what that something is, other than fingerprints, that fingerprints identify. Let us next try memory. Surely each individual has his own experiences of life. What happened at a certain moment at a certain place happened to him alone. He alone did something for which he alone is guilty or praiseworthy. While the reputation attached to events may be conventional, are not the events themselves natural, being occurrences within space and time? Did not Thomas Aquinas say that this alone is denied even to God to make that which has been not to have been? And does not each individual as a maker of that eternal record have an identity? But this brings us back to the same question that faced us in the case of the fingerprints. For the record of events that make up our lives, the memory of which we now say is our identity, also assumes the reality of that very identity. What is it, after all, that links the events in our memory? It is the "I." And is not memory after all a notoriously treacherous thing? Does it not falsely attribute actions? Do we not wrongly claim credit for good actions, and wrongly disclaim the blame for bad ones all the time? We do this deliberately when we think we can get away with it. But as these same actions recede into the past memory replaces will as the servant of desire. Even Aristotle concedes that the great-souled man, as a very element of his virtue, tends to forget the benefits he has received, and remembers only the good deeds he has done for others. Moreover, Aristotle proceeds to illustrate the point with a misquotation from Homer! Of course, in saying all this we again fall into the habit of assuming the point in question, namely, that there is memory because there is identity, however distorted our perception of it.

Neither our names, our bodies, nor our memories supply a ground for establishing that identity we all believe ourselves to possess. Finger-prints, like the DNA molecules which are now said to remain with us all our lives, cannot be the ground or cause of identity, because they are only signs or symbols of an identity that has been already assumed. When the FBI establishes the identity of a criminal, it means that the man with these fingerprints *did* something. That is, it is believed or alleged that he is *guilty* of something. Now it is interesting that in Greek, the original word for cause, *aitia*, is also the word for guilt. The quest for the cause or causes of things comes first to light as a quest for responsibility. "Who did it?" turns out to be a question of primeval concern, indicating that the ground of the legal order and that of the natural order have their roots in the same elements of the human consciousness, as the Declaration of Independence incidentally maintains. To be an individual, to have an identity, means to be an *aitia*, a cause, to be capable of guilt, or a record in virtue of which one deserves punishment, or, alternatively, reward. Indeed, it is our ability to deserve either reward or punishment which enables us to have identities, to be able to answer the question, Who am I? A name is a matter of convention only when it is a mere label. It is a label to the infant who is as yet unconscious of his name, just as our fingerprints are an unconscious label—although one provided somehow by nature—to us who know ourselves only on other grounds. But when a name is a symbol of a reputation then it is no longer a mere convention. It is conventional only as the word "dog" or "tree" is conventional. Another word with a different sound could mean the same thing, as in fact happens when they are translated into other languages. But the fact that such words can be translated without any misunderstanding of their meanings shows that the substances underlying the substantives are natural and stable, even if their symbols are not. As it is with names, so is it with identities.

Now the question remains, what is the reason for assuming the existence of an identity, a unity set over against all plurality, that underlies the many actions that make up a reputation, and thereby a name? To be an individual with an identity means to be the same cause of many events in a world external to the individual. But how do we perceive this cause? Has not the foregoing argument shown in each case that the identity appears as an assumption, for which no antecedent evidence or experience can be adduced as justification? The answer to this is, of course, yes. But let us bear in mind that every chain of argument, if it is to progress to a conclusion, must stop somewhere. To progress to a conclusion would be impossible if every proposition were to be carried back to another, *ad infinitum*. An argument progresses only as it approaches an assumption that appears to be necessary to all explanation, and which itself does not appear to depend upon any further assumption. To say that such a final assumption is necessary means that any alternative assumption would make the experience it underlies unintelligible, whereas this assumption makes it intelligible.

The most radical philosopher of modernity, in the matter of denying our knowledge of natural causality, was David Hume. According to Hume, all the conceptions of the mind are either impressions or ideas, and ideas are copies of impressions. Impressions are those consequences inside the mind that result from the impact of the external world upon the senses. What we call causality, said Hume, is nothing but the habit acquired by the mind in expecting B to follow A, because experience has shown that B always follows A. We say that the sun will rise tomorrow because of a system of causes, a nature, which we attribute to the solar system. What this really means, however, is that because, in our experience, the sun has always risen, we expect it to do so again. Similarly, when we see one billiard ball strike another, we say that the first is the cause of the movement of the second. Yet what has happened, according to Hume, is only that the second has moved after the first, and we have attributed to causality what is nothing but a sequence of impressions. It is the subjective habit of the mind which is said to represent itself to us as the objective order of the external world. Hume's account of causality has had an unbounded effect upon what is today called the methodology of the social sciences. But let us reflect. Who is it—or, in other words, what is the cause—that tells us that all causality lies wholly within the mind, and that it is no property of an objective world outside of that mind? Is it not David Hume? And what is the impression that corresponds to the idea of David Hume? Is it not a book, called *A Treatise of Human Nature*, which I believe David Hume to have written? Why should I believe that the remarkable progression of his arguments, from page to page, lies in the fact that he caused this progression? I have no idea of David Hume except these impressions. I am aware that his treatise *could* have been written by many different authors—like *Naked Came the Stranger*—just as I realize that monkeys with typewriters might in infinite time produce all the books ever written by men. Anything that art or rational purpose might do, might equally well result from chance. However, it is well to remember that a universe without rational purpose is also a universe without chance. The very possibility of designating chance as a cause, or a possible cause, itself depends upon the prior existence of rational purpose. That is to say, chance can be a cause only in a purposeful universe. Without purpose there is no chance, since chance itself comes to light only as the unintended cause of the fulfillment of a purpose, as Aristotle demonstrates in the second book of his *Physics*. Skeptical reason properly warns us against assigning reason to everything that appears artful or purposeful, but this same reason tells us that the distinction between art and chance is itself not arbitrary.

Now none of us will ever suppose that David Hume himself ever had a moment's doubt that he was the author of the *Treatise of Human Nature*. Yet the evidence by which I am convinced of this, the close concatenation of purposeful signs, is what leads me to attribute intelligible causality to any system of effects in the external world. Skepticism is not only possible, but necessary, to rationality. That is why we do not place simple trust in our memories, or even to our observations of ordinary experiences. Who does not know how ten witnesses to a street corner accident in broad daylight can give ten different accounts of what happened? But surely that is no reason to think that street corner accidents are figments of the imagination. The sensible view is that by astute examination of the witnesses, an approximation to the truth might be winnowed from the conflicting accounts. But skepticism becomes self-defeating when, instead of insisting upon the possibility of error in our account of the external world, it denies the possibility of truth. Hume's attack on natural causality ultimately reaches the identity of the observer who makes this denial. We are finally invited to disbelieve in the identity of the skeptic himself. Carried to this extreme, skepticism devours itself, leaving dogmatism unchallenged in the world. Our young people, suffering identity crises, have become the victims of this monster.

I would conclude then that I am indeed, not my name, in the sense that the label on the bottle is not the bottle or the contents of the bottle. But I am my name in the sense in which that name has become a symbol of the actions of my life. I am my name in that a real agent is the inward cause of actions that flow outward upon a world of which I am a part, but which is affected by me. The quality of the actions imputed to the agent and represented by a name, becomes then an identity. But actions compelled by necessity, whether conscious or unconscious, are not actions of the one compelled. To be an agent, as distinct from an instrument, means to be possessed of freedom. And to be possessed of freedom means to be possessed of dignity—or indignity. The possibility of a name depends upon the possibility of voluntary actions, which being voluntary may be recognized as praiseworthy or blameworthy. It depends upon actions that are recognized either as wise or foolish, noble or base, just or unjust. Only as the names applied to such actions can be regarded as realities, can our names be thought to represent realities. Only so can we have identities.

Personal identity cannot then be demonstrated in the way in which we can point to objects in the external world. Yet every discussion of the external world presupposes such an identity, and indeed a system of such identities. For we believe in the world only as we are able to discuss it with other selves like us. What we call objectivity is in fact the consequence of intersubjectivity. The primary data of the senses—which are indeed the ground of all ideas and of all speech—are themselves never transmitted by language. We never see through another's eyes, or hear through another's ears. How then do we find intelligible another's speech about what he has heard or seen? It is because we believe in the genuineness of his subjective impressions, which in turn serve as confirmations to us of our own. In short, we become subjects of independent consciousness by a process in which we attribute to others the same kind of consciousness. As genuine selves, we achieve a certain independence of our senses; that is to say, we learn when and how our sight and our hearing go awry by trusting the judgment of others. We realize, of course, that if everyone went colorblind in the same way at the same time, no one could ever discover the fact, even though we were shocked for the moment by the change in the appearance of the world. By the discovery of other selves, as dependent upon their senses as we are, we gain a certain independence of our senses, since we do communicate our awareness of sense perception to these others. Our inwardness, our sense of detachment—and therewith freedom—from the external world, is a consequence of our perception that there are other selves having the same tenuous combination of dependence and independence. We become objects in the world, both to ourselves and to others, by the same process by which we become aware of our own inwardness, and the dependence of that inwardness upon the inwardness of others.

But what of the reality of the world revealed by science, whose truth is testified by nuclear explosions and space travel? Does not this reality imply the superiority of scientific methodology to prescientific forms of perception, upon which the sense of identity rests? But the nuclear scientist, speaking about atoms and the nuclei of atoms, which he apprehends by the medium of instruments, communicates his discoveries by language which utilizes the same media by which all of us communicate in the non or prescientific world. The scientist, reading the dials in the laboratory like the astronauts in their space ships, confides in the power of his eyes to read numbers. He writes such things upon blackboards for students whose existence he takes for granted, and who he does not regard merely as bundles of molecules or aggregates of energy. Unless at some point in the process of learning and teaching, prescientific sense perception and reasoning were reliable, then science itself would have no place to dwell.

The goodness of science as a human vocation, and the status of scientific truth among the kinds of truth accessible to man as man, cannot be established by science itself. Whether the scientist is therefore to be regarded with veneration or contempt, with awe or anger, can be decided only in a human conversation, in which the matters in question are in no way begged. The power of science, great as it is, can not decide the issue.

When Crito begged Socrates to take heed of the opinion of the many, since they had such great power, Socrates denied that the power to put him to death was anything great. Only that was great, he held, that can make men either wise or foolish. In what wisdom, or more generally, in what virtue consists, is of course still *the* question. That question, in turn, is only a form of the question, What is man? Of this much we can, at this point, be certain. Man is the being that can ask the question, What is man? In asking that question, he has a better assurance than has been commonly supposed, that the universe—of which after all he is himself a manifestation—is not without purpose, and that it is not blind to his fate. In taking seriously that question, we return to the liberal arts, the condition of human freedom.

CRITICISM AND CONTROVERSY

12 | SLAVERY
A Battle Revisited

One hundred years ago—on the evening of June 16, 1858—the delegates to the Illinois State Republican Convention assembled in the House of Representatives of the Illinois State House. Earlier in the day, the same delegates had voted unanimously "that Abraham Lincoln is the first and only choice of the Republicans of Illinois for the United States Senate, as the successor of Stephen A. Douglas." Now they were to hear their candidate.

In the speech that followed—one of the very few, I believe, which can be said to have changed the course of a nation's history—an old-line Whig was heard to pronounce sentiments which would have been expected from the wildest-eyed radicals of the Free Soil or Liberty parties:

" 'A house divided against itself cannot stand.' I believe this government cannot endure, permanently half *slave* and half *free.* "

The ensuing campaign, whose main themes were established in the "House Divided" speech, involved the seven joint debates with Lincoln's redoubtable antagonist, Douglas. They constitute perhaps the most famous forensic episode in the history of democratic discussion. The dust has not settled upon the issues that were debated upon the prairies of that hot and dry summer; and it is fitting that, in the year of their centennial, the text of the debates, which have been out of print for many years, is made available again. Concerning the edition itself, there is little to say, except that it is handsome and eminently readable. We are given not only the complete text of the seven joint debates, but also the opening speeches by Lincoln at Springfield and Douglas at Chicago, and the two subsequent speeches by Lincoln and Douglas at Springfield on July 17, in which major lines of their arguments are elaborated. Professor Paul Angle has followed the precedent of the Sparks edition, published in 1908, by including press comments heralding the debaters. He has done this on a smaller scale than Sparks did. But he has added four chapters—"Taking the Stump," "The Campaign Progresses," "Touches of Temper" and "The Campaign Ends"—which give the reader a sense of the place of the debates in the context of the whole campaign, which lasted more than five months, and in which the joint debates were a minor fraction of the

Review of Paul M. Angle (ed.), *Created Equal? The Complete Lincoln-Douglas Debates of 1858* (Chicago: University of Chicago Press, 1958). Reprinted by the kind permission of the publisher from *The New Leader* 41, no. 30 (Aug. 18-25, 1958): 21-23.

campaigners' engagements. There is also an appendix listing the dates and places of all the rivals' speaking engagements, and a thirty-page introduction by the editor.

It would be difficult to make suggestions for a better single-volume edition, except, perhaps, that it should be made available to students at a more modest price, since earlier, cheaper editions can readily be had in secondhand bookstores. Yet the scholar must lament that, although the other major speeches by Lincoln, which must be read to grasp his position fully, are easily available in inexpensive editions, we have no such access to Douglas' works. Reading through these debates one can easily see why Douglas was the most feared debater of his day, perhaps the hardest political infighter the country has produced. Yet in the debates Lincoln is much nearer his best than Douglas. Douglas' Senate speeches in January and March 1854, for example, when he was driving his Nebraska bill through to victory—which covers much of the same ground as the ones in the present volume—are much keener and harder hitting. All Lincoln students know the Cooper Union speech; yet few know Douglas' essay in *Harper's* magazine, "Popular Sovereignty in the Territories," to which the Cooper Union speech is largely a reply. Let us hope that Douglas' works will soon become available somewhere.

Douglas, the political giant of 1858, has now become the historical appendage of his antagonist. Yet in the eyes of professional historians, he has fared much better than Lincoln. On the issues that divided them, contemporary historiography pronounces Lincoln wrong and Douglas right. This is true in spite of, rather than because of, the relative esteem in which the men are held. Angle, for example, is an unstinted admirer of Lincoln. Yet, like most other commentators, he thinks that the conspiracy charge in the "House Divided" speech, upon which Lincoln's entire campaign hinged, was inconsequential. Lincoln charged that the four "workmen," Stephen, Franklin, Roger, and James (Douglas, Pierce, Taney, and Buchanan), had collaborated in a policy which logically pointed to the legalization of slavery in "all the States, old as well as new, North as well as South." Lincoln did not say he "knew" they had conspired; he merely arrayed the evidence to show that their actions produced a "tendency" toward that result.

Professor Angle says of the conspiracy charge that Lincoln "failed to support it with evidence, and gave it diminishing emphasis in his later speeches." The first part of this statement is certainly not true. The entire "House Divided" speech is nothing but evidence to support it. Angle, like most historians, has failed to distinguish the legal sense of "conspiracy," which means an unlawful combination, from the nonlegal sense which, according to Webster, means "combination or union (of persons or things) for a single purpose or end; harmonious action." Lincoln's rhetoric is deliberative, not forensic. Its forensic quality—for he was a lawyer—is metaphoric. He is not trying to convict Douglas and the others of a crime; he is attempting to convince the American people that these men collaborated upon policies which make them untrustworthy guardians of the nation's liberties. However, the crucial point is not whether Douglas and the others actually "conspired" together, but whether their policies amounted to a "tendency" toward making slavery lawful throughout the nation.

Historians have in fact rejected the conspiracy charge because they have doubted that there was such a tendency; and, of course, it is impossible to believe the former while doubting the latter. In my judgment, neither Professor Angle nor his historical preceptors—the revisionist historians Randall, Craven, Milton, Hodder, Ramsdell, to mention leading names—have justified their doubts. The substance of their position is that slavery would not have spread further no matter what Lincoln did or said. Yet Lincoln argued that the defeat of the proslavery Lecompton Constitution for Kansas, in the winter and spring of 1857–58, could not have been accomplished without the Republicans in the House of Representatives. And the Republicans would never have been there if Douglas' popular sovereignty principle had been accepted by northern free-soilers. Hence Lincoln believed it essential to end the flirtation of Douglas and the eastern Republicans that had been going on all spring. Greeley and others wanted Lincoln to support Douglas for reelection, not oppose him.

Angle's contention that Lincoln gave the conspiracy charge diminishing emphasis in his speeches is correct. But the reason is that, as the campaign progressed and the pugnacious Douglas attacked the "Black Republicans" with increasing ferocity, Lincoln saw that the bridges between Douglas and the main body of the party were burned. He had nothing more to fear from a rapprochement between Douglas and the national leaders of the Republican party. Historians have generally failed to see how much of Lincoln's early speech-making in the campaign was designed to split Douglas and the *Republicans,* rather than appeal to free-soil Democrats. Lincoln felt that only a simon-pure Republicanism could guarantee the continued existence of a party which could defeat future Lecomptons.

A good deal of misunderstanding has been spread through the history books concerning Lincoln's stand on racial equality. It is regrettable that Angle has added to it. He says Lincoln's "attitude toward the Negro, whether slave or free, was essentially the same as that of Douglas." This is completely untrue. Lincoln insisted that the Negro was a man, and as a man entitled to all the *natural* rights enumerated in the Declaration of Independence, including the right to a government in which he had an equal voice. Douglas, on the contrary, believed that the Negro belonged to an "inferior race" which lacked, and forever must lack, any right to be governed by a government founded upon the consent of the governed. Douglas also believed this to be true of Indians, Orientals, and mixed or "mongrel" races.

The great difficulty concerning Lincoln's position arises from a failure to grasp the distinction between natural and civil rights. It has been alleged that Lincoln was inconsistent or insincere because he was not in favor of immediately making citizens of Negroes. As a matter of fact, Lincoln, in the 1858 campaign, said that he "was not, and never had been" in favor of giving full political equality to Negroes; he never said that he *would* not in future favor it. If this equivocation seems to detract from the fervor of Lincoln's faith, let us remember that he believed the antislavery movement depended vitally upon the kind of leadership he was attempting to furnish; and that it would have been madness to wreck his party—as he certainly would have done—by espousing a program of complete political equality.

But apart from this, Lincoln did not believe that Negroes had any natural right to United States citizenship any more than did resident aliens. Citizenship was a privilege which need be bestowed upon those whom the community wished, *in their own interests,* to accept as new members. The only political right possessed by free Negroes, implied in the abstract right to freedom, was to leave the country and form political associations of their own, just as the colonists had left Europe to found new political associations in the new world. Lincoln's colonization idea—which he had inherited from Jefferson via Clay—was always correlated with his aim of eventual complete emancipation. It should also be remembered that prior to the Fourteenth Amendment freed Negroes were not citizens, and that the rights of citizens were determined by the states. Each state legislature could determine who, residing within its boundaries, should be added to the body politic. In a government based upon the consent—or opinion—of the governed, Lincoln saw an obligation to respect what he believed to be a "universal" opinion in Illinois which then opposed adding freed Negroes to that body.

There is one other point. Lincoln's advocacy of colonization, as a solution of the problem of the freed Negro, was not as impractical and hollow as Angle, like most other historians, thinks. Whatever the intrinsic merit of the proposal, it served a vital rhetorical and political function in 1858 and thereafter. Lincoln's political following was overwhelmingly antislavery. It was also overwhelmingly anti-Negro. Lincoln's platform was to oppose the spread of slavery, not to abolish it. Yet Lincoln tried as much as, if not more than, any of his contemporaries to link opposition to the spread of slavery with the idea of its gradual extinction. If Lincoln was vague on plans as to how this was to be accomplished, it was because he knew from experience that any concrete plan would meet with over-whelming opposition, and might fatally disrupt the antislavery cause. Indeed, if it had become known that ultimate extinction of slavery would mean that four million Negroes would be free to move around the country, and compete with white labor, it is doubtful that many elements in the free-soil movement would have continued to oppose even the extension (and perpetuation) of slavery. The colonization idea—which Lincoln believed in sincerely—played the vital role of making that vague "ultimate" extinction of slavery seem reasonable and palatable.

Lincoln found the gulf between himself and Douglas in Douglas' "don't care" attitude concerning what, Lincoln believed, all true men did and must care about, namely, labeling human slavery for the evil it was. Free government, then and now, depends upon keeping alive in the hearts of men a deep concern for the principles of political right. Those princi-ples have never been more dramatically affirmed and tested than upon the Illinois prairies, in that summer of 1858. There is no better guide to the problems of 1958 than to contemplate and ponder that drama and test.

13 | LETTERS OF A PATRIOT

This is the first, and undoubtedly, the definitive collection of Douglas' letters. It comes only after a long and arduous search into every known repository, public or private, of Douglas' papers. Every letter by Douglas (but none to him) is either printed here, calendared, or briefly noted. Letters judged to be merely routine are recorded by the editor in their proper chronological order. Letters by Douglas alluded to in other sources, but which cannot be located, are summarized on the basis of whatever information about them exists and also placed as nearly as possible in proper order. The identification of addressees and other necessary information is given with great succinctness in notes following each letter. A number of documents which could not be strictly called letters (e.g., Autobiographical Sketch, September 1, 1838; Call for Democratic Convention, March 26, 1840; Autobiographical Notes, April 17, 1859; Statement, April 14, 1861) are also printed with pertinent notes. The editorial standard, established with tremendous assiduity and devotion, is in every way equal to that of the great editions, completed or in process, of the works of Lincoln, Clay, Calhoun, and others of Douglas' contemporaries. It is, moreover, the work of one man and not, as is today customary, that of a team or staff. This, of course, is not an *opera omnia*. Douglas' speeches, which are his principal political testament, have been omitted, as have legal briefs, drafts of speeches, resolutions and bills, and other manuscripts. Many of Douglas' speeches are widely available in the *Congressional Globe,* Sheahan's Life (1860), as well as in the several editions of the *Lincoln-Douglas Debates. In the Name of the People: Speeches and Writings of Lincoln and Douglas in the Ohio Campaign of 1859* (1959) contains Douglas' three Ohio speeches and his great Harper's essay, "The Dividing Line between Federal and Local Authority," to which Lincoln's Ohio speeches and his Cooper Union speech were replies. The only regret of the present reviewer is that the very excellence of this volume of letters, while it demands a companion, will probably preclude a collected edition, similar to that of Lincoln's works, where every letter, speech, and paper can be read in consecutive order. The decision to proceed with the letters was, the editor tells us, based upon practical considerations of time and space and the belief that these most urgently

Review of Robert W. Johannsen (ed.), *The Letters of Stephen A. Douglas* (Urbana, Ill.: University of Illinois Press, 1961). Reprinted by the kind permission of the publisher from *The Journal of Southern History* 28, no. 2 (May 1962): 251-53.

required collection. In such a matter we defer to the judgment of Professor Johannsen; and, our appetite whetted by his excellent introduction, we now look to him with increasing anticipation for *the* life of Douglas.

Concerning the letters themselves, we speak with some particular pleasure and some disappointment. Inevitably, comparison with Lincoln will be made, and we must say that, from the literary and personal standpoint, there is no comparison. Douglas was a public man and, although in some measure a great public man, nothing more. His autobiographical sketch of 1838 is brilliantly written and fascinating to read. It is the Horatio Alger story of a man, written by himself, at twenty-five years of age! But there is nothing like the record of inner torment of Lincoln's letters to Speed. Douglas is a man who seems never to have hesitated or to have doubted. In the heat of a fight he is magnificent; otherwise he is rather ordinary. The present reviewer must record his regret at finding not a single word in Douglas' letters concerning the morality of slavery. In comparing Lincoln and Douglas, we have observed that Lincoln's position on the Know-Nothings paralleled that of Douglas on slavery: Douglas denounced the Know-Nothings publicly and slavery privately; Lincoln denounced slavery publicly and the Know-Nothings privately. But Douglas' denunciation of slavery is in passing oral comments (see George Fort Milton's biography, p. 150); Lincoln's denunciation of the Know-Nothings in the letter to Speed (August 24, 1855) is a poignant record of moral and intellectual consistency that will stand in eternity.

On the whole then we would pronounce this volume to be indispensable to the historian, but only occasionally possessed of considerable interest to the historical buff. The human interest of Douglas is as a tough little fighter, frequently the underdog, and appealing to the traditional American interest in the underdog. His Senate speeches in defense of the Kansas-Nebraska Bill in the spring of 1854 are probably his fighting best; they are certainly superior in this respect to those in the debates with Lincoln. In the present volume, the reviewer's favorite item is the scathing polemic addressed "To Twenty-Five Chicago Clergymen," April 6, 1854. In it, the attempt of the brethren of the cloth to invoke the authority of Almighty God, as distinct from the right of American citizens, to denounce a political measure, is treated in a manner that would have delighted the heart of Tom Paine. Still, it could be compared to its disadvantage with Lincoln's remarks to a group of clergymen who during the Civil War attempted to assure him it was God's will that he issue an emancipation proclamation. He hoped, he said, that it was not irreverent to suggest that it was probable that, if God would reveal His will on a point so connected with *his* duty, it might be supposed that he would reveal it directly to *him*.

14 | PORTRAIT OF A PATRIOT

Robert W. Johannsen's *Stephen A. Douglas* should take its place in the tradition of magisterial biographies—along with Freeman's *Lee* and *Washington,* Brant's *Madison,* Wiltse's *Calhoun,* and Randall's *Lincoln*—in which so much of the best writing on American history is to be found. Notwithstanding the passionate advocacy of George Fort Milton, and the measured praise of James G. Randall and his school, Douglas has hitherto remained in the giant shadow of Abraham Lincoln. Yet with the exception of the final chapter of his life, Douglas was in the foreground and Lincoln in the background of nearly all the important events that occurred during the twenty-five years in which they were rival politicians in Illinois. To some degree, Douglas' eclipse followed his ill fate in passing from the scene, just as the war began. What part he might have played in that tremendous drama, no one, of course, can say. Yet it almost certainly would have been a powerful one. At his death he was but forty-eight years old, and at the height of his career. But Lincoln became the central figure of the war years—years that have dominated our historic memories ever since—at once its principal actor and, by the majesty of his language, its principal interpreter.

Yet Douglas' domination of the immediate antebellum political scene was nearly as great as Lincoln's during the war. It is doubtful if anyone who has not occupied the presidential chair, not even Webster, Clay, or Calhoun, has played so prominent a role in such great events. The present volume, as nearly definitive as a work of its kind can well be, goes far toward restoring the perspective that these events must have presented to contemporaries.

During the joint debates of 1858 the tall and angular Lincoln was wont to compare himself to his stubby opponent by saying, "Judge Douglas is a great man, and I am only a little one." But Lincoln could also say, with less of humor and more perhaps both of melancholy and envy, that "Judge Douglas is of worldwide renown. All the anxious politicians of his party . . . have been looking upon him as certainly, at no distant day, to be President of the United States. . . .On the contrary, nobody has ever expected me to be President. On my poor, lean, lank face, nobody

Review of Robert W. Johannsen, *Stephen A. Douglas* (New York: Oxford University Press, 1973). Reprinted by the kind permission of the publisher from *National Review* 25, no. 21 (May 25, 1973): 587-89.

has ever seen that any cabbages were sprouting out." It is difficult to divest ourselves of all recollection of the presidential Lincoln, and to see him as one on whose countenance no one envisioned the cabbages that one day would—contrary to expectations—sprout therefrom. In 1858, in every respect but one, Lincoln did seem to be a little man in comparison with his antagonist. Indeed, Douglas' celebrity was a decisive factor in Lincoln's rise to power. Had Douglas been a senator from Indiana or Ohio, for example, it is inconceivable that Lincoln would have become president. Professor Johannsen enables us to see why this is so.

The story of Douglas' meteoric political rise is testimony to his remarkable personal qualities, and symbolic as well of the dynamism of the state and section—the new west of that day—that he represented. His easy manners and ready wit engendered quick friendships. His loyalty to popular causes, and his pugnacity in behalf of them, made him a champion others were anxious to follow. Born in Vermont and raised partly in Canandaigua, New York, Douglas arrived in Winchester, Illinois in the summer of 1832, at the age of nineteen, a penniless migrant, without friends or family to assist him. He established a school, worked as a clerk, and in a short time was able to hang out his lawyer's shingle. Throwing himself energetically into Democratic politics, he had by 1835 maneuvered himself into the office of state's attorney. In the following year he was elected to the legislature. He resigned his seat, however, to become registrar of the Springfield Land Office, a position of considerable political influence. In 1838 he ran for Congress against John T. Stuart, senior partner to Abraham Lincoln. The contest had been regarded as a hopeless one. "We have adopted it as part of our policy here, to never speak of Douglas at all," Lincoln wrote to a friend. "Isn't that the best mode of treating so small a matter?" Although Douglas lost the election, he surprised everyone by how close he came to winning it—Stuart's margin was 36 out of more than 36,000 votes cast. In 1840 Douglas was appointed secretary of state of Illinois, another post that he promptly resigned, this time to take a seat upon the newly enlarged—or newly packed, as some would say—Supreme Court of the state. In 1842 he was narrowly defeated in a contest for the United States Senate, but was elected in the following year to the House of Representatives. He remained in the House until his elevation to the Senate in 1848, a place for which he was twice again chosen—the second time in the great contest with Lincoln—and which he occupied until his death in 1861.

From the time he entered Congress, Douglas seemed to command the limelight. In the crisis of 1850—the greatest the nation was to face until the Civil War—Douglas played a prominent role. Although Henry Clay is credited with devising the compromise of the year, it was Douglas who devised the tactics that enabled the compromise measures to pass the Congress. Clay himself said that Douglas "more than any other individual" was responsible for their success. And Jefferson Davis, who had opposed them, declared that "if any man has a right to be proud of the success of these measures, it is the Senator from Illinois." Little wonder then that, in 1852, at the age of thirty-nine, Douglas was already a prominent candidate for his party's presidential nomination.

The lives of Lincoln and Douglas were closely linked for a generation. The debates of 1858 were no novelty to the two men. They had met in such encounters as early as 1838—during the Stuart-Douglas contest. In 1839 and 1840, in response to popular demand, they debated across the state. There are no stenographic reports of these exchanges, but we can get a fair sample of Lincoln's style from the report of his December 1839 address on the subtreasury, printed in his *Collected Works*. In this speech, as in others of the period, Lincoln's comic genius is at its rollicking best. His animadversions on Democratic subtreasurers who had absconded with public funds are hilarious. But it is notable that even then, his specific rebuttals are directed at arguments that had been set forth by Douglas. Lincoln had already discovered that Douglas, so far from being someone to ignore, was someone whose prominence could gain attention for himself. From the time of Lincoln's return to politics in 1854 until his election to the presidency, *every* major speech he delivered was an attack upon Douglas, usually in the form of a reply to a speech Douglas had previously given. In the 1858 campaign, Lincoln began by following Douglas around the state, attending his meetings, and rising to tell the assemblages that he would address them later on. It was in part to compel Lincoln to stop "borrowing" his audiences, that Douglas agreed to the joint debates. Lincoln's Cooper Union address, February 27, 1860, his principal contribution to the fateful presidential campaign of that year, was a reply both to an earlier speech by Douglas in Columbus, Ohio, and to Douglas' *Harper's* essay, on "The Dividing Line between Federal and Local Authority." The editor of the pamphlet edition of Lincoln's speech attempted to emend it, substituting at one point the word "Democrats" for "Douglas." But Lincoln corrected him, writing, "But what I am saying there is *true* of Douglas, and is not true of 'Democrats' generally; so that the proposed substitution would be a very considerable blunder." It is almost literally the case that Lincoln rode Douglas' back to the White House.

Lincoln's speeches during the period 1854-60 constitute what may be the greatest intellectual achievement of American statesmanship. They may indeed be the greatest example of forensic rhetoric that the court of public opinion has ever heard. It is doubtful if any single book—perhaps

not even *The Federalist* or *Democracy in America*—reveals as much of the
inner nature of the American regime as the *Political Debates* between
Abraham Lincoln and Stephen A. Douglas. Yet this book can be understood only within the context within which the debates themselves were
but an episode. One must understand the great struggle in which Douglas
was engaged, from 1854, to persuade the nation to adopt his conception
of popular sovereignty as the solution of the territorial problem, the
problem upon which the ship of state—the Union—was split. At first
Douglas was an object of vilification almost beyond belief by the antislavery forces, because of the repeal of the Missouri Compromise's restric-
tion of slavery in the Kansas-Nebraska Act of 1854. But in little more
than three years—by one of history's supreme ironies—he became the very
head and front of those same forces in the struggle against the Lecompton
Constitution, which he regarded as a mockery of popular sovereignty. Yet
Douglas was perfectly consistent throughout: he had said repeatedly that
it was not his business, as an Illinois senator, to decide that Kansas, or any
other territory, either have or not have slavery. That was a question for
each territory to decide for itself. It was for him—and the United States
government—to see to it only that the people of the territories did decide
this question freely and fairly, and without force or fraud.

Douglas certainly believed in popular sovereignty as he understood
it. Whether it was defensible as a theory of government is, however, not
the sole question. Douglas accurately perceived that the slavery question,
on the national level, was simply not susceptible to political solution.
There was no middle ground—either moral or logical—between those who
thought slavery was right and should be extended, and those who thought
it was wrong, and should be restricted. But if the partisans in the national
forum could only be persuaded to agree to disagree, and to allow the
decision between slavery and freedom in the territories to be made by the
inhabitants of each of the territories themselves, then perhaps a national
collision could be avoided. For this policy to have any chance of acceptance, Douglas of course could not appear to belong to either of the
contending forces. Hence his much-repeated assertion that he cared not
whether slavery was voted up or voted down. His concern was that those
immediately concerned should do the voting, and that the vote be free
and fairly counted. As time went on, it appeared more and more likely
that the settlers in the territories, if given that fair chance, would vote to
keep slavery out. Thus there seemed less reason for the Republicans, any
more than the Free State Democrats, to reject Douglas' leadership. Douglas was then not simply an antagonist of Lincoln, but one who represented
what many perceived as a viable alternative to what Lincoln himself stood
for. No man has been more profoundly challenged to justify himself in a

public forum than Lincoln was by Douglas in 1858. And no man has ever risen to greater heights in defense of a policy, and the convictions upon which that policy depended.

But this is Douglas' book, and one that helps us understand the awesome power of the Little Giant in action. It is an astounding story, particularly as we see that, even while the Lincoln-Douglas debates were in progress, Douglas was devoting as much, if not more, time and attention to the assault upon his other flank by President Buchanan and his southern proslavery cohorts.

It is well to record that, when the balloting was over, and the bullets began their deadly work, the old rivals stood side by side. After the firing on Fort Sumter, and Lincoln's call for 75,000 volunteers, Douglas' only objection was that Lincoln should have asked for 200,000 men. Douglas at the moment probably guessed better than Lincoln the deadliness of the contest that was beginning. But Douglas fell ill soon thereafter, and died on June 3, 1861. He was in Chicago, on a trip rallying support for Lincoln's government—for the government of the man he had fought politically for a quarter of a century. As he lay mortally ill he was asked to give a message to his young sons. "Tell them," he said, "to obey the laws and support the Constitution of the United States." Douglas' brilliant career thus came to a premature end, but its manner was worthy of the patriot that he was. Professor Johannsen has done us all a great service in telling his tale so well.

15 | LINCOLN AND THE CAUSE OF FREEDOM

In his "Lincoln Without Rhetoric" in the August 24, 1965, issue of *National Review,* Frank Meyer has achieved something that is, so far as I can recall, absolutely without precedent: he has written a critical essay on Abraham Lincoln and the Civil War without mentioning or even alluding to the subject of slavery. I respect his bold rejection of received opinion about Lincoln, but I believe his conclusions are based upon mistakes and omissions as to facts, and upon inferences from the present that give erroneous impressions of the past. Most important, his strange silence about the central cause of the war, represents a default of his own deepest conviction, so often and so eloquently affirmed, of the absolute value of human freedom.

Meyer charges Lincoln with responsibility for the weakening, if not the destruction of the "Constitution in its original form." Essential to that Constitution, says Meyer, was "what has usually been called 'checks and balances,' but is more accurately designated as the setting up of a state of tension between all the political centers of power so that effective final power rests in none of them." That this was the conception of the Founding Fathers, Meyer will undoubtedly argue, with supporting evidence, in his forthcoming book. He certainly has his work cut out for him. At the very least, and as a starting point, he must discredit the arguments of Hamilton and Madison in *The Federalist* papers, as authority for the meaning of the original Constitution. From the point of view of these Fathers, it was the Articles of Confederation in which the political centers were so disposed that effective final power was not to be found. It was above all to remedy that deficiency that the Constitutional Convention was called.

The doctrine that the federal government has many more implied powers than those enumerated in the Constitution is the juridical basis upon which most of the aggrandizement at the expense of the states has proceeded. If this doctrine is not in *The Federalist,* as I am convinced it is, it is assuredly to be found in Hamilton's opinion on the constitutionality of the first Bank of the United States. Jefferson, who was not at the Convention, opposed Hamilton's opinion; but President Washington who,

Reprinted by the kind permission of the publisher from *National Review* 17, no. 38 (Sept. 21, 1965): 827-28, 842.

like Hamilton, was a member of the Convention, adopted it, and signed the bill chartering the bank into law. Hamilton's conceptions of the federal supremacy later became the foundation of John Marshall's jurisprudence, as they became the basis of the indivisible and indestructible unionism of Webster and, through him, of Andrew Jackson. Meyer writes: "Until the Civil War no one knew whether a state could secede as its last sanction, and this was of the utmost necessity if the Federal Government were not to grow so strong as to destroy the tension that guaranteed liberty." If by this he means that no one knew if a state could secede until one had tried, he merely affirms a truism. But if he means that no one knew whether a state could *lawfully* secede, that is, whether the Constitution itself permitted a state to secede, then he is saying what no one could safely say in the presence of President Jackson. In 1832 South Carolina passed a Statute of Nullification, forbidding federal agents to collect the tariff in that state. Jackson responded by declaring that any idea, either of nullification or of secession, was "incompatible with the existence of the Union, contradicted expressly by the letter of the Constitution, unauthorized by its spirit, inconsistent with every principle on which it was founded, and destructive of the great object for which it was formed." And he promptly asked for and received from Congress an act authorizing him to send an army into South Carolina, if necessary, to collect the tariff there. In the nullification crisis Jackson moved more decisively, and much more uncompromisingly, to assert federal supremacy, than Lincoln did in 1861, prior to the firing on Fort Sumter. I believe that Jackson's opinion on the supposed right of secession, based squarely on the major pronouncements of Hamilton, Madison, Washington, Marshall, and Webster, and many others, was in accord with the dominant tradition of American statesmanship, and of an overwhelming majority of Americans, North and South, who had any opinion at all upon the subject. Most historians doubt that the secessionist theory was ever held by a majority of the people who formed the Confederacy, on the eve of the Civil War, although it may have been held by a majority in South Carolina. Many Confederate leaders, including Robert E. Lee, did not believe in it. For Lee the South, in 1861, was exercising the right of revolution, as it had in 1775. Mr. Meyer has as much right as George Washington ever had, to say what he thinks the Constitution ought to be. But when he says what it was, he is bound by the record. I do not know of a single authority who ever held that the actual Constitution ever depended for its efficacy upon uncertainty as to whether a state could secede.

"Confounding almost every school of political theory, the American Constitution rested sovereignty nowhere (unless it were in every individual citizen) . . . " writes Meyer. In fact, the doctrine of the sovereignty of the people is to be found plainly upon the face of nearly every great document of the period. The Virginia Bill of Rights, of June 12, 1776, states "That all power is vested in, and consequently derived from, the people; that magistrates are their trustees and servants, and at all times amenable to them." The Declaration of Independence and the Constitution are both authorized by reference to the people as the sovereign power. In the long contest as to the relative primacy of states and nation, no one seriously questioned the indefeasible authority of the people. The disagreement concerned, not the people's unequivocal sovereignty, but exactly who the people were who had formed the Union and had authorized the Constitution. Did sovereignty reside in the several peoples of the several states, or in the one people of the United States? From the former point of view, the Union was a compact among several peoples; from the latter, the states were subdivisions of and by one people.

It is historically incorrect to imply that the attempts to limit the powers of the federal government were attempts to produce or preserve limited government, that is, government which simply exempted private life as much as possible from every form of political control. Many of those who tried hard to keep federal hands off state governments, wished the state governments to lay strong hands upon private activities. The main opposition to the Alien and Sedition Acts was not on the grounds that they were improper acts for any government, but that they were improper acts for the federal government. The most important and durable basis of the hostility to a strong central government, from the debate on the ratification of the Constitution until the firing on Fort Sumter, was the fear that such a government might some day have the power and the inclination to emancipate the slaves. Mr. Meyer's conception of the original Constitution as a system of multiple tensions seems somewhat tenuously to reflect the theories of John C. Calhoun, but Calhoun was the most famous of those who declared that slavery was, not a necessary evil, but a positive good. And is not slavery the most unlimited of all forms of government? How can one identify theories devised to protect slavery with the cause of limited government?

The genius of Abraham Lincoln consisted above all in the clarity with which he perceived and demonstrated the inner connection between free, popular, constitutional government, and the mighty proposition, "that all men are created equal." Questions concerning the construction of the Constitution were absolutely subordinate to the principle which gave life and meaning to the whole regime. The sovereignty of the people, Lincoln argued, was itself an inference from the primordial tenet of human equality. Men originally equal in authority consent to form a people, and consent thereby to the authority of government. But how can consent be given to slavery, which denies the requirement of consent? How can one man enslave another, without conceding that the other might, if he can, enslave him? If states can declare their right to enslave human persons within their borders, what principle is it that they appeal to in denouncing arbitrary power in the federal government? The principle of a free constitution rests not in any particular distribution of the powers of government, but in the recognition that *all* men have rights which *no* government should infringe. But Lincoln was no abolitionist; he was the least doctrinaire man who ever lived, Mr. Meyer to the contrary notwithstanding. He conceded the immense difficulties that obstructed the path to Negro freedom. All he demanded was that we place our feet on that path, and not on one that faced toward the spread and perpetuation of slavery. The issue which led to his election was *not,* "Shall slavery be abolished?" but "Shall slavery *or freedom* be abolished?" It was not to end slavery in the South, but to prevent its extension into free territories, and its legalization in free states, that the Republican Party was formed. If the states of the Confederacy had not sought to reverse the results of the election of 1860 by force and violence, Lincoln neither could nor would have taken any of those steps which led to the violent demise of slavery.

Meyer suggests that the right policy for Lincoln in 1861 was to let the erring brothers depart in peace, and to rely "upon the passage of time, the congruity of natural interest, and the exercise of statesmanship to reunite the federal structure." Of course, such a possibility was considered and debated thoroughly at the time. Meyer forgets that the United States nearly went to war with Great Britain over Oregon in 1845; and that the French attempted to install a puppet government in Mexico during the Civil War. The whole policy of the Confederacy was directed toward foreign alliances, and the European vultures waiting to descend upon the corpse of the American Union were ravenous. How would North and South have agreed to partition the territories, as foreign powers, when they could not agree upon their division when fellow citizens? How would they have dealt with fugitive slaves? How would they have dealt with each other's shipping, if the South reopened the slave-trade, regarded by the North as piracy? If one formed a military alliance with one European power, would not the other have done so with another? The wars that would have followed the Balkanization of the continent cause the imagination to boggle. The Civil War might have been a tea party by contrast. And where would the mighty power have been that today can defend freedom around the world? Meyer's theories of peaceful coexistence for the 1860s have all the political realism of Bertie Russell's for the 1960s.

The purpose of all government—to secure the rights to life, liberty, and the pursuit of happiness—is not itself the result of government. Today it is positivism and relativism, so characteristic of our self-proclaimed liberals, which lead to the notion that "man makes himself," and see no purpose outside the will of man, which ought to inform the government of man. From positivism and relativism come the opinion that whatever a sufficient mass can be persuaded to desire, it is right for them to desire. And if ends can be freely chosen, so can means. From this it follows that morality should be governed by opinion, not opinion by morality. Hence the Constitution, too, may mean whatever enough people (or the judges) think it should mean. Against this debased, plebiscitary version of supposed free government, Lincoln is the great prophet of our tradition. He is at once the greatest of our true liberals, and the greatest of our conservatives. It was he, more than anyone, who said clearly that just government must be controlled by moral purpose, and that no counting of heads can turn wrong into right. If slavery was a positive good, he observed, then it was strange that no man ever sought the good of it for himself!

Jefferson before him had denied that slavery could be justified because of any supposed inferiority in the Negro. "Because Sir Isaac Newton was superior to others in understanding, he was not therefore lord of the person or property of others," Jefferson had written. Slavery robbed a man of his labor, and in the perpetual, unrelieved, hopeless bondage of the antebellum American Negro slave, it robbed him of all his labor, and therefore of his life. Under the laws of American slavery, which had grown steadily harsher in the decades before the Civil War—manumission had become practically impossible, and it was a felony to teach a Negro to read or write in many states—the moral imperatives of the Ten Commandments were abrogated as far as slaves were concerned. Chief Justice Taney summed it up when, in the Dred Scott decision, he said that, under the Constitution, the Negro (free or slave) had no rights which the white man was bound to respect. I can therefore think of no good objection to either Nazism or communism, that would not apply to the chattel slavery that once existed in this country. That the horrors inherent in the system might be tempered by the humanity of individuals is, I take it, no more excuse for slavery than for communism. Meyer thinks that the Constitution of the United States as it resulted from the Civil War was less apt an instrument for liberty than it was before. Whatever the debit side of the ledger might show, certainly the credit side must show a mighty entry: the destruction of that reproach to everything sacred to the American mission in the world, American Negro slavery.

Meyer says that, in the conduct of the war, Lincoln intended "the permanent destruction of the autonomy of the states." Nothing could be further from the truth. To give but one example: Lincoln strove, with might and main, for gradual, compensated emancipation, by state, not federal action. The role of the federal government, as he recommended it during the war, would have been limited to underwriting the costs to the states. But he would have left the entire administration of the process in the hands of the states, which would have had until the year 1900 to complete the process. Lincoln strove in a thousand ways to preserve what was best in the political structure he had inherited. Emancipation by military proclamation was not a calculated means to abolish slavery, it was an obligation to the men in the ranks to neglect no means to end the war. The options available to a commander in chief, in the middle of a terrible conflict, are not what may appear to the leisurely commentator. Lincoln himself said, "I have not controlled events, events have controlled me." In many respects, Lincoln's leadership was a failure. His influence with Congress varied, but was seldom very great. He could not compel the government under his direction, or the people whose government it was, to live on the level of his own powerful logic, or his own transcendent compassion. Perhaps, in the end, it was far more important that he lived on that level himself; and that, in the manner of one of Shakespeare's tragic heroes, he revealed human possibilities that might not otherwise have come to light. As Woodrow Wilson once said, the phenomenon of Lincoln has made it possible to believe in democracy.

16 | RECONSTRUCTION Old and New

American historical writing has in recent years taken an increasingly reflective and self-critical turn. The proportion of the writing about the writing of history has steadily increased. Much of this literature has been marked by genuine distinction, and by a sophistication that distinguishes it from both the old-style debunking and the traditional warfare of the schools. Two outstanding examples that come to mind are Thomas J. Pressly's *Americans Interpret Their Civil War* (Princeton, 1954), and Merrill D. Peterson's *The Jeffersonian Image in the American Mind* (Oxford, 1960). The latter, although it purports only to be a book about the books about Jefferson, taught me more about Jefferson himself than any of the standard biographies. The reason, I believe, is that from the variety of highly plausible viewpoints about Jefferson, one learns why the study of Jefferson is such a problem.

Pressly's book reminds us of the man who wrote "An Impartial History of the War Between the States from a Southern Point of View." Pressly documents the existence not merely of Union and Confederate historiography, but of historiography corresponding to the points of view of abolitionists, ex-northern Whig Republicans, Constitutional Unionists, ex-southern Whig Democrats, and so forth. Moreover, he shows how these different viewpoints have recurred, in a kind of cyclical pattern, during the century following the war. This should not be too surprising, of course, to anyone who sees in the civil rights movement the lineal descendants of the old abolitionists. Whoever does so will also discover today most of the other counterparts (political and historiographical) of the party spectrum of circa 1860.

Pressly's book also points out that the thesis that the Civil War was a "needless war" flourished during the period between World Wars I and II, when American neutralism and isolationism were at their zenith. If Mr. Wilson's war was not really a war to make the world safe for democracy, but was rather a war to make J. P. Morgan's loans to the Allies safe, then maybe Mr. Lincoln's war was not a war to make men free either. Perhaps it only represented, as the title of a famous monograph of the period suggested, the "triumph of American capitalism." The rediscovery of moral purpose, or moral significance, in the Civil War has coincided more

Review of Kenneth M. Stampp, *The Era of Reconstruction, 1865–1877* (New York: Alfred A. Knopf, 1965). Reprinted by the kind permission of the publisher from *National Review* 17, no. 16 (Apr. 20, 1965): 330-33.

or less with a parallel evaluation of World War II. Whatever dissatisfaction there may be with the aftermath of World War II, there have been few among us who have doubted that, as Winston Churchill put it, Adolf Hitler was "a bad man." (When Churchill first said that, in the 1930s, he was laughed at by sophisticates of the day and told that he was living in the world of Grimm's fairy tales. Later on, of course, he was duly celebrated for using the only language which fit the facts of the case.) And so the reality of the evil of Nazism has retrospectively convinced our historians of the reality of the evil of slavery. The perspective of today's historians more nearly resembles that of the immediate postbellum generation than of almost any other time in the intervening period.

The "revisionism" which has restored something of the perspective of the Civil War period has naturally had a similar effect upon writing about the Reconstruction. Professor Stampp, in the excellent book before us, gives an account of the main phases of Reconstruction historiography which, while not so detailed or precisely documented as Pressly's work, does nonetheless complement it. Stampp's starting point is a paradox. In the bulk of our historical writing, the Civil War itself appears as an age of tragic heroism and tragic nobility. Notwithstanding the brutality of the fighting and the sordidness of the profiteering, it was a war of demigods and heroes, a conflict of men transcendent both in the purity of their ideals, and the ability and the devotion with which they pursued them. Yet the era of Reconstruction, immediately following the war, involving many of the same actors, is generally portrayed as a period of virtually unrelieved meanness, depravity, and mediocrity. Surely, professor Stampp suggests, human nature is not so erratic that the Civil War could have been as exalted a conflict, or the Reconstruction so degenerate an episode, as this tradition would indicate.

Such exaggeration, he admits, is common enough in the history books, and is generally harmless. However, the legend about Reconstruction is not harmless, because it is a legend about the political corruption and irresponsibility of the American Negro during the one period when a serious effort was made to guarantee him equal political rights in the states of the old Confederacy. That is to say, it concerns the one period when such an attempt was made *before 1965.* So Stampp's book is, quite deliberately, a contribution to the consummation of the *new* Reconstruction, quite as much as it it is an attempt to correct misunderstanding of the old.

On the whole, I believe Stampp's effort is successful. But it is an ambiguous kind of success. That carpetbaggers and scalawags were corrupt he does not question; but they were not conspicuously more corrupt than the officeholders in states which had never rebelled at all. The sparse examples of enlightened government, and the plentiful examples of moral dissoluteness and unbridled chicanery are found distributed among all the states, old as well as new, North as well as South, with a random impartiality. Moreover, Stampp makes an impressive argument that the behavior and misbehavior of Negro voters and officeholders did not, so far as available evidence goes, depart from the national norms. From all this I think it fair to draw the inference that Stampp intends: that nothing in the history of Reconstruction is a ground for believing that the enfranchisement today of the American Negro in the states of the old Confederacy will alter the political character of those states for the worse.

But what about the broad *historical* picture that Stampp sets out to revise? That, I believe, emerges substantially unchanged. The Reconstruction was a deplorable period, even if no significant difference exists between the Radical governments of the period and other governments. Moreover, the Civil War was a period of nobility and heroism, not because human nature changed, and not because there wasn't just as much political corruption, but because great and fundamental decisions concerning the future of the American Republic were being made then: the indissolubility of the American Union, the end of chattel slavery, and the nationalization of American citizenship.

Nothing so fundamental was being decided during Reconstruction, and probably nothing so fundamental could have been decided then. In 1860 the American people had moved toward a crisis by electing Abraham Lincoln president and thus deciding, not to end slavery, but to end its territorial extension. In fighting a war to make that decision stick, they abolished slavery. Having made the decision stick, they stuck with all the necessary consequences. Full immediate political equality for Negroes was simply not one of those necessary consequences, and the attempt to make it one at that time was a political mistake by the Radicals. Nothing in Stampp's book upsets this traditional view of the Reconstruction.

Professor Stampp finds in the Fourteenth and Fifteenth Amendments to the Constitution the enduring positive achievements of Reconstruction. This is because they are the foundation stones upon which the Negro revolution of today—the New Reconstruction—is building. Yet it seems to me, at least, that the fact that these portions of the Constitution could be dead as far as Negro rights are concerned, for so long, is evidence that their presence in the Constitution is not crucial. While I would certainly admit that these amendments are a great convenience in the prosecution of this revolution today, it is difficult for me to believe that the present interpreters of the Supreme Court would not be sufficiently ingenious to discover them elsewhere in the Constitution, were they under sufficient inducement to do so. In any event, Professor Stampp does not know, and I do not know, whether the relations of the races today might not be much healthier than they are, if there had been no Radical Reconstruction.

17 | THE TRUTH ABOUT WAR

In *My Early Life*, published in 1930, Churchill wrote that "the years 1895 to 1900 exceed in vividness, variety, and exertion anything I have known—except of course the opening months of the Great War." Here are the wars of those early years, as young Winston experienced them, in all the vigor of youthful consummation. All the great Churchillian themes are present: war and peace, barbarism and civilization, empire and freedom. There was in Churchill, even from his early years, a Shakespearean response to life in its totality. He wanted to be where the action was, but he was no jingo or romanticizer. War was a part of life. It was that part in which the fates of empires, nations, and heroes—good and bad—were determined. And Churchill was determined to learn about it at first hand.

The editor of this collection has chosen two epigraphs, drawn from the writings themselves. The first is: "I have cared only to write what I thought was the truth about everybody." And the second: "War, disguise it as you may, is but a dirty, shoddy business, which only a fool would play at." Despite some opinions to the contrary, Churchill never played at war. There was about him, from the outset, far more of Prince Hal than of Hotspur. Young Winston, like Hal, knows that "rule shows the man," and that men rule, and are ruled, above all, in war. Therefore he who would tell "the truth about everybody" must discover the truth about war.

However evil a thing war might be, it was yet the place in which, more than any other, men's courage was tested and shown. And Churchill always admired courage above all other human qualities. In the dark days of World War II, his ability to pay tribute, with matchless eloquence, to those who had borne the battle was one of the great gifts of his leadership. Here is an example of the genre, which Churchill early raised to the level of art. There is in it not a touch either of exaggeration or false sentiment. We have instead a medallion, a permanent reminder of the fleeting moment of a life, of action, and of honor. The spirit of a man is captured in a few, brief lines, and a noble death made quaint and individual in the quiet, ironic beauty of the self-chosen epitaph from 2 Kings 4:26.

Review of Frederick Woods (ed.), *Young Winston's Wars: The Original Despatches of Winston S. Churchill, War Correspondent, 1897–1900* (New York: Viking Press, 1973). Reprinted by the kind permission of the publisher from *National Review* 25, no. 31 (Aug. 3, 1973): 847, 849.

I think this death of Major Childe was a very sad event even among the inevitable incidents of war. He had served many years ago in the Blues, and since then a connection with the Turf had made him not unknown and well liked in sporting circles. Old and grey as he was, the call to arms had drawn him from home and wife and comfort, as it is drawing many of all ages and fortunes now. And so he was killed in his first fight against the Boers after he had performed an exploit—his first and last in war—which would most certainly have brought him honorable distinction. He had a queer presentiment of impending fate, for he had spoken to us of the chances of death, and had even selected his own epitaph, so that on the little wooden cross which stands at the foot of Bastion Hill—the hill he took himself and held—there is written: "Is it well with the child? It is well."

Who now reading these lines, even across the vast anonymous slaughter pens of the twentieth century, can forget Major Childe of Bastion Hill?

Of the three wars that are the subject of this book, two are waged against barbarians. Such a distinction is much against the temper of our times. The later Churchill would certainly have rejected the assumption of an implicit harmony between the progress of science and of civilization, which the young Victorian seems to make. Yet his outlook here has much in common with that of the Jefferson of the Declaration of Independence, who began by declaring the equality of all men, but ended by denouncing both "barbarous ages" and "merciless Indian Savages."

According to Young Winston, the rising on the Indian frontier was excited by "the hostility of the priesthood," whose "wealth and influence" depended upon the "extraordinary credulity of the people," which, in turn, was being undermined by the "civilizing, educating rule" of Great Britain. The filthy habits and unspeakable morals of the tribesmen could claim no right against the great structure of civilized law and government embodied in the British Empire. Notwithstanding their "odious vices," however, Young Winston "will yet ungrudgingly admit that [these same tribesmen] are a brave and warlike race."

Similar remarks are made about the Dervishes of the Sudan. Although they too lived lives that were, in certain respects, of unutterable depravity, still they "were as brave men as ever walked the earth." Surveying the carnage of the field of Omdurman, he writes: "The conviction was borne in on me, that their claim beyond the grave in respect of a valiant death was as good as any of our countrymen could make." Since the Young, like the Old, Winston seems to have respected this claim, perhaps even above all others, the superiority of civilization to barbarism, in the decisive respect is left surprisingly open to question.

Although the claim of the valiant comes close to being a Churchillian absolute, it is by no means clear that the conviction upon which it appears to rest is equally deserving of regard. When Churchill at one point registers his disgust at the mutilation of the corpses of their enemy by the tribesmen, he confesses that his revulsion has something irrational in it, as he does not really believe that harm can come to the dead. But Churchill respects myths consistent with human dignity, and is repelled by myths inconsistent with it. The ground of human dignity however is independent of the myths. He describes the ceremonies that accompany the remains of a soldier of a civilized power to the grave, above all "the triumphant words of the Funeral Service." These, he says, "divest the act of its squalor [and] the spectator sympathizes with, perhaps almost envies the comrade who has found this honorable exit." But the honor of the exit is itself different from the spectator's sympathy, even as the triumph of the Service is different from the squalor of the act.

We have, in the letters from the Sudan, the first reactions to Kitchener's brutal treatment of the defeated Dervishes. We can, however, anticipate Churchill's fury, because here is a British commander doing exactly the same degrading kind of thing that had horrified him when done by tribesmen or Dervishes. Here are some sentences concerning the destruction of the Mahdi's tomb that are not unworthy of the youthful disciple of Gibbon, Burke, and Macaulay.

> This place had been for more than ten years the most sacred and holy thing that the people of Sudan knew of. Their miserable lives had perhaps been brightened, perhaps in some ways ennobled, by the contemplation of something which they did not quite understand, but which they believed exerted some protecting influence. It had gratified that instinctive desire for the mystic which all human creatures possess, and which is perhaps the strongest reason for believing in a progressive destiny and a future state.

It is not certain how strong is that "strongest reason." The British Empire seems at this juncture to fulfill the same kind of specifications for providential patronage that, according to Dante and others, had earlier been met by the Roman Empire. And Churchill seems to be demanding a policy of imperial toleration of alien gods similar to that of the Augustan Age. He has an imaginary correspondent presume to defend the destruction of the tomb, on the grounds that the Mahdi was, after all, only a false prophet. But, Churchill responds, that only means that *you* do not believe him. " 'False' is the epithet which all religious sects have applied to all others since the beginning of things." To find a politically intelligible *via media* between the opposing evils of mere skepticism and mere credulity was an enterprise upon which the Young Churchill was engaged with utmost seriousness.

The Boers were challengers of the Empire of an entirely different order of dignity. At moments, Churchill shows a romantic attachment to them, not unlike that which he obviously felt for Lee and Jackson, when he studied the American Civil War. He admired their independence and their skill, "moving like the wind, and supported by iron constitutions and a stern, hard, Old Testament God." On the night of his capture, as he lay wet and cold, and heard them sing their evening hymn, a chill was struck in his heart, "so that I thought after all that the war was unjust, that the Boers were better men than we, that Heaven was against us. . . ." But morning, and the sun, brought better—or more optimistic— thoughts. In retrospect, Young Winston's escape from the Boer's—here described for the first time, although not with the circumstantial detail of later accounts—takes on symbolic meaning. Both Churchill and the Empire were to escape, and the enemies he held in such regard were to become comrades in far greater and more deadly conflicts.

This review would be misleading if it were to seem that the thoughts we have selected for notice were all in the foreground. This is a narrative of actions, above all the actions of men in battle. But he who would command men in battle must come to terms with death, which means laying hold upon a purpose in life which can sometimes be fulfilled only by that "honorable exit." These despatches are a priceless starting point for the study of the education of perhaps the greatest leader "into battle" that the world has seen.

18 | WHAT ABOUT THE DARDANELLES?

When Randolph Churchill died in 1968, having completed only the first two volumes of his father's life (to 1914), the role of official biographer of the late Sir Winston Churchill passed to his research assistant, Martin Gilbert. Gilbert is a young scholar, still in his thirties, but already established as among the most distinguished of a new breed of extraordinarily well trained professional historians coming from the school of A. J. P. Taylor. Among Gilbert's earlier works is one entitled *The Appeasers* (with Richard Gott), another, *The Roots of Appeasement,* and still another, *The European Powers: 1900-1945.* Gilbert is also the author of a fine series of historical atlases, and his home in Oxford is called The Map House. All this indicates a preoccupation with themes and vocations eminently Churchillian. Still, the change in tone accompanying the change in authorship is striking and profound. It was not possible for Gilbert to retain the epigraph that Randolph Churchill, borrowing from Lockhart, had chosen for his work: "He shall be his own biographer."

Randolph Churchill had found an unusual tone in writing about his father's childhood and early career, which involved writing about his grandparents and their circle as well. Notwithstanding the undoubted filial (and familial) piety, there was a certain amused detachment, a kind of robust enjoyment of a remarkable spectacle, free from petty partisanship in regard to issues and personalities of a distant past. Scattered through Sir Winston's own writings as the years rolled on were certain wry observations about the younger Winston. It was the spirit of these, rather than the elaborate self-justifications of the later years, by which Randolph seemed to be guided. Still, when the work fell from his hands, the tales of world-shattering events and cosmic quarrels were yet to be told.

It is said that once, in debate in the House, Sir Winston retorted to a critic, "We'll leave that to history," adding in a loud aside, "And I'll write the history." But Churchill always called his accounts of contemporary events, not history, but a contribution to history. No man, he knew, can be a spectator of himself, or be permitted to be a judge in his own

Review of Martin Gillbert, *Winston S. Churchill,* vol. 3: *The Challenge of War: 1914–1916* (Boston: Houghton Mifflin Company, 1971); and Martin Gilbert (ed.), *Winston S. Churchill,* Companion vol. 3: *July 1914–December 1916* (Boston: Houghton Mifflin Company, 1973), parts 1 and 2. Reprinted by the kind permission of the publisher from *National Review* 25, no. 47 (Nov. 23, 1973): 1307-9.

cause. Churchill had, moreover, devoted much thought to that ancient conundrum—who will judge the judges?—in its application to the high court of history. Many things, he knew, turn out well or ill not because of intelligent forethought—or its absence—but because of chance. It is always easy, after the fact, to attribute wisdom to success, and folly to failure. It is always hard to see success or failure emerging from their true causes, in which wisdom and folly often play roles entirely different from those which seem so evident in the afterlight.

> Documents written at the time and before the event are the only foundation upon which the judgment of history can be erected. They alone reveal the perplexities of the situation at the moment. They alone show how far it was understood. By their aid we can recall the light which then played over the immense battlefield with partial fleeting gleams. We can revive again and try to gauge the pressure under which the men responsible lived, and from which action emerged. We can not only discern the points where judgment was right or wrong, but whether such judgment, right or wrong, was reasonable or even inevitable at the time and with the knowledge of the time.

So wrote Churchill in 1923, in the preface to the second volume of *The World Crisis*. Gilbert is his own man in giving his account here of events recorded earlier by his subject. But he does so in the presence of powerful admonitions.

In 1923 Churchill thought that the events of the year 1915 had been, and would thereafter prove to be, the most fateful of the twentieth century. At the outset of that year it was still possible, he thought, to contain the conflict which had begun a year earlier. Statesmanship might yet have resolved the issues of the war so as to preserve the great progressive civilization of Europe and the European empires of the late Victorian era. The rising tides of radical modernity—of nationalism, democracy, and technology—might yet have been accommodated within a framework of older, but evolving, political structures. In the event, the terrible bloodletting of 1916, 1917, and 1918 led to the collapse of the Ottoman and Austro-Hungarian empires and the fall of the Russian and German monarchies, and to an exhaustion of victors and vanquished alike that ushered in an era of political and economic instability, of totalitarianism and revolutionary change.

If 1915 was a year of disaster for civilization, so also was it a year of disaster for Churchill. Although no one could have foreseen it, it was the beginning of the end for the Liberal regime which had governed England since 1906 and for the prime minister who had held office through hitherto unparalleled difficulties since 1908. The cabinet, which included Asquith, Sir Edward Grey, Lloyd George, Kitchener, and Churchill, might possibly have been the most talented assemblage to have governed a great nation in the modern world. Still, it was an assemblage ill qualified to direct a great war. The multiplicity of its talents and the power of its personalities left it a committee, at best artfully managed. But the war required decision rather than management, and that Asquith could not give. Although Asquith's judgment nearly always supported Churchill, he would not act, or act consistently, in support of that judgment. In the end, he gave Churchill up to his critics—Churchill as a turncoat Tory was the sacrifice for which the Tory Party hungered—and what was perhaps worst, Asquith refused Churchill the explanation to the public of what had really happened.

"What about the Dardanelles?" was a cry to follow Churchill for nearly a generation. Yet Churchill did not originate the Dardanelles strategy (which made its first appearance in a cabinet memorandum by Colonel Hankey), nor was he its early proponent. He always preferred, as an alternative, the invasion of the island of Borkum off the German coast in the North Sea. This was a strategy for neutralizing—or destroying—the German High Seas Fleet, preparatory to an invasion of the German heartland behind the lines of the existing western front, from a point less than one hundred miles from Berlin. For the War Council was entirely agreed on the necessity, at the end of 1914, of finding some new initiative in the war. The western front then presented a continuous set of fortified lines, more than three hundred miles long, from the North Sea (near the Channel) to the Swiss frontier. These lines were an intricate set of manned trenches, protected by barbed wire and by minefields, whose approaches could be swept by machine guns. Neither the tank nor any other form of effective armor for the foot soldier then existed. Offensive tactics consisted of little more than sending waves of unarmored men against these positions, to be mowed down with almost unvarying precision.

"Battles are won by slaughter and maneuver," Churchill has written. "The greater the general, the more he contributes in maneuver, the less he demands in slaughter." But not all strategy is directed toward the battlefield. "The maneuver which brings an ally into the field is as serviceable as that which wins a great battle." At the end of 1914, all of the Balkan states except Serbia were neutral, as was Italy. The significance of the Dardanelles lay in the possibility that it would unite all of these by the lure of Turkish plunder. The rivalries among them were great, but so were the temptations which the Entente could lay before them, if it could mount a successful operation in the eastern Mediterranean. Almost any plan of attack against Turkey had many of the elements that go into the making of a self-fulfilling prophecy. If any of the Balkan states—e.g., Greece—had joined the campaign, one after another of the other Balkan states would almost surely have joined. And a decisive move by any one of them would almost certainly have assured success. In fact, the Dardanelles campaign came very close to success on a dozen occasions even without any overt move of the neutrals to join the Entente. Of all the historic ironies, none is greater than that it was Russian imperial opposition to the possibility of a Greek army entering Constantinople—at a moment when Venizelos had just about overcome the Greek king's pro-German sentiments—that kept the Balkan dominoes from falling into place. The effective beginning of the Dardanelles was an urgent request by the Russians, early in January 1915, for relief from the pressure of Turkish armies upon them in the Caucasus. And among the glittering rewards promised was a reopening of the Russian Black Sea ports, giving Russia access to badly needed Western military supplies, and the West access to badly needed Russian grain.

The centerpiece of Gilbert's volume is a brilliant retelling of the tale of this great and tragic operation, as seen from the perspective of the British War Council. The main lines of policy were agreed to by all. But in the execution, there was a constant tug-of-war, with Kitchener, secretary of state for war (but a field marshal, and Britain's most prestigious military figure), on the one side, and Fisher, first sea lord (and Britain's most famous sailor), on the other. And it fell to Churchill, first lord of the Admiralty—a brilliant young Liberal politician, but with no military or naval prestige at all—to find the *media via* between them. It was Kitchener who, first of all, called upon the navy to make some demonstration at the Dardanelles, as a gesture to relieve the Russians. Moreover, it was Kitchener who, as the reigning authority on the Middle East (his whole career had been spent there), assured the War Council that if a British fleet entered the Marmora and appeared before Constantinople, the shock would utterly disorganize the Turks. Churchill never believed in an unsupported naval attack if any combined operation were possible. But he had enough confidence in Kitchener's judgment that, when Kitchener declared that no troops were available, he went ahead with the plans for that attack "by ships alone." That is, he went ahead with it when a plan had been worked out, and declared feasible, by his professional naval advisers. But whenever it appeared that troops might become available, Churchill always pressed for the maximum military force to assist the navy—or to realize those fruits of the navy's success that could only be achieved by putting troops ashore.

The Dardanelles operation was agreed to at every stage by Fisher. Like Churchill, he preferred the attack on the northern flank of the Central Powers. Although the Borkum scheme had the advantage of permitting the British navy to remain wholly concentrated in the North

Sea, it required many times the number of troops ever contemplated at the Dardanelles. It was never a real possibility. But the first task of the British navy in World War I was always to maintain its unquestioned domination of the German High Seas Fleet. Upon this its control of Britain's lifelines—and everything else—depended. This meant maintaining at all times a battle fleet in the North Sea of absolutely assured superiority to that of the Germans. Neither Churchill nor Fisher forgot for a moment that Britain could lose everything in one short action, if the Grand Fleet ever lost its domination of the High Seas Fleet. With a single exception, the big ships used at the Dardanelles were predreadnought battleships, of no use whatever in a general fleet action, and most of them already destined for the scrap heap. Still, Churchill had again and again to reassure Fisher that nothing sent to the east weakened the Grand Fleet in its vigil. Moreover, the sending of the *Queen Elizabeth,* the newest and most powerful British warship, was Fisher's idea. Her guns had still to be tested, and he suggested testing them on the forts at the Dardanelles instead of on practice targets at sea. But the old guard at the Admiralty—whether prodding Fisher or prodded by him is not always clear—never ceased their nagging, as they would have nagged at any operation not designed purely to enhance the navy's own superiority. In the end, Fisher's irrational fears, his erratic and devious behavior, and his fantastic notion that if Churchill were driven from the Admiralty he would replace him, led the way to ruin.

What the Grand Fleet was to Fisher, the western front was to Kitchener. In the case of the former, the reality was that its firepower was always overwhelmingly dominant. In the case of the latter, the reality was that defensive firepower—on both sides—was dominant. Not only was a German breakthrough unlikely, but it was unlikely that the small number of troops originally asked to go with the fleet to the east would make any difference in France. But Kitchener, who was convinced that an attack by ships alone on the Dardanelles would cause the collapse of European Turkey, would not (until too late) risk the 29th Division—the only regular army division in reserve in England—to assist the navy. Thus while Kitchener at the War Office kept calling for the navy to go it alone, Fisher at the Admiralty kept calling for troops.

The worst that can be said of Churchill is that he tried to make the best of a bad bargain. In fact, the bargain, or the series of bargains, was not too bad. It was the chopping and changing of the principals that ruined a basically sound strategy. The naval attack on March 18, 1915, was inconclusive. There is a great mass of evidence that, had the navy got through, many of the desired political results would have followed. But late in the day, three battleships—one French and two British—struck mines in a field that had not been charted, and sank. Although almost all the French crew was lost, virtually all the British sailors were saved. But an unforeseen technical problem had arisen. While the ships could dominate the forts, they could not find and silence a large number of concealed mobile batteries firing from the hills and brush nearer the water's edge. And these batteries, although not posing much danger to the warships, kept driving off the minesweepers. The minesweeping force of March 18 had consisted almost entirely of merchant fishing trawlers from the North Sea with civilian crews. And they would not do their work under fire. To return to the attack with destroyers fitted with mine bumpers was no great difficulty. The trawlers had fled without suffering any casualties at all. And the Admiralty knew from secret but certain sources, confirmed after the war, that the Turkish forts were desperately short of ammunition, and could hardly have kept firing another day. At the end of March 18 the British admiral commanding, de Robeck, fully expected to return to the attack. The losses had been well within the bounds anticipated. No new fact, then or soon thereafter, presented itself. But bit by bit, doubt and hesitation crept in. And every tremor of de Robeck's became a loud reverberation in Whitehall. Then, as the Admiralty wavered, troops were found, and as troops were found, all will power to carry the fleet alone through the straits disappeared. When, six weeks later, the expeditionary force to invade the Gallipoli Peninsula was finally assembled, the Turkish positions, under an able German general, had been immeasurably strengthened. The soft underbelly had been case-hardened to the temper of Flanders steel.

Partly because Churchill became the political scapegoat of the Dardanelles, he has been, by and large, the historiographical scapegoat as well. Gilbert tells his story from the greatest array of sources yet brought to bear upon this episode. Still, elements of the older historiography creep into his judgments, perhaps unawares. At the end of a chapter entitled, "The Search for Men," he writes:

> Churchill had helped to add to the War Council's self-deception by his earlier willingness to make the operation purely naval; he now believed that ships alone would be inadequate, and that the more troops that could be found, the greater the chance there would be of victory. But he so believed in the need for victory that he was prepared to go ahead with the plans for the entirely naval attack. However much he continued to argue that these plans might fail, by agreeing to go ahead with them, he made himself responsible for the very disaster that he forecast.

In a fine dissertation, recently completed, Professor Jeffrey Wallin of Arkansas State University has pointed to the startling inconsistency of these judgments with the actual material of Gilbert's narrative. In the first place, there was no disaster. Gilbert himself later acknowledges that there was no "massive naval disaster." The British navy had suffered exactly seventy-three casualties, killed and wounded, on the 18th, and two old ships that had been destined for scrap were lost. Gilbert also later admits that there had been no "conclusive sign that a naval victory was impossible." But in truth, there was no sign at all. De Robeck never pointed to a single reason for not attacking *after* the 18th, that would not have been a reason for not attacking *before* the 18th. There simply were no new facts, just a failure of nerve.

Churchill's reputation in later years also suffered from the military disasters—the genuine disasters—that took place upon the Peninsula. But as Gilbert points out, for these operations he never had any direct responsibility. The failures there were mainly failures in the command structure, over which Kitchener alone had absolute control. As long as he was a member of the War Council, Churchill gave the expedition all the political support he could. And he never ceased to believe that, if it had had a fraction of the concentrated support that went into the vain—and vastly more costly—offensives on the Somme, it too might have succeeded. As we have noted, it came within a hairsbreadth of success a number of times. Perhaps the last words on the Dardanelles remain those of John Masefield's poem, which Churchill himself used as an epigraph to his own account.

Even so was wisdom proven blind,
So Courage failed, so strength was
   chained,
Even so the gods, whose seeing mind
Is not as ours, ordained.

Yet this may not be altogether the last word. Thirty years later, a far greater amphibious expedition than that at Gallipoli landed upon the beaches of Normandy. Churchill's and Fisher's "Borkum plan" finally had its chance. Few of Lord Kitchener's mistakes would not have been repeated, had the American chiefs been permitted to make this attempt in 1942 or 1943, as they wished. But Churchill, now with an authority greater than Kitchener's had been, never forgot a single mistake that had been made in 1915. The perfection of all the elements of the attack—including the element of tactical surprise—before the first step was taken assured a master stroke in the art of war.

19 | AMORAL AMERICA AND THE LIBERAL DILEMMA

During the Lincoln-Douglas debates, Abraham Lincoln remarked that "Judge Douglas is a man of vast influence, so great that it is enough for many men to profess to believe anything when they once find out that Judge Douglas professes to believe it."[1] The essays to which the following critique is addressed are by men of unusual eminence in the world of the American university. On the topic they treat—moral education—their views, however, far from being unusual, seem to be perfectly representative of the most influential opinions—liberal and radical—within that world. Each in his own way, and both together, point to a crisis of confidence in the traditions, not merely of the university, but of Western civilization altogether.

* * *

My esteemed colleague, Dr. George C. S. Benson, in the inaugural issue of *Res Publica*,[2] has invited us to "stop pointing the finger" at unethical conduct, and do something. What we are asked to do is to pay "more attention to education in ethical fundamentals." Like Socrates, however, Dr. Benson seems better at exhorting us to education in virtue, than in instructing us in what it is. But unless we know what it is, or how to find it, the old dilemmas remain.

When Dr. Benson is asked how ethics can be taught, he points out that "an excellent start was made on Mt. Sinai when the Ten Commandments were laid down." He also mentions Thomas Aquinas, John Bunyan, and McGuffey (of the Readers) as successful practitioners of the art of ethical instruction. All of them, however, would have been taken aback, to say the least, by the reference to the Mosaic pronouncements as an "excellent start." For all of them the Decalogue was in some sense not merely a beginning, but an end, in fact a permanent last word. Dr. Benson

Reprinted from *A Symposium* (Claremont, Calif.: Committee for Academic Freedom, Fall 1973).

[1] Roy P. Basler (ed.), *The Collected Works of Abraham Lincoln* (New Brunswick, N.J.: Rutgers University Press, 1953), 3: 27.

[2] All indicated quotations in the first part of this essay are from George C. S. Benson, "Amoral America," *Res Publica* 1, no. 1: 10-15. All quotations in the second part are from Joseph C. Hough, Jr., "Dilemma: The Liberal and the Church," ibid., pp. 33-40.

differs decisively from the tradition he seems to invoke, and what it is to which we are being called remains at best uncertain.

An effective ethical teaching depends upon at least two things. First, intrinsic excellence; and second, sanctions. By the first we mean that if men obey commands that are really good, then they can live good lives by obeying them. Conversely, if they refuse to obey such commands, their lives suffer by an absence of goodness. That is to say, the precepts of true virtue are their own reward, and of vice their own punishment. However, nearly all moralists of the tradition agree that the difficulty for most human beings of perceiving the goodness of virtue, and the evil of vice, make it necessary that there should be auxiliary rewards and punishments. If men believe, for example, that an all-knowing and all-powerful God both punishes and rewards, in this world and the next, for disobedience and obedience to the moral code, then that code is much more likely to be a potent force in their lives.

In the modern world, the heart of the ethical problem—or the problem of ethical education—is that there has been a catastrophic decline in the belief, either in the intrinsic rightness of morality or in the existence of any sanctions for morality—other than those resulting from getting caught. The whole focus of concern with morality has shifted away from the objective question of recognizing what is right, and of how to bring it to bear within our lives. In its place we find a concern with the subjective accommodation to whatever anyone thinks is right. The only unconditional commandment now seems to be: Thou Shalt Not Impose Anyone's Ethical Code on Anyone Else or, in short, Thou Shalt Not Say No!

The dilemma into which this leads is well illustrated by Dr. Benson, when he attempts to define "ethical teaching." "By 'ethical teaching,'" he writes, "we do not mean doctrinaire theological views or even rigid moral codes; we mean simply a consciousness that each individual has some responsibility for trying to think out for himself a code of conduct that puts him in harmony with his own ideals and with the overall goals of the society of which he is a part." Let us observe first the exclusion of "doctrinaire theological views." Now doctrinaire has become a popular pejorative these days. No one would defend a foolish or impractical application of theological views. But doctrinaire is also a cognate of doctrine, which means nothing more than teaching. And Dr. Benson professes to be defining a teaching. A nondoctrinal teaching would be a nonteaching teaching. But I suspect that his objection is more to the theology than to the doctrinairism. I think it is therefore worth recalling that the precepts of the first table of the Decalogue (with the possible exception of the fifth commandment) are not moral commandments at all. They direct our relationship not toward our fellow men, but toward

God. The initial commandments establish the identity and authority of God, and it is only in virtue of such authority that the moral commandments become commandments.

But Dr. Benson also has objections to a "rigid moral code." Now certainly no one would defend rigidity as such, any more than one would defend an unreasonable application of a doctrine. But all the evidence Dr. Benson presents, not to mention the evidence of the world around us, suggests that moral rigidity is the last thing we have to worry about. Moral laxity is what we have to contend with. Perhaps a little rigidity now might even be a useful corrective. But Dr. Benson's formula has no starch in it at all. He asserts as a primary ethical datum, "a consciousness that each individual has some responsibility for trying to think out for himself a code of conduct." But how much responsibility is "some"? And why does each individual have such a responsibility? Who lays it down that each individual ought to do this thinking out of a code of conduct? God? Nature? The rational self-interest of each? The greatest good of the greatest number? But assuming that each individual obeys the imperative to try to think out a code of conduct for himself, what kind of a code shall it be? One, we are told, that is in harmony with his own ideals and with the overall goals of the society of which he is a part. But suppose he has communist ideals in a capitalist society? Or Nazi ideals in a Jewish society? Or democratic ideals in a totalitarian society? Unless we know what are good ideals and a good society, we don't know when they *ought* to harmonize. In principle, good men ought to be in conflict with bad societies, and good societies ought to be in conflict with bad men.

Dr. Benson also poses a dichotomy between personal ideals and a moral code that is inadmissible. A moral code ought not to be distinct from one's personal ideals, but a vital element of them. Also, the goals of one's society, if they are worthy of respect, ought to be part of one's moral code. "As I would not be a slave, so I would not be a master," wrote Abraham Lincoln. "This expresses my idea of democracy; whatever differs from this, to the extent of the difference, is not democracy." Respect for the rights of others thus becomes a condition, not merely of respect by others, but of self-respect. The political foundations of a free society, of a society postulating equal human rights as its axiomatic premise, and its moral foundations, are one and the same.

That Dr. Benson has little confidence in his definition is shown by the sequel. "Such a code," he writes, "would almost certainly exclude murder, forcible rape, armed robbery, and the corruption we are now enduring." The Ten Commandments were only a good beginning, and now we see how they would be amended. Under the new dispensation, the sixth commandment would read, "Thou Shalt Almost Certainly Not Commit Murder." Now those who are moved to deeds of murder, rape, and robbery, are moved as well by the passions of anger, avarice, and lust. Such passions, like wild beasts, must learn to obey the checks and reins of reason. To state a rule as here is done, with permission to make an exception given in the prohibition itself, is perfectly self-defeating. It simply gives to wrongdoing the license of conscience.

There is certainly nothing wrong in someone "thinking out for himself a code of conduct." In fact, however, very few people, at any time of life, have the leisure, the competence, or the inclination to do such a thing. The great moralists have been greatly honored among the benefactors of the human race, and they have been few. But the decisive period of moral education is in early childhood. Both the gifted and the ungifted need to be well brought up, and they need the authority of a firm moral code long before they can possibly think it out for themselves. Neither young nor old, in this age of divided souls, will find healing in do-it yourself ethical code kits.

Dean Hough gives us a very different insight into the problem of morality in the modern world. For him that problem appears to be primarily one of producing radical social change. The moral life is essentially the life committed—not to reforming—but to transforming man and his world. And the task of the moralist appears to be that of providing an *ethos* of commitment to such a life. Dean Hough describes his project as that of setting "a pattern of representative participation in social-action ministries." A true church is a "social action ministry." "Church involvement," he writes, "requires group decision and mobilization. The committed are no *cadre* until they are gathered and moved." A church animated by *cadres* of the committed, making group decisions, while mobilizing for social action, is a very far cry from what most of us had thought was the traditional—but essential—function of a church. That function Dean Hough however dismisses as "the personal salvation style of conservatism."

Dean Hough's main argument, as we shall see, is with liberals, not conservatives. The latter belong to the legions of the damned, and there is no good news for them, or about them. He cites with approval the work of Adorno on *The Authoritarian Personality*. The most important conclusion of this work, as reported by Hough, was that "this authoritarian personality 'type' was positively correlated with right-wing conservatism on politico-economic matters and showed a high degree of anti-Semitism and generally strong ethnocentrism." Translated, this means that people who favor limited, constitutional government, who profess patriotism, and who generally favor the free market over a government-regulated economy, also as a rule hate Jews, Negroes, and foreigners. Now Hough concedes that "there was some dissatisfaction in the social scientific community with the Adorno study." Indeed there was, and Hough, with one exception, reports none of it. It would go beyond the limits of this essay to make that report in any detail, beyond the observation that Adorno seemed to many observers to have circulated loaded questionnaires to support pre-existing opinions. One can hardly imagine a more specious "study" than one that implies that whatever makes one a follower of Milton Friedman in economics, or Barry Goldwater in politics, also causes anti-Semitism and ethnocentrism.

Dean Hough cites one critic of the Adorno study, one Milton Rokeach. But Hough's disagreement is not with Adorno, but with Adorno's critic. Rokeach had argued that there were in fact authoritarians of the left as well as the right. As a result many liberals, fearing to be called authoritarians, began to eschew left-wing radicalism. Rokeach's criticism "pushed the image of the liberal much more to the center." And the main thrust of Hough's argument is to overcome the liberals' fear of the authoritarian label, and get them away from merely "centrist" politics.

On one point, however, we would agree with Dean Hough's criticism of liberals and liberalism. According to Rokeach—as reported by Hough—"*Any* belief held too tenaciously could function as an indication of the rigidity and authoritarianism that seems causally related to prejudice." Liberals, then, eschew "any belief held too tenaciously." But let us (and Dean Hough) ask: can the belief that any belief held too tenaciously causes prejudice, itself be held too tenaciously? If it can, then it too can cause prejudice. If it cannot, then it is not true that *any* belief can be held too tenaciously. From this we would conclude that the whole idea of a "personality type" being the index of the validity of anyone's social, economic, or political convictions is the purest nonsense. Milton Friedman's economic teachings can be refuted—if they can be refuted—only by an economic argument. And political teachings can be refuted only by political arguments. Dean Hough's rejection of the Adorno thesis when applied to the left wing, is sufficient grounds for rejecting it when applied to the right. There never was any justification for introducing it in the first place. It was a mere appeal to prejudice.

Dean Hough rightly criticizes liberal leaders for "their failure to find the limits of tolerance." Certainly tolerance cannot be tolerant of everything, including intolerance. We see no inconsistency in denying to Nazis the right to destroy those they deem enemies of the master race, nor in denying to Communists the right to destroy those they consider enemies of the proletariat.[3] But Dean Hough finds liberalism objection-

---

[3] See my essay "On the Nature of Civil and Religious Liberty," in *Equality and Liberty* (New York: Oxford University Press, 1965).

able because it is present-oriented rather than future-oriented. He cites with disapproval, as a manifestation of the liberal "style," the slogan, "Let the World Set the Agenda." By this he means responding only to those ills that press themselves upon our attention, and dealing with them in what he (quoting Amitai Etzioni) calls "bit" or piecemeal fashion. This, he says, is "essentially a rearguard morality," and "it falls far short of the initiating power of a moral style that focuses on the process of transformation." The true morality, Dean Hough tells us, is a "transformative morality," one that embraces "a totally new moral vision." Without this totally new vision, which Dean Hough also calls a "contextuating vision," liberalism "has little hope of transformative power."

Now in the Book of Revelation the prophet sees a new heaven and a new earth, and a new Jerusalem in which God himself will dwell, where death itself shall be no more. For the believer, this is testimony of a high order concerning the future. But Dean Hough addresses to us no testimony, and offers no argument, either of reason or of revelation, which tells us either why the present order is insufficient (or wrong), or why we ought to transform it. Moreover he does not tell us *into what* we are to transform ourselves. It hardly seems enough to criticize liberals for "bit" decisions which, by definition, are responses to rationally perceived defects in the *status quo*. If the "bits" don't fit into a totally new vision perhaps it is because most of us just don't have one, or know why we need one. Unlike the author of Revelation—or other utopians from Plato to Marx—Dean Hough never tells us (even in parables) what his vision is. In fact, we don't even know that he has such a vision.

Only at one point do we have a hint of what the source and substance of the transformative vision, and the transformative morality, might be. This occurs in a discussion of the conservative understanding of the function of religion. Such an understanding, Dean Hough tells us, still dominates the church. It is peculiarly concerned with personal salvation, and sees religious meaning as "essentially private and interior." "At best, the social aspect is seen to be the sharing of private and interior meaning with others of like mind or similar needs, and any wider social effectiveness is epiphenomenal." That is to say, conservative churchmen aim at converting and saving individual souls; but society benefits from such conversions only indirectly, if the converted live (and share) better lives with others. But Dean Hough clearly believes that this is the wrong order to proceed: he thinks that individuals can be benefited primarily by reforming (or transforming) society, not that society can be benefited by improving individuals. Salvation is essentially social, not individual.

For Dean Hough, the priority of the social to the individual, is paralleled by the priority of the practical to the theoretical. This is indicated in the context of his rejection of the conservative understanding.

"What is never argued," he writes about such views, "is whether a non-political vision of meaning is really adequate for contemporary man or for the church. One wonders whether the neo-Marxist criticism of the separation of meaning from action is taken seriously at all." Now Dean Hough clearly takes this "neo-Marxist criticism" with utmost seriousness, and it behooves us therefore to be clear about what that criticism is.

In attempting to state what Dean Hough refers to as neo-Marxist, however, we find ourselves at a loss to distinguish the "new" (or "neo-") from the old, or classical Marxism. As far as we know, there is no ground of difference between the different sects of Marxists on this fundamental issue. All of them hold that thought is fundamentally derivative—or epiphenomenal, as Dean Hough would say—and that its ultimate meaning is to be sought, not in the analysis of ideas, but in the analysis of the role of ideas within the system of society. In general, Marx held that men are conditioned by their environment, and that even their most private thoughts are consequences of that environment, and not the free choices of their souls. The very idea of souls—and of salvation—is but an element of ideology, of a way of thinking induced in men by the environment. But of the varied elements of a given environment, only one is of decisive importance, and that is something Marx called "the relations of production." These relations arise from the possession of the tools or instruments which are the dominant means, in any era, for producing what is, in that era, the dominant form of wealth. Such, for example, would be land in the Middle Ages, commercial capital in the eighteenth century, industrial capital in the nineteenth, and financial capital in the twentieth. When Marx called religion the opiate of the people, he meant something like this. Both feudalism and capitalism induced "relations of production" in which the mass of mankind were exploited for the benefit of the possessors of land and capital. By such relations, the exploited were compelled to forego the consumption of real wealth—beyond the minimum needed to keep them alive, working, and reproducing—in favor of the owning classes. If however they remained docile in this world, they were promised eternal bliss in another. Such promises of course cost nothing—apart from the cost of the churches, which were built and maintained with exploited labor anyway—and were vital to the preservation of an exploitative social order. But the point central for us is this: the real content of "interior and private" religious experience is not to be found within that experience, but only in the external objective social conditions which such experience helps both to produce and to preserve. If then a man seeks truth in "interior and private" experience, he simply cannot find it. Traditional religion is a mere symptom of human "alienation," of the separation of men into social classes as a consequence of the private ownership of the means of production. To overcome alienation means then to overcome the system resulting from private ownership; it means to become a revolutionary.

We must ask then if this is why Dean Hough rejects traditional religion and traditional morality. If it is, we can see why he finds the liberal so unsatisfactory—and his dilemma so unnecessary. To be a liberal is to be like someone who lances the boils upon the surface of the body, but will do nothing about the infection within. The transformation that Dean Hough calls for would then properly be called revolution. And the desirability of that revolution would be guaranteed by the truth of certain fundamentals of Marxism. We will not be so ungracious as to characterize these fundamentals as the private, interior thoughts of Marx and his followers. We point out only that they imply the priority, not only of society to the individual, and of action to thought, but of matter to mind. Marxism is not only materialistic, but because it is, atheistic. It would be strange indeed for a Professor of Christian Ethics, Chairman of a Faculty of Religion, and Dean of a School of Theology, to take his bearings by such a doctrine.[4] We would be compelled to wonder whether he, his school, and his department were being called by their right names. But we must not concern ourselves unduly with names. We must instead invite Dean Hough to tell us, in his own words, what he understands by a "transformative morality." And we must then proceed, with the utmost detachment, and without prejudice, to examine the question of whether or not it would indeed help us to lead the better life that we all so earnestly seek.

[4] We are aware that there are those today who speak of "Christian Marxism." We suggest that they do so in the same sense as one may speak of "hot ice" or "frozen flame."

Library of Congress Cataloging in Publication Data

Jaffa, Harry V
    The conditions of freedom.

    1. Liberty—Addresses, essays, lectures. 2. Equality
—Addresses, essays, lectures. 3. United States—
Politics and government—Addresses, essays, lectures.
I. Title.
JC599.U5J237   323.44   74-24389
ISBN 0-8018-1631-9

o